FAIR TRIAL RIGHTS

by
RICHARD CLAYTON
Barrister, Devereux Chambers, London

HUGH TOMLINSON
Barrister, Matrix Chambers, London

D1477392

OXFORD
UNIVERSITY PRESS

OXFORD
UNIVERSITY PRESS

Great Clarendon Street, Oxford OX2 6DP

Oxford University Press is a department of the University of Oxford.
It furthers the University's objective of excellence in research, scholarship,
and education by publishing worldwide in

Oxford New York

Athens Auckland Bangkok Bogotá Buenos Aires Calcutta Cape Town
Chennai Dar es Salaam Delhi Florence Hong Kong Istanbul Karachi
Kolkata Kuala Lumpur Madrid Melbourne Mexico City Mumbai Nairobi
Paris São Paulo Shanghai Singapore Taipei Tokyo Toronto Warsaw

with associated companies in Berlin Ibadan

Oxford is a registered trade mark of Oxford University Press
in the UK and in certain other countries

Published in the United States
by Oxford University Press Inc., New York

© Richard Clayton, Hugh Tomlinson, and Carol George 2001

The moral rights of the authors have been asserted
Database right Oxford University Press (maker)

First published 2001

Crown copyright material is reproduced with the permission of the
Controller of Her Majesty's Stationery Office

British Library Cataloguing in Publication Data

Data available

Library of Congress Cataloging in Publication Data

Data available

ISBN 0–19–924634–3

3 5 7 9 10 8 6 4 2

Typeset in Garamond by
Cambrian Typesetters, Frimley, Surrey

Printed in Great Britain
on acid-free paper by
Antony Rowe Ltd.
Chippenham, Wilts.

PREFACE AND UPDATE

The right

Article 6 provides the fair trial guarantees under the European Convention. Article 6(1) confers several express rights which must be secured where there is a determination of a civil right or where a defendant faces a criminal charge. Article 6(2) and 6(3) contain a number of additional rights which are specific to criminal cases. The European Court of Human Rights has also recognized a number of rights can be implied out of Article 6.

Fair procedure is of course a principle which is fundamental to the common law. The critical question posed by the Human Rights Act is the extent to which Article 6 adds something of value to these well established principles.

This book is a reprint of the Chapter on Fair Trial Rights from our book on *The Law of Human Rights*.[1] It sets out to provide a comprehensive and systematic treatment of human rights law and practice in the UK in relation to these areas, including detailed analysis of the impact of the incorporation of the European Convention on Human Rights into domestic law by the Human Rights Act 1998.

The book is divided into five sections. After an introduction, there is a discussion of the right in English law before the coming into force of the Human Rights Act 1998. This is followed by an analysis of the case law under the European Convention on Human Rights. The likely impact of incorporation on English law is then examined. The general impact is considered with an examination of the effect of Article 6 on access to the courts and immunities, independence and impartiality, the impact on civil proceedings and the impact on judicial review. Specific subject areas of impact are then examined: business and commerce, criminal law and justice, education, employment, discrimination and disciplinary bodies, family law, heath care, housing, local government law, planning and environment law, police, prisoners and social security. The book concludes with an Appendix surveying the case law under the Canadian Charter of Rights, the New Zealand Bill of Rights Act and the constitutional jurisprudence in other common law jurisdictions.

In the next section of this introduction we will discuss developments concerning Article 6 decided over the first 7 months of the operation of the Human Rights Act 1998.[2]

---

[1] Oxford University Press, 2000.
[2] The Act came into force on 2 Oct 2000, this Introduction covers cases decided up to 1 May 2001.

Article 6 case law

Article 6 is the Convention right most often raised in applications before the European Court of Human Rights. It is therefore not surprising that a large number of claims under the Human Rights Act have concerned fair trial rights. Two particular decisions stand out. Perhaps the most important analysis of terms of Article 6 was undertaken by the Privy Council in *Brown v Stott*.[3] In reversing the decisions of the Scottish courts, the Privy Council decided that a confession made by a driver, who was compulsorily questioned under section 172 of the Road Traffic Act 1972, did not infringe the right against self discrimination. Lord Bingham emphasized that the requirements of a fair trial cannot be the subject of a single, unvarying rule or collection of rules but must take account of the facts and circumstances of a particular case. More controversially, he said that the express rights in criminal trials conferred by Article 6(2) and 6(3) are not absolute.[4] Nevertheless, in *R v Forbes*[5] the House of Lords held that whereas the right to a fair trial under Article 6 is absolute, the subsidiary rights are not: so that it is always necessary to consider all the facts and the whole history in a particular case to judge whether a defendant's right to a fair trial has been breached.

The effect of Article 6 on administrative decisions was analysed in *R v Environmental Secretary ex p Alconbury*.[6] Any breach of Article 6 by the decision maker can be rectified by subsequent court procedures. Whether the nature of the review in judicial review proceedings is sufficient for these purposes depends on the subject matter of the decision, the manner it is arrived at and the content of the dispute.[7] In reversing the Divisional Court, the House of Lords held that planning procedures were compatible with Article 6; and that judicial review proceedings satisfied Article 6 in relation to policy decisions but would not do so in relation to a factual adjudication.

The rights under Article 6(1) are triggered by a dispute involving the applicant's civil right or a criminal charge. Under the Human Rights Act it has been held that the right to education[8] does not fall within the scope of a civil right and that anti-social behaviour orders[9] and the prison disciplinary procedure[10] do not constitute a criminal charge. Article 6 requires an adjudication before an independent and impartial hearing. The impact of Convention principles to the domestic law of

---

[3] [2001] 2 WLR 817.
[4] Ibid at 836; contrast the views of Lord Hope at 851; and see para 11.235 below.
[5] [2001] 2 WLR 1.
[6] *The Times*, 10 May 2001.
[7] See para 1.197ff in *The Law of Human Rights*, OUP 2000.
[8] *R v Richmond LBC ex p JC*, *The Times*, 10 Aug 2000.
[9] *R v Manchester Crown Court ex p McCann*, *The Times*, 9 Mar 2001.
[10] *Greenfield v Secretary of State for Home Department*, *The Times*, 7 Mar 2001.

bias was considered by the Court of Appeal in *Director General of Fair Trading v Proprietary Association of Great Britain*.[11] In *R v Environmental Secretary ex p Alconbury*[12] the House of Lords appear to reject a complaint of bias based on a complaint that a decision maker is predisposed to apply his own policy.

The criminal courts have considered a number of cases where the right to a fair trial is said to be breached. It is almost inevitable that a conviction will be regarded as unsafe if a defendant is denied a fair trial.[13] However, a defect at trial which renders the trial unfair can be cured by a fair and proper consideration by the Court of Appeal of all the evidence available to it including evidence which was unavailable at trial.[14] Where a judge fails to give a required direction to a jury, the Court of Appeal has to be satisfied that no reasonable jury could have come to a different conclusion if they had been properly directed.[15] The compatibility of Article 6 with the rape shield protecting the complainant was examined in *R v Y (Sexual Offence: Complainant's sexual history)*.[16] Article 6 is not breached by a public interest immunity hearing.[17] The question of whether pretrial publicity breached the right to a fair trial was discussed in *Montgomery v HM Advocate*.[18]

The Privy Council in two Commonwealth cases expressed divergent views about the right to a fair trial within a reasonable time. In *Darnalingum v State*[19] it stated that right comprised three separate guarantees so that even if a defendant's guilt was manifest, the factor could not excuse a failure to hear the case within a reasonable time. However, in *Flowers v The Queen*[20] it said that the three elements form part of one all embracing protection which must be balanced against the public interest in the attainment of justice; in deciding whether to quash a conviction after a lengthy delay, a court is entitled to take account of the fact that a defendant was clearly guilty of a very serious crime.

Article 6 does not confer upon a litigant an unfettered choice of the tribunal in which to pursue or defend his civil rights.[21] The express obligation under Article 6 to give reasoned decisions was analysed by the Court of Appeal in *Hyams v Plender*.[22]

---

[11] [2001] 1 WLR 700.
[12] *The Times*, 10 May 2001.
[13] *The Times*, 24 Nov 2000.
[14] *R v Craven, The Times*, 2 Feb 2001.
[15] *The Times*, 24 Oct 2000.
[16] *The Times*, 13 Feb 2001; the decision of the House of Lords is awaited.
[17] *R v Smith (Joe), The Times*, 20 Dec 2000.
[18] *The Times*, 6 Dec 2000
[19] [2000] 1 WLR 2303.
[20] [2000] 1 WLR 2396.
[21] *OFT Africa v Fayad Hijazy, The Times*, 28 Nov 2000.
[22] [2001] 1 WLR 32.

Article 6 creates a number of implied rights. In *Brown v Stott*[23] the Privy Council took the view that implied rights were not absolute and depended on whether a fair balance had been struck between the general interest of the community and the personal rights of the individual. The Court of Appeal itself took the point that the bar against enforcing a credit agreement breached the right of access to the court.[24] Complaints concerning breaches of the presumption of innocence have failed in several occasions in relation to provisions in the Misuse of Drugs Act and Homicide Act,[25] confiscation orders[26] and an irrefutable presumption in the Road Traffic Offenders Act.[27]

There have been a large number of decisions of the European Court since October 2000. A two year delay in sentencing a defendant breached the reasonable time requirement under Article 6[28] whereas a three year delay did not in complex and protracted custody proceedings.[29] The use of statements in criminal proceedings which defendants were compelled to give inspectors appointed by the Department of Trade and Industry breached the right against self incrimination.[30] The domestic courts had breached Article 6(1) when dealing with a complaint of bias since it held that there was a real risk of bias but allowed the decision to stand because of the doctrine of necessity.[31] The European Court held that an application for judicial review following a planning inquiry was sufficient to meet the requirements of Article 6.[32]

Conclusion

The significance of Article 6 has been demonstrated by the large number of cases where it has been canvassed. Its implications will continue, in particular, to be scrutinized in the criminal field. However, it is too early to tell whether Article 6 will radically alter domestic principles of fair procedure.

Richard Clayton

Devereux Chambers
Devereux Court
London WC2R 3JJ

Hugh Tomlinson

Matrix Chambers
Gray's Inn
London WC1R 5LN

10 May 2001

---

[23] [2001] 2 WLR 817.

[24] *Wilson v First County Trust* (No 2), *The Times*, 16 May 2001.

[25] *R v Lambert* [2000] 2 WLR 211.

[26] *R v Benjafield* (CA), *The Times*, 28 Dec 2000; *HM Advocate v McIntosh* (PC), *The Times*, 8 Feb 2001.

[27] s 15(2): see *Parker v DPP*, *The Times*, 26 Jan 2001.

[28] *Howarth v United Kingdom*, *The Times*, 10 Oct 2001.

[29] *G v United Kingdom*, *The Times*, 1 Nov 2000.

[30] *IJKGMR and AKP v United Kingdom*, *The Times*, 13 Oct 2000.

[31] *Kingsley v United Kingdom*, *The Times*, 9 Jan 2001.

[32] *Chapman v United Kingdom*, *The Times*, 30 Jan 2001.

CONTENTS

11

FAIR TRIAL RIGHTS

A. The Nature of the Rights

11.01 The closely related principles of 'due process' and 'the rule of law' are fundamental to the proection of human rights. Such rights can only be protected and enforced if the citizen has recourse to courts and tribunals which are independent of the state and which resolve disputes in accordance with fair procedures. The fairness of the legal process has a particular significance in criminal cases but 'fair trial rights' must also be applied in other proceedings which deal with disputes between citizen and state. The protection of procedural due process is not, in itself, suficient to protect against human rights abuses but it is the foundation stone for 'substantive protection' against state power. The protection of human rights therefore begins but does not end with fair trial rights.

11.02 One of the earliest and most well known provisions is to be found in the 'Bill of Rights' comprising the first ten amendments to the United States Constitution.[1] The Fifth Amendment[2] provides that:

---

[1] For a discussion of American due process rights, see generally, L Tribe, *American Constitutional Law* (2nd edn, Foundation Press, 1988) Chap 10 in relation to procedural due process rights and at Chap 8 in relation to substantive due process rights.

[2] The Fifth Amendment applies to the laws and actions of the federal government; however, due process rights are extended to the states under the Fourteenth Amendment.

No person shall . . . be deprived of life, liberty, or property, without due process of law.

The Sixth Amendment includes the provision that:

In all criminal prosecutions, the accused shall enjoy the right to a speedy and public trial, by an impartial jury . . .

Over 150 years later the need for 'fair trial' or 'due process' rights was recognised by the drafters of the Universal Declaration. Article 10 provides:

Everyone is entitled in full equality to a fair and public hearing by an independent and impartial tribunal, in the determination of his rights and obligations and of any criminal charge against him.

The Convention was the first international human rights instrument to set out **11.03** detailed protection for fair trial rights.[3] The rights were dealt with under four headings (which have been followed in many other international instruments):

- general rights to procedural fairness, including a public hearing before an independent and impartial tribunal which gives a reasoned judgment;[4]
- the presumption of innocence in criminal proceedings;[5]
- specific rights for those accused of criminal offences, including rights to be informed of the charge, to trial within a reasonable time, to legal assistance and to cross-examine witnesses;[6]
- the right to be free from retrospective criminal laws.[7]

Other 'legal process' rights were added by the Seventh Protocol to the Convention and have also been recognised by other instruments:

- the right of appeal in criminal matters;[8]
- the right to compensation for wrongful conviction;[9]
- the right not to be tried or punished twice for the same offence.[10]

---

[3] Art 6, see para 11.150 below, and Art 7, see para 11.152 below.
[4] Convention, Art 6(1); Covenant, Art 14(1); American Convention on Human Rights, Art 6(1).
[5] Convention, Art 6(2); Covenant, Art 14(2), American Convention on Human Rights, Art 6(2); African Charter, Art 7(1)(b).
[6] Convention, Art 6(3); Covenant, Article 14(3); American Convention on Human Rights, Art 14(2).
[7] Convention, Art 7; Covenant, Article 15; American Convention on Human Rights, Art 9; African Charter, Art 7(2).
[8] Seventh Protocol, Art 2; Covenant, Art 14(5); American Convention on Human Rights, Art 7(2)(h).
[9] Seventh Protocol, Art 3; Covenant, Art 14(6); American Convention on Human Rights, Art 10.
[10] Seventh Protocol, Art 4; Covenant, Art 14(7); American Convention on Human Rights, Art 8(4).

Although the Seventh Protocol has not been ratified by the United Kingdom, it has ratified the Covenant and is, therefore, obliged to give effect to these additional rights as a matter of international law.[11]

11.04 'Fair trial rights' give rise to a large number of difficult issues. The following can be highlighted:

The extent of the right of access to the courts. It is always necessary to prescribe some limits on access to the courts, for example, in relation to stale or vexatious claims. The state has, traditionally, sought to restrict access to the courts by, for example, 'ouster clauses', and the use of special procedures and immunities; and this requires examination of the extent to which 'fair trial rights' include a right of access to the courts for the resolution of disputes.

The types of dispute subject to 'fair trial rights'. Although it is generally accepted that 'fair trial rights' should apply in the ordinary criminal courts, there is no clear consensus as to which other 'determinations' should attract protection. The extension of procedural rights into the area of 'administrative' decision-making is controversial and its limits have been worked out in varying ways in different contexts.

The nature of the tribunal. It is clearly established that a fair tribunal should be independent of the parties and impartial; but there has been considerable debate concerning the content of these notions and there is no generally accepted definition of either. 'Independence' gives rise to problems when the members of the tribunal are appointed on a temporary basis or can be removed by the executive. A variety of tests for 'impartiality' have been suggested— including 'real likelihood', 'real danger' or 'reasonable suspicion'. Their application continues to give rise to practical difficulties.

The content of due process rights. The principle of 'natural justice', *audi alteram partem* (hear the other side) is generally accepted but there is no consensus as to what this entails. Questions arise, for example, as to whether there should be advance disclosure of evidence, a public oral hearing, legal representation, cross-examination of witnesses and a reasoned judgment.

Restrictions on fair trial rights. In criminal cases, it is often necessary to balance the rights of the individual defendant against the wider interest. When considering fair trial provisions, courts are repeatedly faced with decisions as the extent to which the rights of defendants should be modified or restricted in the wider interest. Three examples can be given of areas which have caused particular controversy: first, the use of statutory provisions which place the burden of proving a defence on the accused; secondly, the circumstances in which the courts should admit evidence obtained by the exercise of state powers of 'compulsion'; and thirdly, the extent to which the courts should exclude evidence or

---

[11] See para 2.09ff above.

stay proceedings when the human rights of suspects have been violated. In all three examples the courts have been called on to balance the interests of the individual suspect against those of the community generally with differing results in different jurisdictions.

These and similar issues have, of course, been explored in the English case law, but **11.05** usually without reference to broader 'fair trial' principles. They have also been considered in other common law jurisdictions; and on many occasions by English judges in the Privy Council. Fair trial rights will be an area in which the case law in other jurisdictions is likely to be of particular assistance in dealing with issues which arise under the Human Rights Act.

B. The Rights in English Law Before the Human Rights Act

(1) Introduction

English law provides no explicit general statement of rights in relation to the con- **11.06** duct of legal process. Nevertheless, it is possible to identify a number of elements which are conventionally regarded as 'fair trial' rights. These have been most thoroughly explored in the context of administrative law but have been increasingly recognised as being of general application.

The right of access to the court in order to have disputes determined in accordance **11.07** with the law is deeply rooted in the common law. Blackstone viewed the right of access to the courts as one of the 'outworks or barriers, to protect and maintain inviolate the three great and primary rights, of personal security, personal liberty and private property'. He described it in these terms:

> A third subordinate right of every Englishman is that of applying to the courts of justice for redress of injuries. Since the law is in England the supreme arbiter of every man's life, liberty and property, courts of justice must at all times be open to the subject and the law be duly administered therein.[12]

The constitutional importance of the rights of the citizen to use the courts has **11.08** been consistently emphasised. As Lord Diplock said:

> Every civilised system of government requires that the state should make available to all its citizens a means for the just and peaceful settlement of disputes between them as to their respective legal rights. The means provided are courts of justice to which *every citizen has a constitutional right of access* in the role of plaintiff to obtain the remedy to which he claims to be entitled . . .'[13]

---

[12] R Kerr (ed), *Blackstone's Commentaries on the Laws of England* (4th edn, John Murray, 1876) 111.

[13] *Bremer Vulkan Schiffbau und Maschinenfabrik v South India Shipping Corporation Ltd* [1981] AC 909, 917.

11.09 More generally, although the phrase 'due process of law' is most familiar in the context of the United States Constitution,[14] it has its origins in the early history of English law. Thus, the right to trial by due process of law is sometimes traced back to clause 39 of the Magna Carta of 1215 which states that:

> No freeman shall be taken and imprisoned or disseised of any tenement or of his liberties or free customs . . . except by lawful judgment of his peers or by the law of the land (*per legem terrae*).[15]

This interpretation has been doubted[16] but the term 'due process' appears in a number of medieval statutes. The most well-known example is the Statute of Edward III which provides that:

> no man of what estate or condition that he be, shall be put out of land or tenement, nor taken, nor imprisoned, nor disinherited, nor put to death, without being brought in answer by due process of the law.[17]

11.10 The doctrine of 'due process of law' was revived in the early seventeenth century by Sir Edward Coke who interpreted the words '*per legem terrae*' as meaning, 'Without being brought in to answer but by due process of the common law'.[18] Coke's view of the importance of 'due process' was extremely influential.[19] Limited statutory provision for 'due process rights' was made by Articles 10 and 11 of the Bill of Rights of 1689 which provided:

> That excessive bail ought not to be required nor excessive fines imposed nor cruel and unusual punishments inflicted.
>
> That jurors ought to be duly impanelled and returned . . .[20]

The independence of the judges was finally confirmed in the Act of Settlement of 1701. During this period, it was emphasised that there must be no punishment except as prescribed by a previously existing law, that all statutes must have only prospective (and not retrospective) operation and that the discretion of magistrates should be strictly circumscribed by law.

11.11 Since the late nineteenth century, procedural forms of justice have been inextricably linked to the concept of the rule of law. The Privy Council has said that the phrase 'due process of law' invokes the concept of the rule of law itself and the universally accepted standards of justice observed by civilised nations.[20a] In Dicey's

---

[14] See generally, H Abraham and B Perry, *Freedom and the Court* (7th edn, Oxford University Press, 1998) Chap 4 'The Fascinating World of Due Process of Law'.

[15] See *Halsbury's Statutes* (4th edn, Butterworths, 1995) Vol 10, 15–16.

[16] See generally, D Galligan, *Due Process and Fair Procedures* (Clarendon Press, 1996) 171–3

[17] 28 Edw II Ch 3 (1354); *Halsbury's Statutes* (n 15 above) Vol 10, 21.

[18] *Coke's Institutes*, Chap 29, 51; see generally, D Galligan (n 16 above) 188ff.

[19] See D Galligan (n 16 above) 174ff.

[20] *Halsbury's Statutes* (n 15 above) Vol 10, 46; Art 10 is reproduced as the Ninth Amendment to the US Constitution.

[20a] *Thomas v Baptiste* [1999] 3 WLR 249, 259 dealing with the 'due process clause' in the Constitution of Trinidad and Tobago.

exposition, the 'rule of law' involved the supremacy of regular law as opposed to arbitrary power and equality before the law.[21] The concept of the rule of law involves a number of ideas which are now seen as part of the 'fair trial' or 'due process' rights. However, as Galligan has pointed out, the notion of 'due process' is not mentioned in Dicey's *Introduction to the Study of the Law of the Constitution*.[22] The procedural aspects of 'due process' were treated as being contained in the procedures of the ordinary courts which were not further analysed.

Over the past 200 years, common law 'due process rights' have received their most **11.12** sustained development not in relation to the procedure of the superior courts, but in connection with inferior tribunals and administrative bodies.[23] The principles of 'natural justice' were developed in cases involving proceedings before justices and the deprivation of public office. By a series of nineteenth century cases, they were applied to 'every tribunal or body of persons invested with authority to adjudicate upon matters involving civil consequences to individuals'.[24] The approach of the courts was classically expressed in *Cooper v Wandsworth Board of Works*[25] in which it was held that a power to demolish buildings was subject to an implied right to be heard. As Willes J said:

> a tribunal which is by law invested with power to affect the property of one of Her Majesty's subjects, is bound to give such subject an opportunity of being heard before it proceeds: and that the rule is of universal application and founded on the plainest principles of justice.[26]

However, in the first third of the twentieth century, the courts drew back from the **11.13** broader application of 'natural justice' principles.[27] In the *Venicoff* case[28] it was held that the Home Secretary's power of deportation was a purely executive function and the deportee had no right to be heard. 'Natural justice' principles were taken to be restricted to decision-makers who were under a duty to 'act judicially', a category which was understood to exclude most administrative decisions.[29] In a

---

[21] A Dicey, *An Introduction to the Study of the Law of the Constitution* (10th edn, Macmillan, 1961), 202–203.

[22] D Galligan, (n 16 above)178–9.

[23] See generally, H Wade and C Forsyth, *Administrative Law* (7th edn, Clarendon Press, 1994) Chap 15; Lord Woolf and J Jowell, *De Smith, Woolf and Jowell, Judicial Review of Administrative Action* (5th edn, Sweet & Maxwell, 1995), Chap 17 and M Beloff, 'Natural Justice—(The Audi Alteram Partem Rule) and Fairness', in M Supperstone and J Goudie, *Judicial Review* (2nd edn, Butterworths, 1997) paras 8.1–8.72.

[24] *Wood v Woad* (1874) LR Ex 190, 196; see generally, *De Smith, Woolf and Jowell* (n 23 above) para 7-012; M Beloff, (n 23 above) paras 8.6–8.10.

[25] (1863) 14 CB (NS) 180.

[26] Ibid 190, see also, Byles J at 194.

[27] See *De Smith, Woolf and Jowell* (n 23 above) para 7–015ff.

[28] *R v Leman Street Police Station Inspector, ex p Venicoff* [1920] 3 KB 72.

[29] *R v Electricity Commissioners, ex p London Electricity Joint Committee Company (1920) Ltd* [1924] 1 KB 171, 205.

series of cases over a period of 40 years, the courts consistently denied 'fair hearing' rights to those affected by administrative decisions.[30]

11.14 The older more vigorous approach was re-asserted by the House of Lords in *Ridge v Baldwin*[31] in which they held that a Chief Constable had an implied entitlement to prior notice of the charge against him and a proper opportunity of meeting it. The House of Lords recognised that any decision which affected a person's rights or interest was subject to the principles of natural justice: any person exercising such power had to act 'judicially'. Over the next three decades, the principles of 'fair hearing' were extended to almost the entire range of public decisions, including decisions under prerogative powers.[32] The scope and extent of the requirements to act fairly in any particular situation depends on the character of the decision-maker, the nature of the decision and the statutory framework.[33] These principles have, increasingly, been applied to the operation of the ordinary courts as the English law has come to recognise the central importance of 'fair trial rights'.

(2) Right of access to the courts

(a) Introduction

11.15 There is a well-established common law presumption of legislative intent that access to the courts in respect of justiciable issues is not to be denied save by clear words in a statute.[34] There is, thus, a 'right' of access to the courts which is, in the familiar way, subject to express or implied statutory provision to the contrary. It is unclear whether the right can be overridden by 'necessary implication'. In *R v Lord Chancellor, ex p Witham*[35] Laws J said he found:

> great difficulty in conceiving of a form of words capable of making it plain beyond all doubt to the statute's reader that the provision in question prevents him from going to court (for that is, what would be required), save in a case where that is expressly stated. The class of cases where it could be done by necessary implication is, I venture to think, a class with no members.[36]

---

[30] See *De Smith, Woolf and Jowell* (n 23 above) paras 7-028–7-030.

[31] [1964] AC 40.

[32] *Council of Civil Service Unions v Minister for the Civil Service* [1985] AC 374 but not to those relating to matters such as the making of treaties, the defence of the realm, the grant of honours, the dissolution of parliament and the appointment of Ministers, *per* Lord Roskill at 415.

[33] *Lloyd v McMahon* [1987] 1 AC 625.

[34] *Pyx Granite Company Ltd v Ministry of Housing and Local Government* [1960] AC 260, 286; and see F Bennion, *Statutory Interpretation* (3rd edn, Butterworths, 1997) s 281, 658ff and *De Smith, Woolf and Jowell* (n 23 above) para 5-017; and, see para 1.34 above.

[35] [1998] QB 575, 586.

[36] Similar views were expressed by Lord Browne-Wilkinson in *R v Secretary of State for the Home Office, ex p Pierson* [1998] AC 539, 575, but see *R v Secretary of State for the Home Office, ex p Leech (No 2)* [1994] QB 198, CA and see also M Supperstone and J Coppel, 'Judicial Review after the Human Rights Act' [1999] EHRLR 301 (in which it is argued that the views of Laws J are inconsistent with the *dicta* in *ex p Leech* and of Lord Reid in *Westminster Bank Ltd v Beverley Borough Council* [1971] AC 508, 529; and see *R v Lord Chancellor ex p Lightfoot* [2000] 2 WLR 318.

This 'right' has been invoked in a number of contexts in order to limit the cir- **11.16**
cumstances in which the 'access to justice' of individual litigants can be restricted.
In *R v Boaler* the right was applied to the institution of criminal proceedings.[37]
The issue was whether the then statutory provisions relating to vexatious litigants
prevented the commencement of a private prosecution. The court held by a majority that they did not. Scrutton J said that:

> One of the valuable rights of every subject of the King is to appeal to the King in his
> Courts if he alleges that a civil wrong has been done to him, or if he alleges that a
> wrong punishable criminally has been done to him, or has been committed by an-
> other subject of the King. This right is sometimes abused and it is, of course, quite
> competent for Parliament to deprive any subject of the King of it either absolutely
> or in part. But the language of any such statute should be jealously watched by the
> Courts, and should not be extended beyond its least onerous meaning unless clear
> words are used to justify such extension . . . I approach the consideration of a statute
> which is said to have this meaning with the feeling that unless its language clearly
> convinces me that this was the intention of the Legislature I should be slow to give
> effect to what is a most serious interference with the liberties of the subject.

The ability of a citizen to bring a private prosecution has been recognised to be an
'important constitutional right'.[38]

The right of access to the courts was invoked by a prisoner who complained that **11.17**
correspondence with his solicitor concerning litigation was being censored by the
prison authorities under the prison rules. The Court of Appeal held that the general 'rule making power' in section 47(1) of the Prison Act 1952 did not extend to
the making of rules which created an impediment to the free flow of communication between solicitor and client about contemplated legal proceedings. Steyn LJ
said:

> It is a principle of our law that every citizen has a right of unimpeded access to a
> court, In *Raymond v Honey* ([1983] 1 AC 1, 13), Lord Wilberforce described it as a
> 'basic right'. Even in our unwritten constitution it must rank as a constitutional
> right.[39]

The impact of this 'constitutional right' on the ability of the executive to make **11.18**
secondary legislation arose in *R v Lord Chancellor, ex p Witham*[40] in which it was
held that rules requiring litigants on income support to pay a minimum Writ fee
were *ultra vires*. Laws J said that:

> the right to a fair trial, which of necessity imports the right of access to the court, is
> as near to an absolute right as any which I can envisage.[41]

---

[37] [1915] 1 KB 21.
[38] *R v Leeds Magistrates' Court, ex p Serif Systems Ltd* [1997] CLY 1373.
[39] *R v Secretary State for the Home Department, ex p Leech (No 2)* [1994] QB 198, 210A-D; see also
R v Secretary of State, ex p Quaquah, The Times, 21 Jan 2000.
[40] [1998] QB 575; see also *R v Lord Chancellor, ex p Lightfoot* (n 36 above).
[41] Ibid 585.

He went on to express the view that:

> the executive cannot in law abrogate the right of access to justice, unless it is specifically so permitted by Parliament; and this is the meaning of the constitutional right.[42]

11.19 Nevertheless, the right of access to the court cannot be absolute. It has long been accepted that it must be regulated and restricted for the benefit of all litigants. As Sullivan J said in *R v Immigration Appeal Tribunal, ex p S*:[43]

> A right to a hearing is rarely unconditional, even where matters of life and liberty are at stake. One may have to appeal within a certain time, appear at a certain time, not be abusive or disruptive, file certain documents in support of the appeal and so forth. Having an opportunity for a hearing does not mean that one may not disentitle oneself from taking up that opportunity if one behaves in a certain manner. I do not consider that it offends any fundamental principle to say that certain breaches of procedural rules may mean that an Appellant loses his right to a hearing in certain circumstances. The more serious the issues . . . the more serious the breaches would have to be in order to justify depriving an Appellant of his right to a hearing.

There are a number of ways in which the right of access to the courts is restricted: a 'leave requirement' for the commencement of proceedings, the granting of 'immunities' to certain litigants, the imposition of time limits and other restrictions such as those relating to costs.

(b) 'Ouster' provisions

11.20 The attitude of the courts towards restrictions on access to justice is illustrated by the long line of cases dealing with 'ouster' or 'finality' clauses. Such clauses seek to prevent access to the courts for the purposes of judicial review.[44] It has been consistently held that such clauses do not prevent access to the courts in cases where decisions are taken without jurisdiction.[45] As Sir John Laws has said:

> The rigour of the court's approach to ouster clauses is a function of the rule of law; the vindication of the rule of law is the constitutional right of every citizen. So if it is to be breached by Parliament or Parliament's permission, the High Court will require express words to be used.[46]

11.21 It is often said that contracts which oust the jurisdiction of the courts are illegal and contrary to public policy.[47] Arbitration agreements were, however, not treated

---

[42] *R v Lord Chancellor, ex p Witham* [1998] 8 QB 57.

[43] [1998] Imm AR 252.

[44] See generally, Lord Woolf and J Jowell, *De Smith, Woolf and Jowell, Judicial Review of Administrative Action* (5th edn, Sweet & Maxwell, 1995) paras 5-015–5-027; Bennion, *Statutory Interpretation* 74ff.

[45] The leading case is *Anisminic Ltd v Foreign Compensation Commission* [1969] 2 AC 147.

[46] J Laws, 'Illegality: The problem of jurisdiction', in M Supperstone and J Goudie, *Judicial Review* (2nd edn, London: Butterworths, 1997) para 4.23.

[47] *Doleman and Sons v Ossett Corporation* [1912] 3 KB 257.

as offending this principle because the courts retained wide powers to review arbitration awards.[48] Nevertheless, the courts would not recognise provisions which sought to exclude this review jurisdiction, because 'There must be no Alsatia in England where the King's writ does not run'.[49] The position is now governed by the Arbitration Act 1996 which binds parties to arbitration agreement and prevents recourse to the courts save in limited circumstances.[50] The courts have recognised the international policy exemplified in this legislation, that the consent of the parties should be honoured by the courts.[51]

(c) Leave to commence proceedings

In a number of cases the access of litigants to the court is restricted by requirements of 'leave', 'permission' or 'prior authorisation'. Such a requirement applies to special categories of litigant and to special types of proceedings. Special types of litigants who require leave or permission include mental patients, minors and vexatious litigants. Permission is required for applications for judicial review of the decisions of public bodies. **11.22**

Under the Civil Procedure Rules,[52] infants and mental patients cannot bring proceedings without a 'litigation friend'. The proceedings may be stayed if a claim is brought without the participation of a 'litigation friend'. A person may act as a litigation friend without a court order provided that he can fairly and competently conduct the proceedings, has no adverse interest and, when a claim is being brought, undertakes to pay the costs.[53] An authorisation and certificate of suitability must be filed.[54] Otherwise, a litigation friend can be appointed by the court.[55] **11.23**

A 'leave' requirement is imposed on mental patients by section 139(2) of the Mental Health Act 1983. This provides that: **11.24**

> No civil proceedings shall be brought against any person in any court in respect of any [act done in pursuance of the Act] . . . without the leave of the High Court; and no criminal proceedings shall be brought against any person in any court in respect of any such act except by or with the consent of the Director of Public Prosecutions.

---

[48] *Scott v Avery* (1856) 5 HLC 811; *Hallen v Spaeth* [1923] AC 684.

[49] Per Scrutton LJ, *Czarnikow v Roth Schmidt and Company* [1922] 2 KB 478, 488 ('Alsatia' being the common name for the Whitefriars area which, until 1697 had certain privileges and was a sanctuary for debtors).

[50] See generally, D Sutton, J Kendall and J Gill, *Russell on Arbitration*, (21st edn, Sweet & Maxwell, 1997).

[51] See eg *Halki Shipping Corporation v Sopex Oils Ltd* [1998] 1 WLR 726.

[52] CPR, Pt 21; formerly, RSC Ord 80.

[53] CPR, r 21.4.

[54] CPR, r 21.5.

[55] CPR, r. 21.6.

Proceedings issued without leave are a nullity.[56] This provision is designed to prevent harassment by 'clearly hopeless actions' so leave should be granted if the case deserves further investigation, even if it is unlikely to succeed.[57] However, leave will be refused if the point is 'virtually unarguable'.[58] The section does not cover applications for judicial review to quash admission decisions.[59] More generally, the court has jurisdiction in all types of case to prevent further applications being made without leave in proceedings which are before the court.[60] It also has jurisdiction to restrain the issue of proceedings which are manifestly vexatious.[61]

11.25 There is also a statutory jurisdiction restricting access to the courts by so-called 'vexatious litigants'. The Attorney-General can apply for an order that a person cannot institute or continue civil or criminal proceedings without the leave of the High Court.[62] This application must be made to the Divisional Court[63] and an order can only be made, if the court is satisfied that the person has 'habitually and persistently and without any reasonable ground' instituted vexatious civil proceedings, made vexatious applications or instituted vexatious prosecutions.[64] Once an order is made against a person then he requires leave to commence proceedings. Leave shall not be given unless the High Court is satisfied:

> that the proceedings or application are not an abuse of the process of the court in question and that there are reasonable grounds for the proceeding or application.[65]

This provision does not, therefore, entirely exclude the vexatious litigant's access to the courts. It is noteworthy that the analogous provision in South Africa has recently been held to be consistent with the 'fair trial' provisions of the Constitution.[66]

11.26 Proceedings to challenge the decisions of public bodies must be brought by way of 'judicial review' applications under CPR Sch 1 R 53.[67] These are subject to a 'permission requirement' under Sch 1 R 53.3(1). The applicant makes an application without notice for permission which will only be granted if the applicant has an

---

[56] *Pountney v Griffiths* [1976] AC 314.
[57] *Winch v Jones* [1986] QB 296.
[58] See eg *James v London Borough of Havering* (1992) 15 BMLR 1.
[59] *ex p Waldron* [1986] QB 824.
[60] *Grepe v Loam* (1887) 37 Ch D 168.
[61] *Ebert v Venvil* [1999] 3 WLR 670.
[62] Supreme Court Act 1981, s 42(1A).
[63] *In Re Vernazza* [1960] 1 QB 197.
[64] s 42(1).
[65] s 42(3).
[66] *Beinash v Ernst and Young* 1999 (2) BCLR 125.
[67] Order 53 was preserved under Sch 1 of the CPR but is being replaced by new rules which take effect on 2 Oct 2000.

'arguable case on the merits'.[68] If permission is refused, the applicant may renew his application at an oral hearing.[69]

(d) Immunities

Introduction.   The English law confers a number of immunities from suit on public authorities and private individuals. These can be considered under six heads:

    11.27

- crown immunity;
- parliamentary immunity;
- judicial immunity;
- proceedings immunity;
- negligence immunity; and
- statutory immunities.

Crown immunity.   The Sovereign can act either in a personal capacity or in a public capacity. In her personal capacity, the Sovereign is not subject to legal process because no court can have jurisdiction over her.[70] This is sometimes described as an application of the maxim 'the king can do no wrong'.[71] Until 1947 it was possible to bring a claim in contract (but not in tort) against the sovereign personally by the petition of right procedure. It seems that the abolition of the petition of right by the Crown Proceedings Act[72] means that it is no longer possible to bring a contractual claim against the Sovereign.[73]

    11.28

The Crown is the Sovereign in her public capacity and is a 'corporation sole'.[74] The Crown Proceedings Act 1947 removed most of the Crown's immunities against ordinary legal process. For the first time it was possible to sue the Crown in tort.[75] It is now clear that injunctions can be granted against the Crown and that the Crown is subject to the ordinary contempt jurisdiction.[76]

    11.29

After 1947, the Crown retained a statutory immunity in relation to tort actions

    11.30

---

[68] *R v Legal Aid Board, ex p Hughes* (1992) 24 HLR 698 and generally, R Clayton and H Tomlinson, *Judicial Review Procedure* (Wiley, 1997) Chap 5; *De Smith, Woolf and Jowell* (n 44 above) para 15–011ff.

[69] Clayton and Tomlinson (n 68 above) 127–129 (the precise procedure depends on whether or not the application relates to a 'civil' or a 'criminal' matter).

[70] *Blackstone's Criminal Practice* (Blackstone Press, 1999) Vol 1, 242.

[71] See generally, H Wade and C Forsyth, *Administrative Law*, 7th edn, Clarendon Press, 1994) Chap 21.

[72] s 13 and Sch 1; cf *Franklin v A-G* [1974] 1 QB 185, 201.

[73] See Wade and Forsyth (n 71 above) 833–834.

[74] Wade and Forsyth (n 71 above) 819.

[75] s 2(1).

[76] *M v Home Office* [1994] 1 AC 377; and see Sir Stephen Sedley, 'The Crown In Its Own Courts', in C Forsyth and I Hare, *The Golden Metwand and the Crooked Cord* (Clarendon Press, 1998) 253–66.

arising out of the acts or omissions of members of the armed forces brought by other members of the armed forces.[77] This extended to claims for medical negligence by military doctors.[78] This immunity has now been removed by statute[79] but can be revived by the Secretary of State if it appears to him necessary to do so by reason of 'imminent national danger or great emergency' or 'for the purposes of warlike operations'.[80]

11.31   **Parliamentary immunity.**   Parliament and its members have a number of ancient but important immunities and privileges.[81] The most important of these privileges derives from Article 9 of the Bill of Rights 1689 which provides that:

> the freedom of speech and debates or proceedings in parliament ought not to be impeached or questioned in any court or place out of Parliament.

This is a provision of high constitutional importance and ought not to be narrowly construed.[82] 'Proceedings in parliament' extend to everything said or done in the House in the transaction of parliamentary business, the giving of evidence before either House or a committe, the presentation or submission of a document to either House or a committee, the preparation of a document for the purposes of such business, the publication of a document including a report by order of either House and ancillary matters.[83] Article 9 goes only to prohibit:

- the attachment by the courts of any form of legal penalty to a member of Parliament (or any person taking part in proceedings in Parliament) for anything said in Parliament. This means that a member cannot be sued for defamation in relation to any statement made in parliament, nor prosecuted for any offence relating to these statements;[84]
- the direct criticism by the courts of anything said or done in the course of Parliamentary proceedings.[85]

11.32   Furthermore, Article 9 is a manifestation of the wider principle that the courts and Parliament are both astute to recognise their respective constitutional roles. This means that the courts will not allow any challenge to be made to what is said or done within the walls of Parliament in performance of its legislative functions

---

[77] Crown Proceedings Act 1947, s 10.

[78] See *Derry v Ministry of Defence* (1999) 49 BMLR 62; see also *Pearce v Secretary of State for Defence* [1988] AC 755.

[79] Crown Proceedings (Armed Forces) Act 1987, s 1.

[80] Ibid s 2(2).

[81] See generally, D Limon and W McKay (eds), *Erskine May, Parliamentary Practice* (22nd edn, Butterworths, 1997); I Loveland, *Constitutional Law: A Critical Introduction* (Butterworths, 1996) Chap 8, see also *In Re Parliamentary Privilege Act 1770* [1958] AC 331.

[82] See *per* Lord Browne-Wilkinson, *Pepper v Hart* [1993] 1 AC 593, 638D.

[83] See, in relation to defamation proceedings, Defamation Act 1996, s 13; and generally, *Halsburys Laws of England* (4th edn, Butterworths, 1997) Vol 34, 'Parliament', para 1008, and see *A-G of Ceylon v De Livera* [1963] AC 103, 121.

[84] *Ex p Wason* (1869) LR 4 QB 573, 576; *Dillon v Balfour* (1887) 20 LR Ir 600.

[85] See *Hamilton v Al Fayed* [1999] 1 WLR 1569.

and protection of its established privileges.[86] Thus, in *Prebble v Television New Zealand*[87] Lord Browne-Wilkinson approved Blackstone's statement that:

> the whole of the law and custom of Parliament has its original from this one maxim, 'that whatever matter arises concerning either House of Parliament ought to be examined, discussed, and adjudged in that House to which it relates, and not elsewhere'.[88]

As a result, it is a breach of parliamentary privilege to allow what is said in Parliament to be the subject matter of investigation or submission.[89] It is not permissible to bring into question anything said or done in Parliament by suggesting (whether by direct evidence, cross-examination, inference or submission) that the actions or words were inspired by improper motives.[90] Although it is legitimate to prove as a matter of history by reference to *Hansard* what happened in Parliament, it is not acceptable to go beyond history so as to suggest impropriety. Witnesses may not be cross-examined by reference to earlier evidence given to a parliamentary Select Committee.[91]

11.33

If the exclusion of material on the ground of parliamentary privilege makes it quite impossible fairly to determine the issues between the parties, the court must stay proceedings altogether. The grant of such a stay in *Hamilton v Guardian Newspapers*[92] led to the enactment of section 13 of the Defamation Act 1996 which provides that, where the conduct of a person in or in relation to proceedings in Parliament is in issue in defamation proceedings, he may waive the privilege for the purposes of those proceedings.[93] This waiver is of the privilege of the member alone,[94] and gives rise to potential problems if there is relevant evidence arising out of the conduct of other members who have not waived their privilege.[95] The fact that Parliament has found an MP guilty of misconduct will not prevent the MP taking advantage of the Defamation Act 1996 to sue his accuser for repeating the allegations of misconduct in the media. This will not be a 'questioning of proceedings in parliament'.[96]

11.34

---

[86] *Burdett v Abbot* (1811) 14 East 1; *Stockdale v Hansard* (1839) 9 Ad & El 1; *Bradlaugh v Gossett* (1884) 12 QBD 271; *Pickin v British Railways Board* [1974] AC 765; *Pepper v Hart* [1993] 1 AC 593; *Hamilton v Al Fayed* [2000] 2 WLR 609.

[87] [1995] 1 AC 321.

[88] *Commentaries on the Laws of England* (17th edn, 1830), Vol 1, 163.

[89] *Church of Scientology of California v Johnson-Smith* [1972] 1 QB 522; approved in *Pepper v Hart* [1993] 1 AC 593.

[90] See *Prebble v Television New Zealand* [1995] 1 AC 321, 333.

[91] See generally, *Hamilton v Guardian Newspapers Financial Times*, 22 Jul 1995, May J.

[92] n 91 above and also in *Allason v Haines The Times*, 25 Jul 1995, *per* Owen J.

[93] For s 13, see generally, P Milmo and W Rogers (eds), *Gatley on Libel and Slander* (9th edn, Sweet & Maxwell, 1998) para 13.30; for the history of the *Hamilton v Guardian, Financial Times*, 22 Jul 1995 litigation (which was discontinued on the first day of the trial).

[94] s 13(3).

[95] See *Hamilton v Al Fayed (No 2)* [2000] 2 WLR 609.

[96] Ibid.

11.35 **Judicial immunity.**   The Crown is not liable in respect of actions done by any person 'while discharging or purporting to discharge any responsibility of a judicial nature'.[97] Judges of the superior courts[98] have special immunity against actions in tort even where they are acting outside their jurisdiction.[99] If such a judge acts in bad faith then an action will only lie if he is acting outside his jurisdiction.[100] A similar immunity applies in relation to properly empanelled jurors who are immune from action arising out of anything said or done in their capacity as jurors.[101]

11.36 However, in relation to other judges and magistrates, the common law rule was that they are liable for acts done outside their jurisdiction.[102] The meaning of 'jurisdiction' in this context caused considerable difficulty. Four categories of case have been distinguished:[103] cases in which there is no 'jurisdiction of cause', cases in which magistrates do 'something quite exceptional' in the course of a summary trial, cases in which there is no proper foundation of law for the sentence or order made and cases where, as a result of a technical defect, a magistrate who would otherwise have jurisdiction to try the case and sentence the defendant, acts without jurisdiction. In the fourth class of case, the magistrate was not liable in damages. Thus, a magistrate who issued a warrant without jurisdiction in the course of properly constituted proceedings was not liable.[104] The common law rule in relation to justices was subsequently reversed by a statute. The Justices of the Peace Act 1997 now makes it clear that no action lies against a justice in relation to any matter within his jurisdiction[105] and, in relation to matters not within his jurisdiction, an action will only lie 'only if, it is proved that he acted in bad faith'.[106] The impact of the Human Rights Act on judicial immunity and claims for damages is discussed in Chapter 5.[106a]

11.37 **'Proceedings immunity'.**   There is also an immunity from civil action attaching to preparing a witness statement or giving evidence in court proceedings.[107] It has long been established that no action lies against parties or witnesses for anything said or done, even if falsely and maliciously and without any reasonable and probable cause, in the ordinary course of any proceeding in a court of justice.[108] This

---

[97] Crown Proceedings Act 1947, s 2(5).
[98] The High Court, Court of Appeal and House of Lords.
[99] See generally, A Olowofoyeku, *Suing Judges: A Study of Judicial Immunity* (Clarendon Press, 1993); and 'State Liability for the Exercise of Judicial Power' [1998] PL 444.
[100] See *Anderson v Gorrie* [1895] 1 QB 668, 670; *Re McC (A Minor)* [1985] AC 528, 540–541.
[101] See *Bushell's* case (1670) 6 State Tr 999; *Henderson v Broomhead* (1859) 4 H&N 569, 579.
[102] *Re McC* (n 100 above) 541B-H.
[103] *R v Manchester City Magistrates' Court ex p Davies* [1989] QB 631.
[104] *R v Waltham Forest Justices, ex p Solanke* [1986] QB 479.
[105] s 51.
[106] s 52.
[106a] See para 5.110ff above and see also para 10.175ff above.
[107] See generally, *Docker v Chief Constable of West Midlands Police, The Times,* 1 Aug 2000 (HL).
[108] *Dawkins v Lord Rokeby* (1873) LR 8 QB 255; *Watson v McEwen* [1905] AC 480.

immunity extends to the preparation of evidence to be given in court[109] including the preparation of expert reports.[110] However, in *Docker v Chief Constable of West Midlands Police*[111] the House of Lords distinguished between what a witness said in court or in a witness statement and fabricating evidence (such as a police officer writing down a false confession). It went on to hold that the immunity did not extend to fabricating evidence. Furthermore, it does not apply to proceedings for malicious prosecution,[112] malicious process or malicious arrest.[113] It seems that the immunity does apply to actions for misfeasance in a public office.[114]

It has been said that the test as to whether the immunity should be extended to   **11.38**
new situations is a strict one: 'necessity must be shown'.[115] However, in recent times the immunity has been extended to publications in documents prepared in the investigation of crime[116] and to the supply of information by the official receiver in bankruptcy in the ordinary course of his duties.[117] It is difficult to see in some cases how the test of 'necessity' is satisfied and there are powerful arguments in support of the more limited immunity which can be displaced on proof of malice.[118] The approach is also difficult to reconcile with *Docker*.

There was formerly a closely related immunity applied to advocates in respect of   **11.39**
their conduct and management of a case in court. This applied to any claim for damages for negligence arising out of what is done or omitted in the course of conducting a case in court.[119] This immunity was to be based on public policy and to be part of the general immunity which attaches to judges, witnesses and others participating in trials.[120] It applied to work 'intimately connected with the conduct of the cause in court'.[121] However, the House of Lords in *Arthur J S Hall v Simons*[122] decided that it was no longer in the public interest in the administration of justice for advocates to be immune from suit in civil or criminal litigation.

---

[109] *Marrinan v Vibert* [1963] 1 QB 528.
[110] *Palmer v Durnford Ford (a firm)* [1992] QB 483; *Stanton v Callaghan* [1998] PNLR 116.
[111] See n 107 above.
[112] *Martin v Watson* [1996] 1 AC 74.
[113] *Roy v Prior* [1971] AC 470; *Gizzonio v Chief Constable of Derbyshire, The Times*, 29 Apr 1998.
[114] See *Silcott* (n 107 above); *Docker* (n 107 above), but see *Bennett v Commissioner of Police* (1997) 10 Admin LR 245, cf *Taylor v Director of the Serious Fraud Office* [1998] 1 WLR 1040, 1053H.
[115] *Per* Lord Hoffmann, *Taylor* (n 114 above) 1052F, citing *Mann v O'Neill* (1997) 71 ALJR 903.
[116] *Taylor v Director of the Serious Fraud Office* (n 114 above).
[117] *Mond v Hyde* [1998] 2 WLR 499.
[118] See Lord Lloyd dissenting in *Taylor* (n 114 above).
[119] *Rondel v Worsley* [1969] 1 AC 191; see generally, *Arthur J S Hall v Simons* [1999] 3 WLR 873 (an appeal to the House of Lords is pending).
[120] *Saif Ali v Sydney Mitchell and Company* [1980] AC 198.
[121] *Rees v Sinclair* [1974] 1 NZLR 180.
[122] See n 119 above.

Nevertheless, it will normally be an abuse of process[123] for a civil court to hold that a subsisting conviction is wrong whereas, in general, it will not be an abuse to make a collateral challenge in a claim arising from civil proceedings.

However, a litigant does not owe a duty of care to the opposite party in relation to the manner in which the litigation is conducted.[124]

11.40   **Negligence immunity.**   Public authorities have immunity from negligence claims in a number of different contexts. A claim in the tort of negligence depends on the existence of a 'duty of care' owed by the defendant to the claimant. Where a claimant can show foreseeability of damage and a relationship of proximity with the defendant, a duty of care will be imposed *provided* the court is satisfied that it is 'just and reasonable' to impose such a duty.[125] This requirement involves considerations of 'public policy'. In a range of cases, the courts have held that it is not 'just and reasonable' to impose a duty of care on public authorities. These authorities have, as a result, been granted immunity from actions in negligence. It has been suggested that a general approach underlies the immunity cases namely:

> a recognition that such a duty [of care] would be inconsistent with some wider object of the law or interest of the particular parties. Thus, if the existence of a duty of care would impede the careful performance of the relevant function, or if investigation of the allegedly negligent conduct would itself be undesirable and open to abuse by those bearing grudges, the law will not impose a duty'.[126]

11.41   At least two difficulties arise from the approach taken by the courts. First, despite some suggestions to the contrary,[127] the language used in the cases suggest that the courts are applying a blanket rule of policy which has the effect of preventing access to the court.[128] Secondly, in reaching policy conclusions, the courts make factual *assumptions* about the practical impact of imposing liability in negligence. The difficulty about applying a priori reasoning to these situations was illustrated by the views expressed in the Court of Appeal in *X (Minors) v Bedfordshire County Council*[129] concerning the impact of imposing a duty of care on psychiatrists; whereas Sir Thomas Bingham MR took the view that imposing a duty of care

---

[123] See *Hunter v Chief Constable of West Midlands Police* [1982] AC 529.

[124] *Business Computers International Ltd v Registrar of Companies* [1988] Ch 229.

[125] *Caparo Industries plc v Dickman* [1990] 2 AC 605, 617H, *per* Lord Bridge.

[126] *Capital and Counties plc v Hampshire County Council* [1997] QB 1004, 1040D-E, *per* Stuart-Smith LJ.

[127] See eg *per* Lord Browne-Wilkinson in *Barrett v Enfield LBC* [1999] 3 WLR 79; see para 11.44 below.

[128] Although the Court of Appeal struck out a negligence claim on this basis in *Osman v Ferguson* [1993] 4 All ER 344, the European Court of Human Rights in *Osman v United Kingdom* (1998) 5 BHRC 293 decided that this breached the right of access to the Court under Art 6. The principles applied by the Court are discussed at para 11.195 below and its impact under the Human Rights Act are discussed at para 11.307 below.

[129] [1995] 2 AC 633.

would maintain high standards,[130] Staughton LJ said[131] that it would result in overkill and defensive practices. Unfortunately, the courts have not received evidence as to the practical impact of imposing duties of care and have relied on judicial 'hunches'. This has led to highly unsatisfactory (and inconsistent) conclusions as to the existence of immunities.[132] The force of this argument was accepted by Lord Slynn in *Phelps v Hillingdon London Borough Council*[132a] where he said that it must *not* be presumed that the imposing liability will interfere with the performance of a public body's duties. The allegation must be proved and will only be established in exceptional circumstances.

One of the first areas in which such an immunity was recognised was in relation **11.42** to police investigations. In *Hill v Chief Constable of West Yorkshire*[133] the House of Lords held that, as a matter of public policy, actions for damages for negligence would not lie against the police 'so far as concerns their function in the investigation and suppression of crime'. It was suggested that there was no need to impose a duty of care on the police because 'the general sense of public duty which motivates police forces is unlikely to be appreciably reinforced by the imposition of such liability'. A number of reasons were suggested as to why, as a matter of public policy, the police should be immune from negligence liability:

- the imposition of liability may lead to the exercise of a function being carried on in a detrimental fashion;
- negligence actions against the police might require an elaborate investigation of the facts with a consequent diversion of police manpower and resources.

This reasoning depends on a number of factual assumptions about which no evid- **11.43** ence had been adduced. Nevertheless, the immunity is now well established. It has been held to apply even in cases in which the negligence alleged related to failures to take care in specific high risk factual situations:

- where there was an identified suspect, known to be a threat to named individuals;[134]
- where burglars were present at premises when the police had been called to the scene by an alarm;[135]
- where the police knew about road hazards and had taken no steps to warn road users about them;[136]

---

[130] Ibid 662.
[131] Ibid 675.
[132] See eg the first instance cases discussed in *Capital and Counties plc v Hampshire County Council* [1997] QB 1004, 1022–1024.
[132a] *The Times*, 28 Jul 2000.
[133] [1989] 1 AC 53.
[134] *Osman v Ferguson* [1993] 4 All ER 344, but see *Osman v United Kingdom* (1998) 5 BHRC 293; and see para 11.307 below.
[135] *Alexandrou v Oxford* [1993] 4 All ER 328.
[136] *Ancell v McDermott* [1993] 4 All ER 355.

- where a person has been exposed to psychological harm whilst acting as an 'appropriate adult' in police interviews under Code of Practice C;[137]
- where the police negligently damage property when searching a suspect's home.[138]

Similar reasoning has been employed to grant immunity to other public authorities in related situations:

- to the Crown Prosecution Service[139] and the police[140] in the conduct of criminal prosecutions;
- to the immigration service in relation to the provision of information;[141]
- to the Home Office in relation to the provision of information to the Parole Board concerning prisoners.[142]

11.44   There is also an immunity from negligence claims for local authorities in relation to the performance of their statutory duties to protect children and deal with special educational needs. In *X (Minors) v Bedfordshire County Council*[143] the House of Lords held that it would not be 'just and reasonable' to impose a common law duty of care on a local authority in relation to the performance of its statutory duties to protect children. Three reasons were advanced for this. First, that such a duty would 'cut across the whole statutory system set up for the protection of children at risk'. Secondly, because the task of the local authority in dealing with children at risk is extraordinarily delicate. Thirdly, if liability in damages were to be imposed 'it might well be that local authorities would adopt a more cautious and defensive approach to their duties'. Analogous reasoning was applied in holding that local education authorities were immune from claims in negligence arising out of the provision for children with special needs.[144] A similar immunity has been held to apply in relation to claims against local authorities for negligence in relation to foster parents.[145] In addition, it has been held that the immunity extends to the individual educational psychologists employed by local authorities to give advice in relation to children with learning difficulties.[146] The same policy reasons which led the House of Lords to hold that the local authority had immunity applied to claims against the individuals. These included the risk of late and vexatious claims, the difficulties of establishing causation and the risk of 'defensive

---

[137] *Leach v Chief Constable of Gloucestershire* [1999] 1 WLR 1421 (but it was held that there was a duty to provide counselling afterwards).
[138] *Kinsella v Chief Constable of Nottinghamshire, The Times*, 24 Aug 1999.
[139] *Elguzouli-Daf v Commissioner of Police of the Matropolis* [1995] QB 335.
[140] *Kumar v Metropolitan Police Commissioner*, unreported, 31 Jan 1995.
[141] *W v Home Office, The Times*, unreported 14 Mar 1997 CA.
[142] *Dixon v Home Office*, unreported 30 Nov 1998 CA.
[143] [1995] 2 AC 633.
[144] Ibid 761–762; for US cases in which claims for 'educational malpractice' were struck out, see *Phelps v Hillingdon London Borough Council* [1999] 1 All ER 421, 435j–436f.
[145] *W v Essex County Council* [1999] Fam 90.
[146] *Phelps v Hillingdon LBC* [1999] 1 All ER 421.

education'.[147] On the other hand, in *Barrett v Enfield LBC*[148] the House of Lords held that the public policy considerations which meant that it would not be fair, just and reasonable to impose a common law duty of care on a local authority when deciding whether or not to take action in respect of a suspected case of child abuse did not have the same force in respect of decisions taken once the child was in care.

However, there has been a shift of emphasis in recent cases, partly under the influence of the decision of the Court of Human Rights in *Osman v United Kingdom*.[148a] The courts have made it clear that local authority defendants are unlikely to establish a defence which relies on a 'blanket immunity': there must be a proper examination of the facts in each case.[148b] This approach does not, however, preclude the court from making a summary determination of the 'duty of care' issue under the CPR.[148c]   **11.44A**

Recent cases have suggested that the police are not immune from liability in negligence if there is 'some form of assumption of responsibility' by them for the plaintiff.[149] Furthermore, there are some cases in which other considerations of public policy, such as the need to protect informers, may prevail.[150] The authorities were reviewed by the Court of Appeal in *Costello v Chief Constable of Northumbria*:[151]   **11.45**

> For public policy reasons, the police are under no general duty of care to members of the public for their activities in the investigation and suppression of crime (*Hill's* case). But this is not an absolute blanket immunity and circumstances may exceptionally arise when the police assume a responsibility, giving rise to a duty of care to a particular member of the public (*Hill's* case and *Swinney's* case). The public policy considerations which prevailed in *Hill's* case may not always be the only relevant public policy considerations (*Swinney's* case).[152]

In that case, the police were found liable in negligence as the result of a failure of a police officer to assist a colleague who was being attacked by a prisoner.

It seems that this type of 'policy immunity' does not extend to negligence claims against fire fighters. In *Capital and Counties plc v Hampshire County Council*[153] the   **11.46**

---

[147] Ibid 441h–442h.
[148] [1999] 3 WLR 79; the views expressed by Lord Browne-Wilkinson concerning the decision in *Osman v United Kingdom* (1998) 5 BHRC 293, 84 and their impact on the development of negligence are discussed at para 11.307 below.
[148a] (1998) 5 BHRC 293, see para 11.307 below.
[148b] See, in particular, *Barrett v Enfield London Borough Council* (n 148 above).
[148c] *Kent v Griffiths* [2000] 2 WLR 1158 paras 37–38 (*per* Lord Woolf).
[149] *Elguzouli-Daf v Commissioner of Police of the Metropolis* (n 139 above) 349.
[150] *Swinney v Chief Constable of Northumbria Police Force* [1997] QB 464, 481H–482B.
[151] [1999] 1 All 550.
[152] Ibid 563f–g.
[153] [1997] QB 1004; see also *OLL Ltd v Secretary of State for Transport* [1997] 3 All ER 897 in which a similar approach was taken to the duties of coastguards answering a call at sea.

Court of Appeal considered and dismissed a range of arguments in favour of the imposition of such an immunity including the risk of encouraging 'defensive fire fighting' and the risk of opening the 'floodgates' of litigation.[154] However, fire fighters owe no duty of care in answering calls for help or merely by attending at the scene of the fire and fighting it. A duty of care only arises if the fire fighters themselves create the danger which causes injury. The ambulance service has no immunity and, once a call is accepted, it owes the person on whose behalf the ambulance has been called a duty to attend within a reasonable time.[154a]

11.47   **Statutory immunities.**   The Mental Health Act 1983 gives a limited immunity from suit to those involved in dealing with mental patients.[155] By section 139(1) it is provided that:

> No person shall be liable, whether on the ground of want of jurisdiction or on any other ground, to any civil or criminal proceedings to which he would have been liable apart from this section in respect of any act purporting to be done in pursuance of this Act or any regulations or rules made under this Act, or in, or in pursuance of anything done in discharge of functions conferred by any other enactment on the authority having jurisdiction under Part VII of this Act, unless the act was done in bad faith or without reasonable care.

This provision does not create a 'personal immunity' but imposes a fetter on the court's jurisdiction to act in such cases.[156]

(e) Restrictions arising in the course of proceedings

11.48   The courts have, in some circumstances, refused to allow litigants who are in contempt of court to take further steps in the action until the contempt was 'purged'.[157] However, the fact that a party has disobeyed a court order is not now of itself a bar to his being heard.[158] It is only actions of the party which impeded the course of justice in the cause which gave the court a discretion to refuse to hear him until the impediment was removed or good reason shown why it should not be. In *Re Swaptronics*[159] it was said that:

> were the courts to refuse to allow those in contempt access to the courts simply on the grounds that they are in contempt, they could well be acting in breach of the provisions of Article 6.1 of the European Convention on Human Rights which entitles everyone to the determination of his civil rights by means of a fair and public

---

[154] Ibid 1043D–1044F.

[154a] *Kent v Griffiths* [2000] 2 WLR 1158 (however, the court recognised that, if what was being attacked was the allocation of resources the position might have been different, see para 47, *per* Lord Woolf).

[155] For consideration of these points under the Convention see para 11.191 below.

[156] *Pountney v Griffiths* [1976] AC 314.

[157] *Hadkinson v Hadkinson* [1952] 2 All ER 567, *per* Romer and Somervell LJJ; *Re Jokai Tea Holdings Ltd* [1992] 1 WLR 1196.

[158] *X Ltd v Morgan-Grampian (Publishers) Ltd* [1991] 1 AC 1.

[159] *The Times*, 17 Aug 1998.

hearing before an independent and impartial tribunal. The 'everyone' in that Article is not subject to an exception in respect of people who are guilty of serious offences or contempt of court.

It has been held that, in the light of Article 6 of the Convention, it is not a proper exercise of the court's power to strike out a case where there has been a breach of the rules or a court order if it can be shown that, notwithstanding the party's conduct, there is no substantial risk that there cannot be a fair trial.[159a]

(f) Limitation periods

The Limitation Act 1980 places a range of time limits on access to the courts. These range from a limit of one year for defamation actions[160] to 30 years for actions for recovery of land brought by the Crown.[161] Actions for personal injury are subject to a limitation period of three years.[162] Other actions in tort and actions in contract are subject to a limitation period of six years.[163] In general, the right of a person from whom goods are stolen to bring an action in respect of the theft is not subject to any limitation period.[164] In relation to persons under a disability,[165] the limitation period is six years from the date when the person ceased to be under a disability.[166] The limitation period may be postponed in cases of fraud, concealment or mistake.[167]   **11.49**

Limitation periods are subject to extension in a number of different circumstances. The limitation period for defamation is subject to discretionary extension under section 32A.[168] The limitation period in personal injuries actions is subject to a discretionary extension.[169] Time limits in actions for negligence are subject to extension where relevant facts are not known at the date of accrual, up to a maximum of 15 years.[170] No similar extension applies in contract cases.   **11.50**

(g) Financial restrictions on access to the courts

There are, of course, practical and financial limitations on access to justice in English law. Any person wishing to institute proceedings must pay court fees. These fees may be so high as to prevent effective 'access' to the courts. In *R v Lord Chancellor, ex p Witham*[171] the court considered regulations for the imposition of   **11.51**

[159a] *Arrow Nominees v Blackledge, The Times*, 8 Dec 1999 (Evans-Lombe J); see also *Annodeous Entertainment v Gibson, The Times*, 3 Mar 2000 (Neuberger J).
[160] Limitation Act 1980, s 2A (as substituted by Defamation Act 1996, s 5(2)).
[161] The period is 12 years in respect of actions brought by other litigants, s 15.
[162] Limitation Act 1980, s 11.
[163] ss 2 and 5.
[164] s 4.
[165] That is, infants and persons of unsound mind, s 38(2).
[166] s 28.
[167] s 32.
[168] See *Oyston v Blaker* [1996] 1 WLR 1326.
[169] s 33.
[170] s 14A.
[171] [1998] QB 575.

new fees for the issue of writs in the High Court. The applicant was unemployed, had no savings and was in receipt of income support. He wished to bring proceedings for malicious falsehood and libel as a litigant in person since legal aid was not available for actions in respect of defamation. The Supreme Court Fees (Amendment) Order 1996 provided for a minimum fee of £120 and repealed provisions under the terms of which those in receipt of income support were not obliged to pay fees. As a result, the applicant was unable to issue proceedings and successfully applied for a declaration that the order was *ultra vires.* However, litigants who are not in receipt of income support are still obliged to pay fees for the issue of court process which can be substantial and seem likely to deter litigants of modest means.

11.52   The high level of legal costs prevents or restricts access by most private individuals using their own resources. The recognition of this led to the introduction of legal aid by the state under the provisions of the Legal Aid and Advice Act 1949.[172] The position has until recently been governed by the provisions of the Legal Aid Act 1988. In 1997-98 the sum of £1,526 million was spent on Legal Aid, £597 million of which was spent on criminal cases. Radical changes have been brought about by the Access to Justice Act 1999. This replaces the Legal Aid system with two new schemes: the Community Legal Service for civil cases[173] and the Criminal Defence Service for criminal cases.[174] The Community Legal Service funded by the 'Community Legal Service Fund' has been given a fixed annual budget.[175] This is divided into two main budgets: family and other civil cases. Certain categories of case are excluded from the fund:[176]

- disputes involving negligent damage to person or property —these are generally considered suitable for conditional fees;
- allegations of defamation or malicious falsehood;
- disputes arising in the course of business;
- matters concerned with the law relating to companies or partnerships, the law of trusts and boundary disputes.

Under the Access to Justice Act there is a controlled contracting scheme for legal service providers. It has been held that this scheme is not an unlawful restriction on the common law right of access to the courts.[176a] In contrast, the Criminal Defence Service is a 'demand led' service.[177]

---

[172] For the background, see Lord Bingham's unpublished Barnett Lecture, 11 Jun 1998, and for criminal legal aid see T Goriely, 'The Development of Criminal Legal Aid in England and Wales', in R Young and D Wall (eds), *Access to Criminal Justice: Legal Aid, Lawyers and the Defence of Liberty* (Blackstone, 1996).

[173] s 1.

[174] s 12.

[175] s 5.

[176] Sch 2.

[176a] See *R v Legal Aid Board, ex p Duncan* (2000) 150 NLJ 276.

[177] s 10.

In some circumstances, litigants can be required to give security for costs before proceeding.[178] There is a discretion to order security if the claimant is ordinarily resident out of the jurisdiction, is a nominal claimant, the claimant's address is not stated in the claim form or the claimant has changed his address with a view to evading the consequences of the litigation.[179]

11.53

(h) Rights of appeal

Civil cases. In all but three types of civil appeal it is now necessary to obtain permission to appeal from the judge or the Court of Appeal.[180] The only cases in which permission is not required are appeals against:

11.54

- the making of a committal order;
- a refusal to grant habeas corpus;
- a secure accommodation order made under section 25 of the Children Act 1989.

Appeals from the Court of Appeal to the House of Lords can only be brought with leave of either court.

Criminal cases. A person who is convicted in the magistrates' court following a plea of not guilty may appeal against conviction and/or his sentence to the Crown Court. A person who pleads guilty can only appeal against sentence.[181] The Crown Court may confirm, reverse or vary any part of the decision appealed against.[182] Furthermore, any party to proceedings in the magistrates' court may question the proceedings on the ground that the decision is wrong in law or in excess of jurisdiction by applying for the magistrates to 'state a case for the opinion of the High Court'.[183]

11.55

In relation to trials on indictment, an appeal against conviction[184] or sentence[185] can only be brought with the leave of the Court of Appeal or if the trial judge certifies that the case is fit for appeal. If it appears to the Registrar of Criminal Appeals that an application for leave or a notice of appeal does not show any substantial ground of appeal, he may refer the appeal or application to the court for summary determination.[186] An unsuccessful applicant for leave to appeal is at risk for a direction for 'loss of time', that is that time spent in custody since the commencement of the appeal proceedings shall not count towards any custodial

11.56

---

[178] CPR, Sch 1 R 23.1.
[179] Ibid.
[180] CPR, Sch 1 R 52.3(1).
[181] Magistrates' Court Act 1980, s 108.
[182] Supreme Court Act 1981, s 48.
[183] Magistrates' Court Act 1980, s 111(1).
[184] Criminal Appeal Act 1968, s 1.
[185] Ibid, s 11.
[186] Ibid, s 20.

sentence.[187] However, there will be no direction for loss of time if the appeal is advised by counsel in writing and the grounds were settled and signed by him[188] and, in practice, a direction for loss of time on an unsuccessful leave application is very unusual. A notice of appeal must be served within 28 days of conviction or sentence although there is a discretion to extend time.[188a]

11.57 If an appeal is unsuccessful, the appellant cannot bring a second appeal on the same matter.[189] But the Criminal Cases Review Commission may refer a conviction or sentence to the Court of Appeal[190] if there is a 'real possibility' that the verdict or sentence would not be upheld if the reference were to be made.[191] The Attorney-General can refer to the Court of Appeal any point of law which arose in a case which resulted in an acquittal[192] or a sentence which he considers to be unduly lenient.[193]

(3) Fair trial rights in general

(a) Introduction

11.58 English law provides a number of general rights in relation to the actual conduct of 'legal process'. The common law provides the parties to both criminal or civil proceedings with a number of protections and safeguards which, taken together, form the framework of a common law 'right to a fair trial'. Many of these rights are familiar to public lawyers but it is only in recent years that they have begun to be articulated as part of ordinary court procedures. The common law has long recognised two minimum 'fair trial' principles: *nemo judex in causa sua* (nobody can be a judge in his own cause) and *audi alteram partem* (hear the other side). These are often known as the principles of 'natural justice' and have been developed over the years in relation to all forms of decision-making;[194] they have evolved as the standards of administrative law when the court is reviewing the decision-making of inferior tribunals and public bodies. It has been said that a decision which offends against the principles of natural justice is outside the juris-

---

[187] Ibid, s 29; in practice, such directions are now extremely rare.

[188] *Practice Direction (Crime: Sentence, Loss of Time)* [1980] 1 WLR 270; see also *Monnell and Morris v United Kingdom* (1987) 10 EHRR 205.

[188a] Criminal Appeal Act 1968, s 18(2) and (3).

[189] *R v Pinfold* [1988] QB 462; even if the House of Lords restores a quashed conviction, *R v Berry* [1991] 1 WLR 125.

[190] Criminal Appeal Act 1995, s 9.

[191] Ibid, s 13.

[192] Criminal Justice Act 1972, s 36.

[193] Criminal Justice Act 1988, ss 35 and 36.

[194] See generally, H Wade and C Forsyth, *Administrative Law* (7th edn, Clarendon Press, 1994) Chap 15; Lord Woolf and J Jowell, *De Smith, Woolf and Jowell, Judicial Review of Administrative Action* (5th edn, Sweet & Maxwell, 1995) Chap 17 and M Beloff, 'Natural justice—(The *audi alteram partem* rule) and fairness', in M Supperstone and J Goudie, *Judicial Review* (2nd edn, Butterworths, 1997) paras 8.1–8.72.

diction of the decision-making authority,[195] and that the 'duty to act fairly . . . lies upon everyone who decides anything'.[196] However, the right to a fair trial comprises a number of elements and the right will be considered under five headings: independent and impartial tribunal, fair hearing, public hearing, hearing within a reasonable time and reasoned judgment.

(b) Independent and impartial tribunal

Independence.   The nature of the 'tribunal' which considers legal disputes in England and Wales depends on the nature of the right in question. Criminal cases are dealt with either by magistrates or by a judge and jury in the Crown Court. The civil courts still deal with a large proportion of civil disputes and the High Court retains a supervisory jurisdiction over other tribunals. Many civil disputes are now dealt with by statutory tribunals. **11.59**

The large majority of criminal case are tried by magistrates courts, most of which consist of benches of lay magistrates. Magistrates are appointed by the Lord Chancellor to the 'commission of the peace'.[197] They can be removed at the discretion of the Lord Chancellor in circumstances which are not clearly defined.[198] In 1946, the Royal Commission on Justices of the Peace were told that justices were removed: **11.60**

> Where, for any reason, the Lord Chancellor decided that it is inexpedient or contrary to the public interest that the justice should continue to act in any way as such.

The removal is effected by deletion of the justice's name from the commission of the peace to which he is assigned. It has been suggested that, by constitutional usage, the power of removal must be exercised in a judicial manner and the Lord Chancellor must show cause for the removal.[199]

Serious criminal cases are dealt with by judge and jury at the Crown Court. The judges are Circuit judges or High Court judges, appointed by the Queen on the recommendation of the Lord Chancellor. High Court Judges and Circuit judges also deal with civil cases. High Court judges hold office 'during good behaviour, subject to a power of removal by Her Majesty on an address presented to Her by both Houses of Parliament'.[200] No High Court judge in England or Wales has ever been removed under this provision. It cannot be circumvented by the court **11.61**

---

[195] *A-G v Ryan* [1980] AC 718.
[196] *Board of Education v Rice* [1911] AC 179.
[197] Justice of the Peace Act 1997, s 5 (lay magistrates), s 11 (stipendiary magistrates), s 15 (metropolitan stipendiary magistrates).
[198] See generally, A Bradley and K Ewing, *Constitutional Law* (12th edn, Longman, 1997) 419.
[199] See generally, T Skyrme, *History of the Justices of the Peace* (Barry Rose, 1994) App VI 'The Power to Remove Justices of the Peace'.
[200] Supreme Court Act 1981; s 11(3).

administration refusing to assign cases to a judge.[201] Circuit judges can be removed by the Lord Chancellor, if he thinks fit, for incapacity or misbehaviour.[202] Part-time judges, known as 'Recorders' may be appointed[203] for a specified term[204] to act as judges of the Crown Court and carry out such other judicial functions as may be conferred on them. The appointment of a Recorder may be terminated on the ground of incapacity or misbehaviour or of a failure to comply with the terms of his appointment concerning availability.[205] As a temporary measure, the Lord Chancellor may appoint deputy High Court Judges,[206] deputy Circuit judges, deputy District judges, deputy Masters or Registrars of the Supreme Court and retired Law Lords, Lords Justices and High Court Judges to carry out judicial functions. In April 2000 it was announced[207] that, in the light of the Scots decision in *Starrs v Procurator Fiscal, Linlithgow*[207a] and in order to comply with Article 6 of the Convention, the arrangements for part time judicial appointments would be as follows:

- appointments to be for a minimum period of five years;
- appointments to be renewed automatically, except for limited and specific grounds such as misbehaviour, incapacity, or failure to comply with sitting and training requirements;
- removal from office to be only on limited and specific grounds similar to those for non-renewal;
- wherever administratively possible, the offer of a minimum number of sitting days would be guaranteed.

11.62   Appeals in both criminal and civil cases are heard by the Court of Appeal and, in a few cases, by the House of Lords. Lords of Appeal and members of the Court of Appeal are appointed, in the name of the Queen, by the Prime Minister[208] and have the same 'security of tenure' as High Court Judges.

11.63   Statutory tribunals[209] now adjudicate on a large range of rights including such important areas as employment rights and discrimination claims,[210] the rights of

---

[201] Cf *Rees v Crane* [1994] 2 AC 173 (the decision of Chief Justice of Trinidad and Tobago to exclude a judge from the roster of judges sitting for the following term was quashed as a judge could only be suspended or removed in accordance with the Constitutional procedure).

[202] Courts Act 1971, s 17(4); see *Ex p Ramshay* (1852) 18 QB 173.

[203] Courts Act 1971, s 21; as from Apr 2000, the separate office of Assistant Recorder is no longer retained.

[204] As from Apr 2000, for a period of not less than five years.

[205] Courts Act 1971, s 21(6)

[206] Supreme Court Act 1981, s 9(4).

[207] Lord Chancellor's Department, Press Release, 12 Apr 2000.

[207a] [2000] 1 LRC 718, see para 11.310 below.

[208] Supreme Court Act 1981, s 10.

[209] See generally, Wade and Forsyth (n 23 above) Chap 23.

[210] Employment Tribunals and the Employment Appeal Tribunal.

immigrants and asylum seekers,[211] the detention of mental patients,[212] income tax assessments,[213] and a wide range of disputes concerning land.[214] Most of these tribunals are now governed by the provisions of the Tribunals and Inquiries Act 1992.[215] The Council on Tribunals has overall responsibility for tribunals covered by the Act:[216] of which there are now 78.[217] Some tribunals deal with only a few cases a year and some deal with tens or hundreds of thousands.[218]

Statutory tribunals are intended to be quick and informal and to bring specialist expertise to the resolution of disputes. There are no fixed rules for the composition of tribunals.[219] One form commonly adopted is the 'balanced tribunal' comprising a legally qualified chairman and two expert lay members. The chairman is selected by the appropriate authority from a panel appointed by the Lord Chancellor.[220] The other members are often appointed from panels nominated by the Lord Chancellor or the relevant ministry. Although the legally qualified chairman are usually permanent appointments, the lay members are usually appointed by Government Ministers on terms specified by the Minister. The remuneration, fees and allowances are determined by the Minister.   **11.64**

Criminal offences by members of the armed forces or members of their families are dealt with by 'Courts-martial'. Depending on their gravity, charges against army law can be tried by district, field or general court-martial. A court-martial is not a standing court: it comes into existence in order to try a single offence or group of offences. The 'higher authority', who is a senior officer, will decide whether any case referred to him by the accused's commanding officer should be dealt with summarily, referred to the 'prosecuting authority', or dropped. Once the higher authority has taken this decision, he or she will have no further involvement in the case. The 'prosecuting authority' is the Services' legal branch. Following the higher authority's decision to refer a case to them, the prosecuting authority has absolute discretion, applying similar criteria as those applied in civilian cases by the Crown Prosecution Service to decide whether or not to prosecute, what type of court-martial would be appropriate and precisely what charges   **11.65**

---

[211] Immigration adjudicators and the Immigration Appeals Tribunal, Immigration Act 1971, Sch 5.

[212] Mental Health Review Tribunals, Mental Health Act 1983, s 65.

[213] The Commissioners for Income Tax.

[214] Lands Tribunal, Lands Tribunal Act 1949, s 1.

[215] The predecessor of which was enacted to implement the recommendations of the *Report of the Committee of Administrative Tribunals and Enquiries* (1957) Cmnd 218—The Franks Report.

[216] s 1; this has 10 to 15 members, appointed by the Lord Chancellor and makes annual reports.

[217] Sch 1.

[218] Many tribunals have no cases in a particular year, while the Traffic and General Income Tax Commissioners each deal with several hundred thousand, see Annual Report of Council on Tribunals, 1997–98.

[219] See generally, Wade and Forsyth (n 194 above) 912ff.

[220] Tribunal and Inquiries Act 1992, s 6.

should be brought.[221] Court administration officers are appointed in each Service and will be independent of both the higher and the prosecuting authorities. They are responsible for making the arrangements for courts-martial, including arranging venue and timing, ensuring that a judge advocate and any court officials required will be available, securing the attendance of witnesses and selection of members. Officers under the command of the higher authority will not be selected as members of the court-martial.[222] Each court-martial includes a judge advocate as a member. His advice on points of law are rulings binding on the court and he will have a vote on sentence (but not on conviction). The casting vote, if needed, will rest with the president of the court-martial, who will also give reasons for the sentence in open court. Findings by a court-martial are no longer subject to confirmation or revision by a confirming officer (whose role has been abolished). A reviewing authority has been established in each Service to conduct a single review of each case. Reasons will be given for the decision of the reviewing authority. As part of this process, post-trial advice received by the reviewing authority from a judge advocate (who will be different from the one who officiated at the court-martial) will be disclosed to the accused. There is a right of appeal against conviction and sentence to the civilian Courts-Martial Appeal Court.

11.66 **Impartiality.**   English law permits parties to any form of dispute to challenge the tribunal on the grounds of actual or apparent bias.[223] This is one of the fundamental principles of 'natural justice' and has been clearly recognised since the seventeenth century.[224] It is rare that actual bias, in the sense of actual partiality is established. The case law is largely concerned with 'apparent bias'.

11.67 The starting point for challenging the appearance of bias is that 'justice should not only be done but should manifestly and undoubtedly be seen to be done'.[225] This principle has two closely related but not identical, applications. First, if a judge or member of a tribunal is a party to litigation or has any direct financial[226] or other interest[227] in a matter in dispute, he is automatically disqualified. The question in each case is 'whether the outcome could, realistically, affect the judge's interest'.[228]

---

[221] See Armed Forces Act 1996, Sch I.

[222] Sch I, Pt III, para 19.

[223] See generally, *De Smith, Woolf and Jowell* (n 194 above) Chap 12; J Goudie, 'Interest and Favour' in M Supperstone and J Goudie, *Judicial Review* (2nd edn, Butterworths, 1997) paras 9.1–9.26; and see P Havers and O Thomas, 'Bias Post-*Pinochet* and Under the ECHR' [1999] JR 111.

[224] For the history, see *De Smith, Woolf and Jowell* (n 194 above) paras 12-001–12-005.

[225] *R v Sussex Justices ex p McCarthy* [1924] 1 KB 256, 259.

[226] See *Dimes v Proprietors of Grand Junction Canal* (1852) 3 HL Cas 759; *Leeson v General Council of Medical Education and Registration* (1889) 43 Ch D 366.

[227] *R v Bow Street Metropolitan Stipendiary Magistrate, ex p Pinochet Ugarte (No 2)* [1999] 2 WLR 272 (promotion of a cause in which Lord Hoffman was involved with one of the parties as a director of a company controlled by Amnesty which was a party to the proceedings).

[228] *Locabail (UK) v Bayfield Properties Ltd* [2000] 2 WLR 870, 881D.

It has been said that the size of the financial interest is irrelevant;[229] however more recent authorities have recognised a *de minimis* exception.[230] In any case giving rise to automatic disqualification a judge should recuse himself from the case before any objection is raised.[231]

Secondly, if the judge's conduct or behaviour gives rise to an appearance of bias   **11.68** then he may be disqualified. There has been considerable uncertainty on the authorities on the appropriate test for ascertaining whether there is bias in this sense.[232] In some instances it has been said that the test for disqualification is whether there is a real likelihood of bias.[233] On other occasions it is said that the appearance of bias is made out if a reasonable person acquainted with the position had reasonable grounds for suspecting bias.[234] In *R v Gough*[235] (a case concerned with the apparent bias of a juror) the House of Lords decided that the correct test for bias was whether there was a real danger of bias. The court should ascertain the circumstances and then:

> the court should ask itself whether, having regard to those circumstances, there was a real danger of bias on the part of the relevant member of the tribunal in question, in the sense that he might unfairly regard (or have unfairly regarded) with favour, or disfavour, the case of a party to the issue under consideration.[236]

The perspective from which the matter must be viewed is that of the 'informed observer' and it will very often be appropriate to enquire whether the judge knew of the matter relied on as appearing to undermine his impartiality.[237] The *Gough* test has been adopted in relation to bias issues in a number of different areas.[238] If

---

[229] *R v Hammond* (1863) 9 LT (NS) 423, 'The interest to each shareholder may be 1/4d but it is still an interest' (shareholders in a railway company disqualified from hearing charges of travelling without a ticket); *R v Camborne Justices, ex p Pearce* [1955] 1 QB 41.

[230] *Locabail (UK) v Bayfield Properties Ltd* (n 228 above), 881, 882 and the cases there cited.

[231] Ibid, 886.

[232] See *R v St Edmundsbury Borough Council, ex p Investors in Industry Commercial Properties Ltd* [1985] 1 WLR 1168.

[233] See eg *R v Rand* (1866) LR 1 QB 230; *Rv Barnsley Licensing Justices ex p Barnsley and District Licensed Victuallers' Association* [1960] 2 QB 167.

[234] *R v Sussex Justices, ex p McCarthy* (n 225 above) 259; *Metropolitan Properties Company (FGC) Ltd v Lannon* [1969] 1 QB 577, 599.

[235] [1993] AC 646.

[236] Ibid 670; this approach has, however, not been followed in Australia, *Webb and Hay v The Queen* (1994) 181 CLR 41; and see *Rv S (RD)* (1997) 151 DLR (4th) 193 and *BOC New Zealand v Trans Tasman Properties* [1997] NZAR 49; see also *Ex parte Pinochet Ugarte (No 2)* (n 227, above) 284D–G, (Lord Browne-Wilkinson), 289H–290G (Lord Hope) and *Roylance v GMC (No 2)* [1999] 3 WLR 541, 545E–546H, see also *Locabail (UK) v Bayfield Properties Ltd* (n 228 above), 884–885.

[237] See *Locabail (UK) Ltd v Bayfield Properties* (n 228 above), 885.

[238] *R v Inner West London Coroner, ex p Dallaglio* [1994] 4 All ER 139 (coroner); *Rv Secretary of State for the Environment, ex p Kirkstall Valley Campaign* [1996] 3 All ER 304 (Urban Development Corporation) *AT & T Corporation v Saudi Cable*, *The Times*, 23 May 2000 (arbitrators); for recent example see Goudie, (n 223 above) para 9.11.

the judge becomes aware of any matter which could arguably be said to give rise to a real danger of bias, disclosure should generally be made in advance of the hearing.[239]

(c) Fair hearing

11.69 **Introduction.** The right to a 'fair hearing' has been extensively analysed in the administrative law context.[240] This right has been said to arise by way of 'statutory implication' so that,

> it is to be implied, unless the contrary appears, that Parliament does not authorise . . . the exercise of powers in breach of the principles of natural justice, and that Parliament does . . . require in the particular procedures, compliance with those principles.[241]

Two general points should be noted about the 'duty to act fairly' in English public law. First, it is a flexible standard. As the House of Lords made clear in *R v Secretary of State for the Home Department, ex p Doody*[242] the standards of fairness are not immutable and change over time, both in general and in their application to particular cases. Furthermore, principles of fairness cannot be applied by rote but depend on the context of the decision in question.[243] Second, the duty goes beyond the areas normally covered by constitutional 'due process rights': the duty does not just lie on those charged with the 'determination of civil rights and obligations or of any criminal charges'[244] but extends to all decisions made by public bodies. In the present context the aim is to examine the common law 'fair hearing rights' which apply to what English public law regards as 'judicial' or 'quasi-judicial' decisions.

11.70 A number of aspects of 'procedural fairness' have been recognised in the cases. Whether or not a particular element applies in a given case will depend on the precise circumstances. There is no established list of the elements of procedural fairness but they include the following: prior notice of the case, adequate time to prepare, disclosure of the material on which the decision is to be based, a hearing, legal representation, calling and cross-examination of witnesses, consideration of evidence and submissions. Procedural fairness may also entail an obligation to give reasons for the decision.[245]

---

[239] *Locabail (UK) v Bayfield Properties Ltd* (n 228 above), 886.
[240] See generally, Lord Woolf and J Jowell, *De Smith, Woolf and Jowell, Judicial Review of Administrative Action* (5th edn, Sweet & Maxwell, 1995) Chap 9; and M Beloff, 'Natural justice— (The audi alteram partem rule) and Fairness' in M Supperstone and J Goudie, *Judicial Review* (2nd edn, Butterworths, 1997); H Wade and C Forsyth, *Administrative Law* (7th edn, Clarendon Press, 1994) Chap 15.
[241] *Fairmount Investments Ltd v Secretary of State for the Environment* [1976] 1 WLR 1255, 1263.
[242] [1994] 1 AC 531.
[243] See also *Lloyd v McMahon* [1987] 1 AC 625.
[244] Contrast Art 6(1) of the Convention.
[245] Contrast para 11.89 below.

However, the duty to act fairly can be waived by an applicant where he chooses not to complain about a breach of his rights.[246] Furthermore, a breach of the duty at a hearing can be cured or remedied at a properly conducted appeal hearing. In *Calvin v Carr*[247] the Privy Council distinguished three types of cases: (i) those where the rules for a re-hearing made it possible to treat the appeal as superseding the initial hearing; (ii) those where the hearing structure required a fair hearing at both the initial and appeal hearing; and (iii) those where the court should not intervene because the parties accepted that a fair result had been achieved by fair methods.

11.71

Prior notice of the case.   It has been said that:

11.72

> One of the principles of natural justice is that a person is entitled to adequate notice and opportunity to be heard before any judicial order is pronounced against him, so that he, or someone acting on his behalf, may make such representations, if any, as he sees fit.[248]

As a result, an individual who is likely to be directly affected by the outcome of a decision should be given prior notification of the action to be taken and be given sufficient particulars of the case against him so he is able to prepare his case to meet them.[249]

Adequate time to prepare.   A party must be allowed sufficient time to prepare a case and must not be taken by surprise. Where an adjournment is reasonably needed it must be granted.[250] In criminal cases, this applies to both prosecution and defence.[251]

11.73

Duty of disclosure.   Parties are entitled to proper notice of material which is to

11.74

---

[246] See eg *R v Comptroller-General of Patents and Designs, ex p Parke, Davies and Company* [1953] 1 All ER 862; *R v British Broadcasting Corporation, ex p Lavelle* [1983] 1 WLR 23, 29; and see generally, Beloff (n 240 above), and Wade and Forsyth (n 240 above) 8.60.

[247] [1980] AC 574 which was concerned with contractual rights of appeal; and in relation to statutory appeals: see *McMahon v Lloyd* [1987] AC 625; and see, generally, *De Smith, Woolf and Jowell* (n 240 above) paras 10-20–10-24.

[248] *Forrest v Brighton Justices* [1981] AC 1038, 1045; see also *Mahon v Air New Zealand Ltd* [1984] AC 808, 821.

[249] See eg *Kanda v Government of Malaya* [1962] AC 322; *Chief Constable of North Wales Police v Evans* [1982] 1 WLR 1155 (police probationer should be given notice of allegations about private life); *R v Secretary of State for the Home Department, ex p Hickey (No 2)* [1995] 1 WLR 734 (a convicted prisoner seeking reference to Court of Appeal should be given notice of material before Home Secretary); *R v Secretary of State for the Home Department, ex p Fayed* [1998] 1 WLR 763 (freestanding obligation to disclose areas of concern in advance of decision in respect of nationality so that representations can be made even though the statute precluded the requirement to give reasons for the decision); see generally, *De Smith, Woolf and Jowell* (n 240 above) paras 9-004–9-011; Wade and Forsyth, (n 240 above) 531ff; Beloff (n 240 above) paras 8.41–8.42.

[250] *R v Thames Magistrates' Court, ex p Polemis* [1974] 1 WLR 1371; see also, *Rv Panel on Take-Overs and Mergers, ex p Guinness plc* [1990] 1 QB 146; Beloff (n 240 above) paras 8.43–8.44.

[251] See *R v Barnet Magistrates, ex p DPP*, *The Times*, 8 Apr 1994.

be put before the tribunal for their consideration. In ordinary civil litigation, this is done by the process of disclosure and the exchange of witness statements.[252] In other cases, the decision-maker must disclose relevant evidence on which he intends to rely and give access to all material relevant to the case[253] including reports and expert evidence supplied to the tribunal.[254]

11.75 **A hearing.** The body determining a dispute must give each party a fair opportunity to put his own case. The obligation to conduct a hearing does not necessarily mean there should be an oral hearing. For example, in *Lloyd v McMahon*[255] Liverpool councillors who were surcharged by the district auditor for wilful misconduct were given full particulars of the misconduct alleged and offered them the opportunity to make written representations. However, the councillors never asked for and were never offered an oral hearing. The Court of Appeal ruled that the procedure adopted was unfair, but the House of Lords decided that the procedure was fair and suitable in all the circumstances.[256]

11.76 **Legal representation.** It has sometimes been held that there is a right to legal representation in formal tribunal or investigatory hearings.[257] However, it seems that the better view is that there is no right to legal representation but only a discretion depending on the circumstances, and, in particular, the nature of the allegations being made.[258] The House of Lords have taken the view that the existence of discretion to grant legal representation rather than the absolute right is consistent with Article 6(3)(c) of the Convention.[259]

11.77 **Calling and cross-examination of witnesses.** When there is an oral hearing, the tribunal should usually allow witnesses to be questioned.[260] However, this right may be limited in more informal hearings[261] such as an investigation carried out

---

[252] CPR, Pts 31 and 32.

[253] *R v Army Board of the Defence Council, ex p Anderson* [1992] QB 169; *De Smith, Woolf and Jowell* (n 240 above) paras 9-018–9-020; Wade and Forsyth (n 240 above) 534; Beloff (n 240 above) paras 8.46–8.47.

[254] *R v Kent Police Authority, ex p Godden* [1971] 2 QB 662.

[255] [1987] 1 AC 625.

[256] See also *Rv Army Board of Defence, ex p Anderson* [1992] QB 169; *De Smith, Woolf and Jowell* (n 240 above) paras 9-012–9-017 and 9-023–9-025; Wade and Forsyth, (n 240 above) 537; Beloff, (n 240 above) paras 8.48–8.49.

[257] *De Smith, Woolf and Jowell*, (n 240 above) paras 9-029–9-034; Wade and Forsyth (n 240 above) 540.

[258] *R v Secretary of State for the Home Department, ex p Tarrant* [1985] QB 251.

[259] *Hone v Maze Prison Board of Visitors* [1988] 1 AC 379.

[260] *R v Newmarket Assessment Committee ex parte Allen Newport* [1945] 2 All ER 371, 373; *R v Deputy Industrial Injuries Commissioner, ex p Moore* [1965] 1 QB 456, 490; *Nicholson v Secretary of State for Energy* (1977) 76 LGR 693 (failure to allow objectors questions led to the decision being quashed); *De Smith, Woolf and Jowell* (n 240 above) paras 9-026–9-028 and 9-035–9-038; Wade and Forsyth (n 240 above) 538–9; Beloff (n 240 above) para 8.49.

[261] Cf *Bushell v Secretary of State for the Environment* [1981] AC 75, 97.

by the Commission for Racial Equality.[262] Nevertheless, a person who is entitled to be heard orally will normally be given an opportunity to put his own case, particularly where there are important factual disputes or where oral argument will assist the decision-maker.[263]

Consideration of evidence and submissions.   However, where there is an oral **11.78** hearing it seems that a tribunal must consider all the relevant evidence submitted, inform the parties of the evidence taken into account, allow witnesses to be questioned and allow comment on the whole case.[264] A tribunal should make clear its views on any material construction of relevant statutes and rules so that the parties could properly decide whether to give or call evidence.[265] The decision-makers must take into account the material submitted to them and must not rely on points not argued or private inquiries.[266]

(d) Public hearing[267]

In relation to court proceedings, the general principle, subject to rare exceptions, **11.79** is that the court must sit in public.[268] It has been said:

> Open justice promotes the rule of law. Citizens of all ranks in a democracy must be subject to transparent legal restraint, especially those holding judicial or executive offices. Publicity whether in the courts, the press or both, is a powerful deterrent to abuse of power and improper behaviour.[269]

In *R v Legal Aid Board, ex p Kaim Todner (a firm)*[270] Lord Woolf MR gave four reasons for the principle of open justice: it deters inappropriate behaviour on the part of the court, it maintains public confidence in the administration of justice and enables the public to know that justice is being administered fairly, it may result in new evidence becoming available, and it makes uninformed and inaccurate comment about court proceedings less likely. Nevertheless, the court has an inherent

---

[262] *R v Commission for Racial Equality ex p Cottrell and Rothon* [1980] 1 WLR 1580.

[263] See, eg *R v Criminal Injuries Compensation Board, ex p Dickson* [1997] 1 WLR 58 (no entitlement to an oral hearing where there was no dispute as to the primary facts); *R v Criminal Injuries Compensation Board, ex p Cook* [1996] 1 WLR 1037; *R v Secretary of State for Wales, ex p Emery* [1996] 4 All ER 1 (conflict of documentary evidence concerning footpath should have been tested at public inquiry).

[264] *R v Deputy Industrial Injuries Commissioner, ex p Moore* [1965] 1 QB 456, 490.

[265] *Dennis v United Kingdom Central Council for Nursing, The Times*, 2 Apr 1993

[266] *R v Mental Health Review Tribunal, ex p Clatworthy* [1985] 3 All ER 699, 704.

[267] For a general discussion, see *Arlidge, Eady and Smith on Contempt* (2nd edn, Sweet & Maxwell, Chap 7.

[268] *R v Felixstowe Justices ex p Leigh* [1987] QB 582, 592; *A-G v Leveller Magazine Ltd* [1979] AC 440, 449–450.

[269] *Ex Parte Guardian Newspapers* [1999] 1 All ER 65, 79, 82.

[270] [1998] 3 WLR 925, 934; and see *Hodgson v Imperial Tobacco Ltd* [1998] 1 WLR 1056.

power to exclude the public where a public hearing would defeat the ends of the justice.[271] There are a number of grounds on which such an order may be made including:[272]

- the fact that the case involves the maintenance and upbringing of minors;[273]
- the need to preserve secret technical processes or other commercial confidences;
- the need to avoid the possibility of disorde;[274]
- the fact that a witness refuses to testify publicly;[275]
- the fact that a public hearing might deter future prosecutions.[276]

However, considerations of public decency[277] or national security will not, of themselves, be sufficient to allow a hearing in private.[278]

11.80   An order for a hearing in private is a most exceptional step in civil litigation. The position is now governed by CPR Part 39. By rule 39.2(1), the general rule is that a hearing is to be in public. However, this rule 'does not require the court to make special arrangements for accommodating members of the public'.[279] The hearing may be in private if:[280]

- publicity would defeat the object of the hearing;
- it involves matters relating to national security;
- it involves confidential information and publicity would damage that confidentiality;[281]
- a private hearing is necessary to protect the interests of any child or patient;
- it is a hearing of a without notice application and it would be unjust to the respondent for there to be a public hearing;
- it involves uncontentious matters arising in the administration of trusts or in the administration of a deceased's person's estate; or
- the court considers this to be necessary in the interests of justice.

---

[271] *Scott v Scott* [1913] AC 417, 438; *R v Governor of Lewes Prison, ex p Doyle* [1917] 2 KB 254, 271; *A-G v Leveller Magazine Ltd* [1979] AC 440, 449H–450D; *R v Chief Registrar of Friendly Societies, ex p New Cross Building Society* [1984] QB 227, 235.

[272] Cf Administration of Justice Act 1960 s 12, which deals which the publication of information in relation to proceedings in private and which gives recognition to the first two categories (see also para 15.67ff below).

[273] See *Scott v Scott* (n 271 above) 437, 483; *Re R (Wardship: Restrictions on Publication)* [1994] Fam 254, 271.

[274] *Scott v Scott* (n 271 above) 445–6.

[275] Ibid 439, but this exception must be treated cautiously, the witness can be protected in other ways, such as the grant of anonymity, see para 11.127 below.

[276] *A-G v Leveller Magazine Ltd* (n 271 above) 471C-D.

[277] *Scott v Scott* (n 271 above) 439.

[278] *A-G v Leveller Magazine Ltd* (n 271 above) 471C-D.

[279] CPR, r 39.2(2).

[280] CPR, r 39.3.

[281] PD39 para 1.5 gives a list of hearings which, in the first instance, shall be listed as hearings in private under this rule.

If a hearing is held in private a non-party can seek the leave of the judge to obtain a transcript.[282]

The position is different in criminal cases. Applications for hearings in camera are regularly made in sensitive cases: for example, those involving terrorism or where criminal investigations have been carried out by members of the security services. A judge can order a criminal trial to be held in private if the case involves issues of national security[283] and the public, but not the press, can be excluded when a child is testifying in a case of alleged indecency.[284] The prosecution can apply for a witness to give evidence from behind a screen.[285] An application for an order that all or part of a Crown Court trial should be held in camera for reasons of national security or for the protection of the identity of a witness must be made on seven days' notice, and a copy of the notice must be displayed in the court building.[286] The notice must be dated and should usually specify the ground relied on.[287] The rule applies to any part of the trial process, including a pre-trial application to stay the proceedings as an abuse of the process.[288] Although the rule is expressed in mandatory terms, it is often not complied with when the need for a hearing in camera is said to arise 'urgently'. In such cases Crown Court judges often proceed on the basis that they have inherent power to order a hearing in camera.[289] A judge should not be left to infer, in the absence of relevant evidence from the Crown, that national security will be at risk if the hearing is not held in camera.[290]

11.81

There is inherent jurisdiction to exclude the public but not the press if the interests of justice require it. Thus, in *R v Richards*[291] it was held that the judge had acted properly (and in accordance with Article 6 of the Convention) in excluding the public because an 18-year-old witness felt intimidated by their presence. In addition, as part of its inherent power to control proceedings, the court can permit the names of witnesses to be withheld in both civil and criminal proceedings.[292] This power is rarely used in civil proceedings but is commonly invoked in criminal cases, particularly in blackmail cases and in cases involving 'terrorism' and national security.[293]

11.82

Under the former procedure, if a civil hearing was held in 'chambers' although the

11.83

---

[282] PD39 para 1.12.
[283] Official Secrets Act 1920, s 8(4).
[284] Children and Young Persons Act 1933, s 37.
[285] See para 11.127 below.
[286] Crown Court Rules 1982, r 24A; cf *R v Crook* (1991) 93 Cr App R 17.
[287] *Ex p Guardian Newspapers* [1999] 1 All ER 65.
[288] Ibid.
[289] Cf *R v Godwin* [1991] Crim LR 302.
[290] *Ex p Guardian Newspapers* (n 287 above).
[291] (1999) 163 JP 246.
[292] See *A-G v Leveller Magazine Ltd* [1979] AC 440, 458; see generally, para 15.65 above.
[293] See para 15.67 above.

public had no right to attend subject to specific statutory exceptions involving children, national security and trade secrets,[294] the proceedings were not 'secret'. As a result, members of the public who wished to attend were, if practicable, given permission.[295] Judgments given in chambers were, subject to the statutory exceptions mentioned, public documents and it was not a breach of confidence to disclose what occurred in chambers.[296]

(e) Hearing within a reasonable time

11.84 The English civil justice system has long been notorious for its delays.[297] However, the past two decades have seen a fundamental change in the attitude of the English courts towards the conduct of litigation. There has been a progressive move away from a 'reactive' system, moving at the pace of the parties, to a 'proactive' system of 'case management'.

11.85 The 'overriding objective' of the Civil Procedure Rules is to deal with cases justly.[298] This entails, dealing with cases, so far as practicable, 'expeditiously and fairly'.[299] The court must further the overriding objective 'by actively managing cases'.[300] The courts have been given extensive powers of management over all proceedings.[301] 'Fast track' cases should be allocated timetables of no more than 30 weeks between commencement and trial.[302]

11.86 Under the former procedural rules the court sought to prevent delay after the commencement of proceedings either by striking out the case for 'want of prosecution'[303] or striking it out under its inherent jurisdiction. However, Lord Woolf MR indicated in *Biguzzi v Rank Leisure*[304] that under the self-contained CPR, the earlier authorities were no longer relevant. He stressed that under the CPR time limits were more important than formerly and that the court now has much broader powers to consider alternatives to striking out the case such as making costs orders (including ordering costs on an indemnity basis), making orders in relation to interest or ordering that money be paid into court.[305] It has, however, been emphasised that the sanction to be invoked by the court to deal with a

---

[294] Administration of Justice Act 1960, s 12.
[295] *Hodgson v Imperial Tobacco Ltd* [1998] 1 WLR 1056, 1072A–C.
[296] Ibid.
[297] For a general discussion, see Lord Woolf, *Access to Justice* (The Stationery Office, 1996), Chap 3, paras 29–42.
[298] CPR, r 1.1(1).
[299] CPR, r 1.1(2)(d).
[300] CPR, r 1.4(1).
[301] CPR, Pt 3.
[302] CPR, r 28.2(4).
[303] See *Birkett v James* [1978] AC 297; there is a large body of case law dealing with these principles, see the survey in *Shtun v Zalejska* [1996] 1 WLR 1270.
[304] [1999] 1 WLR 1926, 1934; see also *Purdy v Cambran* [1999] CPLR 843.
[305] Ibid 1932, 1933.

particular case of delay should be proportionate and that the court should hesitate before striking out an apparently meritorious claim.[305a]

Criminal cases. In criminal cases, there is no general right to a trial within a reasonable time. However, it has been said that constitutional provisions in relation to trial within a reasonable time 'do no more than codify in writing the requirements of the common law which ensure that an accused person receives a fair trial'.[306] There is no general limit on the length of time that can elapse between charge and trial but certain time limits have been laid down under the Prosecution of Offences Act 1985:[307]   **11.87**

- 70 days between first appearance in the magistrates' court and committal proceedings;
- 56 days from first appearance in the magistrates' court to the opening day of the trial;
- 112 days between committal for trial and arraignment.

Furthermore, the courts have an inherent jurisdiction to stay prosecutions on the ground of prejudice resulting from delay even though that delay has not been occasioned by fault on the part of the prosecution.[308] However, a stay should not be imposed on the ground of delay unless the defendant shows, on the balance of probabilities that he will suffer serious prejudice to the extent that no fair trial can be held.[309] In cases involving constitutional rights to a speedy trial it has been suggested that the court should look at four factors: the length of delay; the reasons given by the prosecution to justify the delay, the responsibility of the accused for asserting his rights and the prejudice to the accused.[310] In general, this right should be asserted on an application to stay for an abuse of the process to the trial judge.[311]   **11.88**

(f) Reasoned judgment

A judge determining an issue of law or fact is under a common law duty to give reasons for his decision. This is a function of 'due process and justice' and has a   **11.89**

[305a] See *Annodeous Entertainment v Gibson, The Times*, 3 Mar 2000.

[306] *Per* Lord Woolf, *Vincent v The Queen* [1993] 1 WLR 862, 867, PC, Jamaica; but see *DPP v Tokai (Jaikaran)* [1996] AC 856, 158; PC, Trinidad and Tobago).

[307] s 22; see Prosecution of Offences (Custody Times Limits) Regulations, 1987, SI 1987/698; see also para 10.60 above.

[308] *R v Telford Justices, ex p Badhan* [1991] 2 QB 78; *A-G's Reference (No 1 of 1990)* [1992] QB 630 for a general discussion of the jurisdiction to stay for abuse of the process see para 11.141ff below.

[309] *A-G's Ref (No 1 of 1990)* (n 308, above) 644; see also *Jago v District Court of New South Wales* (1989) 168 CLR 23, High Court of Australia and *Tan v Cameron* [1992] 2 AC 205, PC, and generally, *Archbold: Criminal Pleading, Practice and Evidence* (Sweet & Maxwell, 1999), 4–64.

[310] *Bell v DPP of Jamaica* [1985] AC 937; referring to *Barker v Wingo* (1972) 407 US 514 ; see also *US v Von Neumann* (1986) 474 US 242; and *Re Mlambo* [1993] 2 LRC 28.

[311] See *DPP v Tokai (Jaikaran)* [1996] AC 856.

two-fold rationale: the parties should be in no doubt why they have won or lost and a fully reasoned judgment is more likely to be soundly based on the evidence.[312] A judgment given after the trial should display:

> the building blocks of the reasoned judicial process, where the evidence on each issue is marshalled, the weight of the evidence analysed, all tested against the probabilities based on the evidence as a whole, with clear findings of fact and all reasons given.[313]

11.90 There is no common law rule that non-judicial decision-makers must always give reasons for their decisions.[314] However, the duty to act fairly will often imply an obligation to provide reasons.[315] In *R v Civil Service Appeal Board, ex p Cunningham*[316] Lord Donaldson took the view that implying an obligation to provide reasons depended on:

- the character of the decision-making body;
- the framework within which the body operates; and
- whether additional procedural safeguards are needed to attain fairness.

In *R v Higher Education Funding Council, ex p Institute of Dental Surgery*[317] the Divisional Court took the position further. Sedley J held that there was an implied duty to provide reasons for a decision where (1) the subject matter is of an interest so highly regarded by the law (for example, personal liberty) that fairness requires reasons as of right or (2) the decision appears aberrant (so that fairness requires reasons so that the recipient can see if the aberration is real and challengeable). In *R v Mayor of City of London, ex p Matson*[318] the Court of Appeal suggested that even where a decision was not aberrant, fairness might require that reasons should be given in appropriate circumstances. The Court of Appeal therefore quashed a decision of the Court of Aldermen refusing to confirm the election of the applicant on the ground that no reasons for its conclusion had been given.

11.91 The Privy Council in *Stefan v General Medical Council*[319] recently summarised the position as follows:

---

[312] *Flannery v Halifax Estate Agencies* [2000] 1 WLR 377.

[313] *Heffer v Tiffin Green, The Times*, 28 Dec 1998.

[314] *R v Secretary of State for the Home Department, ex p Doody* [1994] 1 AC 531, 564 *per* Lord Mustill; *R v Kensington London Borough Council, ex p Grillo* (1996) 28 HLR 94, 105 *per* Neill LJ; *R v Ministry of Defence, ex p Murray* [1998] COD 134.

[315] See generally, Lord Woolf and J Jowell, *De Smith, Woolf and Jowell, Judicial Review of Administrative Action* (5th edn, Sweet & Maxwell, 1995) paras 9-039–9-053; H Wade and C Forsyth, *Administrative Law* (7th edn, Clarendon Press, 1994) 541–5; M Beloff, 'Natural Justice— (The audi alteram partem rule) and Fairness' in M Supperstone and J Goudie, *Judicial Review* (2nd edn, Butterworths, 1997) paras 8.54–8.57; D Toube, *Requiring Reasons at Common Law* [1997] JR 68; and see *Stefan v General Medical Council* [1999] 1 WLR 1293.

[316] [1992] 2 ICR 816; see also *R v Secretary of State for the Home Department, ex p Doody* [1994] AC 531.

[317] [1994] 1 WLR 242.

[318] [1996] 8 Admin LR 49.

[319] [1999] 1 WLR 1293.

The trend of the law has been towards an increased recognition of the duty upon decision-makers of many kinds to give reasons. This trend is consistent with current developments towards an increased openness in matters of government and administration. But the trend is proceeding on a case by case basis (*R v Royal Borough of Kensington and Chelsea, Ex parte Grillo* (1996) 28 HLR 94), and has not lost sight of the established position of the common law that there is no general duty, universally imposed on all decision-makers. . . . There is certainly a strong argument for the view that what were once seen as exceptions to a rule may now be becoming examples of the norm, and the cases where reasons are not required may be taking on the appearance of exceptions.[320]

Lord Clyde went on to say that a review of the general principles should take place in the context of a case arising out of the Human Rights Act.[321]

The duty to act fairly obliges the Crown Court to give reasons where it is dealing **11.92** with appeals from the magistrates' courts, identifying the main issues in dispute and how each of them was resolved[322] including appeals in licensing applications.[323] The reasons given must be intelligible and adequate so that the reader knows what conclusions the decision-maker came to on the principal controversial issues.[324] However, this principle is not always applied in criminal cases. It is clear that the decisions of magistrates, even professional stipendiary magistrates, do not call for reasons.[325] A jury does not give reasons for its decisions and Crown Court judges often do not give reasons for decisions made in the course of trials.

(4) Fair trial rights in criminal cases

(a) Introduction

It is a fundamental principle of criminal law that 'the court is under the duty to en- **11.93** sure the accused a fair trial'.[326] This is an 'elementary right of every defendant'[327] and is properly described as a 'constitutional right'.[328] The right to fair trial of an accused in criminal cases has a number of components: the right to legal advice, the right to pre-trial disclosure of evidence, the right to a speedy trial, the right to

---

[320] Ibid, 1300F–1301B.

[321] Ibid 1301.

[322] *R v Harrow Crown Court, ex p Dave* [1994] 1 WLR 98; *DPP v Pullum* unreported, 17 Apr 2000.

[323] *R v Snaresbrook Crown Court, ex p Lea*, The Times, 5 Apr 1994.

[324] See *Save Britain's Heritage v Number 1 Poultry Ltd* [1991] 1 WLR 153, 166, 167.

[325] *R v Civil Service Appeal Board; ex p Cunningham* [1992] ICR 816; *Rey v Government of Switzerland* [1998] 3 WLR 1, 10C-H (no implied duty on magistrates to give reasons in extradition proceedings).

[326] *R v Sang* [1980] AC 402.

[327] *Per* Lord Hope, *R v Brown (Winston)* [1998] AC 367, 374F.

[328] *Per* Steyn LJ, *R v Brown (Winston)* [1994] 1 WLR 1599, 1606E; see generally, Lord Steyn, 'The Role of the Bar, the Judge and the Jury' [1999] Public Law 51, 55; and also *Dodd v Chief Constable of Cheshire*, unreported, 22 Oct 1997 ('the plaintiff's constitutional right is for a fair trial . . .'.

silence and presumption of innocence. These rights can be protected by the power of the court to stay proceedings which are an abuse of its process:[328a] serious breaches of such rights may lead to the court ordering a stay. In addition, the court has a general power to exclude evidence whose admission would result in unfairness.

(b) Right to legal advice

11.94 At common law, a person in custody was entitled to consult a solicitor at an early stage of the investigation unless this would caused unreasonable delay or hindrance to the investigation or the administration of justice.[329] This has been described as a 'fundamental right'[330] but its precise ambit at common law was unclear. In relation to individuals held in police custody,[331] the right is now to be found in section 58 of the Police and Criminal Evidence Act 1984 which provides that:

> A person arrested and held in custody in a police station or other premises shall be entitled, if he so requests, to consult a solicitor privately at any time.[332]

This is subject to statutory exceptions, most importantly, if this will lead to harm or interference with evidence or the alerting of other suspects.[333] As was pointed out in *R v Samuel*[334] the officer:

> must believe that a solicitor will, if allowed to consult with a detained person, thereafter commit a criminal offence. Solicitors are officers of the court. We think that the number of times that a police officer could genuinely be in that state of belief will be rare.

There is, however, no established common law right to have a solicitor present at a police interview although it is possible that such a right could be developed.[335] Under paragraph 6.8 of the Code of Practice C (Detention, Treatment and Questioning of Persons), if a suspect has exercised his statutory right to legal advice at a police station and the solicitor is available, the solicitor must be allowed to be present at the interview. The fact that an accused is denied legal advice in a police station, in breach of section 58, does not, necessarily, mean that the

---

[328a] See para 11.141ff below.

[329] *R v Lemsatef* [1977] 1 WLR 812; *R v Chief Constable of South Wales, ex p Merrick* [1994] 1 WLR 663.

[330] Cf *R v Samuel* [1988] QB 615, in relation to the statutory provision.

[331] That is, whose custody has been authorised by a custody officer, see *R v Kerawalla* [1991] Crim LR 451.

[332] s 58(1).

[333] s 58(8); see also s 58(8A) in relation to 'drug trafficking' offences and s 58(13) in relation to 'terrorism provisions'.

[334] [1988] QB 615; see also *R v Silcott, The Times*, 9 Dec 1991.

[335] *R v Chief Constable of the Royal Ulster Constabulary, ex p Begley* [1997] 1 WLR 1475.

evidence obtained in interview will be excluded.[336] The court will consider whether to exclude the confession under the provisions of the Police and Criminal Evidence Act 1984.[337]

There was no 'right to legal assistance' in criminal cases at common law.[338] **11.95** Nevertheless, legal advice has been provided for a considerable period under various statutory schemes. Assistance in criminal cases was first made available, in very limited terms, by the Poor Prisoner's Defence Act 1903. It was slightly improved by the Poor Prisoner's Defence Act 1930. Legal aid was granted by magistrates and was paid by local ratepayers. Its availability was gradually increased.[339] The position now is governed by Part I of the Access to Justice Act 1999.[340] The competent authority to grant legal aid is generally the court before which the proceedings take place.[341] A right to representation shall always be granted in such circumstances as may be prescribed.[342] Any question as to whether a right to representation should be granted shall be determined according to the interests of justice.[343] The factors to be taken into account include the following:[344]

- whether the individual would, if any matter arising in the proceedings is decided against him, be likely to lose his liberty or livelihood or suffer serious damage to his reputation;
- whether the determination of any matter arising in the proceedings may involve consideration of a substantial question of law;
- whether the individual may be unable to understand the proceedings or to state his own case;
- whether the proceedings may involve the tracing, interviewing or expert cross-examination of witnesses on behalf of the individual;
- it is in the interests of someone other than the accused that the accused be represented.

The general rule is that an individual for whom services are funded by the Commission as part of the Criminal Defence Service shall not be required to make any payment in respect of the services.[345] However, where representation for

---

[336] *R v Alladice* (1988) 87 Cr App R 380 (defendant aware of rights and able to cope with interview), see generally, *Archbold: Criminal Pleading, Practice and Evidence* (Sweet & Maxwell, 1999) para 15–218ff.

[337] See para 11.111 below.

[338] But see *Dietrich v R* (1992) 177 CLR 292.

[339] See T Goriely, 'The Development of Criminal Legal Aid in England and Wales', in R Young and D Wall (eds), *Access to Criminal Justice: Legal Aid, Lawyers and the Defence of Liberty* (Blackstone Press, 1996) 26–54.

[340] Replacing Part V of the Legal Aid Act 1988.

[341] Access to Justice Act 1999, Sch 3, para 2.

[342] Ibid Sch 3, para 5(4).

[343] Ibid Sch 3, para 5(1).

[344] Ibid Sch 3, para 5(2).

[345] Access to Justice Act 1999, s 17(1).

an individual in respect of criminal proceedings in any court other than a magistrates' court is funded the court may make an order requiring him to pay some or all of the costs of representation.[346]

(c) Pre-trial disclosure

11.96 The prosecution owe a duty to the courts to ensure that all relevant evidence which assists an accused is either led by them or made available to the defence.[347] This right is part of the more general right to a 'fair trial':

> The rules of disclosure which have been developed by the common law owe their origin to the elementary right of every defendant to a fair trial. If a defendant is to have a fair trial he must have adequate notice of the case which is to be made against him. Fairness requires that the rules of natural justice must be observed.[348]

The prosecution was under a common law duty to provide material which had or might have some bearing on the offences charged. All 'material' evidence was discloseable. This was defined as the evidence:

> which can be seen on a sensible appraisal by the prosecution (1) to be relevant or possibly relevant to an issue in the case; (2) to raise or possibly raise a new issue whose existence is not apparent from the evidence which the prosecution proposes to use; (3) to hold out a real (as opposed to fanciful) prospect of providing a lead on evidence which goes to (1) or (2).[349]

There was a duty to provide all statements which have been taken, whether or not the witnesses were apparently credible.[350] This includes material relevant to the credibility of prosecution witnesses[351] but not material which relates only to the credibility of defence witnesses. This is because:

> Fairness, so far as the preparation of the defence case and the selection of the defence witnesses are concerned is preserved by the existing rules of disclosure and by ensuring that the defendant has adequate time and facilities for the preparation of his defence. That right, which is to be found also in article 6.3(b) of [the Convention] has for long been part of our law relating to the conduct of criminal trials.[352]

11.97 The position has now been modified by the complex provisions of the Criminal Procedure and Investigations Act 1996 ('the CPIA') and the Code of Practice issued under it. These replace the common law rules in relation to prosecution disclosure.[353] The effect of these provisions is, in summary:[354]

---

[346] Ibid s 17(2), this is subject to regulations made under s 17(3).
[347] *R v Ward (Judith)* [1993] 1 WLR 619, 645.
[348] *Per* Lord Hope, *R v Brown (Winston)* [1998] AC 367, 374F.
[349] *R v Keane* [1994] 1 WLR 746.
[350] *R v Mills* [1998] AC 382; cf *R v Stinchcombe* (1991) 68 CCC (3d) 1.
[351] Cf *Wilson v Police* [1992] 2 NZLR 533.
[352] *R v Brown (Winston)* [1998] AC 367, 381A-B.
[353] CPIA, s 21(1).
[354] For a full account, see *Archbold: Criminal Pleading, Practice and Evidence* (Sweet & Maxwell, 1999) para 12–52ff; P Murphy (ed), *Blackstone's Criminal Practice 1999* (Blackstone Press, 1999) D6.

- the person investigating the offence must record and retain information or material gathered or generated during the investigation;[355]
- the prosecution must disclose the material on which it intends to rely at trial;
- in addition, the prosecution must make 'primary disclosure' of the other material which, 'in the prosecutor's opinion might undermine the case for the prosecution against the accused';[356]
- the defence must then provide a 'defence statement' setting out 'in general terms the nature of the accused's defence' and 'indicating the matters on which he takes issue with the prosecution' and why;[357]
- the prosecution then comes under a duty to make 'secondary disclosure' of any previously undisclosed material 'which might reasonably be expected to assist the accused's defence' as disclosed by the defence statement;[358]
- the prosecutor is under a continuing duty to review questions of disclosure.[359]

Although the disclosure provisions do not apply until after committal, it is envisaged that some disclosure may be required before then although this would not normally exceed primary disclosure.[360]

The prosecutor may, at any time, make an application to the court for an order **11.98** that material should not be disclosed on the grounds that 'it is not in the public interest to disclose it'.[361] The common law rules as to whether disclosure is in the public interest continue to apply.[362] A number of categories of documents are covered:

- documents which would tend to disclose the identity of informers;[363]
- documents which might reveal the location of police observation posts;[364]
- police reports[365] or manuals.[366]

The procedure to be followed was established in *R v Davis*[367] in which the following principles were set out:

---

[355] Code of Practice, para 5.1, see *Archbold: Criminal Pleading, Practice and Evidence* (Sweet & Maxwell, 1999) para 12–105.
[356] CPIA, s 3(1).
[357] CPIA, s 5.
[358] CPIA, s 7.
[359] CPIA, s 9.
[360] See *R v Director of Public Prosecutions, ex p Lee* [1999] 2 All ER 737.
[361] CPIA, s 8.
[362] CPIA, s 21(2).
[363] *Marks v Beyfus* (1890) 25 QBD 494 and see *Savage v Chief Constable of Hampshire* [1997] 1 WLR 1061.
[364] *R v Rankine* [1986] QB 861; *R v Johnson (Kenneth)* [1989] 1 All ER 121.
[365] *Evans v Chief Constable of Surrey* [1988] QB 588; *Taylor v Anderton (Police Complaints Authority Intervening)* [1995] 1 WLR 447.
[366] *Gill and Goodwin v Chief Constable of Lancashire*, The Times, 3 Nov 1992.
[367] [1993] 1 WLR 613.

n general, the prosecution has a duty to make disclosure voluntarily;

f the prosecution wishes to rely on public interest immunity it should, wherver possible, notify the defence that it will be applying for a court ruling and indicate the category of material in question, so that the defence has the opportunity of making representations to the court;

- where the disclosure of the category of material would itself reveal the information which the prosecution does not wish to reveal, the prosecution should notify the defence of the application but this will be made *ex parte*;[368]
- in highly exceptional cases, the prosecution may apply to the court *ex parte*, without any notice to the defence.

The procedure now is set out in rules made under the CPIA.[369] The court should study the material before making an order.[370]

11.99   The test to be applied by the court on an application for an order for 'non-disclosure' is unclear. In the leading case of *Marks v Beyfus*[371] it was said that:

> if upon the trial of a prisoner, the judge should be of the opinion that the disclosure of the name of the informant is necessary or right to shew the prisoner's innocence, then one public policy is in conflict with another public policy and that which says that an innocent man is not to be condemned when his innocence can be proved is the policy that must prevail.

This suggests that material which assists the defence should always be disclosed. However, in *R v Keane*[372] the Court of Appeal held that the court must carry out a balancing exercise: between the public interest in the non-disclosure of the documents and the public interest in the proper administration of justice. It is clear that public interest immunity may be overridden

> in order to prevent the possibility that a man may, by reason of the exclusion, be deprived of the opportunity of casting doubt upon the case against him.[373]

Disclosure should always be ordered if the witholding of the information 'may prove the defendant's innocence or avoid a miscarriage of justice'.[374]

11.100   The obligation to make pre-trial disclosure does not apply to trials in the magistrates' court. The absence of such disclosure does not affect the fairness of any

---

[368] No *ex parte* application should be made where there is nothing that cannot be said in the presence of defence counsel: *R v Smith (David)* [1998] 2 Cr App R 1.

[369] Crown Court (Criminal Procedure and Investigations Act 1996) (Disclosure) Rules 1997, *Archbold: Criminal Pleading, Practice and Evidence* (Sweet & Maxwell, 1999), para 12–77.

[370] *R v Brown (Winston)* [1994] 1 WLR 1599; but see *Balfour v Foreign and Commonwealth Office* [1994] 1 WLR 681.

[371] (1890) 25 QBD 494, 498; see also *R v Governor of Brixton Prison, ex p Osman* [1991] 1 WLR 281, 290.

[372] [1994] 1 WLR 746.

[373] *R v Agar* (1990) 90 Cr App R 318.

[374] *R v Keane* [1994] 1 WLR 746, 484; see also *R v Turner (Paul)* [1995] 1 WLR 264; and generally, *Archbold: Criminal Pleading, Practice and Evidence* (Sweet & Maxwell, 1999) para 12–44e.

trial, provided that justices appreciate the need to grant reasonable adjournments to enable the defendant to deal with the evidence.[375] Nevertheless, such disclosure ought to be given if requested unless there are good reasons for a refusal, such as protection of a witness (at least where the offences charged could possibly lead to imprisonment).[376] The disclosure position is not affected by the provisions of the CPIA.[377] It has been held that this approach is consistent with Article 6 of the Convention.[378]

(d) The right to silence and the privilege against self-incrimination

Introduction.   The 'right to silence' and the 'privilege against self-incrimination' are closely related rights which are deeply embedded in the common law.[379] The right to silence has been analysed by the House of Lords as including the following:

    (1) A general immunity, possessed by all persons and bodies, from being compelled on pain of punishment to answer questions posed by other persons or bodies.

    (2) A general immunity, possessed by all persons and bodies, from being compelled on pain of punishment to answer questions the answers to which may incriminate them.

    (3) A specific immunity, possessed by all persons under suspicion of criminal responsibility whilst being interviewed by police officers or others in similar positions of authority, from being compelled on pain of punishment to answer questions of any kind.

    (4) A specific immunity, possessed by accused persons undergoing trial, from being compelled to give evidence, and from being compelled to answer questions put to them in the dock.

    (5) A specific immunity, possessed by persons who have been charged with a criminal offence, from having questions material to the offence addressed to them by police officers or persons in a similar position of authority.

    (6) A specific immunity . . . possessed by accused persons undergoing trial, from having adverse comment made on any failure (a) to answer questions before the trial, or (b) to give evidence at the trial.[380]

In addition, there is a specific immunity from answering questions or providing evidence in the course of an action which might expose the party to contempt proceedings in that action.[380a]

11.101

---

[375] *R v Kingston-upon-Hull Justices, ex p McCann* (1991) 155 JP 569.
[376] Ibid 573E–574B; *R v Stratford Justices, ex p Imbert* (1999) 2 Cr App R 276.
[377] See *R v Stratford Justices ex p Imbert* (n 376 above).
[378] Ibid.
[379] See generally, I Dennis, 'Instrumental Protection, Human Right or Functional Necessity? Reassessing the Privilege Against Self-incrimination' (1995) 52 CLJ 342.
[380] *Per* Lord Mustill, *R v Director of Serious Fraud Office, ex p Smith* [1993] AC 1, 30F–31B; see also *Bishopsgate Investment Management v Maxwell* [1993] Ch 1.
[380a] *Memory Corporation v Sidhu* [2000] 2 WLR 1106.

11.102 **The right to refuse to answer questions.**   The first aspect of the right to silence has been subject to substantial statutory encroachment over recent years.[381] Witnesses can now be compelled to give evidence in a number of situations where financial irregularity and fraud are being investigated. The Director of the Serious Fraud Office ('SFO') has the power to require a person under investigation or any other person who he has reason to believe has relevant information to produce documents and to provide an explanation of them.[382] The powers can be exercised at any time.[383] SFO do not have to provide the person being interviewed with advance information as to the subject matter of the interview.[384] Legal professional privilege provides a ground for refusing to produce.[385] It was held that the effect of these statutory provisions was to override the privilege against self-incrimination.[386] The privilege has now been restored by statute.[386a]

11.103 Inspectors appointed by the Department of Trade and Industry have powers to compel witnesses to give them assistance, to attend before them and to answer questions on oath.[387] Such inspections are conducted in private and information disclosed to the inspectors is not generally to be made public.[388] A witness cannot refuse to answer such questions on the grounds of self-incrimination.[389] By section 434(5):

> An answer given by a person to a question put to him in exercise of powers conferred [by section 434] . . . may be used in evidence against him.

It was held that such evidence could not be excluded under section 78 of the Police and Criminal Evidence Act 1984[390] simply because the statute overrode the principles against self-incrimination.[391] The privilege has now been restored by statute.[391a] The evidence obtained by inspectors can be used in directors disqualification proceedings.[392] Any refusal to comply with the requirement of an inspector is a contempt of court.[393]

---

[381] See generally, O Davies, 'Self-Incrimination, Fair Trials and the Pursuit of Corporate and Financial Wrongdoing' in B Markesinis (ed), *The Impact of the Human Rights Bill in English Law* (Oxford University Press, 1998) 31.

[382] Criminal Justice Act 1987, s 2.

[383] *R v Turner, The Times*, 2 Jul 1993 (after service of defence statement).

[384] *R v Serious Fraud Office, ex p Maxwell, The Independent*, 7 Oct 1992.

[385] *In Re Barlow Clowes Gilt Managers Ltd* [1992] Ch 208.

[386] *R v Director of Serious Fraud Office, ex p Smith* [1993] AC 1.

[386a] See para 11.107 below.

[387] Companies Act 1985, s 434(2), and (3); and generally, *Re Pergamon Press Ltd* [1971] Ch 388.

[388] See *Hearts of Oak Assurance Co v A-G* [1932] AC 392.

[389] *Re London United Investments plc* [1992] Ch 578.

[390] See para 11.132 below.

[391] *R v Saunders (Ernest)* [1996] 1 Cr App Re 463, 475–477.

[391a] See para 11.107 below.

[392] *R v Secretary of State for Trade and Industry, ex p McCormick* [1998] BCC 379; *Official Receiver v Stern* [2000] UKHRR 332.

[393] s 434.

Comparable powers of compulsion are found in the Insolvency Act 1986.[394] By **11.104**
section 433 it is provided that:

> In any proceedings (whether or not under this Act) . . .
>
> > (b) any . . . statement made in pursuance of a requirement imposed by or
> > under any [provision of this Act] or by any rules made under this Act;
>
> may be used in evidence against any person making or concurring in making the
> statement.

As a result, the witness cannot rely on the privilege against self-incrimination to
refuse to answer questions[395] and it was possible to use the written record of the examination in criminal proceedings.[396] The common law position has now been restored by statute.[396a]

The Financial Services Act 1986 gives similar **powers of compulsion** to inspectors **11.105**
investigating insider dealing.[397] It is expressly provided that a statement made by
a person in compliance with a requirement imposed on him by an inspector 'may
be used in evidence against him'.[398] It was held that there is no power to exclude
such evidence.[399] The position has, however, been reversed by statute.[399a]

There are similar powers of compulsion in relation to insurance,[400] banking,[401] **11.106**
financial services,[402] planning enforcement[403] and the regulation of waste on
land.[404] It has been held that the power to require the provision of information in
relation to the supply of waste was conferred not merely for the purposes of obtaining evidence but also for the broad public purpose of protecting public health
and the environment and that, as a result, those questioned should not be entitled
to rely on the privilege against self-incrimination.[404a] The question of exclusion of
potentially incriminating answers on the ground of prejudice was a matter for the
discretion of the trial judge.

---

[394] For example, s 236 (provision of information to liquidators by officers of companies in liquidation); s 290 (public examination of a bankrupt), s 366, (examination of bankrupt by receiver).
[395] *Bishopgate Investment Management Ltd v Maxwell* [1993] Ch 1.
[396] *R v Kansal* [1993] QB 244.
[396a] See para 11.107 below.
[397] s 177.
[398] s 177(6).
[399] *R v Morisey* (1997) 2 Cr App R 426 (despite the fact that the provision is incompatible with Art 6 of the Convention).
[399a] See para 11.107 below.
[400] Insurance Companies Act 1982, s 43A.
[401] Banking Act 1987 ss 41 and 42, see *Riley v Bank of England* [1992] Ch 475.
[402] Financial Services Act 1986, ss 94 and 105.
[403] Town and Country Planning Act 1990, ss 171C and 171D.
[404] Environmental Protection Act 1990, ss 34(5) and 71.
[404a] *R v Hertfordshire County Council, ex p Green Environmental Industries* [2000] 2 WLR 373 (HL).

11.107 **Privilege against self-incrimination by provision of evidence.** The 'privilege against self-incrimination' has been described as one of the 'basic freedoms secured by English law'.[405] The privilege entitles a party to civil litigation to refuse to give discovery of documents which may incriminate him[406] and may entitle an individual to refuse to provide documents to comply with a production order made under section 9 of the Police and Criminal Evidence Act 1984.[406a] However, as has been indicated, privilege can be overridden by a wide range of statutory provisions. Thus the use of evidence obtained by compulsion by DTI Inspectors in a subsequent criminal trial was held by the European Court of Human Rights to be a violation of Article 6.[407] As a result, the Attorney-General issued guidance to prosecuting authorities making it clear that the prosecution

> should not normally use in evidence as part of its case or in cross-examination answers obtained under compulsory powers.[408]

All the statutory provisions allowing for the use of compelled evidence in criminal proceedings[408a] have now been amended by section 58 and Schedule 3 of the Youth Justice and Criminal Evidence Act 1999. These amendments have inserted into each statute provisions to the effect that, in relation to completed statements:

(a) no evidence relating to the statement may be adduced, and
(b) no question relating to it may be asked, by or on behalf of the prosecution, unless evidence relating to it is adduced, or a question relating to it is asked, in the proceedings by or on behalf of that person.

In each case an exception is made for prosecutions for perjury or for failure to answer questions.

11.108 **Adverse inferences from silence.** Until 1994, the prosecution in a criminal trial was not permitted to comment on the defendant's failure to give evidence[409] or on his decision to remain silent in the police station.[410] Any comment by the judge had to be measured and the jury had to be warned that guilt must not be assumed on the basis of silence.[411] The position has now been radically altered by sections 34 to 37 of the Criminal Justice and Public Order Act 1994 ('the 1994 Act').

---

[405] *In Re Arrows Ltd (No 4)* [1995] 2 AC 75.

[406] *Rank Film Distributors Ltd v Video Information Centre* [1982] AC 380; *A T & T Istel Ltd v Tully* [1993] AC 45.

[406a] See *R v Central Criminal Court ex p Bright, The Times*, 26 Jul 2000; and in relation to production orders, see para 15.123ff below.

[407] See *Saunders v United Kingdom* (1996) 23 EHRR 313.

[408] Attorney-General's Chambers *News Release*, 3 Feb 1998.

[408a] The following English provisions have been amended: Insurance Companies Act 1982, s 43A and s 44; Companies Act 1985, s 434; Insolvency Act 1986, s 433; Company Directors Disqualification Act 1986, s 20; Financial Services Act 1986, s 105; Banking Act 1987, s 39; Criminal Justice Act 1987, s 2; Companies Act 1989, s 83; Friendly Societies Act 1992, s 67.

[409] Criminal Evidence Act 1898, s 1(b).

[410] *Hall v R* [1971] 1 WLR 298.

[411] *R v Bathurst* [1968] 2 QB 99.

Section 34 deals with the effect of an accused's failure to mention facts when ques-   **11.109**
tioned or charged. Where evidence is given that the accused:

(a) at any time before he was charged with the offence, on being questioned under
    caution by a constable trying to discover whether or by whom the offence had
    been committed, failed to mention any fact relied on in his defence in those
    proceedings; or
(b) on being charged with the offence or officially informed that he might be pros-
    ecuted for it, failed to mention any such fact[412]

then, if the fact is one which the accused might reasonably have been expected to
mention, the court may, in specified circumstances, including at the trial, 'draw such
inferences from the failure as appear proper'.[413] However, these provisions do not
apply if the accused had not been allowed an opportunity to consult a solicitor prior
to being questioned, charged or informed.[413a] The Court of Human Rights has rejected the argument that the caution administered under the 1994 Act is ambiguous
or unclear about the effect of a refusal to answer police questions.[413b]

Section 35, deals with the effect of an accused's silence at trial. Subject to narrow   **11.109A**
exceptions,

> the court or jury, in determining whether the accused is guilty of the offence
> charged, may draw such inferences as appear proper from the failure of the accused
> to give evidence or his refusal, without good cause, to answer any question.[414]

The section does not, however, render the accused a compellable witness[415] and he
will have 'good cause' to refuse to answer a question if he relies on privilege.[416] Section
36 provides that inferences may be drawn from an accused's failure or refusal to account for 'objects, substances or marks' on his person, clothing or in his possession or
in any place in which he is arrested. Section 37 provides that inferences may be drawn
from an accused's failure or refusal to account for his presence at a particular place.
The various statutory conditions must be fulfilled before these sections can operate.[417] Section 34 only applies to 'facts', not theories, possibilities or speculations advanced by the accused.[418] It is reasonable for the defendant to ask for details of the
charge before answering, but the police are not required to reveal their whole case
before interview.[419] The defendant is now entitled to have the opportunity to
consult counsel or a solicitor before adverse inferences can be drawn from his

---

[412] The 1994 Act, s 34(1).
[413] Ibid s 34(2).
[413a] s 34(2A), added by Youth Justice and Criminal Evidence Act 1999, s 58.
[413b] *Condron v United Kingdom, The Times*, 9 May 2000, para 59.
[414] Ibid s 34(3).
[415] Ibid s 34(4).
[416] Ibid s 34(5).
[417] See *R v Argent* [1997] 2 Cr App R 27, 32–33.
[418] *R v N, The Times*, 13 Feb 1998.
[419] *R v Imran and Hussain* [1997] Crim LR 754.

silence.[419a] Legal advice to remain silent cannot prevent an adverse inference being drawn.[420] However, if the defendant leads evidence as to the solicitor's reasons for giving such advice, this will be a waiver of legal professional privilege in respect of communications between solicitor and client at the time of the interview.[421] The fact that the privilege is waived in this situation is not inconsistent with Article 6.[421a]

11.110 The 1994 Act provides that a person cannot be found to have a case to answer or be convicted of an offence solely on the basis of inferences drawn from failures or refusals to mention facts, testify or provide explanations.[422] It has been suggested that inferences of guilt should not be drawn from a failure to give evidence to contradict a prosecution case of 'little evidential value'.[423] However, the Court of Appeal have refused to restrict the impact of section 35 and have said that the judge should only direct or advise the jury against drawing an adverse inference where there is some evidential basis for doing so or some exceptional factors.[424]

(e) The admissibility of confessions

11.111 The common law rule that a confession was only admissible in evidence if the prosecution proved beyond reasonable doubt that it was freely and voluntarily given is closely related to the privilege against self-incrimination:

> That privilege aims to protect all citizens against being compelled to condemn themselves. But the law has never set out to protect a subject who condemns himself whilst acting of his own free will. Its only concern has been to ensure that he really does so act, by the general rule which excludes from evidence any confession which is not proved to have been voluntary.[425]

This rule appears to have derived from a determination to eradicate the oppressive and often barbaric methods of interrogation employed by the Star Chamber to extract confessions from accused persons. From the abhorrence of those methods there developed the privilege against self-incrimination, and the right of silence, one aspect of which is the exclusion of compelled confessions, with the onus placed on the prosecution to prove beyond reasonable doubt that any confession relied on was voluntary. The law relating to proof of the voluntariness of confessions was particularly important at a time when an accused was not entitled to give evidence on his own behalf—a disability removed in England only in 1898.[426]

[419a] s 34(2A), s 36(4A) and s 37(3A) of the 1994 Act, inserted by Youth Justice and Criminal Evidence Act 1999, s 58.

[420] *R v Condron (William)* [1997] 1 WLR 827.

[421] *R v Bowden* [1999] 1 WLR 823.

[421a] *Condron v United Kingdom, The Times,* 9 May 2000, para 60.

[422] The 1994 Act, s 38(3).

[423] *Murray v DPP* [1994] 1 WLR 1 (on the comparable Northern Ireland provisions); see also *Waugh v The King* [1950] AC 203.

[424] *R v Cowan* [1996] QB 373.

[425] *Per* Lord Mustill, *R v Director of Serious Fraud Office, ex p Smith* [1993] AC 1, 42.

[426] Ibid 34; and see generally, A Zuckerman, *The Principles of Criminal Evidence* (Clarendon Press, 1989) 311ff.

The principle that a confession was only admissible if voluntary was formulated **11.112** by the Privy Council in *Ibrahim v R*[427] and became Principle (e) of the Judges Rules.[428] Its importance was emphasised in a number of cases. For example, in *Lam Chi-ming v R*[429] Lord Griffiths said that the English cases established:

> that the rejection of an improperly obtained confession is not dependent only upon possible unreliability but also upon the principle that a man cannot be compelled to incriminate himself and upon the importance that attaches in a civilised society to proper behaviour by the police towards those in their custody. All three of these factors have combined to produce the rule of law . . . that a confession is not admissible in evidence unless the prosecution establish that it was voluntary.

Nevertheless, the practical application of this principle caused difficulty and it was criticised by the Phillips Commission on Criminal Procedure in 1981.[430]

The position as to the admissibility of confessions is now governed by the Police **11.113** and Criminal Evidence Act 1984.[431] Section 76(2) provides that:

> If, in any proceedings where the prosecution proposes to give in evidence a confession made by an accused person, it is represented to the court that the confession was or may have been obtained—
>
> (a) by oppression of the person who made it;
> (b) in consequence of anything said or done which was likely, in the circumstances existing at the time, to render unreliable any confession which might be made by him in consequence thereof,
>
> the court shall not allow the confession to be given in evidence against him except in so far as the prosecution proves to the court beyond reasonable doubt that the confession (notwithstanding that it may be true) was not obtained as aforesaid.

The Court may, of its own motion, require the prosecution to prove that the confession was not obtained in this way.[432] A 'confession' includes any statement wholly or partly adverse to the person who made it, whether or not it is in words.[433]

'Oppression' includes 'torture, inhuman and degrading treatment and the use or **11.114** threat of violence'.[434] In general, it must involve the exercise of authority in a 'burdensome, harsh or wrongful manner'[435] and will almost always involve impropriety

---

[427] [1914] AC 599, 610.
[428] See *Practice Note (Judges' Rules)* [1964] 1 WLR 152).
[429] [1991] 2 AC 212, 220; PC; see also *Wong Kam-ming v R* [1980] AC 247, 261, *per* Lord Hailsham.
[430] *Royal Commission on Criminal Procedure* (1981), Cmnd 8092 para 4.73.
[431] For a full discussion, see *Archbold: Criminal Pleading, Practice and Evidence* (Sweet & Maxwell, 1999), para 15–337ff; *Blackstone's Criminal Practice, 1999* (Blackstone Press, 1999) s F17.1ff; M Zander, *The Police and Criminal Evidence Act 1984* (3rd edn, Sweet & Maxwell, 1995) 217ff.
[432] PACE, s 76(3).
[433] Ibid, s 82(1); but it does not exclude statements which were initially self-serving but are, later, the accused's detriment (*Rv Sat-Bhambra* (1988) 88 Cr App R 55).
[434] PACE, s 76(8).
[435] *R v Fulling* [1987] QB 426; see also *R v Emmerson* (1991) 92 Cr App R 284.

on the part of the interrogator.[436] However, not every breach of the Codes of Practice in relation to detention and questioning will be oppressive.[437] Confessions have been excluded under this head where there has been hectoring and bullying questioning[438] or where the evidence has been misrepresented. A wide range of matters have been held to be likely to render a confession unreliable including an offer of bail[439] and minimising the significance of the offence.[440]

(f) The presumption of innocence

11.115   The principle that the prosecution must prove the prisoner's guilt has been said to be the 'golden thread' running through the web of English criminal law:

> the principle that the prosecution must prove the guilt of the prisoner is part of the common law of England and no attempt to whittle it down can be entertained.[441]

This has been described as an 'undoubted fundamental rule of natural justice'.[442] The prosecution has to prove all the elements of the offence, including proving 'negatives', such as the absence of consent on a charge of rape. If a defendant raises defence such as provocation, self-defence or duress then, provided there is some evidence of such a defence, the prosecution must prove that there is no such defence. The only common law exception is the defence of insanity. If a defendant raises this defence he must prove it on the balance of probabilities.[443] This exception has not been extended to the defence of automatism.[444]

11.116   However, the general common law principle is subject to statutory exceptions, whether these are express or implied.[445] A distinction must be drawn between provisions which place an 'evidential burden' on the accused and those which place him under a 'persuasive burden'.[446] Statutory provisions which place only an 'evidential burden' on the accused, requiring him to raise a reasonable doubt, do not breach the presumption of innocence and are likely to be compatible with Article

---

[436] *R v Fulling* (n 435 above) 432.
[437] *R v Parker* [1995] Crim LR 233, and the commentary by D J Birch.
[438] *R v Paris* (1993) 97 Cr App R 99.
[439] *R v Barry* (1992) 95 Cr App R 384.
[440] *R v Delaney* (1988) 88 Cr App R 338.
[441] *Woolmington v DPP* [1935] AC 462, 481, *per* Lord Sankey; see also *Mancini v DPP* [1942] AC 1, 11; and see generally, P Roberts, 'Taking the Burden of Proof Seriously' [1995] Crim LR 783; Ashworth and Blake, 'The Presumption of Innocence in English Criminal Law' [1996] Crim LR 306.
[442] *Haw Tua Tau v Public Prosecutor* [1982] AC 136.
[443] *Sodeman v The King* (1936) 55 CLR 192.
[444] See *Hill v Baxter* [1958] 1 QB 277, 285; the position is the same in Scotland (*Ross v HM Advocate* 1991 SLT 564 and Northern Ireland (*Bratty v A-G for Northern Ireland* [1963] AC 386).
[445] *R v Hunt (Richard)* [1987] AC 352.
[446] See the general discussion by Lord Hope in *R v DPP, ex p Kebilene* [1999] 3 WLR 972, 991–993.

6(2) of the Convention.[447] Statutory provisions which place a 'persuasive' burden on the accused can be divided into three types:[448]

- provisions which place the burden on the accused to show that he has the benefit of an exemption or proviso;
- presumption of guilt as to an essential element of the offence which is 'discretionary' in the sense that the tribunal of fact may or may not rely on the presumption;
- 'mandatory' presumption of guilt as to an essential element of the offence, based on proof of a particular fact.

In such cases, the burden is on the defence to prove the requisite fact or knowledge 'on the balance of probabilities'.[449]

11.117 The first class of case often involves an implied statutory reversal of the burden of proof. In relation to summary trials the matter is governed by section 101 of the Magistrates' Court Act 1980 which provides that, in such a case:

> the burden of proving the exception, exemption, proviso, excuse or qualification shall be on [the defendant] . . . notwithstanding that the information or complaint contains an allegation negativing the exception, exemption, proviso, excuse or qualification.

This sets out the common law rule, established in the case of *R v Edwards*[450] However, the presumption is against an inference that the burden was to be placed on the defendant and the courts should be slow to draw such inference from the language of a statute.[451]

11.118 In the second class of case the court has a discretion as to whether or not to rely on the presumption. In *R v Killen*[452] the Northern Ireland Court of Appeal held that such provisions should not be used unless, having done so, the court would be left satisfied beyond reasonable doubt of the guilt of the accused. It has been suggested that a similar approach should be applied in England.[453]

11.119 The third class of case involves a clear breach of the presumption of innocence. There are a number of statutory provisions in this category including:[454]

---

[447] Ibid.
[448] Ibid.
[449] *R v Carr-Briant* [1943] KB 607.
[450] [1975] QB 27; see also *Rv Hunt (Richard)* [1987] AC 352.
[451] *R v Hunt* (n 450 above) 374.
[452] [1974] NI 220.
[453] See *R v DPP, ex p Kebilene* [1999] 3 WLR 972, 995 *per* Lord Hope; in relation to s 16A(4) of the Prevention of Terrorism (Temporary Provisions) Act 1989.
[454] For a full list, see *R v DPP, ex p Kebilene* (n 453 above) 995H–996B.

- a defence that a person did not believe or suspect that a substance in his possession was a controlled drug;[455]
- that a person in possession of articles in circumstances giving rise to a reasonable suspicion that this is for a purpose connected with terrorism does not have them in his possession for this purpose;[456]
- that a person in possession of information which is likely to be useful to terrorists has a lawful authority or reasonable excuse for the possession of the information.[457]

It is arguable that such provisions are in breach of Article 6(2) of the Convention. This was the view of the Divisional Court in *R v DPP, ex p Kebilene*[458] in relation to the offences under sections 16A and 16B of the Prevention of Terrorism (Temporary Provisions) Act 1989.[459] The House of Lords, in overruling the decision on other grounds, declined to express a view on this point. However, Lord Hope suggested that, in order to decide whether a particular statutory provision was in breach of the presumption of innocence it was necessary to consider, in each case, the balance between the interests of the individual and those of society as a whole. This, in turn, involved the consideration of three questions:

- what does the prosecution have to prove in order to transfer the onus to the defence?
- what is the burden on the accused, does it relate to something which is likely to be difficult for him to prove or something likely to be within his own knowledge?
- what is the nature of the threat faced by society which the provision is designed to combat?[460]

Lord Hope declined to express a concluded view on the facts of that case. It seems likely that this approach will be adopted to 'reverse onus' provisions under the Human Rights Act.[461]

(g) The right to jury trial

11.120 The right to trial by jury is often regarded as central to the rights of criminal

---

[455] Misuse of Drugs Act 1971, s 28.
[456] Prevention of Terrorism (Temporary Provisions) Act 1989, s 16A (as inserted by CJPOA 1994, s 82(1)).
[457] Prevention of Terrorism (Temporary Provisions) Act 1989, s 16B (as inserted by CJPOA 1994, s 82(1)).
[458] n 453 above.
[459] See para 11.118 above.
[460] *R v DPP, ex p Kebilene* (n 453 above) 998–999.
[461] See para 11.347 below.

defendants[462] and has been described as a 'constitutional right'.[463] To many commentators it is the most important fair trial right of all. In Lord Devlin's well known words:

> trial by jury is more than an instrument of justice and more than one wheel of the constitution: it is the lamp that shows that freedom lives.[464]

The adoption of the institution of the jury reflected 'a fundamental decision about the exercise of official power'.[465] As Deane J put it in the High Court of Australia:

> The institution of trial by jury also serves the function of protecting both the administration of justice and the accused from the rash judgment and prejudices of the community itself. The nature of the jury as a body of ordinary citizens called from the community to try the particular case offers some assurance that the community as a whole will be more likely to accept a jury's verdict than it would be to accept the judgment of a judge or magistrate who might be, or be portrayed as being, over-responsive to authority or remote from the affairs and concerns of ordinary people. The random selection of a jury panel, the empanelment of a jury to try the particular case, the public anonymity of individual jurors, the ordinary confidentiality of the jury's deliberative processes, the jury's isolation (at least at the time of decision) from external influences and the insistence upon its function of determining the particular charge according to the evidence combine, for so long as they can be preserved or observed, to offer some assurance that the accused will not be judged by reference to sensational or self-righteous pre-trial publicity or the passions of the mob.[466]

However, this right is only available for prosecutions for certain classes of offences. **11.121** Criminal offences are divided into three categories: summary only, triable either way and indictable. Offences in the first category are tried in the magistrates' courts. Offences in the second category are tried either in the magistrates' court or in the Crown Court on indictment. Offences in the third category can only be tried on indictment. Trial on indictment is, in all cases, by a judge and jury.

In relation to a wide range of conduct, the prosecution can, therefore, control **11.122** whether or not a defendant has a right to jury trial by the selection of the charge. For example, the same conduct may constitute both assault occasioning actual

---

[462] See P Devlin, *Trial by Jury* (Stevens, 1966); and *The Judge*, (Oxford University Press, 1979), Chap 5, 'The Judge and the Jury'; see also R Kerr (ed), *Blackstone's Commentaries on the Laws of England*, (4th edn, John Murray, 1876) Vol IV, 360.

[463] see *Rv Islington North Juvenile Court ex p Daley* [1983] AC 347; and see *per* Lord Denning MR in *Rothermere v Times Newspapers* [1973] 1 WLR 448, 452, 'Every defendant has a constitutional right to have his guilty or innocence determined by a jury' (said in the context of defamation proceedings).

[464] Devlin Trial by Jury (n 462 above)164.

[465] See *Duncan v Louisiana* (1968) 391 US 145, 156; and generally, A Amar, *The Constitution and Criminal Procedure: First Principles* (Yale University Press, 1997) 120–124.

[466] *Per* Deane J, *Kingswell v The Queen* (1985) 62 ALR 161, 188 (in a dissenting judgment); see also *Brown v The Queen* (1986) 160 CLR 171.

bodily harm and assaulting a police officer in the execution of his duty but only the former charge carries the right to jury trial. It is not an abuse of the process for the prosecution to present a lesser summary only charge appropriate to the nature of the offence when they could have charged an offence which would have carried a right to jury trial.[467] This is so even where the prosecution make it clear that they are substituting a lesser charge because it carries no right to jury trial.[468]

11.123 Juries are now selected at random from all the names appearing on the electoral register. In order to be eligible for jury service, a person must be between the ages of 18 and 70,[469] must have been ordinarily resident in the United Kingdom for a total period of at least five years since the age of 13 and must not be ineligible or disqualified.[470] The judiciary, those concerned with the administration of justice, the clergy and the mentally ill are ineligible.[471] A person is disqualified if he has ever been sentenced to a period of imprisonment of five years or more or if he has served any part of a sentence of imprisonment or detention within the past 10 years.[472] However, the fact that a juror was disqualified, ineligible or unfit to serve cannot be a ground of appeal against a jury verdict.[473] A number of persons, including peers, serving members of the armed forces and various medical professionals are excusable from jury service as of right.[474]

11.124 The police can, in appropriate circumstances, check the criminal convictions of potential jurors.[475] In two classes of case, additional checks may be carried out:[476]

- cases in which national security is involved and part of the evidence is likely to be heard in camera;
- terrorist cases.

Such 'jury vetting' should only be carried out on the personal authority of the Attorney-General. Only in the most exceptional cases is the defence permitted to put questions to potential jurors concerning matters which might lead to prejudice or bias.[477]

---

[467] See *Rv Canterbury and St Augustine Justices, ex p Klisiak* [1982] 1 QB 398.
[468] See *Rv Liverpool Stipendiary Magistrate, ex p Ellison* [1990] RTR 220.
[469] Juries Act 1974, s 1(a) and Criminal Justice Act 1988, s 119.
[470] Juries Act 1974, s 1 and Sch 1.
[471] Juries Act 1974, Sch 1, Pt I.
[472] Juries Act 1974, Sch 1, Pt II.
[473] Juries Act 1974, s 18, and see *R v Chapman (William)* (1976) Cr App R 75.
[474] Juries Act 1974, Sch 1, Pt III.
[475] *R v Mason* [1981] QB 881; and see *A-G's Guidelines on Jury Checks* (1978) 88 Cr App R 123.
[476] See *A-G's Guidelines* (n 475 above) paras 3 and 4.
[477] See generally, *R v Andrews (Tracey)* [1999] Crim LR 156; a case in which this was done was *Rv Kray* (1969) 53 Cr App R 412; see also *Murphy v The Queen* (1989) 167 CLR 94, 103.

(h) Other rights in relation to the trial

There is no specific 'right' to the assistance of an interpreter under English law. **11.125**
However, it has often been said that the accused should be 'capable of understanding the proceedings' which implies a right to an interpreter if a defendant is
unrepresented.[478] A trial is a nullity if the accused cannot comprehend the charges
and instruct his lawyers.[479] The Crown Court has a discretion to order an accused
to pay the costs of an interpreter.[480]

In general, a criminal trial must take place in the presence of the accused.[481] As a **11.126**
result, no part of the trial should take place in camera in the absence of the accused.[482] However, there is jurisdiction, in exceptional circumstances, to proceed
with a trial in the absence of an accused who has entered a plea. These circumstances include misbehaviour by the accused[483] and the voluntary absence of the
accused.[484] If the accused is absent for reasons beyond his control then the trial
cannot continue in his absence unless he consents.[485]

There is a fundamental right of a defendant to see and to know the identity of his **11.127**
accusers, including witnesses for the prosecution brought against him.[486] This is a
right which should only be denied in rare and exceptional circumstances.
Whether or not these circumstances exist is a matter for the discretion of the trial
judge. The following factors are relevant:[487]

- there must be real grounds for being fearful of the consequences if the evidence
  is given and the identity of the witness is revealed;
- the evidence must be sufficiently relevant and important to make it unfair to the
  prosecution to compel them to proceed without it;
- the prosecution must satisfy the court that the creditworthiness of the witness
  has been fully investigated and the results of that enquiry disclosed to the defence so far as is consistent with the anonymity sought;
- the court must be satisfied that no undue prejudice is caused to the defendant;
- the court can balance the need for protection, including the extent of any necessary protection, against the unfairness or appearance of unfairness in the particular case.

---

[478] *R v Lee Kun* [1916] KB 337; *Kunnath v The State* [1993] 1 WLR 1315.
[479] *R v Iqbal Begum* (1991) 93 Cr App R 96.
[480] *Practice Direction (Crime Costs)* [1991] 1 WLR 498.
[481] *R v Lee Kun* [1916] KB 337.
[482] *R v Preston* [1994] 2 AC 130.
[483] *R v Lee Kun* (n 481 above).
[484] *R v Jones (Robert) (No 2)* [1972] 1 WLR 887; *R v O'Nione* [1986] Crim LR 342; see generally,
Blackstone's Criminal Practice, 1999 (Blackstone Press, 1999) s D12.25.
[485] *R v Jones (No 2)* (n 484 above); see also, *R v Howson* (1981) 74 Cr App R 172.
[486] See *R v Taylor and Crabb* [1995] Crim LR 253; and also *R v Watford Magistrates' Court, ex p
Lenman* [1993] Crim LR 388; see also *Arlidge, Eady and Smith on Contempt* (2nd edn, Sweet &
Maxwell, 1999) para 7–45, n 80 and the cases there cited.
[487] See *Rv Taylor and Crabb* (n 486 above).

Furthermore, in exceptional circumstances, screens may be used to protect the anonymity of witnesses.[488]

11.128   The criminal courts have power, under the Criminal Justice Act 1988, to receive evidence in the form of written statements from witnesses who do not attend court[489] if:

- the witness is dead, unfit to attend court, abroad or cannot be found;[490]
- the witness does not give oral evidence through fear or because he is kept out of the way (provided that the statement was made to a police officer or other investigator.[491]

The prosecution must prove beyond reasonable doubt that one of these grounds applies.[492] In relation to a witness who does not give oral evidence 'through fear', the prosecution does not have to show that the fear is reasonable,[493] but the 'fear' must be proved by admissible evidence.[494] The court must consider whether it is in the interests of justice that such a statement be admitted,[495] and must have regard to the following factors: the nature and source of the document containing the statement and its likely authenticity, the extent to which the statement appears to supply evidence which would otherwise not be readily available, the relevance of the evidence and to any risk that its admission or exclusion will result in unfairness to the accused.[496] Where a statement has been prepared for the purposes of pending or contemplated criminal proceedings or a criminal investigation, then the statement shall not be given in evidence without the leave of the court, 'unless it is of the opinion that the statement ought to be admitted in the interests of justice'.[497]

11.129   The courts have considered the exercise of the statutory discretion on a number of occasions.[498] The cases establish that:

- the fact that the accused loses his right to cross-examine is not, of itself, unfair;

---

[488] *R v DJX* (1990) 91 Cr App R 36; *R v Schaub and Cooper, The Times,* 3 Dec 1993; see also *Rv Murphy and Maguire* [1990] NI 306 and *Doherty v Ministry of Defence* [1991] 1 NIJB 68 and generally, B Dickson, 'The European Convention in Northern Irish Courts' [1996] EHRLR 496, 508–509.

[489] See also 1988 Act, s 26 which deals with evidence contained in documents.

[490] Ibid s 23(2).

[491] Ibid s 23(3).

[492] See *R v Acton Justices, ex p McMullen* (1990) 92 Cr App R 98.

[493] Ibid *R v Martin* [1996] Crim LR 589.

[494] See *Neill v North Antrim Magistrates' Court* [1992] 1 WLR 1220.

[495] 1988 Act, s 25(1).

[496] Ibid s 25(2).

[497] Ibid s 26.

[498] See most recently, *R v Radak (Jason)* [1999] 1 Cr App R 187 and see generally, *Rv Cole* [1990] 1 WLR 866; and P Murphy (ed), *Blackstone's Criminal Practice 1999* (Blackstone Press, 1999) F16.17.

- an important factor is the quality of the evidence contained in the statement;[499]
- there is no general rule that a statement which is 'crucial' to the case must be excluded;[500]
- there is no general rule against admitting a statement which will force the accused to testify in order to 'controvert' it.[501]

It has been held that the provisions of sections 23 to 26 of the Criminal Justice Act 1988 are consistent with the right to a fair trial[502] under Article 6 of the Convention. In *R v Gokal*[503] the Court of Appeal concluded that:

> Since the whole basis of the discretion conferred by section 26 is to assess the interests of justice by reference to the risk of unfairness to the accused, our procedures appear to us to accord fully with [Article 6].

This decision was followed by the Court of Appeal in *R v Thomas*.[504] Roch LJ pointed out that the European Court of Human Rights had made clear that its task was 'to ascertain whether the proceedings considered as a whole, including the way in which evidence was taken, were fair'.[505] He concluded that:

> the narrow ground which the trial judge has to be sure exists before he can allow a statement to be read to the jury coupled with the balancing exercise that he has to perform and the requirement that having performed that exercise he should be of the opinion that it is in the interest of justice to admit the statement having paid due regard to the risk of unfairness to the accused means that the provisions of sections 23 to 26 of the 1988 Act are not in themselves contrary to Article 6 of the Convention.[506]

The Law Commission has also concluded that Article 6 of the Convention does not require direct supporting evidence where it is sought to prove a particular element of the offence by hearsay.[507]

11.130 A statement tendered at committal may, 'without further proof be read as evidence on the trial of the accused'.[508] If the accused objects the statement cannot be read,[509] but the court may order that the objection shall have no effect 'if it

---

[499] *R v Cole*, (n 498 above), *Scott v Queen* [1989] AC 1242.

[500] See *R v Patel (Sabhas)* (1993) 97 Cr App R 294, *R v Setz-Dempsey* (1993) 98 Cr App R 23; this may be a factor in favour of receiving the evidence, *R v Batt* [1995] Crim LR 240.

[501] *R v Moore* [1992] Crim LR 882.

[502] See para 11.204ff below.

[503] [1997] 2 Cr App R 266.

[504] [1998] Crim LR 887.

[505] Citing, *Kostovski v Netherlands* (1989) 12 EHRR 434.

[506] It was pointed out that the Commission had taken the same view in *Trivedi v United Kingdom* (1997) 89 DR 136, EComm HR.

[507] Law Commission, *Report on Evidence in Criminal Proceedings: Hearsay and Related Topics* (Law Com No 245, 1997) (the Law Commission was persuaded to reverse the contrary view taken in its Consultation Paper); see also *McKenna v Her Majesty's Advocate* 2000 SCCR 159.

[508] Criminal Procedure and Investigations Act 1996, Sch 2, para 1(2).

[509] Ibid Sch 2, para 1(3)(c).

considers it to be in the interests of justice'.[510] No statutory criteria are laid down for the exercise of this discretion.[511] A defendant may not examine, in person, a child who is the victim of or a witness to a violent or sexual offence.[512]

11.130A The trial of children and young persons in the Crown Court gives rise to potential difficulties in relation to the right of an accused to participate effectively in his trial. The Court of Human Rights has held that a trial of a ten-year-old for murder violated this right.[512a] As a result, a *Practice Direction* was issued[512b] making it clear that the overriding principle was that all possible steps should be taken to assist the young defendant to understand and participate in the proceedings. These steps include matters such as all the participants being on the same level, the young defendant being free to sit with members of his family, full explanation of the proceedings, no wigs or robes and restricted attendance.

(i) Exclusion of illegally obtained evidence

11.131 The position at common law was that a judge had no discretion to refuse to admit relevant evidence on the ground that it was obtained by improper or unfair means. As Lord Diplock said *R v Sang*:[513]

> (1) A trial judge in a criminal trial has always a discretion to refuse to admit evidence if in his opinion its prejudicial effect outweighs its probative value.
> (2) Save with regard to admissions and confessions and generally with regard to evidence obtained from the accused after commission of the offence, he has no discretion to refuse to admit relevant admissible evidence on the ground that it was obtained by improper or unfair means. The court is not concerned with how it was obtained.

As a result, evidence is admissible even if obtained by theft,[514] unlawful search[515] or the use of agent provocateurs.[516] Even though evidence has been unlawfully obtained from the accused after the commission of the offence, the evidence will not be excluded where it was obtained by someone acting in good faith.[517] It may, however, be excluded if the persons who obtained the evidence used trickery or deception.[518]

---

[510] Ibid Sch 2, para 1(4).

[511] During parliamentary debate on this provision, the Government indicated that it was anticipated that the courts would turn to s 26 of the Criminal Justice Act 1988 for guidance, *per* Baroness Blatch, *Hansard*, HL, 26 Jun 1996, cols 951–952.

[512] Criminal Justice Act 1988, s 34A.

[512a] *T v United Kingdom* (2000) 7 BHRC 659, see para 11.293 below.

[512b] *Practice Note (Trial of Children and Young Persons: Procedure)* [2000] 2 All ER 285.

[513] [1980] AC 402, 437; see also *Kuruma v The Queen* [1955] AC 197.

[514] *R v Leathem* (1861) 8 Cox CC 498, 501.

[515] *Jeffrey v Black* [1978] QB 490.

[516] *R v Sang* [1980] AC 402.

[517] *R v Fox* [1986] AC 281; *Rv Trump* [1980] RTR 274.

[518] See for example *Rv Mason (Carl)* [1988] 1 WLR 139.

The position is now governed by section 78(1) of the Police and Criminal **11.132**
Evidence 1984 which provides:

> In any proceedings the court may refuse to allow evidence on which the prosecution
> proposes to rely to be given if it appears to the court that, having regard to all the cir-
> cumstances, including the circumstances in which the evidence was obtained, the
> admission of the evidence would have such an adverse effect on the fairness of the
> proceedings that the court ought not to admit it.

In exercising this discretion, the court will look at all the circumstances, including
unlawful searches, questioning or detention.[519] The approach of the courts has
been summarised in the following terms:

> . . . proceedings may become unfair if, for example, one side is allowed to adduce
> relevant evidence which, for one reason or another, the other side cannot properly
> challenge or meet, or where there has been an abuse of process, eg because evidence
> has been obtained in deliberate breach of procedures laid down in an official code
> of practice.[520]

The fact that conduct is 'unlawful' or 'oppressive' does not necessarily mean that
evidence obtained thereby should be excluded. The sole test is fairness.[521] Unlike
abuse of process applications, no 'balancing exercise' is involved:

> The exercise for the judge under section 78 is not the marking of his disapproval of
> the prosecution's breach, if any, of the law in the conduct of the investigation or the
> proceedings by a discretionary decision to stay them, but an examination of the
> question whether it would be unfair to the defendant to admit that evidence.[522]

In considering fairness the court looks both at the trial and at the fairness of pre-
trial proceedings.[523] The English courts have taken the view that this approach is
consistent with the right to a fair trial[524] under Article 6 of the Convention. As
Lord Nicholls said in *R v Khan*:[525]

> the discretionary powers of the trial judge to exclude evidence march hand in hand
> with Article 6(1) of the European Convention on Human Rights. Both are con-
> cerned to ensure that those facing criminal charges receive a fair hearing.
> Accordingly, when considering the common law and statutory discretionary pow-
> ers under English law, the jurisprudence on Article 6 can have a valuable role to play.

This approach was approved by the European Court of Human Rights in *Khan v
United Kingdom*.[525a]

---

[519] For an analysis of the substantial case law, see R Stone, 'Exclusion of Evidence Under Section
78 of the Police and Criminal Evidence Act: Practice and Principles' [1995] 3 Web JCLI.
[520] *R v Quinn* [1990] Crim LR 581.
[521] *R v Chalkley* [1998] QB 848.
[522] Ibid at 876C.
[523] See *Matto v Wolverhampton Crown Court* [1987] RTR 337.
[524] See para 11.204ff below.
[525] [1997] AC 558, 583B-D.
[525a] *The Times* 23 May 2000.

11.133   The relevant factors to be taken into account include apparent breaches of the Convention or the law of a foreign country[526] and the extent to which evidence was obtained as the result of the activities of an agent provocateur.[527] Evidence from 'interviews' is likely to be excluded if the defendant has been detrimentally deprived of legal advice[528] or if the provisions of the Code of Practice relating to interviews have not been complied with.[529] The exclusionary discretion can be exercised even if there has been no bad faith.[530] The fact that evidence has been obtained by a trick[531] or by agent provocateurs[532] will not, of itself, render it inadmissible. In *Nottingham City Council v Amin*[532a] police officers had flagged down a taxi which was not licensed for use in the area and the driver picked them up and carried them to their destination for a fare. The Divisional Court accepted that the officers had 'given the defendant the opportunity' to break the law. Lord Bingham CJ considered the Convention authorities and went on to hold that the proper test was whether or not the effect of admitting the evidence was to deny the respondent a fair trial. On the facts this was not the case and the evidence was admitted.

11.134   The court does not use section 78 to 'discipline' the police or prosecuting authorities.[533] English judges have consistently refused to countenance an approach whereby evidence obtained in breach of fundamental rights of the suspect should always be excluded.[534] The Privy Council has recently rejected a *prima facie* rule against admitting confessions obtained in breach of basic rights whilst accepting that the breach of a constitutional right is a cogent factor militating in favour of exclusion.[535] It is arguable that the courts should adopt a somewhat stricter approach in relation to breaches of the Human Rights Act.[536]

(j) Rule against double jeopardy

11.135   A person cannot, at common law, be prosecuted twice for the same offence. If

---

[526] *R v Khan* [1997] AC 558.
[527] *R v Smurthwaite* [1994] 1 All ER 898.
[528] See para 11.94ff above; and see R Kirk [1999] 4 All ER 698 (interview excluded when defendant who was being interviewed for theft was not told he was suspected of robbery and manslaughter arising out of the same incident).
[529] *R v Absalom* (1988) 88 Cr App R 332.
[530] *R v Alladice* (1988) 87 Cr App R 380; *DPP v McGladrigan* [1991] RTR 297.
[531] *R v Bailey* [1993] 3 All ER 513 (co-accused placed in same cell and conversation 'bugged').
[532] *R v Christou* [1992] QB 979 (Police 'shop' staffed by undercover officers bought stolen goods); see also *Williams v DPP* [1993] 3 All ER 365 (insecure unattended van containing cigarettes left in busy street, accused seen removing them); *LB of Ealing v Woolworths* [1995] Crim LR 58 (purchase of video by underage child acting on instructions of prosecutor); and see *Rv Maclean* [1993] Crim LR 687.
[532a] [2000] 1 WLR 1071; see generally, para 21.142ff below.
[533] *R v Mason (Carl)* [1988] 1 WLR 139.
[534] The approach of the US Supreme Court, see *Miranda v Arizona* (1966) 384 US 436.
[535] *Mohammed (Allie) v The State* [1999] 2 WLR 552, 561B-563A (Trinidad and Tobago).
[536] See para 21.144ff below.

such a prosecution takes place, the accused can raise the plea of *autrefois acquit* or *autrefois convict*.[537] The principles were restated by the House of Lords in *Connelly v DPP*[538] in which it was made clear that, in order for the rule to apply, the offence charged in the second indictment must have been committed at the time of the first charge and that there must have been an adjudication of guilt or innocence, resulting from a valid process in a court of competent jurisdiction.[539] Where a conviction has been quashed on appeal without an order for re-trial, the accused 'is in the same position for all purposes as if he had actually been acquitted'.[540] Civil contempt proceedings do not constitute a conviction for these purposes.[541] The verdict of a foreign court will generally be sufficient for a plea of *autrefois*, but not if the accused was convicted in his absence abroad and has not served any sentence.[542]

The doctrine applies where the crime charged in the second indictment is the same as that previously adjudicated upon, where he could have been convicted by way of a verdict of guilty of a lesser offence, where proof of the second crime would necessarily entail proof of the crime for which he was acquitted.[543] Furthermore, a person cannot be tried for a crime which is substantially the same as one of which he was acquitted. It appears that this last power does not fall within the strict doctrine of *autrefois* but involves the use of a discretionary power to prevent abuses of the process.[544] **11 136**

There is, however, a statutory exception in the case when a person is convicted of an administration of justice offence involving interference with or intimidation of a juror or a witness[545] in the proceedings which led to an acquittal. In that case, if it appears to the convicting court that: **11.137**

> there is a real possibility that, but for the interference or intimidation, the acquitted person would not have been acquitted[546]

and it is not contrary to the interests of justice to bring fresh proceedings[547] then it must certify that this applies and an application can be made to the High Court

---

[537] See generally, *Archbold: Criminal Pleading, Practice and Evidence* (Sweet & Maxwell, 1999) para 4–116ff.
[538] [1964] AC 1254.
[539] See *R v West* [1964] 1 QB 15.
[540] *R v Barron* [1914] 2 KB 570; see also *Sambasivam v Public Prosecutor, Federation of Malaya* [1950] AC 458, 479.
[541] *R v Green* [1993] Crim LR 46.
[542] *R v Thomas (Keith)* [1985] QB 604.
[543] *Connelly v DPP* [1964] AC 1254, 1332.
[544] Ibid 1340, 1358, 1364; see also *R v Moxon-Tritsch* [1988] Crim LR 46.
[545] As defined by CPIA, s 54(6).
[546] CPIA, s 54(2)(a).
[547] CPIA s 54(2)(b) and (5).

for an order quashing the acquittal. The High Court must make such an order if it is satisfied that four conditions are fulfilled,[548] namely:

- it is likely that, but for the interference or intimidation, the acquitted person would not have been acquitted;
- it does not appear that it would be contrary to the interests of justice to take fresh proceedings;
- the acquitted person has been given a reasonable opportunity to make written representations to the court;
- it appears likely that the conviction for the administration of justice offence will stand.

(k) Compensation for miscarriages of justice

11.138 There is no general right to compensation for those who have been mistakenly prosecuted or convicted. For a number of years, compensation was awarded under a non-statutory *ex gratia* scheme. In a written Answer to a Commons Question on 29 November 1985[549] the Home Secretary, Mr Douglas Hurd MP, stated the principles governing the non-statutory scheme:

> For many years . . . it has been the Practice for the Home Secretary, in exceptional circumstances, to authorize on application ex gratia payments from public funds to persons who have been detained in custody as a result of a wrongful conviction . . .
>
> I remain prepared to pay compensation to people . . . who have spent a period in custody following a wrongful conviction or charge, where I am satisfied that it has resulted from serious default on the part of a member of the police force or of some other public authority.
>
> There may be exceptional circumstances that justify compensation in cases outside these categories.

A payment under this provision is made under the royal prerogative and the Secretary of State is not obliged to give reasons for refusing to make a payment.[550]

11.139 In 1988, the scheme under the Statement was partially replaced (but not superseded) by section 133 of the Criminal Justice Act 1988[551] which provides that:

> when a person has by a final decision been convicted of a criminal offence and when subsequently his conviction has been reversed, or he has been pardoned, on the ground that a new or newly discovered fact shows beyond reasonable doubt that there has been a miscarriage of justice, the Secretary of State shall pay compensation for miscarriage of justice to the person who has suffered punishment as a result of such conviction . . . unless the non-disclosure of the unknown fact was wholly or partly attributable to the person convicted.

---

[548] CPIA, s 55.
[549] See *Hansard*, HC, Vol 87, col 689
[550] *R v Secretary of State for the Home Department, ex p Harrison* [1988] 3 All ER 86.
[551] Which gives statutory effect to Art 14, para 6 of the International Covenant on Civil and Political Rights, see App J in Vol 2.

The question whether there is a right to compensation under the section is determined by the Secretary of State.[552] By section 133(4):

> If the Secretary of State determines that there is a right to such compensation, the amount of the compensation shall be assessed by an assessor appointed by the Secretary of State.

Schedule 12 makes provision as to the appointment and qualifications of the assessor. Section 133 does not give any guidance as to the principles to be applied by the assessor in assessing the amount of compensation.

11.140 A case in which a person has been wrongly convicted as a result of judicial error does not fall within section 133. Furthermore, it cannot be dealt with under the second paragraph of the Statement as a judge is not a 'public authority' whose serious default can give rise to a claim for compensation.[553] However, judicial conduct can be of such quality as to give rise to exceptional circumstances under the second limb of the Statement.[554]

(l) Protection of fair trial rights: abuse of the process

11.141 The English courts now recognise a wide jurisdiction to halt criminal proceedings on the ground that there has been an abuse of the process. In *Connelly v DPP*[555] Lord Devlin said:

> Are the courts to rely on the executive to protect their processes from abuse? Have they not themselves an inescapable duty to secure fair treatment for those who come or are brought before them? . . . The courts cannot contemplate for a moment the transference to the executive of the responsibility for seeing that the process of law is not abused.

The power of the court to prevent a prosecution which amounts to an abuse of its processes is 'of great constitutional importance and should be jealously preserved'.[556] An abuse of process is something so unfair and wrong that the court should not allow a prosecutor to proceed with what is in all other respects a regular proceeding.[557] However, common law fair trial rights must give way to statutory provision to the contrary. Thus, it could not be an abuse of the process to try the 17-year-son of a soldier by court-martial because this procedure was authorised by the Army Act 1996.[558]

---

[552] s 133(3).
[553] See eg *Rv Secretary of State for the Home Department, ex p Harrison* [1988] 3 All ER 86, 89e; *R v Secretary of State for the Home Department, ex p Bateman, The Times*, 10 May 1993.
[554] *R v Secretary of State for the Home Department, ex p Garner*, (1999) 11 Admin LR 595.
[555] [1964] AC 1254, 1354.
[556] *Per* Lord Salmon, *R v Humphrys* [1977] AC 1, 46.
[557] See *Hui Chi-ming v The Queen* [1992] 1 AC 34, 57B.
[558] See *R v Martin (Alan)* [1998] AC 917.

11.142   The court has jurisdiction to stay a prosecution as an abuse of the process if either

- the defendant cannot receive a fair trial; or
- it would not be fair to try the defendant.[559]

The jurisdiction can be exercised if adverse publicity has made a fair trial imposs-ible.[560] or the conviction can be quashed on this ground.[561] The court has juris-diction to halt a criminal trial as an abuse of the process if the prosecution has deliberately manipulated the criminal process to take unfair advantage of the de-fendant.[562] This includes matters such as a breach of an undertaking or represen-tation that a person would not be prosecuted if he co-operated.[563] In considering whether a prosecution should be stayed as an abuse of process because it is sug-gested that the accused cannot have a fair trial the court could, prior to the com-ing into force of the Human Rights Act, have regard to Article 6 of the Convention.[564]

11.143   The broad basis of the jurisdiction to stay proceedings for abuse of the process was confirmed by the House of Lords in the case of *R v Horseferry Road Magistrates' Court, ex p Bennett*.[565] The defendant was a citizen of New Zealand who claimed to have been brought forcibly to England from South Africa in order to stand trial for certain criminal offences, in disregard of the ordinary procedures for securing his lawful extradition, and in breach of international law. The House of Lords held that the High Court has a wide responsibility for upholding the rule of law where, on the assumed facts, there had been a deliberate abuse of extradition proce-dures.[566] Lord Griffiths said:

> In the present case there is no suggestion that the appellant cannot have a fair trial, nor could it be suggested that it would have been unfair to try him if he had been re-turned to this country though extradition procedures. If the court is to have the power to interfere with the prosecution in the present circumstances it must be be-cause the judiciary accept a responsibility for the maintenance of the rule of law that embraces a willingness to oversee executive action and to refuse to countenance

---

[559] See *R v Horseferry Road Magistrates' Court ex p Bennett* [1994] 1 AC 42.

[560] *R v Magee*, 23 Jan 1997, Kay J (see *Arlidge, Eady and Smith, On Contempt* (2nd edn, Sweet & Maxwell 1999) para 2–100, n 69).

[561] *R v McCann* (1991) 92 Cr App R 239 (Winchester Three convictions quashed in the light of publicity given to comments by the Secretary of State on right to silence); *R v Taylor (Michelle)* (1993) 98 Cr App R 361.

[562] *R v Derby Crown Court, ex p Brooks* (1984) 80 Cr App R 164; *R v Willesden Justices, ex p Clemmings* (1987) 87 Cr App R 280.

[563] *R v Croydon Justices, ex p Dean* [1993] QB 769; *R v Liverpool Stipendiary Magistrates' Court, ex p Slade* [1998] 1 WLR 531.

[564] See *R v Stratford Justices, ex p Imbert* (1999) 2 Cr App R 276.

[565] [1994] 1 AC 42; see also *R v Mullen (Nicholas Robert Neil)* [1999] 3 WLR 777 (conviction quashed due to fact that police and security services had procured defendants's unlawful deportation from Zimbabwe).

[566] Following *R v Hartley* [1978] 2 NZLR 199; *S v Ebrahim* 1991 (2) SA 553.

behaviour that threatens either basic human rights or the rule of law. . . . In my view your Lordships should now declare that where process of law is available to return an accused to this country through extradition procedures our courts will refuse to try him if he has been forcibly brought within our jurisdiction in disregard of those procedures by a process to which our own police, prosecuting or other executive authorities have been a knowing party.[567]

Lord Lowry took the view that it was

essential to the rule of law that the court should not have to make available its process and thereby indorse (on what I am confident will be a very few occasions) unworthy conduct when it is proved against the executive or its agents, however humble in rank.[568]

The Divisional Court subsequently held that there had, on the facts been an abuse[569] but on further investigation of the facts a similar application was refused in Scotland.[570] The Court of Appeal can quash a conviction as being 'unsafe' if it finds that the prosecution was an abuse of the process, even if the point was not taken before the trial judge.[571]

The categories of 'abuse' are not closed but include the following: **11.143A**

- unjustifiable delay which results in the defendant suffering serious prejudice to the extent that no fair trial can be held;[571a]
- the prosecution of a defendant the police having given a promise, undertaking or representation that he would not prosecuted;[571b]
- the prosecution of a defendant who has already faced criminal charges arising out of the same facts;[571c]
- the trial of a defendant after there has been substantial prejudicial pre-trial publicity;[571d]
- the trial of a defendant after the loss or destruction of relevant material by the prosecution;[571e]
- where it would be contrary to the public interest in the integrity of the criminal justice system that a trial should take place because the prosecution have been

---

[567] At 61H–62A and 62G.
[568] See n 566 above.
[569] See *R v Horseferry Road Magistrates' Court, ex p Bennett (No 2)* [1995] 1 Cr App R 147.
[570] See *Bennett v HM Advocate* 1995 SLT 510.
[571] See *Rv Mullen (Nicholas Robert Neil)* [1999] 3 WLR 777.
[571a] *A-G's Reference (No. 1 of 1990)* [1992] QB 630; see generally, D Corker and D Young, *Abuse of Process and Fairness in Criminal Proceedings* (Butterworths, 2000) Chap 1.
[571b] *R v Croydon JJ, ex p Dean* (1993) 98 Cr App Rep 76; see generally, Corker and Young (n 571a above) Chap 2.
[571c] *DPP v Humphrys* [1977] AC 1; see generally, Corker and Young (n 571a above) Chap 3.
[571d] *R v Taylor and Taylor* (1993) 98 Cr App Rep 361; see generally, Corker and Young (n 571a above) Chap 4.
[571e] *R v Beckford* [1996] 1 Cr App Rep 94; see generally, Corker and Young (n 571a above) Chap 5.

guilty of 'investigative impropriety'.[571f] This category is often known as '*Bennett* type abuse'.

- where the prosecution have otherwise been guilty of manipulation or misuse of the process of the court.[571g]

The principles to be applied for granting a stay under the Human Rights Act are considered in Chapter 22.[571h]

(5) Retrospective criminal laws

11.144 The common law presumes that statutes are not intended to have retrospective effect.[572] As Blackstone[573] observed, if:

> after an action (indifferent in itself) is committed, the legislator then for the first time declares it to have been a crime, and inflicts a punishment upon the person who has committed it. Here it is impossible that the party could foresee that an action, innocent when it was done, should be afterwards converted to guilt by a subsequent law: he had therefore no cause to abstain from it; and all punishment for not abstaining must of consequence be cruel and unjust. All laws should be therefore made to commence in futuro, and be notified before their commencement; which is implied in the term 'prescribed'.

It has therefore been said that:

> It is a fundamental rule of English law that no statute shall be construed to have a retrospective operation unless such a construction appears very clearly in the terms of the Act, or arises by necessary or distinct implication.[574]

This principle is often said to rest on the idea of 'fairness'. As Staughton LJ stressed in a case involving recovery of overpaid social security benefits:

> the true principle is that Parliament is presumed not to have intended to alter the law applicable to past events and transactions in a manner which is unfair to those concerned in them, unless a contrary intention appears.[575]

It has been suggested that the presumption against retrospectivity is an aspect of the 'principle against doubtful penalisation': a person should not be penalised except under clear law.[576]

[571f] *R v Horseferry Road Magistrates' Court, ex p Bennett* [1994] AC 42; see generally, Corker and Young (n 571a above) Chap 6.
[571g] See generally, Corker and Young (n 571a above) Chap 7.
[571h] See para 21.117ff.
[572] See eg *Yew Bon Tew v Kenderaan Bas Mara* [1983] 1 AC 553, 558; and see generally, F Bennion, *Statutory Interpretation* (3rd edn, Butterworths, 1997) 235ff.
[573] See *Commentaries on the Laws of England*, (1830), Vol I, 45–46.
[574] P Maxwell, *Maxwell on the Interpretation of Statutes* (12th edn Sweet & Maxwell, 1969), 215.
[575] *Secretary of State for Social Security v Tunnicliffe* [1991] 2 All ER 712, 724f (in that case the statute was held to have retrospective effect).
[576] See Bennion *Statutory Interpretation* (3rd edn, Butterworths, 1997) 236 and generally, Pt XVII, 637ff.

The cases give some support to the argument that the presumption against retro- **11.145**
spectivity is of no application to 'matters of procedure'[577] and that an enactment
fixing the penalty or maximum penalty for a criminal offence is procedural for this
purpose.[578] A different approach was taken by the Northern Ireland Court of
Appeal in *R v Deery*[579] in which it was held that the maximum sentence should be
that prevailing at the time the offence was committed.

The confiscation provisions in the Drug Trafficking Offences Act 1986 apply in **11.146**
relation to offences committed before the Act came into force. This led to an adverse finding in the Court of Human Rights.[580] However, in *R v Taylor*[581] it was
held that a confiscation order could be made on a conviction in 1994 in respect of
'benefits' gained between 1970 and 1979. The offences for which the appellant
was tried in 1994 were committed in the early 1990s and 1993 at which time the
1986 Act was fully in force. As a result, the Court of Appeal held that:

> he must therefore be deemed to have committed them with his eyes open as to the
> possible consequences which were no more severe at the time when he was sen-
> tenced than at the time when he offended.[582]

The Court therefore concluded that the confiscation orders did not breach Article
7 of the European Convention on Human Rights.

There remain a number of criminal offences which are not defined by statute but **11.147**
arise under the common law. The most well known of these is murder. The courts
have, until recently, retained the power to devise new common law offences.[583]
Thus, in *Shaw v DPP*[584] the House of Lords upheld a conviction for conspiracy to
corrupt public morals and did not disapprove the Court of Appeal's view that
there was a substantive offence of corrupting public morals. Lord Simonds said
that:

> In the sphere of criminal law I entertain no doubt that there remains in the courts
> of law a residual power to enforce the supreme and fundamental purpose of the law,
> to conserve not only the safety and order but also the moral welfare of the State, and
> that it is their duty to guard it against attacks which may be the more insidious be-
> cause they are novel and unprepared for.[585]

---

[577] *Re Athlumney* [1898] 2 QB 547, 551; see generally, Bennion (n 572 above) s 98, 238–240.
[578] *DPP v Lamb* [1941] 2 KB 89; *R v Oliver* [1944] KB 68.
[579] [1977] NI 164; see also *R v Penrith Justices ex p Hay* (1979) 1 Cr App Rep (S) 265.
[580] *Welch v United Kingdom* (1995) 20 EHRR 247.
[581] [1996] 2 Cr App R 64.
[582] Ibid 70.
[583] See generally, A T H Smith, 'Judicial Law-Making in the Criminal Law' (1984) 100 LQR 46.
[584] [1962] AC 220; for criticism see A Goodhart, 'The Show Case: The Law of Public Morals'
(1961) 77 LQR 560; J Hall Williams, 'The Ladies Directory and Criminal Conspiracy. The Judge
Custos Morum' (1961) 24 MLR 626.
[585] *Shaw v DPP* (n 584 above) 267.

However, in the subsequent case of *Knuller (Publishing, Printing and Promotions) Ltd v DPP*[586] the House of Lords held that there was no residual power to create new common law offences. The task of the courts is limited to recognising 'the applicability of established offences to new circumstances in which they are relevant'.

11.148   The essence of judge made law is that it applies retrospectively. As Lord Woolf MR said in a recent case:

> any authoritative decision of the courts stating what is the law operates retrospectively. The decision does not only state what the law is from the date of the decision, it states what it has always been. This is the position even if in setting out the law the court overrules an earlier decision which took a totally different view of the law.[587]

This 'fiction' applies as much in the field of criminal law as in civil law. Thus, if the courts take a different view of the common law or of statutory interpretation, conduct which was previously lawful may become unlawful and attract criminal penalties. An important recent illustration of this principle involved the so-called 'marital rape exemption'. It had long been understood that a husband could not be guilty of raping his wife because of the 'matrimonial consent'.[588] However, this was challenged in a number of cases[589] culminating in the decision of the House of Lords in *R v R*[590] which made it clear that 'a rapist is a rapist . . . irrespective of his relationship with his victim'. They agreed with the Court of Appeal's view that:

> This is not the creation of a new offence, it is the removal of a common law fiction which has become anachronistic and offensive.[591]

11.149   Article 7 of the Convention strengthens the presumption against judge made retrospectivity since it requires that an individual can, to a reasonable degree, foresee from the wording of a provision what acts or omissions will make him liable of a criminal offence.[592] As Brooke LJ observed in relation to a conviction for a criminal offence based on a breach of a rule by Westminster Council that the licensee shall maintain good order in the premises:

> The Council could do well, in my judgment, to tighten up the language of Rule 9 if it wishes to be able to prohibit activities like these on the licensed premises after the Human Rights Act 1998 comes into force. The extension of the very vague concept of the maintenance of good order to the control of the activities of the prostitutes

---

[586] [1973] AC 435.
[587] *R v Governor Brockhill Prison, ex p Evans (No 2)* [1999] 2 WLR 103, 107E-F.
[588] The proposition deriving from Hale's *Pleas of the Crown*, 1736 and being confirmed by subsequent case law, *R v Clarence* (1888) 22 QBD 23; *R v Roberts* [1986] Crim LR 188.
[589] *R v C (Rape: Marital Exemption)* [1991] 1 All ER 755 (exemption misconceived), *R v J (Rape: Marital Exemption)* [1991] 1 All ER 759 (exemption upheld).
[590] [1992] 1 AC 599.
[591] [1991] 2 All ER 257, 266.
[592] *Kokkinakis v Greece* (1993) 17 EHRR 397 para 52; see generally, para 11.260ff below.

may have passed muster in the days when the English common law offences did not receive critical scrutiny from national judicial guarantees of a rights-based jurisprudence, but these days will soon be over. English judges will then be applying a Human Rights Convention which has the effect of prescribing that a criminal offence must be clearly defined in law. I do not accept [Counsel's] submission that it is impossible to define the kind of conduct his clients wish to prohibit with greater precision, or that it is satisfactory to leave it to individual magistrates to decide, assisted only by some arcane case-law, whether or not activities of the type which the Council complains in this case amounts to a breach of good order so as to render the licensees liable to criminal penalties.[593]

C. The Law Under the European Convention

(1) Introduction

Article 6 of the Convention provides that: **11.150**

(1) In the determination of his civil rights and obligations or of any criminal charge against him, everyone is entitled to a fair and public hearing within a reasonable time by an independent and impartial tribunal established by law. Judgment shall be pronounced publicly but the press and public may be excluded from all or part of the trial in the interest of morals, public order or national security in a democratic society, where the interests of juveniles or the protection of the private life of the parties so require, or to the extent strictly necessary in the opinion of the court in special circumstances where publicity would prejudice the interests of justice.

(2) Everyone charged with a criminal offence shall be presumed innocent until proved guilty according to law.

(3) Everyone charged with a criminal offence has the following minimum rights:

- (a) to be informed promptly, in a language which he understands and in detail, of the nature and cause of the accusation against him;
- (b) to have adequate time and facilities for the preparation of his defence;
- (c) to defend himself in person or through legal assistance of his own choosing or, if he has not sufficient means to pay for legal assistance, to be given it free when the interests of justice so require;
- (d) to examine or have examined witnesses against him and to obtain the attendance and examination of witnesses on his behalf under the same conditions as witnesses against him;
- (e) to have the free assistance of an interpreter if he cannot understand or speak the language used in court.

In the most general terms, Article 6 applies to proceedings which constitute a determination of criminal charges or the civil rights and obligations of accused persons. As the Convention provides no definition of 'criminal charge', 'civil rights and obligations' or 'determination', the interpretation of those phrases has fallen   **11.151**

---

[593] *Westminster City Council v Blenheim Leisure* (1999) 163 JP 401.

to the Commission and Court. They have affirmed the centrality of the rights of due process and an expansive view of Article 6 as fundamental to the consideration of these issues:

> In a democratic society within the meaning of the Convention, the right to a fair administration of justice holds such a prominent place that a restrictive interpretation of Article 6(1) would not correspond to the aim and the purpose of that provision.[594]

11.152 Article 7 of the Convention provides:

> (1) No one shall be held guilty of any criminal offence on account of any act or omission which did not constitute a criminal offence under national or international law at the time when it was committed. Nor shall a heavier penalty be imposed than the one that was applicable at the time the criminal offence was committed.
>
> (2) This article shall not prejudice the trial and punishment of any person for any act or omission which, at the time when it was committed, was criminal according to the general principles of law recognised by civilised nations.

This article not only embodies the principle against retrospectivity but also the principle that only the law can define a crime and prescribe a penalty.[595] No derogations from this Article are permitted.[596]

11.153 In this section we will begin by considering the scope of Article 6. The nature of the 'guarantees' in Article 6(1) will then be considered. Articles 6(2) and (3) deal with matters which are specific to those charged with criminal offences and are considered together. Finally, we will consider the effect of the prohibition in Article 7.

(2) Proceedings covered by Article 6

(a) Introduction

11.154 Article 6 applies to the determination of 'civil rights and obligations' and 'criminal charges'. Both terms have autonomous meanings under the Convention.[597] These are considered in the next two sections. In order for the guarantees to apply there must be a right, obligation or charge in play and the proceedings must involve its *determination.*

11.155 As a result, Article 6 does not apply to proceedings subsequent to the conviction of an offence of an individual, as they cannot be determinative of the charge.

---

[594] *Delcourt v Belgium* (1970) 1 EHRR 355 para 25; see also *Moreira de Azevedo v Portugal* (1990) 13 EHRR 721.
[595] *Kokkinakis v Greece* (1993) 17 EHRR 397 para 52.
[596] See Art 15(2).
[597] See generally, para 6.17 above, and see paras 11.163ff and 11.174ff below.

Neither are proceedings determinative where they relate to the appointment of a legal aid lawyer,[598] assessment of costs,[599] revocation of a suspended sentence,[600] application for clemency[601] or conditional release,[602] classification of a prisoner,[603] payment for prison work[604] or the recording of an offence.[605]

Proceedings are determinative in relation to civil rights and obligations when the outcome of the proceedings is *decisive* for them, whether or not such determination is the primary purpose of the proceedings.[606] Thus, administrative tribunals that primarily determine questions of purely public concern may also 'determine' civil rights and obligations for the purposes of Article 6.[607] However, the proceedings must be *directly* decisive for civil rights and obligations and a 'tenuous connection or remote consequences do not suffice'.[608] Thus, a decision to deport an alien, which was also decisive for the applicant's private rights pursuant to an employment contract in the deporting state, was not protected by Article 6, because the connection between the deportation and the employment contract was too remote.[609]   **11.156**

Determination or 'decisiveness' in relation to civil rights and obligations refers to the decision on the merits of a case and its finality. Proceedings which are not determinative are not subject to Article 6 guarantees. It has been held that the following are not 'determinative': applications for interim relief ,[610] enforcement proceedings,[611] awards of costs,[612] the re-opening of a case,[613] application for leave to appeal[614] and an official report of an investigation into facts relating to the civil   **11.157**

---

[598] *X v United Kingdom* (1982) 5 EHRR 273, EComm HR.
[599] *X v Germany* (1971) 39 CD 20, EComm HR.
[600] *X v Germany* (1967) 25 CD 1, EComm HR.
[601] *X v Austria* (1961) 8 CD 9, EComm HR.
[602] *X v Austria* (1966) 9 YB 112; *Aldrian v Austria* (1990) 65 DR 337, EComm HR.
[603] *X v United Kingdom* (1979) 20 DR 202, EComm HR.
[604] *Detained Persons v Germany* (1968) 11 YB 528, EComm HR.
[605] *X v Germany* (1960) 3 YB 254, EComm HR.
[606] *Ringeisen v Austria (No 1)* (1971) 1 EHRR 455 (this case greatly expanded the scope of Art 6 in this context).
[607] In particular, *Benthem v Netherlands* (1985) 8 EHRR 1.
[608] *Le Compte, Van Leuven and De Meyere v Belgium* (1982) 5 EHRR 183 para 47.
[609] Ibid.
[610] *X v United Kingdom* (1981) 24 DR 57; *Alsterlund v Sweden* (1988) 56 DR 229, EComm HR.
[611] Art 6 will apply, though, where the proceedings raise new issues in connection with the applicant's rights: *K v Sweden* (1991) 71 DR 94 EComm HR and *Jensen v Denmark* (1991) 68 DR 177, EComm HR.
[612] *Asterlund v Sweden* (1988) 56 DR 229 EComm HR; but the position will be different where the costs proceedings are the continuation of a substantive dispute: see *Robins v United Kingdom* (1997) 26 EHRR 527 EComm HR paras 25–29.
[613] *X v Austria* (1978) 14 DR 200, EComm HR.
[614] *Porter v United Kingdom* (1987) 54 DR 207, EComm HR.

rights and obligations of the applicant.[615] However, Article 6 has been found to apply where a point of constitutionality[616] or a preliminary decision in the case[617] is crucial to the applicant's claim and to separate court proceedings for the assessment of damages.[618]

11.158　**Stage at which Article 6 applies.**　There is no strictly defined point in the criminal process at which Article 6 guarantees must be in place. The protections apply as soon as a person is the subject of a criminal charge and continue to apply until the charge is finally determined or discontinued.[619] Furthermore, Article 6 guarantees cover applications for leave to appeal,[620] appeal proceedings themselves[621] and any sentencing hearing that may follow trial or appeal.[622]

11.159　In relation to the determination of civil rights and obligations, Article 6 guarantees will normally apply from the point at which proceedings are commenced. In some circumstances, however, they may be applicable before the claim form is filed.[623] For example, Article 6 was held to apply where compliance with an administrative procedure was required before a public decision could be appealed to a court;[624] and where the dispute arose upon objection by the applicant to a draft land consolidation plan that would substantially affect his real property rights.[625] Where civil rights and obligations are decided by an administrative, executive or professional disciplinary body that is not a tribunal for the purposes of Article 6, the guarantees need not be applied at the initial decision stage, so long as the decision-making body is ultimately subject to a judicial body that meets the Article 6 requirements.[626] Article 6 continues to apply through appeal and judicial review proceedings[627] and the assessment of damages relevant to the applicant's

---

[615] In *Fayed v United Kingdom* (1994) 18 EHRR 393 para 61 the Court found that Art 6 did not apply because the findings in the report were not 'dispositive of anything' but established evidence for use in any legal proceedings that might later be brought.

[616] *Deumeland v Germany* (1986) 8 EHRR 448; *Ruiz-Mateos v Spain* (1993) 16 EHRR 505; *Kraska v Switzerland* (1993) 18 EHRR 188; *Lombardo v Italy* (1992) 21 EHRR 188.

[617] See *Obermeier v Austria* (1990) 13 EHRR 290 (the preliminary question of the validity of the applicant's dismissal from his employment was pivotal to his claim and thus Art 6 applied).

[618] *Silva Pontes v Portugal* (1994) 18 EHRR 156 para 33.

[619] *Eckle v Germany* (1982) 5 EHRR 1 para 78; *Orchin v United Kingdom* (1983) 6 EHRR 391, EComm HR.

[620] *Monnell and Morris v UK* (1987) 10 EHRR 205.

[621] This whether the appeal is based on the law or the facts: *Delcourt v Belgium* (1970) 1 EHRR 355; or against conviction or sentence.

[622] *Eckle v Germany* (1982) 5 EHRR 1; *Ringeisen v Austria (No 1)* (1971) 1 EHRR 455.

[623] *Golder v United Kingdom* (1975) 1 EHRR 524.

[624] *König v Germany* (1978) 2 EHRR 170; *Schouten and Meldrum v Netherlands* (1994) 19 EHRR 432 para 62 (the Court held that if the procedure was required it should be carried out expeditiously).

[625] *Erkner and Hofauer v Austria* (1987) 9 EHRR 464 para 64.

[626] *LeCompte, Van Leuven and De Meyere v Belgium* (1981) 4 EHRR 1.

[627] *König v Germany* (n 624 above) para 98; *Pretto v Italy* (1983) 6 EHRR 182 para 30; but see para 11.197 below.

claim. The guarantees only cease to apply when the civil rights and obligations have been fully determined, the time for an appeal by the parties expires and the judgment is finalised.[628]

(b) Civil rights and obligations

Introduction. The guarantees in Article 6(1) apply to the determination of civil rights and obligations. The position is complicated by a material difference between the French and English texts of the Article. The French text refers to '*contestations* sur ses droits et obligations de caractère civil'. The word 'contestations' (disputes) has no equivalent in the English text. In this section we will consider the following issues: **11.160**

- the extent to which it is necessary that there be a 'dispute' before Article 6(1) applies;
- the nature of civil rights and obligations to which Article 6(1) applies;
- the rights and obligations to which Article 6(1) does not apply.

Disputes. Despite the absence of the word 'dispute' from the English text of Article 6(1), it is clear that the guarantees are only applicable if there is a dispute in domestic law. The applicable principles have been summarised as follows:[629] **11.161**

- the term 'dispute' must be given a substantive, rather than a formal or technical meaning;[630]
- the dispute may be one which relates not only to the existence but also to the scope or manner of exercise of a right[631] it may also relate to questions both of fact and law;[632]
- the dispute must be genuine and serious;[633]
- there must be a direct link between the dispute and the right in question.[634]

To benefit from Article 6, the applicant must have an arguable right under domestic law. Article 6(1) does not guarantee any particular substantive content for **11.162**

---

[628] *Pugliese v Italy (No 2)* (1991) Series A No 206; *Lorenzi, Bernardini and Gritti v Italy* (1992) Series A No 231-G.

[629] *Benthem v Netherlands* (1985) 8 EHRR 1 para 32.

[630] See also *Le Compte, Van Leuven and De Meyere v Belgium* (1981) 4 EHRR 1 para 45; the burden of the requirement is not seen to be great because there is no English counterpart to the French term, leading to questions as to its importance: *Moreira de Azevedo v Portugal* (1990) 13 EHRR 721 para 66 expressed doubt as to whether it exists at all.

[631] *Le Compte, Van Leuven and De Meyere v Belgium* (n 630 above).

[632] *Albert and Le Compte v Belgium* (1983) 5 EHRR 533.

[633] 'Genuine' might exclude hypothetical or moot cases; 'serious' may exclude cases of minimal interference with the civil right, but does not require that damages be claimed: *Helmers v Sweden* (1991) 15 EHRR 285; see also *Oerlemans v Netherlands* (1991) 15 EHRR 561.

[634] The dispute must be justiciable: see D Harris, M O'Boyle and C Warbrick, *Law of the European Convention on Human Rights* (Butterworths, 1995) 188; and *Van Marle v Netherlands* (1986) 8 EHRR 483 (applicants' registration as accountants is not a dispute that inherently lends itself to judicial resolution).

civil rights and obligations in national law,[635] but provides only the procedural guarantees for the determination of tenable rights.[636] Although Article 6(1) cannot be used to create a substantive civil right which has no legal basis in the state, it may apply in cases where domestic law contains immunities or procedural bars which limit the possibility of bringing potential claims to court.[637] In such cases, the Convention provides a degree of 'constraint or control' on states' abilities to remove civil rights from the jurisdiction of the courts or to provide immunity to particular groups of persons.

11.163   **The nature of 'civil rights and obligations'.**   It is well established that 'civil' does not mean merely 'non-criminal': not all of the rights and obligations that might arguably be claimed by an individual in national law attract the protection of Article 6. The word 'civil' has an autonomous Convention meaning so that the classification of a right in domestic law is not decisive.[638]

11.164   The basic problem in defining the scope of the phrase 'civil rights and obligations' is whether it is also intended to cover certain rights which, under some continental systems of law, fall under administrative law rather than private law.[639] Although the Court initially adopted the distinction between private and public law as the basis for its definition, with civil rights and obligations corresponding to rights and obligations in private law,[640] it is strongly arguable, in the light of the 'drafting history' of the provision, that this approach is misconceived.[641] Subsequent cases show a willingness to extend the scope of Article 6 to include many rights and obligations in a manner that is not easy to explain by reference to the distinction between private and public law. It is widely acknowledged that no clear principles can be derived from the case law; and it has been suggested that the Court should adopt a new approach to the problem.[642] At least three options are available:

- the reclassification of some rights and obligations (such as Convention rights) as 'private law' rights, receiving the benefit of Article 6;

---

[635] *H v Belgium* (1987) 10 EHRR 339.

[636] *James v United Kingdom* (1986) 8 EHRR 123, para 81; *Powell and Rayner v United Kingdom* (1990) 12 EHRR 288.

[637] *Fayed v United Kingdom* (1994) 18 EHRR 393; *Osman v United Kingdom* (1998) 5 BHRC 293 (but see the criticism of this case in *Barrett v LB Enfield* [1999] 3 WLR 79, 84A–85F (*per* Lord Browne-Wilkinson).

[638] *König v Germany* (1978) 2 EHRR 170 para 89.

[639] F Jacobs and R White, *The European Convention on Human Rights* (2nd edn. Clarendon Press, 1996) 128; F Jacobs, 'The Right to a Fair Trial in European Law' [1999] EHRLR 141.

[640] *Ringeisen v Austria (No 1)* (1971) 1 EHRR 455, para 94; *König v Germany* (n 638 above) para 95.

[641] See P van Dijk, 'Access to the Court' in R St J Macdonald, F Matscher and H Petzold (eds), *The European System for the Protection of Human Rights* (Kluwer, 1983) 347–351.

[642] See Harris, O'Boyle and Warbrick (n 634 above) 184ff; P van Dijk and G van Hoof, *Theory and Practice of the European Convention on Human Rights* (3rd edn, Kluwer, 1998) 404–406.

- the abandonment of the private/public distinction and formulation of a new definition of 'civil rights and obligations';
- the extension of the application of Article 6 to 'all cases in which a determination by a public authority of the legal position of a private party is at stake, regardless of whether the rights and obligations involved are of a private character'.[643]

The last approach is supported by the drafting history[644] and has the merit of simplicity.

The Court has, nevertheless, consistently held that the basis for the definition of civil rights and obligations is the distinction between public and private law. The meaning attributed to 'civil rights and obligations' is autonomous from that used in national law.[645] The Court has not advanced its own definition of 'civil rights and obligations'. It is sufficient, for the application of Article 6, that the outcome of the proceedings should be *decisive for private rights and obligations*.[646] In deciding whether a 'civil right or obligation' is in issue, it is necessary to consider:[647]   **11.165**

- the character of the right or obligation in issue;[648]
- any consensus that can be gleaned from national law of European states[649] in connection with the classification of the matter as public or private;
- the classification of the right or obligation in domestic law.[650]

Private law. Proceedings which determine rights and obligations as between private persons are governed by private law and will therefore, in every case, deal with 'civil rights and obligations' requiring the safeguards of a fair trial. Thus it has been held that disputes concerning competition law,[651] insurance law,[652] tort law,[653] the law of succession,[654] family law (including both divorce[655] and cases involving the   **11.166**

---

[643] van Dijk and van Hoof (n 642 above) 406.

[644] See P van Dijk, 'Access to the Court', in Macdonald, Matscher and Petzold (n 641 above) 347–351.

[645] *König v Germany* (1978) 2 EHRR 170.

[646] See the formulation in *H v France* (1989) 12 EHRR 74 para 47.

[647] See generally, Harris, O'Boyle and Warbrick (n 634 above) 176ff.

[648] *Konig v Germany* (1978) 2 EHRR 170 para 90; see also the Commission decision in *Muyldermans v Belgium* (1991) 15 EHRR 204 (which was subject to a friendly settlement) and *Schouten and Meldrum v Netherlands* (1994) 19 EHRR 432.

[649] *Feldbrugge v Netherlands* (1986) 8 EHRR 425 and *Deumeland v Germany* (1986) 8 EHRR 448 refer to any 'uniform European notion' where the Court had to choose how to characterise social security rights.

[650] See *König v Germany* (n 648 above) para 89.

[651] *Barthold v Germany* (1981) 26 DR 145, EComm HR.

[652] *Feldbrugge v Netherlands* (1986) 8 EHRR 425.

[653] *Axen v Germany* (1983) 6 EHRR 195 (negligence).

[654] *X v Switzerland* (1976) 7 DR 104, EComm HR.

[655] *Airey v Ireland* (1979) 2 EHRR 305.

care of,[656] adoption[657] or access[658] to children) and employment law[659] involve the determination of civil rights and obligations. The position is the same if the features of private law are 'predominant'.[660]

11.167   *Disciplinary proceedings.* It has been said that disciplinary proceedings do not ordinarily involve disputes over civil rights and obligations.[661] However, the right to continue in professional practice is a civil right and Article 6 will, therefore, apply when the disciplinary tribunal could suspend a person from professional practice.[662] As a result, Article 6(1) has been applied to disciplinary proceedings involving:

- temporarily suspending a doctor from practice[663] or preventing a doctor from running a clinic;[664]
- removing an avocate from the roll,[665] or disbarring a barrister;[665a]
- a refusal to allow a person to enrol as a pupil advocate;[665b]
- an application to be reinstated as an advocate after suspension;[665c]
- suspending an architect from practice for a period of one year.[665d]

However, Article 6 will not apply if the professional is not at risk of being prevented from practising[666] or if the nature of the 'proceedings' is confined to the assessment of professional ability.[667]

11.168   *Private individuals and the state.* The position is less clear cut when there are proceedings that involve relations *between* the private individual and the state. Not every action or claim involving rights as against a public authority is 'public' in nature so as to be excluded from the fair trial requirements of Article 6. This was made clear by the Court in *Ringeisen v Austria*[668] in which it was held that proceedings before the Regional Land Commission, an administrative tribunal, were

---

[656] *Olsson v Sweden (No 1)* (1988) 11 EHRR 259.
[657] *Keegan v Ireland* (1994) 18 EHRR 342 (adoption); *Eriksson v Sweden* (1989) 12 EHRR 183 (fostering).
[658] *W v United Kingdom* (1987) 10 EHRR 29; *Eriksson v Sweden* (n 657 above).
[659] *Bucholz v Germany* (1981) 3 EHRR 597 (unfair dismissal).
[660] *Feldbrugge v Netherlands* (1986) 8 EHRR 425 para 18 (statutory sickness benefit).
[661] *Albert and Le Compte v Belgium* (1983) 5 EHRR 533 para 25.
[662] Ibid para 28; *Le Compte, Van Leuven and De Meyere v Belgium* (1981) 4 EHRR 1 para 48.
[663] *Albert and Le Compte v Belgium* (n 661 above) para 28.
[664] *König v Germany* (1978) 2 EHRR 170.
[665] *H v Belgium* (1987) 10 EHRR 339.
[655a] *Ginikanwa v United Kingdom* (1988) 55 DR 251.
[665b] *De Moor v Belgium* (1994) 18 EHRR 372.
[665c] *H v Belgium* (1987) 10 EHRR 339.
[665d] *Guchez v Belgium* (1984) 40 DR 100.
[666] *X v United Kingdom* (1983) 6 EHRR 583, EComm HR (barrister reprimanded, Art 6 inapplicable).
[667] *Van Marle v Netherlands* (1986) 8 EHRR 483.
[668] (1971) 1 EHRR 455.

subject to Article 6. It found that it was not necessary to a characterisation of 'private rights and obligations' that both parties to the proceedings should be private persons, and held the determinative factor to be whether the result of the proceedings was 'decisive for private rights and obligations'.

The basic principle is that public law matters are not excluded from being 'civil rights and obligations' if they are directly decisive[669] of private law rights. The most important consideration is whether the applicant has a *financial* interest at stake, in relation to which the action of the state is directly decisive:[670] the existence of such an interest is usually determinative (although in a limited class of cases it may be held to have a 'public law' nature).[671] The following have been held to be 'civil rights': the right to real[672] and personal[673] property rights arising in the context of planning,[673a] the right to engage in commercial activity,[674] to practice a profession[675] and to obtain compensation for monetary loss resulting from illegal state acts.[676]

11.169

However, if compensation is payable on a *purely* discretionary basis, then the applicant will have no 'right' which brings him within the scope of Article 6(1). Thus, it has been held that Article 6 does not apply to a criminal injuries compensation scheme which is discretionary[676a] or which is only *ex gratia*,[676b] similarly, Article 6 could not be invoked in relation to a non statutory disaster fund[676c] or to a discretionary hardship award.[676d] Where, on the other hand, a statute defines in clear

11.169A

---

[669] See para 11.156 above.

[670] See *Le Compte, Van Leuven and De Meyere v Belgium* (1981) 4 EHRR 1 para 45.

[671] See *Schouten and Meldrum v Netherlands* (1994) 19 EHRR 432 para 50 (the examples of 'public law' pecuniary obligations are criminal fines and tax obligations) and *Pierre-Bloch v France* (1997) 26 EHRR 202 para 51 (forfeiture of national assembly seat because the applicant had exceeded the permitted level of election expenditure).

[672] See eg *Ringeisen v Austria (No 1)* (1971) 1 EHRR 455; *Håkansson and Sturesson v Sweden* (1990) 13 EHRR 1 (permission to own land); *Zander v Sweden* (1993) 18 EHRR 175 (extraction of water); *Sporrong and Lonnroth v Sweden* (1982) 5 EHRR 35 (expropriation of land).

[673] See eg *RR and GR v Netherlands* (1991) 69 DR 219, EComm HR (withdrawal of goods from circulation); *Anca v Belgium* (1984) 40 DR 170, EComm HR (bankruptcy); *Lithgow v United Kingdom* (1986) 8 EHRR 329 (expropriation of shares).

[673a] *Bryan v United Kingdom* (1995) 21 EHRR 342.

[674] See eg *Tre Traktörer Aktiebolag v Sweden* (1989) 13 EHRR 309 (restaurant liquor licence) *Pudas v Sweden* (1987) 10 EHRR 380 (public service licence for private passenger carrier); *Axelsson v Sweden* (1989) 65 DR 99, EComm HR (taxi licence); *Benthem v Netherlands* (1985) 8 EHRR 1 (licence to operate a liquid petroleum gas installation).

[675] See eg *König v Germany* (1978) 2 EHRR 170 (medicine); *H v Belgium* (1987) 10 EHRR 339 (law); *Guchez v Belgium* (1984) 40 DR 100, EComm HR (architecture).

[676] See eg *X v France* (1992) 14 EHRR 483 (claim for damages for negligence of the government authority in the administration of a blood transfusion resulting in contraction of AIDS came within Art 6); *Editions Periscope v France* (1992) 14 EHRR 597 (losses resulting from a wrongful refusal of a tax concession).

[676a] *Masson and van Zon v Netherlands* (1996) 22 EHRR 491.

[676b] *B v Netherlands* (1985) 43 DR 198.

[676c] *Nordh v Sweden* (1990) 69 DR 223.

[676d] *Machatova v Sweden* (1997) 24 EHRR CD 44.

terms the pre-conditions for entitlement, an applicant who arguably fulfills those conditions has a right to compensation; and falls within the ambit of Article 6(1).[676e]

11.170 *Social security cases.* The nature of social security and social assistance claims has caused considerable difficulties. In two pivotal cases,[677] the Court found that social security benefits were predominantly private in nature. These benefits were statutory, funded in part by employee contributions, linked to a private employment contract, and had significant consequences for the economic well-being of the applicant. A strong dissenting view in each of the cases, emphasising the limited private law connections, strong collective benefit and diversity of approach across Europe, said that the Court ought not to extend the application of Article 6 to include judicial procedures to determine disputes about social security matters.

11.171 Nevertheless, it is now clear that there is a 'general rule'[678] that Article 6(1) will apply to all welfare benefits (whether contributory[679] or noncontributory).[680] The test with respect to each is whether the grant of the benefit is statutorily required rather than with the discretion of the state.[681] If the former, Article 6 will apply and the Court will not resort to the public and private law balancing process, even in relation to the obligation to pay social security contributions.[682]

11.172 **Cases outside Article 6.** The most obvious examples of disputes considered outside of the reach of Article 6 concern employment in the public sector[683] (although Article 6 *does* apply where a public employee works under a contract of

---

[676e] *Gustafson v Sweden* (1998) 25 EHRR 623.

[677] In *Feldbrugge v Netherlands* (1986) 8 EHRR 425 the applicant's sick pay under a Dutch health benefits scheme was found by a 10 to 7 majority to be a private law matter; in *Deumeland v Germany* (1986) 8 EHRR 448 the Court held 9 to 8 that industrial injuries benefits under German social security law were private law rights.

[678] *Schuler-Zgraggen v Switzerland* (1993) 16 EHRR 405 para 46.

[679] *Lombardo v Italy* (1992) 21 EHRR 188 (a police officer's public service pension not associated with a private employment contract); *Nibbio v Italy* (1992) Series A No 228-A (a disability pension); *McGinley and Egan v United Kingdom* (1998) 27 EHRR 1 (an invalidity pension).

[680] See *Salesi v Italy* (1993) 26 EHRR 187 para 19.

[681] *Lombardo v Italy* (1992) 21 EHRR 188 and *Salesi v Italy* (1993) 26 EHRR 187 were each cases of statutorily-defined rights.

[682] In *Schouten and Meldrum v Netherlands* (1994) 19 EHRR 432 the Court, balancing the public and private law nature of an employer's obligation to pay contributions on behalf of his employees, categorized it as private law.

[683] A large number of claims by public employees in civil law systems have been rejected at the admissibility stage eg *X v Portugal* (1981) 26 DR 262 (members of armed forces); *Leander v Sweden* (1983) 34 DR 78, EComm HR (civil servants); *X v Portugal* (1983) 32 DR 258, EComm HR (judges); *X v Italy* (1980) 21 DR 208, EComm HR (state school teachers); *X v Belgium* (1969) 32 CD 61, EComm HR (employees of public corporations); *X v. United Kingdom* (1980) 21 DR 168 (police officers); *Neigel v France* RJD 1997-II 399 (local authority employee).

employment),[684] the liability of individuals for payment of tax[685] and eligibility for fiscal advantages.[686] Nevertheless, even in this area the position is not clear cut, thus Article 6 does apply:

- to a judge's right to a statutory pension;[687]
- to a claim for compensation for loss of a fiscal benefit (as the result of a refusal to allow a tax exemption).[688]

Other kinds of disputes excluded from the requirements of Article 6 include: immigration and nationality,[689] liability for military service,[690] legal aid in civil cases,[691] court reporting,[692] government funding for research,[693] state education benefits,[694] tax assessments[695] (but not compensation for the refusal to grant tax concessions[696] or restitution for overpaid tax[697] which fall within the scope of Article 6), patent applications,[698] discipline of prisoners,[699] rights of tenants associations[700] public compensation funds,[701] state medical treatment,[702] hereditary peerages,[703] right to stand for public office[704] and the validity of parliamentary elections.[705] **11.173**

---

[684] *Darnell v United Kingdom* (1993) 18 EHRR 205 (doctor employed by the NHS); *C v United Kingdom* (1987) 54 DR 162, EComm HR (janitor at state school).

[685] *X v France* (1983) 32 DR 266, EComm HR; see also *S and T v Sweden* (1986) 50 DR 121, EComm HR (tax on corporate benefits).

[686] *X v Austria* (1980) 21 DR 246, EComm HR (export incentive tax exemption).

[687] See *Lombardo v Italy* (1992) 21 EHRR 188 — even though employment matters in relation to the judiciary are generally considered outside the purview of Art 6, see also *Scuderi v Italy* (1993) 19 EHRR 187.

[688] *Editions Periscope v France* (1992) 14 EHRR 597.

[689] See eg *X, Y, Z, V and W v United Kingdom* (1967) 10 YB 528 (entry); *P v United Kingdom* (1987) 54 DR 211, EComm HR (asylum); *Agee v United Kingdom* (1976) DR 164, EComm HR (deportation); *S v Switzerland* (1988) 59 DR 256, EComm HR (nationality).

[690] *Nicolussi v Austria* (1987) 52 DR 266, EComm HR.

[691] *X v Germany* (1970) 32 CD 56, EComm HR.

[692] *Atkinson Crook and The Independent v United Kingdom* (1990) 67 DR 244, EComm HR.

[693] *X v Sweden* (1974) 2 DR 123, EComm HR.

[694] *Simpson v United Kingdom* (1989) 64 DR 188, EComm HR; *X. Germany* (1984) 7 EHRR 141, EComm HR.

[695] *X v France* (1983) 32 DR 266.

[696] *Editions Periscope v France* (1992) 14 EHRR 597.

[697] *National and Provincial Building Society v United Kingdom* (1997) 25 EHRR 127.

[698] *X v Austria* (1978) 14 DR 200, EComm HR; note that disputes with respect to existing patents are protected by Art 6.

[699] *McFeeley v United Kingdom* (1980) 20 DR 44, EComm HR; note that disciplining of prisoners may also involve a 'criminal charge'.

[700] *X v Sweden* (1983) 6 EHRR 323, EComm HR; *K Association v Sweden* (1983) 33 DR 276, EComm HR.

[701] *Berler v Germany* (1989) 62 DR 207, EComm HR (compensation for Nazi persecution); *B v Netherlands* (1985) 43 DR 198, EComm HR (criminal injuries); *Nordh v Sweden* (1990) 69 DR 223, EComm HR (natural disaster compensation).

[702] *L v Sweden* (1988) 61 DR 62, EComm HR.

[703] *X v United Kingdom* (1978) 16 DR 162, EComm HR (a claim to enter the House of Lords).

[704] *Habsburg-Lothringen v Austria* (1989) 64 DR 210, EComm HR (office of head of state).

[705] *Priorello v Italy* (1985) 43 DR 195, EComm HR; *I Z v Greece* (1994) 76-A DR 65.

(c) Criminal charges

11.174 **'Criminal'.**   Article 6(1) also applies to the determination of criminal charges. As a result of the lack of uniformity in the classification of offences in different national legal systems, this phrase has been given a meaning autonomous[706] from that used in domestic jurisdictions. The Court has set out three criteria in order to assess wheher the allegation made is in fact of a criminal nature:

- the categorisation of the allegation in domestic law;
- whether the offence applies to a specific group or is of a generally binding character;
- the severity of the penalty attached to it.[707]

The classification of the offence by the respondent state is a relevant starting point for the assessment, but is not decisive of the nature of the allegation. In practice, if an offence has been treated by the national court as criminal, the Court will, in light of the sanctions and stigma attributable to criminal charges, subject it to the requirements of a fair trial under Article 6.

11.175 If an allegation is not criminalised in national law, the Court must determine whether it is nevertheless criminal in character and subject to the protection of Article 6 by assessing the two 'more important' criteria: the nature of the offence and the severity of the penalty attached to it.[708] These criteria are alternative, not cumulative, although the cumulative approach may be adopted where the analysis of each criterion does not lead to a clear conclusion.[709]

11.176 The second criterion involves consideration of whether or not the 'offence' applies to a specific group or is of a general binding character. In *Oztürk*,[710] the regulatory offence of careless driving was found to be criminal, despite its decriminalisation in German law. This was because the offence was of general application to the public. The Court was apparently unconcerned that the penalty, though punitive and deterrent, was relatively modest: a fine, rather than imprisonment. The failure of Germany to provide the accused with an interpreter was held to be a violation of Article 6. However, in that case several dissenting judges asserted that decriminalisation of 'minor offences' is in the general interests of individuals and ought to be recognised as legitimate. More recently Austrian

---

[706] *Engel v Netherlands (No 1)* (1976) 1 EHRR 647 para 81.

[707] See *Engel v Netherlands (No 1)* (n 706 above) para 82; *Oztürk v Germany* (1984) 6 EHRR 409; *Campbell and Fell v United Kingdom* (1985) 7 EHRR 165; *Weber v Switzerland* (1990) 12 EHRR 508.

[708] *Engel v Netherlands (No 1)* (n 706 above) para 82.

[709] See *Garyfallou AEBE v Greece* (1999) 28 EHRR 344 para 33; see also *Lauko v Slovakia* [1999] EHRLR 105 para 56.

[710] *Öztürk v Germany* (1984) 6 EHRR 409.

'administrative criminal proceedings' for matters such as breach of planning permission and road traffic offences have been held to fall within Article 6.[711]

Other examples of 'regulatory' offences which have been found to be 'criminal' for the purposes of Article 6 are price-fixing regulations,[712] rules governing competition for contracts,[713] police regulations governing demonstrations[714] and customs codes.[715] Cases dealing with parliamentary privilege[716] and tax evasion[717] have also been treated as 'criminal', for the purposes of Article 6. However, in general, 'disciplinary proceedings' will not be 'criminal' on the basis of this criterion because professional disciplinary matters are essentially matters concerning the relationship between professional associations and individuals rather than a law of general application.[718] Similar reasoning applies to 'regulatory proceedings'.[719] **11.177**

The third criterion concerns the severity of the penalty. The Court has placed great emphasis on the seriousness of the penalty or imprisonment attached to the offence in matters otherwise considered disciplinary in nature. In *Engel* it stated that criminal matters are those characterised by: **11.178**

> deprivations of liberty liable to be imposed as punishment, except those which by their nature, duration or manner of execution cannot be appreciably detrimental.[720]

In that case the proceedings were applicable to armed forces personnel alone, and therefore, in principle, disciplinary rather than criminal. However, the Court's emphasis on the severity of the impending penalty resulted in a finding that a 'criminal charge' was involved. In the disciplinary context, if violations place the accused at risk of 'light arrest' without deprivation of liberty, or confinement of short duration, the offence will not belong to criminal law.[721] A more serious form of punishment involving deprivation of liberty will, however, generally mean that the proceedings are 'criminal' and that the authorities are obliged to afford

---

[711] *Schmautzer v Austria* (1995) 21 EHRR 511; *Umlauft v Austria* (1995) 22 EHRR 76; *Pfarrmaier v Austria* (1995) 22 EHRR 175; Noted [1996] EHRLR 181; see also *Lauko v Slovakia* RJD 1998–VI 2492.

[712] *Deweer v Belgium* (1980) 2 EHRR 239.

[713] *Société Stenuit v France* (1992) 14 EHRR 509.

[714] *Belilos v Switzerland* (1988) 10 EHRR 466.

[715] *Salabiaku v France* (1988) 13 EHRR 379.

[716] See *Demicoli v Malta* (1991) 14 EHRR 47 (journalist was convicted of the non-criminal offence of breach of parliamentary privilege for criticising Members of Parliament; the offence was of general application and generated a penalty of fine or imprisonment).

[717] *Bendenoun v France* (1994) 18 EHRR 54.

[718] *Wickramsinghe v United Kingdom* [1998] EHRLR 338, EComm HR.

[719] See eg *APB Ltd, APP and AEB v United Kingdom*, (1998) 25 EHRR CD 14; *X v United Kingdom* (1998) 25 EHRR CD 88.

[720] (1976) 1 EHRR 647, 679 para 82; see also, *Benham v United Kingdom* (1996) 22 EHRR 293 and *Parks v United Kingdom* Judgment, 12 Oct 1999 which held that proceedings to recover community charge involved a criminal charge: see para 11.284 below.

[721] See for example *Eggs v Switzerland* (1978) 15 DR 35, 65, EComm HR (five days of strict arrest in a civil prison).

Article 6 guarantees. This approach was followed in *Campbell and Fell v United Kingdom*[722] in relation to disciplinary proceedings in an English prison where the Court declined to decide whether other types of punishment such as loss of privileges, might in some circumstances render an offence 'criminal'. However, the imposition of a substantial fine in disciplinary proceedings will not render the charges 'criminal' in nature.[722a]

11.179 Nevertheless, the definition of 'criminal' remains unclear. This is illustrated by a series of 'contempt of court' cases. In *Weber v Switzerland*[723] the applicant was convicted of a non-criminal offence under Swiss law for revealing confidential information relating to a criminal investigation that had resulted from his complaint. This was held to be a 'criminal charge'.[724] In contrast, in *Ravensborg v Sweden*[725] the applicant was fined, without a hearing three times for making improper statements in written observations to the court. It was held that no 'criminal charge' was involved and the 'criminal charge' provisions of Article 6 did not apply.[726] On the basis of *Engel* and *Campbell and Fell*, it is possible that only military or prison disciplinary sentences will meet the test of severity of sentence. Other types of disciplinary proceedings, such as the liberal professions or civil service are unlikely to carry a penalty of imprisonment[727] and will not be covered by Article 6.[728]

11.180 **The nature of a 'charge'.** The 'criminal provisions' of Article 6 only apply if the allegation is both criminal in nature and constitutes a 'charge'. This is an issue that only becomes relevant in connection with the requirement of 'trial within a reasonable time' and the question of access to a criminal court.[729] The word 'charge' has also been given an autonomous meaning under the Convention[730] determined by reference to substance rather than form.[731] 'Charge' has been defined in general terms as 'the official notification given to an individual by the competent

---

[722] (1984) 7 EHRR 165.

[722a] *Brown v United Kingdom* (1998) 28 EHRR CD 233 — the fact that a £10,000 fine was imposed by Solicitors Complaints Tribunal did not render the proceedings 'criminal'.

[723] (1990) 12 EHRR 508.

[724] Ibid paras 31–35.

[725] (1994) 18 EHRR 38.

[726] Ibid para 34; see also, to the same effect, *Putz v Austria*, RJD 1996-I 312 paras 34-38.

[727] See *X v United Kingdom* (1980), 21 DR 168, EComm HR and *Dimitriadis v Greece* (1990) 65 DR 279, EComm HR (where the penalty was dismissal); *Saraiva de Carvalho v Portugal* (1981) 26 DR 262, EComm HR (involving transfer of soldier to a reserve) and *Kremzow v Austria* (1990) 67 DR 307 (a risk of loss of pension by way of disciplinary sanction).

[728] However, they may be protected by Art 6(1) on the basis that there is a determination of 'civil rights and obligations'.

[729] *Deweer v Belgium* (1980) 2 EHRR 439.

[730] Ibid.

[731] It is necessary for the Commission or Court to look beyond what is apparent and investigate the realities: *Deweer* (n 729 above) para 44.

authority of an allegation that he has committed a criminal offence',[732] but it may also take the form of other measures which imply such an allegation and substantially affect the suspect's situation.[733] Whether the proceedings resulting in criminal prosecution are initiated by an individual or by public authorities is irrelevant for the purposes of the applicability of Article 6.[734]

Most of the case law relates to civil law systems. A person is charged when he is first notified or affected by an investigation: a 'charge' has been found to exist when there is arrest,[735] official information as to prosecution[736] or knowledge of an investigation,[737] a request for production of evidence,[738] the freezing of a bank account[739] or closing of a shop pending payment or the outcome of criminal proceedings,[740] and the applicant's retention of a defence lawyer following a police report against him.[741] The Commission has, on a number of occasions, found that the mere fact that police are investigating an offence or that a preliminary enquiry has been made by a judicial body is not tantamount to the existence of a criminal charge.[742] On the other hand, the negotiation of a friendly settlement may imply that a criminal charge is already in issue.[743]   **11.181**

In relation to the position in England, a person has been found to be charged when he is arrested[744]or has police charges laid against him;[745] but because the test of substance over formality applies here too, the point at which an accused is 'substantially affected' may not always be so obvious. For example, an applicant serving a prison sentence for a separate offence was found to be charged with another from the time of conviction on the first, as it was then that he became aware that further charges were imminent.[746] Given the anxiety and uncertainty potentially caused, it is possible that police questioning or investigation of an individual prior   **11.182**

---

[732] *Deweer* (n 729 above) para 46; see also *Eckle v Germany* (1982) 5 EHRR 1; *Serves v France* (1997) 28 EHRR 265 para 42.

[733] *Foti v Italy* (1982) 5 EHRR 313; *Deweer v Belgium* (1980) 2 EHRR 439; *Adolf v Austria* (1982) 4 EHRR 313; and see *Re Mlambo* [1993] 2 LRC 28 which reaches a similar result from a 'common law' perspective, see para 11.520 below.

[734] *Minelli v Switzerland* (1983) 5 EHRR 554 para 26ff.

[735] *Wemhoff v Germany* (1968) 1 EHRR 55; *Foti v Italy* (1982) 5 EHRR 313.

[736] *Neumeister v Austria (No 1)* (1968) 1 EHRR 91.

[737] *Eckle v Germany* (1982) 5 EHRR 1.

[738] *Funke v France* (1993) 16 EHRR 297.

[739] Ibid.

[740] *Deweer v Belgium* (1980) 2 EHRR 439.

[741] *Angelucci v Italy* Series A No 196-C (1991); see also *P v Austria* (1989) 71 DR 52, EComm HR.

[742] See eg *X v Germany* (1972) 38 CD 77, EComm HR; *X v Germany* (1974) 46 CD 1, EComm HR.

[743] *Deweer v Belgium* (1980) 2 EHRR 439.

[744] *X v United Kingdom* (1979) 17 DR 122, EComm HR.

[745] *Ewing v United Kingdom* (1986) 10 EHRR 141.

[746] *X v United Kingdom* (1978) 14 DR 26, EComm HR.

to his arrest or formal charge could constitute a 'charge' in substance for the purposes of Article 6.[747]

(3) Article 6(1) guarantees

(a) Introduction

11.183   Article 6 provides a general right to a 'fair hearing' and a number of specific rights and elaborates further rights in relation to those facing criminal charges. The fair trial rights guaranteed by Article 6 can usefully be divided into two categories: express and implied rights. Article 6 contains the following specific *express* rights:

- the right to a hearing within a reasonable time;[748]
- the right to a independent and impartial tribunal established by law;[749]
- the right to a public hearing unless it is necessary to exclude the press and public from all or part of the trial in the interest of morals, public order, national security, to protect juveniles or private life or where publicity would prejudice the interests of justice;
- the right to the public pronouncement of judgment;[750]
- the right to minimum standards of fairness in *criminal* proceedings which consist of

  (i)   the presumption of innocence;[751]
  (ii)   the right to information as to the accusation;[752]
  (iii)   the right to adequate time and facilities to prepare a defence;[753]
  (iv)   the right of the accused to defend himself in person or through legal assistance;[754]
  (v)   the right to examine witnesses;[755]
  (vi)   the right to assistance from an interpreter.[756]

These rights are 'absolute' in the sense that it will always be unfair if a person is deprived of them.

11.184   In addition, the Strasbourg authorities have interpreted Article 6 as providing, as aspects of the general right to a fair hearing, the following *implied* rights:

---

[747] See D Harris, M O'Boyle and C Warbrick, *Law of the European Convention on Human Rights* (Butterworths, 1995) 172–73; and see *Re Mlambo* [1993] 2 LRC 28 (Zim SC).
[748] See para 11.219ff below.
[749] See para 11.222ff below.
[750] See para 11.230ff below.
[751] See para 11.236ff below.
[752] See para 11.241ff below.
[753] See para 11.243ff below.
[754] See para 11.245ff below.
[755] See para 11.252ff below.
[756] See para 11.255ff below.

- the right of access to the courts;[757]
- the right to be present at an adversarial hearing;[758]
- the right to equality of arms;[759]
- the right to fair presentation of the evidence;[760]
- the right to cross examine;[761] and
- the right to a reasoned judgment.[762]

These rights are subject to inherent limitations in the sense that a breach of any one of them does not always mean that there has been a violation of Article 6. The fairness of the proceedings as a whole can be considered[763] and it is often necessary to carry out a 'balancing exercise' between the interests of the individual and those of society as a whole.[764] Although the point has not been fully developed in the case law it is often helpful to consider, in each case of apparent violation, whether it is necessary and proportionate in pursuit of a legitimate aim.

(b) Right of access to the courts[765]

General. In one of its most important early decisions, *Golder v United Kingdom*,[766] the Court recognised the existence of an implied right of access to the court. This right was recognised because:

    11.185

> It would be inconceivable . . . that Article 6, paragraph 1 should describe in detail the procedural guarantees afforded to parties in a pending lawsuit and should not first protect that which alone makes it in fact possible to benefit from such guarantees, that is, access to the court. The fair, public and expeditious characteristics of judicial proceedings are of no value at all if there are no judicial proceedings . . . it follows that the right of access constitutes an element which is inherent in the right stated by Article 6, paragraph 1.[767]

The right of access to a court is most significant in the context of the determination of private law claims, but also arises in criminal proceedings[768] and in claims

    11.186

---

[757] See para 11.185ff below.
[758] See para 11.205ff below.
[759] See para 11.208ff below.
[760] See para 11.214ff below.
[761] See para 11.217ff below.
[762] See para 11.218 below.
[763] See para 11.204 below.
[764] See generally, para 6.124 above.
[765] For a general discussion of recent cases, see S Phillips, 'The Court v the Executive: Old Battles on New Battlegrounds?' [1996] EHRLR 45; for the English law, see para 11.15 above.
[766] (1975) 1 EHRR 524; for comments on this case, see R Lawson and H Schermers, *Leading Cases of the European Court of Human Rights* (Ars Aequi Libri, 1997) 24–27.
[767] (1975) 1 EHRR 524, 536; see also *Kaplan v United Kingdom* (1980) 4 EHRR 64, EComm HR.
[768] *Deweer v Belgium* (1980) 2 EHRR 439 paras 48, 49.

against the state, including claims arising out of executive decisions.[769] The right overlaps with the Article 13 right to an effective national remedy if the Convention right in question is also a 'civil' right under Article 6.[770]

11.187 Waiver of the right of access to court is possible,[771] but must be 'subjected to careful review'.[772] Whereas voluntary arbitration agreements do not fall within the scope of Article 6, the position is different for compulsory arbitration where the parties have no choice but to refer their dispute to arbitration.[773] However, the Commission has taken a sceptical approach where one party alleges that an arbitration was not voluntary because of duress.[774]

11.188 Settlements of a claim may amount both to a waiver of the right of access to the court and prevent the applicant from proving he is a victim.[775] Three conditions must be satisfied to ensure that a settlement is valid for the purposes of depriving the applicant of his rights under the Convention:

- the waiver must be established in an unequivocal manner; and in relation to procedural rights, a waiver to be effective must provide minimum guarantees commensurate with its importance;[776]
- the settlement will not prevent a claim against the state in proceedings which are based on a complaint that the law is inadequate in regulating the subject area;[777] and
- the settlement does not offend the fundamental principles of the Convention.[778]

11.189 **Effectiveness.** The right of access must be an effective one. In *Golder*, even though the prisoner was not denied a legal right to sue in libel, a failure to allow him contact with a solicitor hindered initiation of proceedings to such an extent that the Court found that he had been precluded access to a court. An effective

---

[769] *Sporrong and Lonnroth v Sweden* (1982) 5 EHRR 35; *Keegan v Ireland* (1994) 18 EHRR 342.

[770] Cases that speak to the interrelationship between the two guarantees are: *Golder v United Kingdom* (1975) 1 EHRR 524 para 33; *Powell and Rayner v United Kingdom* (1990) 12 EHRR 355; and *W v United Kingdom* (1987) 10 EHRR 29: see the separate opinions of Judges Pinheiro Farinha and De Meyer.

[771] See *Deweer v Belgium* (1980) 2 EHRR 439 para 49 (in which the parties contracted out of their access to court by agreeing to an arbitration provision); see also *R v Switzerland* (1987) 51 DR 83; and for the doctrine of waiver generally, see para 6.148ff above.

[772] *Deweer v Belgium* (n 771 above) para 49; cf the requirement that a waiver be 'unequivocal' in relation to other Art 6 rights.

[773] *Bramelid and Malmstrom v Sweden* (1986) 8 EHRR 116 Com Rep paras 30 and 32.

[774] *R v Switzerland* (1987) 51 DR 83.

[775] See generally, para 22.14ff below for a discussion of *locus standi* under the Convention (and the Human Rights Act).

[776] *Pfeifer and Plankl v Austria* (1992) 14 EHRR 692 para 37; *Oberschlick v Austria (No 1)* (1995) 19 EHRR 389.

[777] See eg *Inze v Austria* (1987) 10 EHRR 394 para 33.

[778] See eg *Donnelly v United Kingdom* (1975) 4 DR 4, 78, EComm HR.

right of access might also require that the state provide legal aid, at least where the nature of the proceedings, if they are to be successful, requires legal representation. In *Airey v Ireland*[779] legal aid was refused to a woman who wished to bring proceedings for judicial separation from her husband in the Irish High Court. The Court held that in light of the complexity of the proceedings, the need to examine expert witnesses and the emotional involvement of the parties, a right of access to the court would be ineffective if she were not legally represented. However, the Court has emphasised that, whilst Article 6(1) guarantees an effective right of access to the courts for the determination of their civil rights and obligations

> it leaves to the state a free choice of the means to be used towards this end. The institution of a legal aid scheme constitutes one of those means but there are others.

It has been said that legal aid will usually be required in civil cases involving family separation or parental rights,[779a] the commission of a person to a psychiatric institution[779b] or the right to liberty.[779c] However in a number of cases it has been found that applicants who have been refused legal aid have not been denied their rights of access[780] and Article 6(1) will not provide a full right of legal aid in civil litigation proceedings comparable to that provided by Article 6(3) for criminal proceedings.[781] The question as to whether the cost associated with litigation might itself infringe the right of effective access to a court has yet to be resolved.[782] Sufficient time is also necessary if the right of access to court is to be effective. A person must receive personal and reasonable notice of a decision interfering with his civil rights and obligations to enable him to challenge it in a court.[783]

Restrictions on access. The Court has developed implied limitations to the right as a corollary to implying the right in the first place. The right of access to the court is not absolute, and states' margin of appreciation in its regulation will vary   **11.190**

---

[779] (1979) 2 EHRR 305; cf *M L B v S L J* (1997) 3 BHRC 47; US Sup Ct (court fees preventing an appeal against a decision removing parental rights, unconstitutional).

[779a] See *Munro v United Kingdom* (1987) 52 DR 158.

[779b] *Megyeri v Germany* (1992) 15 EHRR 584 para 23.

[779c] *Aerts v Belgium* [1998] EHRLR 777.

[780] *Munro v United Kingdom* (1987) 52 DR 158, EComm HR (defamation proceedings); *X v United Kingdom* (1980) 21 DR 95, EComm HR (denial of legal aid where there was 'no reasonable prospect of success' would not be considered a denial of access to court unless the decision was an arbitrary one); *Andronicou and Constantiou v Cyprus* (1997) 25 EHRR 491 (offer of *ex gratia* assistance by the state defendant was sufficient); *X v Germany* (1986) 45 DR 291.

[781] See para 11.245ff below.

[782] Cf *X and Y v Netherlands* (1975) 1 DR 66, 71, EComm HR; *X v United Kingdom* (1981) 2 Digest 333, EComm HR; *X v Sweden* (1979) 17 DR 74.

[783] See *De Geouffre de la Pradelle v France* (1992) Series No A 253-B para 33 (the national publication of a decree issued as a result of environmental protection proceedings in relation to the applicant's land was not sufficient communication where the time for appeal had expired before the applicant was directly informed of the decision); *Pérez de Rada Cavanilles v Spain* RJD 1998–VIII 3242 (violation of right of access when applicant allowed only three days for an appeal).

depending on the 'needs and resources of the community and individuals'.[784] Restrictions must not, however, impair the essence of the right of access: they must have a legitimate aim, and the means used must be reasonably proportionate to the aim sought to be achieved.[785] The test for assessing the acceptability of limitation on the right of access is to a large extent similar to the basic requirements when justifying restrictions on interferences with the qualified rights defined under Articles 8 to 11.[786] In a concurring judgment in *De Geoffre de la Pradelle v France*[787] Judge Martens argued that the two tests should be the same; and this appears to be the approach adopted by the Court in *Fayed v United Kingdom*.[788]

11.191   In *Ashingdane v United Kingdom*,[789] the applicant was precluded from challenging an administrative decision to continue his detention in a mental institution. The legislative requirement was leave of the court on a finding of 'substantial grounds' for believing that either bad faith or absence of reasonable care on the part of the administrative authority were present. The Court found that these limitations had the 'legitimate aim' of protecting carers from being unduly targeted by the claims of psychiatric patients, while leaving intact the essence of the right of access, and so were not a violation of Article 6. Restrictions on the access to court of other types of litigants have been justified on the same grounds: these include minors,[790] 'vexatious litigants',[791] prisoners[792] and bankrupts.[793] Various measures to prevent abuses of the right of access, such as the imposition of reasonable time limits on proceedings,[794] the requirement that legal representation be obtained for the lodging of an appeal[795] and payment of security for costs[796] have been held to be permissible. The Court has also held that where the general procedures for telephone tapping comply with Article 8,[797] the lack of a court

---

[784] *Golder v United Kingdom* (1975) 1 EHRR 524.

[785] *Ashingdane v UK* (1985) 7 EHRR 528 para 57; *Lithgow v United Kingdom* (1986) 8 EHHR 329 para 194; *Tolstoy Miloslavsky v United Kingdom* (1995) 20 EHRR 442 para 59; *Tinnelly & Sons and McElduff and others v United Kingdom* (1998) 27 EHRR 249 para 72.

[786] R A Lawson and H Schermers, *Leading Cases of the European Court of Human Rights* (Ars Aequi Libri, 1997) 26.

[787] (1992) Series A No 253-B para 4.

[788] (1994) 18 EHRR 393 para 67.

[789] (1985) 7 EHRR 528

[790] *Golder v United Kingdom* (1975) 1 EHRR 524 para 39.

[791] *H v United Kingdom* (1985) 45 DR 281, EComm HR.

[792] *Campbell and Fell v United Kingdom* (1984) 7 EHRR 165.

[793] *M v United Kingdom* (1987) 52 DR 269, EComm HR.

[794] *X v Sweden* (1982) 31 DR 223, EComm HR.

[795] *Grepne v United Kingdom* (1990) 66 DR 268, EComm HR.

[796] *Tolstoy Miloslavsky v United Kingdom* (1995) 20 EHRR 442 (order for security for costs of defamation appeal, no violation); but see *Ait-Mouhoub v France* RJD 1998–VIII 3214 (requirement of security for costs of 80,000FF infringed right of access to court).

[797] See para 12.105 below.

remedy to question the legality of telephone tapping in a particular case can be justified in order to ensure the effectiveness of the system.[798]

In contrast, a regulation which precluded a professional person from suing a client for fees by requiring that he leave the claim in the hands of his professional organisation deprived him of the 'essence' of his personal right to access to court.[799] Similarly, a law that precluded monasteries from suing in relation to their property rights except through the Greek Church was a violation of their right to access, even though the Church itself had an interest in the actions.[800]   **11.192**

Although limitation periods for proceedings restrict access to the court they serve important purposes and will, generally, not impair the essence of the right. Thus, in *Stubbings v United Kingdom*[800a] the Court held that the limitation periods applicable under English law in sex abuse cases pursued a legitimate aim and were proportionate. There was, therefore, no violation of Article 6. There may, however, be a breach of the right of access to the court if limitation periods are unduly short and rigidly enforced. As a result the Court has found breaches where a three-month time limit had expired before the applicant was effectively notified of the decision,[800b] and where the time limit for lodging an appeal was three days.[800c]   **11.192A**

A defence of privilege or immunity raised by states has been treated as a restriction on the right of the claimant's access to court, rather than going to the substance of the claim and the existence of a 'contestation' or dispute under Article 6. The Court has stressed in a number of cases that total restrictions on access will be carefully scrutinised because: **11.193**

> The right guaranteed to an applicant under art 6(1) of the convention to submit a dispute to a court or tribunal in order to have a determination on questions of both fact and law cannot be displaced by the *ipse dixit* of the executive.[801]

Thus, it has been held that the right of access will not be displaced by a certificate that matters of national security are involved.[802]

The privilege or immunity defences have been upheld in a number of cases on the basis of the *Ashingdane* test. Thus, the Court has upheld the immunity from suit   **11.194**

---

[798] *Klass v Germany* (1978) 2 EHRR 214 para 56.
[799] *Philis v Greece* (1991) 13 EHRR 741.
[800] *Holy Monasteries v Greece* (1994) (1994) 20 EHRR 1.
[800a] (1996) 23 EHRR 213 paras 53–55, see also para 11.277 below.
[800b] *De Geoffre de la Pradelle v France* (1992) A 253 (notification by publication in *Official Journal* insufficient).
[800c] *Perez de Rada Cavanilles v Spain* [1999] EHRLR 208.
[801] *Tinnelly and Sons Ltd and McElduff and others v United Kingdom* (1998) 27 EHRR 249 para 77.
[802] *Tinnelly and Sons Ltd* (n 801 above) see para 11.301 below (the Court took the view that it was possible to modify judicial procedures to safeguard national security and yet accord the individual a substantial degree of procedural justice, para 78).

of an international institution.[803] In *Fayed v United Kingdom*[804] a defence of privilege in relation to a claim that the Government had promulgated a false inspection report was acceptable because it facilitated the investigation of public companies, a matter of public interest which warranted the means used for its protection. The applicants had themselves attempted to bring the contentious subject matter of the report into the public forum and the remedy of judicial review was available to them in relation to the inspector's activities. The *Ashingdane* approach could equally be used to justify parliamentary privilege[805] or diplomatic and state immunity[805a] from suit.

11.195 However, the public policy immunity from liability in negligence[806] was held to be in breach of the right of access to the court in the important case of *Osman v United Kingdom*.[807] The plaintiff had brought proceedings which had been struck out[808] on the basis of the police immunity for actions in negligence arising out of the 'investigation and suppression of crime'[809] The Court rejected the Government's argument that Article 6 had no application. It accepted that the 'immunity' pursued the legitimate aim of the avoidance of defensive policing and the diversion of police manpower but held that it was not proportionate: the applicant's claim had been struck out without any consideration of the different policy considerations at issue. The Court said that:

> the application of the rule in this manner without further enquiry into the existence of competing public interest considerations only serves to confer a blanket immunity on the police for their acts and omissions during the investigation and suppression of crime and amounts to an unjustifiable restriction on an applicant's right to have a determination on the merits of his or her claim against the police in deserving cases . . . it must be open to a domestic court to have regard to the presence of other public interest considerations which pull in the opposite direction to the application of the rule.[810]

As a result, the Court held that there was a violation of Article 6. Other applications are pending; and the Commission has ruled as admissible an application in relation to public authorities' immunities from actions in negligence by children and has found for the applicants on the merits.[811]

---

[803] See *Beer and Regan v Germany* Judgment of 18 Feb 1999 (European Space Agency).

[804] (1994) 18 EHRR 393.

[805] *X v Austria* (1969) 12 YB 246, EComm HR; *Young v Ireland* [1996] EHRLR 326.

[805a] A number of cases relating to state immunity have been found to be admissible: *McElhinney v Ireland* Application 31253/96, 9 Feb 2000; *Al-Adsani v United Kingdom* Application 35763/97, 1 Mar 2000; and *Fogarty v United Kingdom* Application 37112/97, 1 Mar 2000.

[806] See generally, para 11.40ff above.

[807] (1998) 5 BHRC 293; the English decision was *Osman v Ferguson* [1993] 4 All ER 344; for criticism see Lord Hoffmann, 'Human Rights and the House of Lords' (1999) 62 MLR 159 and *Barrett v Enfield LB* [1999] 3 WLR 79, 84–85.

[808] *Osman v Ferguson* [1993] 4 All ER 344.

[809] See para 11.42 above.

[810] (1998) 5 BHRC 293 para 151.

[811] *T P and K M v United Kingdom* Application 28945/95 26 May 1998 (admissibility), 10 Sep 1999 (merits), EComm HR.

The decision in *Osman* has attracted considerable criticism.[812] Article 6(1) does **11.196** not guarantee any particular substantive content for civil rights and obligations in national law;[813] it simply gives procedural guarantees for the determination of *tenable* rights.[814] It has therefore been strongly argued that the Court have unjustifiably extended the scope of Article 6 by interfering in the substantive law of a domestic state. This objection, in turn, depends on whether the policy immunities can properly be characterised as blanket immunities, a view which was sharply criticised by Lord Browne-Wilkinson in *Barrett v Enfield LBC*.[815]

Access following administrative decisions. When decisions are taken by ad- **11.197** ministrative bodies which affect a person's civil rights, he is entitled to a hearing which satisfies the conditions of Article 6. This can be done in two ways:[816]

- the decision-making body must itself comply with the requirements of Article 6 (internal Article 6 compliance) or
- the decision-making body must be subject to control by a judicial body which provides Article 6 guarantees (external Article 6 compliance).

There will be sufficient 'access to the court' where the decision-making body does not comply with Article 6(1) in some respects *provided* that the body exercising judicial control 'has full jurisdiction and does provide the guarantees of Article 6(1)'.[817] In assessing the sufficiency of the review, it is necessary to have regard to matters such as the subject matter of the decision appealed against, the manner in which it was arrived at and the content of the dispute.[818]

However, the difficult question is whether it is necessary for an appeal to consider **11.198** *both* issues of fact and law or whether it is sufficient to satisfy Article 6 if only issues of law can be canvassed. In *Bryan v United Kingdom*[819] the Court held that a

---

[812] See eg T Weir 'Downhill — All the Way' [1999] 1 FLR 193; Lord Hoffmann, 'Human Rights and the House of Lords' (1999) 62 MLR 159; Sir Richard Buxton, 'The Human Rights Act and Private Law' (2000) 116 LQR 48.

[813] *H v Belgium* (1987) 10 EHRR 339.

[814] *James v United Kingdom* (1986) 8 EHRR 123 para 81; *Powell and Rayner v United Kingdom* (1990) 12 EHRR 355; see para 11.162 above.

[815] [1999] 3 WLR 79; see para 11.44 above.

[816] See *Albert and Le Compte v Belgium* (1983) 5 EHRR 533 para 29.

[817] Ibid; *Bryan v United Kingdom* (1995) 21 EHRR 342 para 40; this only applies to decisions of an administrative or disciplinary nature, not to ordinary civil and criminal cases: see *De Cubber v Belgium* (1984) 7 EHRR 236 para 32.

[818] *Bryan v United Kingdom*, (n 817 above) para 45; *Zumtobel v Austria* (1993) 17 EHRR 116 para 32.

[819] n 817 above; see also *ISKCON v United Kingdom* (1994) 76-A DR 90, EComm HR which also concerned an enforcement notice where the only remedy available to the applicant was judicial review; the Commission said it is 'not the role of Article 6 to give access to a level of jurisdiction which can substitute its opinion for that of the administrative authorities on questions of expediency and where the courts do not refuse to examine any of the points raised'.

planning appeal (which is confined to appealing on a question of law)[820] was sufficient to ensure that a planning inspector's decision[821] complied with Article 6. In addition to attaching significance to the procedural safeguards in the planning procedure[822] the Court stressed:

> In the present case there was no dispute as to the primary facts . . .. [However, even if there was such a challenge], the Court notes that while the High Court could not have substituted its own findings of fact for those of the inspector, it would have the power to satisfy itself that the inspector's findings of fact or the inferences based on them were neither perverse nor irrational.
>
> Such an approach by an appeal tribunal on questions of fact can reasonably be expected in specialist areas of law such as the one at issue, particularly where the facts have already been established in the course of a quasi-judicial procedure governed by many of the safeguards required by Article 6(1). It is also a feature in the systems of judicial control of administrative decisions found throughout the Council of Europe Member States. Indeed, in the instant case, the subject matter of the contested decision by the inspector was a typical example of the exercise of discretionary judgment in the regulation of citizens's conduct in the sphere of town and country planning.
>
> The scope of review of the High Court was therefore sufficient to comply with Article 6(1)

It appears that the decision in *Bryan* is a narrow one, turning primarily on the question of whether the applicant disputes the primary facts.[823]

11.199   The Commission has, nevertheless, rejected several recent complaints that recourse to judicial review is insufficient to meet the requirements of Article 6(1): where proceedings were brought following a determination by the Secretary of State that the applicant was not a fit and proper person to be the managing director of an insurance company;[824] and, again, following a finding by the Investment Managers Regulatory Organisation that the applicants were not fit and proper persons to carry on investment business.[825] The Commission also took the same approach about the effect of the availability of an appeal to the Privy Council from a decision of the health committee of the General Medical Council.[826]

---

[820] Under s 289(1) of the Town and Country Planning Act 1990.

[821] *Bryan v United Kingdom* (n 817 above); see also *Oerlermans v Netherlands* (1991) 15 EHRR 561.

[822] *Bryan v United Kingdom* (n 817 above) para 46; the Court referred to uncontested safeguards at the procedure before the planning inspector; the quasi judicial character of the decision-making process; the duty on the inspector to exercise independent judgment, the requirement that the inspector must not be subject to improper influence; the stated mission of the Inspectorate to uphold the principles of openness, fairness and impartiality; and the fact that any alleged shortcomings were subject to review by the High Court.

[823] See eg *Fischer v Austria* (1995) 20 EHRR 349 paras 33, 34.

[824] *X v United Kingdom* (1998) 25 EHRR CD 88.

[825] *APB Ltd, APP and AEB v United Kingdom* (1998) 25 EHRR CD 141.

[826] *Stefan v United Kingdom* (1997) 25 EHHR CD 130; *Wickramsinghe v United Kingdom* [1998] EHRLR 338.

In contrast, there have been several occasions where administrative decisions fol- **11.200**
lowed by an appeal on a point of law (rather than an appeal on the merits) have resulted in breaches of Article 6: on the ground that decisions of administrative
bodies that do not satisfy the requirements of Article 6 must be subject to subsequent control by a 'judicial body which has full jurisdiction'. In *Albert and Le
Compte v Belgium*[827] doctors challenging disciplinary decisions against them succeeded in arguing that failure of the appeals procedure to comply with Article 6
guarantees (and, in particular, an appeal confined to points of law) breached the
right of access to the court. The Court has held that judicial review does not provide sufficient scope to examine the merits of the case in relation to a local authority's decision as to access to a child;[828] and has reached the same conclusion in
a number of other cases.[829]

The question of whether a particular administrative decision maker (which is **11.201**
subject to judicial review) breaches Article 6 will depend on the extent to which
the administrative body *itself* meets the procedural safeguards achieved by a
quasi-judicial procedure.[830] A number of administrative decisions are made
through tribunal procedures (such as planning inquiries) which give an applicant
and interested parties extensive opportunities to dispute the facts in issue. Some
administrative decisions, on the other hand, have only very rudimentary procedures for allowing the applicant to put his case. The procedural guarantees conferred by Article 6 are comprehensive; and include the right to be present at an
adversarial hearing;[831] the right to equality of arms;[832] the right to fair presentation of the evidence;[833] the right to cross examine;[834] the right to a reasoned judgment;[835] the right to a hearing within a reasonable time;[836] the right to an
independent and impartial tribunal established by law;[837] and the right to a public hearing and the public pronouncement of judgment.[838] The critical issue in

---

[827] (1983) 5 EHRR 533 para 36.
[828] *W v United Kingdom* (1987) 10 EHRR 29 paras 80-83.
[829] See *Obermeier v Austria* (1990) 13 EHRR 290 para 70 (inadequate as no appeal on merits
against dismissal decision); *Schmautzer v Austria* (1995) 21 EHHR 511 para 34 and *Umlauft v
Austria* (1995) 22 EHRR 76 para 37 (road traffic conviction followed by appeal to Constitutional
Court which can only consider whether conviction conformed to constitution was insufficient to
satisfy Art 6).
[830] Cf Sir Stephen Richards;' The Impact of Article 6 of the ECHR on Judicial Review' [1999] JR
106.
[831] See para 11.206 below.
[832] See para 11.208ff below.
[833] See para 11.214 below.
[834] See para 11.217 below.
[835] See para 11.218 below.
[836] See para 11.219ff below.
[837] See para 11.222ff below.
[838] See para 11.230ff below.

every case will be whether an administrative procedure provides the applicant with a fair opportunity which is sufficient to dispute the primary facts.[839]

11.202 **Criminal charges.** In criminal proceedings, the right to access to a court means that the accused has a right to be tried on the charge against him in a court.[840] As the right is not absolute, it does not imply that a victim can himself lay a criminal charge,[841] or that every criminal charge must end in a judicial decision. In some instances, such as a decision by the prosecution to discontinue the proceedings, a criminal matter will not be submitted to a court and Article 6 will be irrelevant so long as no factual or formal 'determination' takes place. Article 6 does not give an accused grounds for demanding continuation of judicial proceedings, but requires only that when he is convicted it is done by a court.[842] Nevertheless, there may be a violation of Article 6 when the dismissal of a charge upon an agreement between the accused and the prosecution amounts to a settlement under duress and de facto denial of access.[843] Similarly, if after withdrawal of a charge there remains some suggestion of guilt on the part of the accused, then there is an arguable breach of Article 6, in light of the presumption of innocence in Article 6(2).[844]

11.203 **Access to appeals.** Under Article 6(1) there is no right of appeal from determinations of civil rights or obligations or criminal charges.[845] However, the guarantees apply to any appeal which does take place.[846]

(c) Right to a fair hearing

11.204 **Introduction.** The concept of fairness in Article 6(1) applies to both criminal hearings and to proceedings in which the determination of civil rights and obligations is involved. A decision as to the fairness of a hearing is based on an assessment of the course of the proceedings *as a whole*.[847] This approach was recently confirmed in *Khan v United Kingdom*[847a] where the Court rejected the argument that Article 6(1) was breached because the only evidence against the applicant was

---

[839] See also Lord Clyde's analysis of the position in *Stefan v General Medical Council* [1999] 1 WLR 1293,1299, 1300 discussed at para 11.91 above.

[840] *Deweer v Belgium* (1980) 2 EHRR 439.

[841] *Kiss v United Kingdom* (1977) 20 YB 156, EComm HR.

[842] It does not require an ordinary court or a trial by jury, but only that the court is established by law and meets the other criteria of Art 6: *X v Ireland* (1981) 22 DR 51; *Crociani v Italy* (1981) 22 DR 147, EComm HR.

[843] In *Deweer v Belgium* (1980) 2 EHRR 439 the applicant was threatened with the closure of his shop if he did not accept the settlement offered by the public prosecutor.

[844] *Adolf v Austria* (1982) 4 EHRR 313.

[845] *Delcourt v Belgium* (1970) 1 EHRR 355; in criminal cases, this is guaranteed by Art 2, Seventh Protocol (which has not been ratified by the United Kingdom).

[846] *Monnell & Morris v United Kingdom* (1987) 10 EHRR 205.

[847] See eg *Kraska v Switzerland* (1993) 18 EHRR 188 para 30; *Barberà, Messegué and Jabardo v Spain* (1988) 11 EHRR 360 para 68; contrast *Stanford v United Kingdom* (1994) Series A No 280-A see also *Khan v United Kingdom The Times*, 23 May 2000.

[847a] n 847 above.

obtained by a secret listening device in breach of Article 8(1). The Court instead held that the domestic courts had considered whether the admission of the evidence created a substantial unfairness so that its admission did not conflict with the requirements of fairness under Article 6(1). However, a particular aspect of a case may contravene the notion of fairness in such a way that it is possible to draw a conclusion without regard to the rest of the proceedings.[848] In criminal cases, all three paragraphs of Article 6 must be read *together*, as the general provision in Article 6(1) supplements the specific guarantees of Article 6(2) and 6(3). Although Article 6 rights are applicable to both civil and criminal cases, in applying them Contracting States have a greater latitude when dealing with civil cases than they have when dealing with criminal cases.[849]

Article 6 does not give any indication of the content of the right to a fair hearing. A number of principles has been developed by the Commission and the Court including: **11.205**

- the right to be present when evidence is being heard;
- the right to enter into adversarial argument and to present his case to the court under conditions that do not place him at substantial disadvantage in relation to his opponent;
- the right to be provided with reasons for judgment that have sufficient clarity to enable him to exercise a right of appeal available to him.

Right to be present at an adversarial oral hearing. The notion of a 'fair hearing' in a criminal case includes the right of the accused to be present at and to take part in an oral hearing[850] which is adversarial.[851] This means that each party must have the opportunity to comment on all evidence adduced, including experts report.[851a] The right does not extend to appeals unless the appeal court is dealing with the facts as well as the law.[852] The waiver of this right must be established in an unequivocal manner.[853] If it is waived, the accused must have   **11.206**

---

[848] *Crociani v Italy* (1981) 24 YB 222, EComm HR.

[849] *Dombo Beheer BV v Netherlands* (1993) 18 EHRR 213 para 32.

[850] See *Collozza and Rubinat v Italy* (1985) 7 EHRR 516 para 27; *Monnell and Morris v United Kingdom* (1987) 10 EHRR 205 para 58, *Zana v Turkey* (1998) 4 BHRC 241 para 68.

[851] *Brandstetter v Austria* (1991) 15 EHRR 378 para 66; *Ruiz-Mateos v Spain* (1993) 16 EHRR 505 para 63.

[851a] See *Mantovanelli v France* (1997) 24 EHRR 370 (applicant denied opportunity to attend interviews of witnesses by court appointed expert and not shown the documents he took into account).

[852] *Monnell v United Kingdom* (n 880 above); *Ekbatani v Sweden* (1988) 13 EHRR 504; contrast the cases where the appeal could be decided on documents alone: see eg *Monnell and Morris v United Kingdom* (1987) 10 EHRR 205; *Andersson v Sweden* (1991) 15 EHRR 218; *Kremzow v Austria* (1993) 17 EHRR 322.

[853] *Colozza and Rubinat v Italy*, (n 880 above) para 28; *Albert and Le Compte v Belgium* (1983) 5 EHRR 533 para 35; *Poitrimol v France* (1993) 18 EHRR 130 para 31; see generally, para 6.149 above.

legal representation.[854] As result, there will be a violation if the accused is not aware of the proceedings and the attempts to trace him are inadequate.[855] The presence of the accused's lawyers will not be sufficient when a person faces a serious criminal charge and has not waived his right to be present.[856] However, a trial in absentia is acceptable if the state has diligently but unsuccessfully given the accused notice of the hearing.[857] In some circumstances it is also permissable to proceed where the applicant is absent through illness.[858]

11.207 In civil cases, there is only a right to be present at an oral hearing in cases in which the 'personal character'[859] or conduct[860] of the applicant is relevant. This right can be waived impliedly by, for example, not attending the hearing after receiving effective notice of it.[861] There may be a right to be present at the hearing of appeals in such cases which consider both the facts and the law.[862]

11.208 **Right to equality of arms.**   In both criminal and civil cases, every party to the proceedings must have a 'reasonable opportunity of presenting his case to the court under conditions which do not place him at substantial disadvantage vis-a-vis his opponent'.[863] This right is particularly important in criminal cases where it overlaps with the specific guarantees in Article 6(3) but, in some respects, goes further. In this context, importance is attached to appearances as well as to the increased sensitivity to the fair administration of justice.[864]

11.209 The right to equality of arms means that all parties must have access to the records and documents which are relied on by the court.[865] It appears that the parties should have the opportunity to make copies of the relevant documents from the court file.[866] The parties must be able to cross-examine witnesses.[867] Thus, breaches have been found where:

---

[854] *Lala v Netherlands* (1994) 18 EHRR 586.

[855] See *Colloza and Rubinat v Italy* (n 850, above) paras 28–29.

[856] See *Zana v Turkey* (n 850 above) para 71 (applicant tried and convicted in his absence because he refused to defend himself in Turkish).

[857] *Colozzo and Rubinat v Italy* (n 850 above).

[858] See eg *Ensslin, Baader and Raspe v Germany* (1978) 14 DR 64, EComm HR where the applicants were on hunger strike.

[859] See eg cases involving access to children: *X v Austria* (1983) 31 DR 66, EComm HR; see also *Xv Germany* (1963) 6 YB 520, 572, EComm HR.

[860] *Muyldermans v Belgium* (1991) 15 EHRR 204 para 64, Com Rep.

[861] See *Cv Italy* (1988) 56 DR 40, EComm HR.

[862] See para 11.198 above.

[863] See eg *De Haes and Gijsels v Belgium* (1997) 25 EHRR 1 para 53; *Delcourt v Belgium* (1970) 1 EHRR 355 para 28.

[864] *Bulut v Austria* (1996) 24 EHRR 84 para 47.

[865] *Lynas v Switzerland* (1977) 10 YB 412, 445–446, EComm HR; *Lobo Machado v Portugal* (1996) 23 EHRR 79 para 31.

[866] See P van Dijk and G van Hoof, *Theory and Practice of the European Convention on Human Rights* (3rd edn, Kluwer, 1998) pp.430–431; relying on *Schuler-Zgraggen v Switzerland* (1993) 16 EHRR 405.

[867] *X v Austria* (1972) 42 CD 145, EComm HR.

- only one of two witnesses to an oral agreement was allowed to be called;[868]
- the applicant was denied a reply to written submissions by counsel for the state;[869]
- the applicant was not given the opportunity to comment on a medical report.[870]

The provision of legal aid could also be seen as a matter of 'equality of arms' with the other party, but has generally been dealt with in terms of the right of access to court.[871]

The right is especially significant in criminal cases. The Commission have held that it means that the prosecution must disclose any material in their possession which 'may assist the accused in exonerating himself or obtaining a reduction in sentence'.[872] Any defence expert must be afforded the same facilities as one appointed by the prosecution.[873] **11.210**

Freedom from self-incrimination. The right of a person charged to remain silent and not to incriminate himself is **11.211**

> generally recognised international standards which lie at the heart of the notion of fair procedure under Art 6 of the Convention. Their rationale lies, inter alia, in protecting the 'person charged' against improper compulsion by the authorities and thereby contributing to the avoidance of miscarriages of justice and to the fulfilment of the aims of Art 6. The right not to incriminate oneself, in particular, presupposes that the prosecution in a criminal case seek to prove their case without resort to evidence obtained through methods of coercion or oppression in defiance of the will of the 'person charged'.[874]

It is incompatible with these immunities to base a conviction solely or mainly on an accused's silence or his failure to answer questions or give evidence.[875] The right has been successfully invoked where the applicant failed to cooperate with authorities in the pre-trial production of documents[876] or refused to answer questions required by law on pain of criminal sanction.[877] In *Funke v France*,[877a] the Court found that the applicant's conviction of the offence of failing to produce bank statements relevant to customs investigations amounted to a compulsion to

---

[868] *Dombo Beheer BV v Netherlands* (1993) 18 EHRR 213.

[869] *Ruiz-Mateos v Spain* (1993) 16 EHRR 505.

[870] *Feldbrugge v Netherlands* (1986) 8 EHRR 425.

[871] See para 11.185 above.

[872] *Jespers v Belgium* (1981) 27 DR 61 para 54, EComm HR; see also *Edwards v United Kingdom* (1992) 15 EHRR 417; *Bendenoun v France* (1994) 18 EHRR 54 (no breach by failure to disclose a bulky file whose contents the applicant was aware of and which was not relied on by the court).

[873] *Bonisch v Austria* (1985) 9 EHRR 191.

[874] *Serves v France* (1997) 28 EHRR 265 para 47; and see *Funke v France* (1993) 16 EHRR 297 para 44, *Murray v United Kingdom* (1996) 22 EHRR 29 para 45, *Saunders v United Kingdom* (1996) 23 EHRR 313 para 68.

[875] *Murray* (n 874 above) para 47.

[876] *Funke v France* (n 874 above).

[877] *Saunders v United Kingdom* (n 874 above).

[877a] n 874 above.

produce incriminating evidence that violated his right to remain silent. In *Saunders v United Kingdom*, where the coercion was the threat of a criminal penalty, the Court stated that the freedom was necessary to safeguard the accused from oppression and coercion during criminal proceedings and was closely linked to the presumption of innocence. It also said that it was necessary to assess the impact of the infringement on the fairness of the trial as a whole before concluding that there had been a breach of Article 6. On the facts, the applicant was convicted of commercial fraud charges and sentenced to imprisonment on the basis of information that he was required to provide to Department of Trade and Industry inspectors and, as a result, there was a breach.

11.212   However, the right to silence is not absolute. It is clear that:

> it cannot and should not prevent that the accused's silence, in situations which clearly call for an explanation from him, be taken into account in assessing the persuasiveness of the evidence adduced by the prosecution.[878]

Whether the drawing of adverse inferences from an accused's silence infringes Article 6 is to be determined in light of all the circumstances of the case, having regard to the situations where inferences may be drawn, the weight attached to them by the national courts in the assessment of the evidence and the degree of compulsion.[879] Following the *Murray* case, the Commission have rejected a series of United Kingdom complaints involving 'inferences from silence' on the basis that there was other evidence and sufficient 'judicial protection' for the accused.[880] However, in *Condron v United Kingdom*[880a] the Court upheld a claim where the judge failed to give adequate directions to the jury about the proper inferences it could draw.

11.213   **Right to legal assistance.**   Legal assistance in criminal cases is guaranteed by Article 6(3)(c).[881] In civil cases, the right to a fair hearing includes a right to legal assistance, albeit a less extensive one.[882] Cases can be selected for legal aid on merit with financial contributions being required.[883] The blanket exclusion of legal aid in defamation cases is not a breach.[884] However, the Court has decided in *Benham*

---

[878] *Murray v United Kingdom* (1996) 22 EHRR 29, para 47.

[879] See *Quinn v United Kingdom (Merits)* [1997] EHRLR 167, EComm HR.

[880] See *Quinn* (n 879 above); *Hamill v United Kingdom (Merits)* (Application 22656/93), 2 Dec 1997 and *Murray v United Kingdom* Application 22384/93, 2 Dec 1997.

[880a] *The Times*, 9 May 2000; see para 11.287 below.

[881] See para 11.245ff below.

[882] See *Airey v Ireland* (1979) 2 EHRR 305; and generally, para 11.189 above.

[883] *X v United Kingdom* (1981) 21 DR 95, 101, EComm HR; *Thaw v United Kingdom* (1996) 22 EHRR CD 100.

[884] *Winer v United Kingdom* (1986) 48 DR 154, EComm HR; *Munro v United Kingdom* (1987) 52 DR 158, EComm HR; *S and M v United Kingdom* (1993) 18 EHRR CD 172 (the 'McLibel' case).

v United Kingdom[885] and *Perks v United Kingdom*[886] that the risk of imprisonment and the complexity of the law in community charge cases meant the interests of justice required legal representation before the magistrates.

Right to fair presentation of evidence.   As a result of the wide variation in rules **11.214** of evidence followed in different European legal systems, the Court has not laid down any specific set of evidential rules as a requirement of the guarantee of the right to a fair trial under Article 6. The Court has, nonetheless, provided some guidelines as to the rules that may be applied and a breach of one of these rules may, on the facts of a case, render a trial unfair. The Court will examine the proceedings as a whole.[887]

Illegally obtained evidence. The admission of illegally obtained evidence will not **11.215** contravene Article 6[888] unless it was obtained by an abuse of police powers. Confessions and statements by the accused during investigation must be obtained in the presence of the accused's lawyer, or adequate trial procedures must be available to ensure that they have not been extracted under duress.[889] Thus, in *Khan v United Kingdom*[889a] the admission of evidence obtained by a secret listening device in breach of Article 8 did not of *itself* render the trial unfair since the domestic courts had the discretion to refuse to admit the evidence if it was unfair to do so under section 78 of the Police and Criminal Evidence Act.

Agents provocateur.[890] The fact that evidence has been obtained by agent provoca- **11.216** teurs will not, of itself, lead to its exclusion in a criminal trial. But the Court has made it clear that:

> A distinction had to be drawn between cases where the undercover agent's actions created a criminal intent that had previously been absent and those in which the offender had already been predisposed to commit the offence.[891]

Thus, criminal proceedings will be unfair if the offence was wholly incited by

---

[885]   (1996) 22 EHRR 293 para 61.

[886]   Application 25277/94, 12 Oct 1999 para 76.

[887]   *Miailhe v France (No 2)* (1996) 23 EHRR 491 para 43.

[888]   *Schenk v Switzerland* (1988) 13 EHRR 242 (no breach where illegally obtained tape recording incriminating the accused admitted in evidence); *X v Germany* (1989) 11 EHRR 84, EComm HR (no breach where evidence of conversations overheard by undercover police officer in prison setting was admitted); *X v United Kingdom* (1976) 7 DR 115, EComm HR (admission of evidence of an accomplice who has been promised immunity is acceptable if the jury is aware of the circumstances).

[889]   *G v United Kingdom* (1983) 35 DR 75, EComm HR (*voire dire* proceedings and burden on the prosecution to prove voluntariness of the statement were sufficient safeguards where accused had been questioned without his lawyer present).

[889a]   *The Times*, 23 May 2000.

[890]   See generally, O Davies, 'The Fruit of the Poisoned Tree — Entrapment and the Human Rights Act 1998' (1999) 163 JP 84; and see para 11.353 below.

[891]   See *Teixeira de Castro v Portugal* (1998) 28 EHRR 101 para 32; Noted [1998] Crim LR 751.

agent provocateurs[892] rather than being detected by undercover agents.[893] The Court has made it clear that, while the rise in organised crime requires appropriate measures, 'the public interest cannot justify the use of evidence obtained as a result of police incitement'.[894]

11.217 *Cross-examination of witnesses.* In criminal trials witnesses must generally be made available for cross-examination by the accused regardless of the form in which their evidence originally comes before the court. For example, in *Unterpertinger v Austria*[895] family members who were allegedly assaulted by the applicant exercised their right under Austrian law not to give oral testimony, and the prosecution obtained a conviction of the accused 'mainly' on the basis of their sworn statements to the police. The Court found a breach of Article 6(1) as the right of the accused to a defence was 'appreciably restricted'. The decision was followed in *Kostovski v Netherlands*[896] where the conviction was 'to a decisive extent' based on the statements of two witnesses who failed to give evidence at trial and remained anonymous out of fear that their testimony would lead to reprisals by organised crime in which the accused had been involved. These cases suggest that an infringement of Article 6 will occur where the evidence of the missing witness is the 'main' or 'decisive' evidence before the Court. However, in *Asch v Austria*[897] the Court appeared to relax the general rule: holding that there would be no breach where the evidence is absolutely uncorroborated unless it is the 'only' piece of evidence on which the conviction was based. However, the defence must be given an 'adequate and proper opportunity to question a witness against him' at some stage of the proceedings.[898] Where there are potential threats to the life, liberty or security of witnesses, it is permissible for them to remain anonymous[899] and to give evidence from behind a screen.[900] The defence must be able to question the witness, in order to test his credibility and the reliability of the evidence.

11.218 **Right to a reasoned judgment.**   A court must give reasons for its judgment so that any party with an interest in the case is informed of the basis of the decision,

---

[892] As in the *Teixeira de Castro* case (n 891 above)

[893] As in *Lüdi v Switzerland* (1992) 15 EHRR 173.

[894] *Teixeira de Castro* (n 891 above) para 36.

[895] (1986) 13 EHRR 175.

[896] *Kostovski v Netherlands* (1989) 12 EHRR 434; see also *Lüdi v Switzerland* (1992) 15 EHRR 173 (breach was found where the evidence was not the sole evidence, but had 'played a part in' the conviction).

[897] *Asch v Austria* (1991) 15 EHRR 597 (no breach was found where other corroborating evidence was present); see also *Artner v Austria* (1992) Series A No 242-A.

[898] *Asch v Austria* (n 897 above) para 27; it is difficult to reconcile this statement of principle with the decision in the case, see the dissenting opinions of Judges Sir Vincent Evans and Bernhardt, see also *Ferantelli and Santangelo v Italy* (1996) 23 EHRR 288 and see generally, O Harris, M O'Boyle and C Warbrick, *Law of the European Convention on Human Rights* (Butterworths, 1995) 212.

[899] *Doorsen v Netherlands* (1996) 22 EHRR 330 paras 68–71.

[900] See *X v United Kingdom* (1992) 15 EHRR CD 113.

so that the public in a democratic society may know the reasons for judicial decisions, and to enable the accused in a criminal trial to exercise the right of appeal available to him.[901] Courts in national jurisdictions are given a great deal of discretion as to the content and structure of their judgments, and a reasoned judgment does not have to deal with every argument raised[902] provided that it indicates the grounds on which the decision is based with 'sufficient clarity'.[903] However, if a point would be *decisive* for the case if accepted, it should be addressed specifically and expressly by the court.[904]

(d) A hearing within a reasonable time

This express right applies to both civil and criminal cases. In a civil case, time begins to run when proceedings are instituted.[905] If, prior to the commencement of proceedings, the applicant has sought to have a right determined by an administrative decision, any delays in such decision will be taken into account.[906] In criminal cases, time runs from the date on which the defendant is subject to a 'charge', which is the date when he is 'officially notified' or 'substantially affected' by proceedings.[907] This will usually be the date on which a person is charged with a criminal offence.[908] In a civil case, the time will stop running when the final appeal decision has been made or the time for appealing has expired.[909] In criminal cases, the period covers the whole of the proceedings, including any appeal[910] but not periods spent unlawfully at large.[911] **11.219**

The reasonableness of the length of proceedings must be assessed in each case taking into account all the circumstances including:[912] **11.220**

- *the complexity of the case*, including matters such as the number of witnesses,[913] the intervention of other parties[914] or the need to obtain expert evidence;[915]

---

[901] *Hadjianastassiou v Greece* (1992) 16 EHRR 219 para 33.
[902] *Van der Hurk v Netherlands* (1994) 18 EHRR 481, para 61.
[903] *Hadjianastassiou v Greece* (n 901 above) para 33.
[904] *Hiro Balani v Spain* (1994) 19 EHRR 565 para 28; and *Ruiz Torija v Spain* (1994) 19 EHRR 542 para 30.
[905] *Scopelliti v Italy* (1993) 17 EHRR 493 para 18.
[906] *Schouten and Meldrum v Netherlands* (1994) 19 EHRR 432 (delay in confirmation of a decision).
[907] *Eckle v Germany* (1982) 5 EHRR 1 para 73.
[908] Cf *Ewing v United Kingdom* (1986) 10 EHRR 141, Comm.
[909] *Vocaturo v Italy* (1992) A 245-D.
[910] *Eckle* (n 907 above) para 76.
[911] *Girolami v Italy* (1991) Series A No 196-E.
[912] See, for example *Yagci and Sargin v Turkey* (1995) 20 EHRR 505 paras 59–70 and see generally, P van Dijk and G van Hoof, *Theory and Practice of the European Convention on Human Rights* (3rd edn, Kluwer, 1998) 446–7; Harris, O'Boyle and Warbrick (n 898 above) 222ff.
[913] *Andreucci v Italy* (1992) Series A No 228-G.
[914] *Manieri v Italy* (1992) Series A No 229-D.
[915] *Wemhoff v Germany* (1968) 1 EHRR 55.

- *The conduct of the applicant and the conduct of the judicial authorities.*[916] Although an accused person is not required to cooperate in criminal proceedings and is entitled to make full use of his remedies, delay resulting from such conduct is not attributable to the state.[917] Procedural rules that provide for the parties to take the initiative with regard to the progress of civil proceedings does not excuse the courts from ensuring compliance with the requirements of Article 6 in relation to time;[918]
- *The conduct of the relevant authorities,*[919] including matters such as delays in commencing proceedings[920] or in transferring proceedings.[921] The mere fact that the state does not comply with the time-limits which are laid down is not, in itself, contrary to Article 6.[922]

The fact that a defendant in a criminal case is detained in custody is a factor to be considered in assessing reasonableness.[923] The personal circumstances of an applicant in a civil case may be taken into account. Thus, claims for compensation by HIV infected haemophiliacs required 'exceptional diligence' on the part of the authorities.[924] Factors such as the workload of the court and a shortage of resources are not a sufficient justification for delays in a trial because Contracting States are under a duty 'to organise their legal systems so as to allow the courts to comply with the requirements of Article 6(1)'.[925] However, the state is not liable for delays resulting from a backlog caused by an exceptional situation when reasonably prompt remedial action has been taken.[926]

11.221 No general guidelines have been laid down for what constitutes a 'reasonable time' in either civil or criminal proceedings. It is submitted that the proper approach is to decide whether the overall delay is 'unreasonable' and then to consider whether the state is able to justify each period of delay.[927] In civil cases, violations on the grounds of delay have included the following periods of delay:

- four years for a personal injury case;[928]

---

[916] *Eckle* (n 907 above) para 80.
[917] *Eckle* (n 907 above) para 82.
[918] *Scopelliti v Italy* (1993) 17 EHRR 493 para 25; *Unión Alimentaria Sanders SA v Spain* (1989) 12 EHRR 24.
[919] *König v Germany* (1978) 2 EHRR 170.
[920] *Eckle v Germany* (1982) 5 EHRR 1.
[921] *Foti v Italy* (1982) 5 EHRR 313 para 61.
[922] *G v Italy* (1992) Series A No 228-F.
[923] *Abdoella v Netherlands* (1992) 20 EHRR 585.
[924] *X v France* (1992) 14 EHRR 483.
[925] *Zimmerman and Steiner v Switzerland* (1983) 6 EHRR 17 para 29; *Muti v Italy* (1994) Series A No 281-C para 15.
[926] *Buchholz v Germany* (1981) 3 EHRR 597 para 51.
[927] See Harris, O'Boyle and Warbrick (n 898 above) 229.
[928] *Guincho v Portugal* (1984) 7 EHRR 223.

- nearly nine years for a claim for unfair dismissal;[929]
- four years for the determination of a dispute about costs;[930]
- 14 years for compulsory purchase proceedings;[931]
- over six years for the determination of a dispute concerning the applicant's pension.[932]

In criminal cases, violations have included the following periods of delay:

- 16 years in complex proceedings;[933]
- five years for relatively simple proceedings.[934]

(e) Independent and impartial tribunal established by law

Introduction.   The express right to a tribunal which is 'independent', 'impartial' and established by law applies to all types of case. A tribunal includes not only ordinary courts, but also disciplinary or other specialised tribunals that have a judicial function and otherwise meet the requirements of Article 6. Most importantly, a tribunal must be competent to take legally binding rather than merely recommendatory decisions.[935] The three requirements will be considered in turn. **11.222**

Independent.   'Independent' means 'independent of the executive and also of the parties'.[936] A court that takes instructions for the determination of the dispute from a member of the executive is not independent.[937] Neither can a decision-making member of the executive be an independent tribunal for the purposes of Article 6, even though the decision may be essentially judicial in nature.[938] **11.223**

In order to determine whether a tribunal can be considered to be independent regard must be had to factors such as the manner of appointment of members, their term of office, the existence of guarantees against outside pressures and whether the body presents an appearance of independence.[939] Questions as to appropriateness **11.224**

---

[929] *Darnell v United Kingdom* (1993) 18 EHRR 205; see also *Obermeier v Austria* (1990) 13 EHRR 290 (claim arising out of a dismissal, nine years).

[930] *Robins v United Kingdom* (1997) 26 EHRR 527.

[931] *Guillemin v France* (1997) 25 EHRR 435.

[932] *Ausiello v Italy* (1996) 24 EHRR 568.

[933] *Ferrantelli and Santangelo v Italy* (1996) 23 EHRR 33; see also *Mitap and Müftüoglu v Turkey* (1996) 22 EHRR 209 (16 years in complex criminal proceedings).

[934] *Philis v Greece (No 2)* (1997) 25 EHRR 417.

[935] *Benthem v Netherlands* (1985) 8 EHRR 1 para 40; *Van der Hurk v Netherlands* (1994) 18 EHRR 481 para 45; other functions do not prevent a tribunal from exercising a judicial one: *Campbell and Fell v United Kingdom* (1984) 7 EHRR 165 para 81.

[936] *Ringeisen v Austria (No 1)* (1971) 1 EHRR 455 para 95.

[937] See *Beaumartin v France* (1994) 19 EHRR 485 para 38 (where a court accepted as binding Foreign Office advice as to the interpretation of a treaty for application in the case).

[938] *Benthem v Netherlands* (1985) 8 EHRR 1 para 42.

[939] See *Bryan v United Kingdom* (1995) 21 EHRR 342 para 37, Noted [1996] EHRLR 184.

of the manner of appointment or election of judges[940] and the criteria upon which appointments are made[941] have been decided both in terms of 'impartiality' and 'independence'. Judges' terms of office are not required to be fixed[942] or of any particular duration, although shorter appointments seem to be more acceptable for members of administrative or disciplinary tribunals[943] than for judges in ordinary courts.[944] A lengthy fixed term would assist with reduction of outside pressures on judges, but that has been accomplished instead by the requirement that tribunal members be protected from dismissal during their term of office, either in law or in practice.[945] Other guarantees against outside pressure include prevention of subjection to instructions from the executive,[946] scrutiny of the use of amnesty or pardon by the executive to guard against abuse that would undermine the judicial function,[947] and provision for secrecy of the tribunal's deliberations.[948] In *Campbell and Fell* the Court formulated an objective test for the 'appearance of independence':[949] were the applicants reasonably entitled to think that the tribunal was dependent on the executive? On the basis of this test, the Board of Visitors was held to be independent in that case. However, in *Sramek v Austria*[950] and *Belilos v Switzerland* it was held that, applying this test, the tribunals were not 'independent'.[951]

---

[940] It is permissible and usual for judges to be appointed by the executive: *Campbell and Fell v United Kingdom* (1984) 7 EHRR 165, or elected by Parliament: *Crociani v Italy* (1981) 22 DR 147, EComm HR.

[941] Arrangements for appointment or substitution of judges in a particular case may be challengeable if there is an indication of improper motives of attempting to influence the outcome of the case: *Zand v Austria* (1978) 15 DR 70, EComm HR; *Crociani v Italy* (1981) 22 DR 147, EComm HR (appointment by reference to judges' political views); *Barberà, Messegué and Jabardo v Spain* (1988) 11 EHRR 360.

[942] *Engel v Netherlands (No1)* (1976) 1 EHRR 647.

[943] *Campbell and Fell v United Kingdom* (1984) 7 EHRR 165 (three-year term of Board of Visitors was acceptable given the difficulty of securing unpaid members for longer duration).

[944] Even in ordinary courts, judges are not necessarily appointed for life: *Zand v Austria* (1978) 15 DR 70, EComm HR.

[945] *Zand v Austria* (1978) 15 DR 70; see also *Campbell and Fell v United Kingdom* (n 943 above) in which the Court was satisfied that the irremovability of a Board of Visitors member during his term of office was recognised in fact, though not formally in law; and *Eccles, McPhillips and McShane v Ireland* (1988) 59 DR 212, EComm HR (the *Campbell* test was applied to judges on the Irish Special Criminal Court; although they could be dismissed at will and have their salaries reduced, the Commission found that in reality the executive was not attempting to undermine the functioning of the Court and that the ordinary courts had the power of review of its independence).

[946] *Sramek v Austria* (1984) 7 EHRR 351: requirement in law; *Campbell and Fell v United Kingdom* (1984) 7 EHRR 165: required only in practice; *The Greek Case* (1969) 12 YB 1, EComm HR: courts-martial found not to be independent because members were to exercise their discretion 'in accordance with the decisions of the Minister of National Defence'.

[947] *The Greek Case* (n 946 above).

[948] *Sutter v Switzerland* (1979) 16 DR 166.

[949] para 81; note that this is different from the objective test applied in relation to impartiality of a tribunal.

[950] (1984) 7 EHRR 351 (immediate superior to the civil servant member of a tribunal was representing the government party to the case).

[951] (1988) 10 EHRR 466 (a Police Board that convicted the accused of a minor criminal offence was composed of one member who was a lawyer from police headquarters and a municipal civil servant).

Impartial. For the purposes of Article 6(1), the existence of impartiality[952] must **11.225** be determined according to two tests:

> a subjective test, that is on the basis of the personal conviction of a particular judge in a given case, and also according to an objective test, that is ascertaining whether the judge offered guarantees sufficient to exclude any legitimate doubt in this respect.[953]

In order to satisfy the subjective test, the applicant must show that the tribunal in fact had personal bias against him.[954] The objective test requires a finding, not of actual bias, but of 'legitimate doubt' as to impartiality that can be 'objectively justified'.[955] The accused's apprehensions are not decisive unless they are objectively justified.[955a] The higher objective standard is necessary to inspire the confidence of the public, and the criminally accused, in the courts and ensures that justice is not only done, but is seen to be done as what is at stake is 'the confidence which the courts in a democratic society must inspire in the public'.[956]

In criminal cases, a judge will not necessarily be partial because he has made pre- **11.226** trial decisions. It is necessary to consider the nature and the extent of such decisions.[957] There is likely to be a 'legitimate doubt' about impartiality where the judge's previous involvement in the case might have facilitated the formation of a considered opinion as to the guilt of the applicant. This is most likely to occur where the pre-trial decisions were made in the context of investigation or prosecution of the case,[958] whereas, in cases in which pre-trial involvement relates to the usual ancillary matters such as bail applications there will be no breach unless some special circumstances are established.[959] A court will not be partial because it hears cases involving different parties arising out of the same set of facts[960] or two different cases involving the same accused.[961] A financial interest in the case

---

[952] That is, prejudice or bias, *Piersack v Belgium* (1982) 5 EHRR 169 para 30.

[953] *Fey v Austria* (1993) 16 EHRR 387 para 28; see also *Pullar v United Kingdom* (1996) 22 EHRR 391 para 30.

[954] The tribunal is presumed to be impartial until the contrary is proved, *Le Compte, Van Leuven and De Meyere v Belgium* (1981) 4 EHRR 1; *Albert and Le Compte v Belgium* (1983) 5 EHRR 533; *Debled v Belgium* (1994) 19 EHRR 506.

[955] *Hauschildt v Denmark* (1989) 12 EHRR 266; *Gautrin v France* (1998) 28 EHRR 196; *Incal v Turkey* RJD 1998–IV 1547.

[955a] *Nortier v Netherlando* (1993) 17 EHRR 273 para 33.

[956] *Ferrantelli and Santangelo v Italy* (1996) 23 EHRR 33 para 58.

[957] *Fey v Austria* (1993) 16 EHRR 387 para 30.

[958] *De Cubber v Belgium* (1984) 7 EHRR 236 (breach where a trial judge was previously an investigating judge on the case though in that role he had been quite independent of the prosecution).

[959] See, eg *Sainte-Marie v France* (1992) 16 EHRR 116 (no special circumstances and no breach of Art 6 where two appeal judges who sentenced an accused convicted of weapons possession had earlier sat on the bench that refused his bail application in proceedings arising out of the same facts).

[960] *Gillow v United Kingdom* (1986) 11 EHRR 335, EComm HR.

[961] *Schmid v Austria* (1987) 54 DR 144; *Brown v United Kingdom* (1985) 8 EHRR 272 (one of the judges in the Court of Appeal Criminal Division had previously granted an injunction freezing the applicant's bank account).

will disqualify a judge, unless the interest is disclosed and no objection made by the applicant,[962] as will non-financial interests in some circumstances.[963] The objective test of impartiality has also been applied in the context of jury trials,[964] where links between members of the jury and the defendants may constitute a breach of impartiality, and to the rules for appointment of arbitrators in compulsory arbitration proceedings.[965]

11.227 There is an obligation on every court to check whether it is an 'impartial tribunal' in accordance with Article 6(1) where the point is raised. Thus, a violation was found when a court refused to investigate the accused's allegation that a juror had made a racist remark.[966]

11.228 There have been findings of violation of Article 6(1) due to failure to meet the objective test of impartiality in a large number of cases, including:

- where the prosecuting officer in a court-martial appointed the members of the court-martial and also had the responsibility of confirming the decision;[967]
- where the Secretary of State was entitled to revoke the power of a planning inspector to hear an appeal at any time;[968]
- where the Bailiff of Guernsey who had presided over the legislature when it had adopted a development plan had subsequently been president of the court which had refused the applicant's planning appeal;[968a]
- where the majority of members of a civil jury were active members of a political party which had close links with the defendant;[969]
- where a trial judge's decision dealt with an allegation of racial bias in a jury trying an Asian defendant by giving directions rather than discharging them;[969a]

---

[962] *D v Ireland* (1986) 51 DR 117, EComm HR.

[963] *Demicoli v Malta* (1991) 14 EHRR 47 (partiality where two members of the tribunal that tried the applicant for breach of parliamentary privilege were the Members of Parliament that had been criticised in the publication that was the subject of the alleged offence); *Langborger v Sweden* (1989) 12 EHRR 416 (breach where lay members of a tribunal adjudicating upon a tenancy agreement had been nominated by and had connections with associations holding partisan interests in the outcome).

[964] *Holm v Sweden* (1993) 18 EHRR 79; *X v Norway* (1970) 35 CD 37, EComm HR (challenges to jury successful and applications admissible).

[965] *Bramelid and Malmström v Sweden* (1983) 38 DR 18, EComm HR.

[966] *Remli v France* (1996) 22 EHRR 253 para 48; contrast *Gregory v United Kingdom* (1997) 25 EHRR 577 (no violation of Art 6 was found because the judge had considered an allegation of racism by a juror and given a clear direction to the jury to decide the case free of prejudice).

[967] *Findlay v United Kingdom* (1997) 24 EHRR 221, see para 11.296 below.

[968] *Bryan v United Kingdom* (1995) 21 EHRR 342 (there was no breach of Art 6(1) because of the availability of judicial review, see para 11.198 above.

[968a] *McGonnell v United Kingdom* (2000) 8 BHRC 56 (the case was decided on a narrow ground based on the Bailiff's actual involvement in the relevant legislative decision and the Court did not consider the broader issue as to whether it was appropriate for the Bailiff to have judicial, legislative and executive functions), see para 11–283 below.

[969] *Holm v Sweden* (1993) 18 EHRR 79.

[969a] *Sander v United Kingdom* Judgment of 9 May 2000; and see para 11.290 below.

- where a trial court judge was previously the head of the public prosecutor's department that investigated and instituted proceedings against the applicant, even though he had no personal knowledge of the investigation;[970]
- where the trial judge had decided, on a bail application, that there was a 'confirmed suspicion of guilt' against the defendant;[971]
- where a judge who had taken part in a decision quashing an order dismissing criminal proceedings subsequently sat in the hearing of an appeal against the applicant's conviction.[972]

A tribunal 'established by law'.   The tribunal should be independent of the executive and should be regulated by law emanating from Parliament.[973] But parts of the judicial organisation may be delegated to the executive, provided that there are sufficient guarantees against arbitrariness.[974] Not only the establishment but also the organisation and functioning of the tribunal must have a basis in law.[975]   **11.229**

(f) Right to a public hearing and the public pronouncement of judgment

Public hearing.   The holding of court hearings in public is a fundamental principle enshrined in Article 6(1). The public character of hearings protects litigants against the administration of justice in secret without public scrutiny, and is also one of the means whereby confidence in the courts can be maintained.[976] It is implicit in the requirement of publicity that the hearing at the trial court level should be an oral one.[977] As the press plays an important role in publicising the hearing, Article 6(1) requires that it should not, as a general rule, be excluded,[978] but there is no positive obligation on the state to advertise the hearing or to otherwise extend an invitation to the media to attend.[979]   **11.230**

However, Article 6(1) provides for a number of express restrictions on this right, allowing for the exclusion of the press and public 'in the interests of morals, public order or national security in a democratic society, where the interests of juveniles or the private life of the parties so require, or to the extent strictly necessary in the opinion of the court in special circumstances where publicity   **11.231**

---

[970] *Piersack v Belgium* (1982) 5 EHRR 169.
[971] *Hauschildt v Denmark* (1989) 12 EHRR 266.
[972] *Oberschlick v Austria (No 1)* (1991) 19 EHRR 389; see also *Castillo Algar v Spain* RJD 1988-VIII 3103 (violation when trial judges had previously sat in chamber hearing appeal against order of investigating judge).
[973] *Zand v Austria* (1978) 15 DR 70, 80, EComm HR.
[974] Ibid.
[975] *Piersack v Belgium* (1986) B 47 23.
[976] *Diennet v France* (1995) 21 EHRR 554 para 33.
[977] *Fischer v Austria* (1995) 20 EHRR 349 para 44.
[978] *Axen v Germany* (1983) 6 EHRR 195.
[979] *X v United Kingdom* (1979) 2 Digest 444, EComm HR.

would prejudice the interests of justice'.[980] These provisions have not received detailed consideration in the case law.

11.232 The exclusion of the public has been permitted in cases involving sexual offences against children;[981] in divorce,[982] and medical[983] and prison[984] disciplinary proceedings for the 'protection of the parties'; and to ensure the safety of witnesses in appropriate situations.[985] It was not permitted for the sole purpose of reducing the Court's workload.[986] In relation to appeals there is no general right to a public hearing, even where the court has the jurisdiction to review the case on the facts as well as on the law.[987] The position is assessed on a case-by-case basis, with respect to the 'special features of the proceedings'[988] concerned.

11.233 Apart from the restrictions on a public hearing which are expressly permitted, a public trial will not be necessary if the accused has unequivocally waived the right in a situation in which there is no important public interest consideration which calls for the public to be present.[989] If there is a practice that hearings will not be held in public unless one of the parties expressly requests one, then a failure to make the application is deemed to be an unequivocal waiver.[990] In particular, the practice may be justified where the subject matter of the dispute does not raise issues of public importance, is highly technical and of a private nature.[991]

11.234 Public pronouncement of judgment. The right to public pronouncement of a judgment, unlike the publicity of the hearing, is not subject to any express restriction or principle of waiver under Article 6(1). It has been restricted only in the sense that the language 'pronounced publicly', which implies an oral presentation in open court, has been interpreted to permit the publication of judgments in

---

[980] These reservations apply to administrative proceedings as well as civil and criminal cases, *Ringeisen v Austria (No 1)* (1971) 1 EHRR 455 para 98.

[981] *X v Austria* (1965) 2 Digest 438, EComm HR (several grounds including 'interests of juveniles' could have applied).

[982] *X v United Kingdom* (1977) 2 Digest 452, EComm HR.

[983] *Guenoun v France* (1990) 66 DR 181, EComm HR.

[984] *Campbell and Fell v United Kingdom* (1984) 7 EHRR 165 para 90.

[985] *X v United Kingdom* (1980) 2 Digest 456, EComm HR; *X v Norway* (1970) 35 CD 37, EComm HR.

[986] *Axen v Germany* (1983) 6 EHRR 195, EComm HR.

[987] *Andersson v Sweden* (1991) 15 EHRR 218 para 27.

[988] *Sutter v Switzerland* (1984) 6 EHRR 272.

[989] *Håkansson and Sturesson v Sweden* (1990) 13 EHRR 1 para 66 (where the applicant failed to ask for a public hearing before a court which conducted itself in private unless it considered a public hearing to be 'necessary'); *Pauger v Austria* (1997) 25 EHRR 105 para 58; cf *H v Belgium* (1987) 10 EHRR 339 para 54 (no waiver to be implied from a failure to demand a public hearing when, as a matter of practice, the hearings were conducted in camera); and see generally, para 6.149 above.

[990] *Zumtobel v Austria* (1993) 17 EHRR 116 para 34.

[991] *Schuler-Zgraggen v Switzerland* (1993) 16 EHRR 405 para 58 (complaint concerning lack of oral hearing to determine invalidity benefit).

some proceedings by filing in the court registry.[992] The form of publicity to be given to the judgment is to be assessed in the light of the special features of the case and by reference to the object and purpose of Article 6(1).[993]

(4) Minimum standards of fairness in criminal proceedings

(a) Introduction

Articles 6(2) and 6(3) provide for specific rights in relation to criminal proceedings. These guarantees are specific aspects of the right to fair trial in Article 6(1).[994] These provisions must be read with those of Article 6(1). A criminal trial could be 'unfair' even if the minimum rights guaranteed by Article 6(3) are respected.[995] In addition, Article 6, read as a whole, guarantees the right of an accused to participate effectively in his trial.[995a] This right was violated when two ten year olds were tried for the murder of a young boy in a highly publicised trial in the Crown Court.[995b] It should be noted that the provisions of Article 6 do not, of themselves, create any right to compensation for miscarriage of justice.[996]

11.235

(b) Presumption of innocence

Article 6(2) provides that a person 'charged with a criminal offence shall be presumed innocent until proved guilty according to law'. This applies to persons subject to a 'criminal charge', which has the same autonomous Convention meaning as it does under Article 6(1).[997] As a result, Article 6(2) is not relevant where a person is merely suspected of a crime, or detained for a purpose, such as extradition[998] or deportation[999] that does not involve criminal prosecution. It has not been applied to practices such as blood tests,[1000] medical examinations[1001] or production of documents.[1002]

11.236

Article 6(2) requires:

11.237

> that when carrying out their duties, the members of a court should not start with

---

[992] *Preto v Italy* (1983) 6 EHRR 182; *Axen v Germany* (1983) 6 EHRR 195 (Court of Appeal proceedings).

[993] *Preto v Italy* (n 992 above).

[994] *Edwards v United Kingdom* (1992) 15 EHRR 417 para 33.

[995] *Jespers v Belgium* (1981) 27 DR 61 para 54, EComm HR, cf, P van Dijk and G van Hoof, *Theory and Practice of the European Convention on Human Rights* (3rd edn, Kluwer, 1998) 463.

[995a] *Stanford v United Kingdom* (1994) A 282-A para 26; *T v United Kingdom* (2000) 7 BHRC 659.

[995b] *T v United Kingdom* (n 995a above) paras 97–98 (concurring opinion of Lord Reed).

[996] *Masson and Van Zon v Netherlands* (1995) 22 EHRR 491; this right is provided for in Protocol 7, Art 3 (not ratified by the United Kingdom); for the English law, see para 11.138 above.

[997] *Adolf v Austria* (1982) 4 EHRR 313 para 30; and see para 11.174 above.

[998] *X v Austria* (1963) 6 YB 484, EComm HR.

[999] *X v Netherlands* (1965) 8 YB 228, EComm HR.

[1000] *X v Netherlands* (1978) 16 DR 184, EComm HR.

[1001] *X v Germany* (1962) 5 YB 192, EComm HR.

[1002] *Funke v France* (1993) 16 EHRR 297.

the preconceived idea that the accused has committed the offence charged; the burden of proof is on the prosecution and any doubt should benefit the accused.[1003]

This also implies that it is for the prosecution to inform the accused of the nature of the case against him.[1004] The presumption will be violated if a judicial decision concerning a person charged with a criminal offence reflects an opinion that he is guilty before he has been proved guilty.[1005] It is not necessary for there to be a formal finding if there is some reasoning suggesting that the Court regards the accused as guilty.[1006]

11.238   Article 6(2) does not prohibit presumptions of fact and law but the State must

confine them within reasonable limits which take into account the importance of what is at stake and maintain the rights of the defence.[1007]

Thus, it has been held that the following do not violate Article 6(2):

- the requirement that a person charged with criminal libel prove the truth of the statement;[1008]
- the presumption that a person, having come through customs in possession of prohibited goods, had smuggled them;[1009]
- the presumption that a man living with a prostitute was knowingly living off immoral earnings;[1010]
- a presumption that a dog was a member of a specified breed;[1011]
- the burden on the accused to establish the defence of insanity.[1011a]

Furthermore, strict liability offences, which require no mens rea element, will not be a violation of Article 6(2).[1012] The presumption of innocence does not require that guilt be proved 'beyond a reasonable doubt': Article 6(2) simply requires evidence 'sufficiently strong in the eyes of the law to establish . . . guilt'.[1013]

[1003] *Barberà Messegué and Jabardo v Spain* (1988) 11 EHRR 360 para 77; *Austria v Italy* (1963) 6 YB 740.
[1004] Ibid.
[1005] *Allenet de Ribemont v France* (1995) 20 EHRR 557 para 35.
[1006] *Minelli v Switzerland* (1983) 5 EHRR 554 para 37 (acquitted defendant ordered to pay the costs on the basis that he would, 'very probably' have been convicted had he not had the advantage of a limitation defence).
[1007] *Salabiaku v France* (1988) 13 EHRR 379 para 28.
[1008] *Lingens and Leitgens v Austria* (1982) 4 EHRR 373, 290–291, EComm HR.
[1009] *Salabiaku v France* (n 1007 above) para 30.
[1010] *X v United Kingdom* (1972) 42 CD 135, EComm HR.
[1011] *Bates v United Kingdom* [1996] EHRLR 312, EComm HR; (the presumption was held to be within reasonable limits because the accused had an opportunity to rebut it).
[1011a] *H v United Kingdom* Application 15023/89, 4 Apr 1990, contrast the position in Canada, see para 11.405A below.
[1012] *Salabiaku v France* (n 1007 above).
[1013] *Austria v Italy* (1963) 6 YB 740, EComm HR.

Other obligations with respect to evidence under Article 6(2) overlap with the **11.239** general 'fair hearing' requirement of Article 6(1), as well as with Article 6(3)(d). The presumption of innocence means that the accused must be able to rebut evidence brought against him.[1014] Article 6(2) was not violated by: the admission of a statement made when the accused was not informed of his right to silence,[1015] disclosure of the accused's criminal record to the court prior to conviction,[1016] the arrest of a defence witness for perjury immediately after his testimony,[1017] re-trial of the accused by the court that heard his bail application,[1018] or procedure providing for a guilty plea.[1019]

Article 6(2) also protects the accused from prejudicial statements by public offi- **11.240** cials which disclose the view that the applicant is guilty before he has been tried and convicted. In *Krause v Switzerland*,[1020] the Swiss Minister of Justice stated on public television that the applicant, who had been held on remand pending trial for aircraft hijacking, had 'committed common law offences for which she must take responsibility', adding later that he did not know whether she would be convicted. In *Allenet de Ribemont v France*,[1021] a senior police officer, supported by other officials, stated at a press conference that the applicant, who had been arrested and hence 'charged ' under Article 6(2), was one of the 'instigators' of a murder. However, Article 6(2) does not preclude the authorities from providing factual information to the public about criminal investigations, as long as this does not amount to a declaration of guilt.[1022]

(c) Information as to the accusation (Article 6(3)(a))

Article 6(3)(a) provides that a person charged with a criminal offence be 'in- **11.241** formed promptly, in a language which he understands and in detail, of the nature and cause of the accusation against him'. It is arguable that the guarantee will apply as soon as the accused is 'charged' in accordance with Article 6[1023] and is certainly applicable no later than at the point of indictment in a civil law system.[1024]

[1014] *Albert and Le Compte v Belgium* (1983) 5 EHRR 533; *Schenk v Switzerland* (1988) 13 EHRR 242.
[1015] *X v Germany* (1971) 38 CD 77, EComm HR.
[1016] *X v Austria* (1966) 9 YB 550, EComm HR.
[1017] *X v Germany* (1983) 5 EHRR 499, EComm HR.
[1018] *X v Germany* (1966) 9 YB 484, EComm HR.
[1019] *X v United Kingdom* (1972) 40 CD 69, EComm HR.
[1020] *Krause v Switzerland* (1980) 13 DR 213.
[1021] (1995) 20 EHRR 557.
[1022] *Krause v Switzerland* (1978) 13 DR 73, EComm HR.
[1023] D Harris, M O'Boyle and C Warbrick, *Law of the European Convention on Human Rights* (Butterworths, 1995) 250–251; the Commission expressly left the question open in *X v Netherlands* (1981) 27 DR 37, EComm HR.
[1024] *Kamasinki v Austria* (1989) 13 EHRR 36; in *Brozicek v Italy* (1989) 12 EHRR 371, neither Commission nor Court made a clear finding that Art 6(3)(a) had to be complied with upon commencement of a preliminary investigation, but held, nevertheless, that judicial notification of the investigation complied with it.

Once an accused has been arrested, the exact point at which Article 6(3)(a) starts to run is less relevant because reasons will also be available to him under Article 5(2).[1025]

11.242 What needs to be communicated to the accused is the 'nature' of the accusation or offence with which he is charged and the 'cause' or relevant facts giving rise to the allegation. This will depend, in part, on what he can be taken to have learned during the investigation process and other circumstances of the case[1026] as well as what he might have gleaned had he taken advantage of existing opportunities to learn of the accusation before him.[1027] The words 'in detail'[1028] imply that the information to be provided under Article 6 is to be 'more specific and more detailed' than that which is provided under Article 5(2).[1029] However, it is not necessary that the accused even be informed as to the evidence on which the charge is based: it is sufficient for the accused to be informed of the offences with which he is charged together with the date and place of their alleged commission.[1030] There is no requirement that the information be provided in writing; Article 6(3)(a) will be complied with where the accused has been given sufficient communication orally. It must, however, be provided in a language understandable to either the accused or his lawyer,[1031] failing which the state must provide an appropriate translation[1032] of key documents or statements in order to meet the information requirements.

(d) Adequate time and facilities to prepare a defence (Article 6(3)(b))

11.243 Article 6(3)(b) provides that a person charged with a criminal offence shall be provided with adequate time and facilities for the preparation of his defence. The time element of this guarantee acts as a safeguard to protect the accused against a hasty trial.[1033] Like the other guarantees as to timeliness under the Convention, Article 6(3)(b) applies from the moment the accused is arrested or is otherwise substantially affected[1034] or when he is given notice of charges against him,[1035] and

---

[1025] See para 10.127ff above.
[1026] *Ofner v Austria* (1960) 3 YB 322.
[1027] *Campbell and Fell v United Kingdom* (1984) 7 EHRR 165: fact that a prisoner failed to attend a preliminary hearing was detrimental to his claim that he had not been adequately informed of the accusation against him.
[1028] Which are not present in Art 5(2).
[1029] *Nielsen v Denmark* (1959) 2 YB 412, EComm HR.
[1030] *Brozicek v Italy* (1989) 12 EHRR 371 para 42.; see also *X v Belgium* (1962) 5 YB 168 ('you are accused of corruption' was sufficient); and see *X v Belgium* (1977) 9 DR 169, EComm HR.
[1031] *X v Austria* (1975) 2 DR 68, EComm HR.
[1032] *Brozicek v Italy* (1989) 12 EHRR 371.
[1033] *Kröcher and Möller v Switzerland* (1981) 26 DR 24, EComm HR.
[1034] *X and Y v Austria* (1978) 15 DR 160, EComm HR.
[1035] *Campbell and Fell v United Kingdom* (1984) 7 EHRR 165.

the adequacy of the time allocation depends on all circumstances of the case.[1036] The right to adequate facilities means that the accused must have the opportunity to organise his defence appropriately, with the view to enabling him to put all relevant arguments before the trial court.[1037] The accused must be allowed to acquaint himself with the results of police or preliminary investigations in the case.[1038] The role of Article 6(3)(b) in this regard is to achieve equality of arms between the prosecution and the defence, a principle also considered an element of fairness under the general fair trial guarantee of Article 6(1).

The most important issue considered under this head is the right to communications with a lawyer. This is of particular significance to those persons in detention on remand pending trial. A prisoner must be allowed to receive a visit from his lawyer in private in order to convey instructions or to pass or receive confidential information relating to the preparation of his defence.[1039] Restrictions on lawyer's visits must be justified in public interests such as prevention of escape or prevention of the obstruction of justice. It may be permissible for a lawyer to be restricted from discussing with his client information about the case that would disclose the name of an informer.[1040]

11.244

(e) Defence in person or through legal assistance (Article 6(3)(c))

Article 6(3)(c) provides that a person charged with a criminal offence is guaranteed the right to 'defend himself in person or through legal assistance of his own choosing or, if he has not sufficient means to pay for legal assistance, to be given it free when the interests of justice so require'. The purpose of the guarantee is to ensure adequate representation in the case, equality of arms to the accused and vigilance by the defence over procedural regularity on behalf of his client and of public interests generally. Its scope does not extend to proceedings concerning detention on remand, which are covered by Article 5(4),[1041] but otherwise applies at the pretrial stage,[1042] during trial[1043] and, subject to special considerations, to appeal proceedings[1044] following conviction. Although this provision does not expressly

11.245

[1036] Relevant factors include the complexity of the case: *Albert and Le Compte v Belgium* (1983) 5 EHRR 533; defence lawyer's workload: *X and Y v Austria* (1978) 15 DR 160, EComm HR; the stage of proceedings: *Huber v Austria* (1974) 46 CD 99; accused's representation of himself: *X v Austria* (1967) 22 CD 96, EComm HR.

[1037] *Can v Austria* (1985) 8 EHRR 121; see also *Twalib v Greece* RJD 1998–IV 1415.

[1038] *Kamasinski v Austria* (1989) 13 EHRR 36; *Kremzow v Austria* (1993) 17 EHRR 322; *Jespers v Belgium* (1981) 27 DR 61, EComm HR.

[1039] *Campbell and Fell v United Kingdom* (1984) 7 EHRR 165; *Can v Austria* (1985) 8 EHRR 121.

[1040] *Kurup v Denmark* (1985) 42 DR 287, EComm HR.

[1041] *Woukam Moudefo v France* (1989) 51 DR 62.

[1042] *S v Switzerland* (1991) 14 EHRR 670.

[1043] *Quaranta v Switzerland* (1991) Series A No 205.

[1044] *Monnell and Morris v United Kingdom* (1987) 10 EHRR 205; *Quaranta v Switzerland* (1991) Series A No 205.

guarantee the freedom to communicate with a defence lawyer 'without hindrance', it has been held that:

> an accused's right to communicate with his advocate out of the hearing of a third person is one of the basic requirements of a fair trial in a democratic society.[1045]

This is because, without confidentiality the lawyer's assistance would lose much of its usefulness, whereas the Convention is intended to guarantee rights which are practical and effective.

11.246   The right of everyone under Article 6(3)(c) to be effectively defended by a lawyer, assigned officially if need be, is one of the fundamental features of a fair trial.[1046] This provision does not provide an absolute right to choose between defending oneself and obtaining legal counsel but it does preclude a state from forcing a person to defend himself in person.[1047] The law of some states precludes the person charged from acting on his own behalf, requiring that a lawyer assist him with his defence at the trial stage[1048] or on appeal.[1049] This is not incompatible with Article 6(3)(c).

11.247   An accused person who lawfully chooses to defend himself in person waives his right to be represented by a lawyer,[1050] and, as a result, the state is entitled to expect that he will exhibit a degree of diligence, failing which the state will not be responsible for any resulting deficiencies in the proceedings.[1051] If the accused does not wish to defend himself in person he is entitled to legal representation by his own lawyer or, subject to certain conditions, by a legal aid lawyer.[1052] He cannot be deprived of the right to legal representation on grounds of his failure to appear in court,[1053] though a state may find such denial to be an effective means of discouraging the unjustified absence of the accused.[1054]

11.248   If an accused person chooses legal assistance, Article 6(3)(c) does not provide him with an absolute right to decide which particular lawyer will be appointed to act

---

[1045] *S v Switzerland* (1991) 14 EHRR 670 para 48.
[1046] *Poitrimol v France* (1993) 18 EHRR 130 para 34.
[1047] *Pakelli v Germany* (1983) 6 EHRR 1.
[1048] *Croissant v Germany* (1992) 16 EHRR 135.
[1049] *Philis v Greece* (1990) 66 DR 260, EComm HR.
[1050] *Melin v France* (1993) 17 EHRR 1.
[1051] Ibid.
[1052] *Poitrimol v France* (1993) 18 EHRR 130.
[1053] Art 6(3)(c) guarantees the accused's right to be present at the trial: *FCB v Italy* (1991) 14 EHRR 909; in *Campbell and Fell v United Kingdom* (1984) 7 EHRR 165 a rule generally denying legal representation before a prison disciplinary body was found to be a breach of Art 6(3)(c), quite apart from the fact that the accused had refused to appear; the absentia of the accused, even without excuse, will not justify depriving him of his right to be defended by counsel under Art 6(3)(c): *Lala v Netherlands* (1994) 18 EHRR 586.
[1054] Denial of legal assistance as a penalty or coercive tactic to ensure the appearance and arrest under warrant of an accused who has absconded after conviction is also an infringement of Art 6(3)(c), on the basis it is not proportionate: *Poitrimol v France* (1993) 18 EHRR 130.

as counsel in the case. The general rule is that the accused's choice of lawyer should be respected.[1055] However, this is not absolute and is subject to limitations where free legal aid is concerned and where the court appoints defence lawyers.[1056] The right is also subject to the regulatory powers of the state, by which it governs qualifications and standards of professional conduct of lawyers.[1057] It is permissible for states to restrict the number of lawyers the accused may appoint, as long as the presentation of the defence is not disadvantaged in relation to the prosecution.[1058]

The right to legal aid under Article 6(3)(c) is subject to two conditions: it will only be provided if the accused lacks 'sufficient means to pay' for the legal assistance and 'where the interests of justice so require'. There is no definition of 'sufficient means' in the Convention and no case law as to the factors to be taken into account in the means test to determine an award of legal aid. the onus is on the applicant to demonstrate at least 'some indications'[1059] that he lacks sufficient means to retain his own counsel. For example, the test was met where the applicant had spent two years in custody prior to the case, had delivered a statement of means upon which the Commission had awarded him legal aid to bring an application under another Article of the Convention, and had proposed to make a similar submission to the German Federal Court.[1060] An accused who is subsequently able to pay for the costs of the free legal assistance may then be required to do so.[1061] **11.249**

Whatever the means of the applicant, the state is not required to provide legal aid lawyers unless it is in the interests of justice to do so. The Court has made its own assessment on the facts.[1062] The test as to whether provision of legal aid is in the 'interests of justice' is not that the presentation of the defence must have sustained actual prejudice, but whether it appears 'plausible in the particular circumstances' that a lawyer would be of assistance on the facts[1063] of the case. The following circumstances are relevant: **11.250**

[1055] *Pakelli v United Kingdom* (1983) 6 EHRR 1; *Goddi v Italy* (1982) 6 EHRR 457.
[1056] *Croissant v Germany* (1992) 16 EHRR 135 para 29.
[1057] *Ensslin, Baader and Raspe v Germany* (1978) 14 DR 64, EComm HR (professional ethics); *X and Y Germany* (1972) 42 CD 139, EComm HR (refusal to wear gown); *X v United Kingdom* (1975) 2 Digest 831, EComm HR (lack of respect for the court); *K v Denmark* Application 19524/92, (1993) unreported (barrister appearing as a witness for the defence); *X v United Kingdom* (1978) 15 DR 242, EComm HR (personal interests involved in barrister son's representation of father).
[1058] *Ensslin, Baader and Raspe v. Germany* (n 1057 above).
[1059] It is not necessary that the lack of sufficient means be shown beyond a reasonable doubt: *Pakelli v Germany* (1983) 6 EHRR 1.
[1060] Ibid.
[1061] *Croissant v Germany* (1992) 16 EHRR 135.
[1062] *Quaranta v Switzerland* (1991) Series A No 205.
[1063] *Artico v Italy* (1980) 3 EHRR 1.

- the complexity of the case;[1064]
- the contribution that the particular accused could make if he defended himself;[1065]
- the seriousness of the offence with which the accused is charged and the potential sentence involved.[1066]

Where deprivation of liberty is at stake, 'the interests of justice in principle call for legal representation'.[1067] Where the effective exercise of a right of appeal under national law requires legal assistance, legal aid must be provided, no matter how slight the accused's chances of success.[1068]

11.251   The legal assistance guaranteed by Article 6(3)(c), whether chosen by the accused himself or provided through legal aid, must be effective. It must actually be delivered[1069] and counsel must be qualified to represent the accused at the particular stage of the proceedings for which the assistance is sought.[1070] If legal assistance is effective it may not have been provided by a qualified lawyer.[1071] A state 'cannot be held responsible for every shortcoming on the part of a lawyer appointed for legal aid purposes'[1072] and will not be obliged to intervene unless inadequacy in the representation is apparent or is sufficiently brought to its attention.[1073] There may be a breach of Article 6(3)(c) where defence lawyers are frequently changed,[1074] inadequate time is allowed for their preparation of the case,[1075] or where the accused is not represented at a hearing because of the failure of the state to notify the correct lawyer.[1076]

[1064] *Granger v United Kingdom* (1990) 12 EHRR 469; *Quaranta v Switzerland* (1991) Series A No 205; *Pham Hoang v France* (1992) Series A No 243.
[1065] *Granger v United Kingdom* (n 1064 above) para 47.
[1066] *Boner v United Kingdom* (1994) 19 EHRR 246; *Maxwell v United Kingdom* (1994) 19 EHRR 97. Where the potential sentence is imprisonment this factor alone may require that legal aid be granted.
[1067] *Quaranta* (n 1064 above) paras 32-38; *Benham v United Kingdom* (1996) 22 EHRR 293 para 61.
[1068] *Boner v United Kingdom* (1994) 19 EHRR 246.
[1069] In *Artico v Italy* (1980) 3 EHRR 1 (violation when the state nominated a lawyer to act for the applicant, but claiming other commitments and sickness, he never met with the accused and the Italian Court of Cassation refused to appoint another lawyer).
[1070] *Biondo v Italy* (1983) 64 DR 5, EComm HR.
[1071] *X v Germany* (1960) 3 YB 174, EComm HR (assistance from a probationary lawyer training in the West German criminal system was satisfactory).
[1072] *Kamasinski v Austria* (1989) 13 EHRR 36 para 65.
[1073] Ibid, *Artico v Italy* (1980) 3 EHRR 1; *Stanford v United Kingdom* (1994) Series A No 280-A; *Tripodi v Italy* (1994) 18 EHRR 295; *Daud v Portugal* RJD 1998-II 739; see also *Imbrioscia v Switzerland* (1993) 17 EHRR 441 para 41.
[1074] *Koplinger v Austria* (1966) 9 YB 240, EComm HR.
[1075] These have also been treated under Art 6(3)(b) (right to adequate facilities): see *X v United Kingdom* (1970) 32 CD 76, EComm HR; *Murphy v United Kingdom* (1972) 43 CD 1, EComm HR.
[1076] *Goddi v Italy* (1984) 6 EHRR 457.

(f) Examination of witnesses (Article 6(3)(d))

Article 6(3)(d) guarantees an accused person the right to examine witnesses for the **11.252**
prosecution and to call and examine witnesses on his behalf under the same conditions as witnesses against him.[1077] The right applies during trial and appeal proceedings, but not at the pre-trial stage.[1078] 'Witness' includes expert witnesses called by
the prosecution or the defence[1079] as well as those persons whose statements are pro-
duced as evidence before a court even though they may not give oral evidence.[1080]

Neither the right of the accused to cross-examine witnesses against him nor to call **11.253**
and examine his own witnesses is absolute; but limitations must not contravene the
principle of equality of arms, which is the essential aim of Article 6(3)(d).[1081]
Where witnesses against the accused are excused from giving oral testimony[1082] the
accused must have the opportunity to confront the person providing the statement
during the preceding investigation,[1083] although statements taken from witnesses
abroad[1084] or evidence from foreign court proceedings against the accused[1085] are
admissible. The court will consider the importance of hearsay evidence in the context of the proceedings as a whole.[1086] The exclusion of the accused himself may be
permissible under Article 6(3)(d) to ensure a candid statement by the witness, if his
lawyer is allowed to remain and conduct a cross-examination.[1087]

The national courts have a wide discretion in the determination as to which de- **11.254**
fence witnesses are appropriate to be called,[1088] and in control over the accused's
questioning of them.[1089] A court must give reasons for not summoning a defence
witness expressly requested by the accused,[1090] and found that if properly called by
the defence, a court must take all steps within its control[1091] to ensure that

---

[1077] See also, para 11.217 above.

[1078] In particular an accused cannot examine a witness being questioned by the police: *X v Germany*
(1979) 17 DR 231, EComm HR; or an investigating judge: *Ferraro-Bravo v Italy* (1984) 37 DR 15,
EComm HR.

[1079] *Bönisch v Austria* (1985) 9 EHRR 191, EComm HR.

[1080] *Kostovski v Netherlands* (1989) 12 EHRR 434.

[1081] *Engel and others v Netherlands (No 1)* (1976) 1 EHRR 647 para 91; see also *Brandstetter v
Austria* (1991) 15 EHRR 378 para 45.

[1082] For example, a police informer (cf *Kostovski v Netherlands* (1989) 12 EHRR 434).

[1083] See *Ferantelli and Santangelo v Italy* (1996) 23 EHRR 288; and see para 11.217 above.

[1084] *X v Germany* (1987) 10 EHRR 521, EComm HR.

[1085] *S v Germany* (1983) 39 DR 43, EComm HR.

[1086] See para 11.204 above; and cf the analysis of Art 6(3)(d) by the English courts, para 11.129
above.

[1087] *Kurup v Denmark* (1985) 42 DR 287, EComm HR.

[1088] *Vidal v Belgium* (1992) Series A No 235-B.

[1089] *Engel and others v Netherlands* (1976) 1 EHRR 647, 706.

[1090] *Bricmont v Belgium* (1989) 12 EHRR 217; *Vidal v Belgium* (1992) Series A No 235-E.

[1091] There is, however, no liability if a defence witness fails to appear for reasons beyond the court's
control or at a time other than that requested by the accused, unless the presentation of the defence
is affected.

witnesses appear.[1092] The state is not liable for the failure of defence counsel to call a particular witness.[1093]

(g) Assistance of an interpreter (Article 6(3)(e))

11.255   Article 6(3)(e) guarantees the right of a person charged with a criminal offence to have the free assistance of an interpreter if he cannot understand or speak the language used in court. The guarantee applies once the individual is 'charged' for the purposes of Article 6, and to the pre-trial,[1094] trial and appeal proceedings. The guarantee is intended to enable the accused to understand the language of the court, and does not entitle him to insist on the services of a translator to enable him to conduct his defence in his language of choice.[1095] Whether the accused is incapable of understanding the language is a determination of fact for the state to make, and the onus is on the accused to show the inaccuracy of its assessment.[1096] Article 6(3)(e) provides an unqualified 'exemption or exoneration'[1097] from any requirement on the part of the accused to pay the cost of providing the interpreter, whether or not his means would allow it, or he is ultimately convicted.[1098] The state must make free interpretation a part of criminal justice facilities so that the financial cost of an interpreter does not deter the accused from obtaining such assistance and thus prejudice the fairness of the trial.

11.256   The substance of the 'assistance' required by Article 6(3)(e) extends beyond provision of an interpreter at the hearing to include translations of 'all statements which it is necessary for him to understand in order to have a fair trial'.[1099] This will not require a written translation of every official document,[1100] but it implies that communications between the accused and his legal aid lawyer must be translated[1101] and that, where a lawyer (but not the accused) understands the language in which the hearing is conducted, that the accused be given a personal translation of the proceedings in order to enable him to properly instruct his lawyer.[1102]

[1092] *X v Germany* Application 3566/68 (1969) 31 CD 31; *X v Germany* Application 4078/69 (1970) 35 CD 125.

[1093] *F v United Kingdom* (1992) 15 EHRR CD 32.

[1094] Police questioning prior to a 'charge' is not covered by Article 6(3)(e), but following the charge an accused is entitled to an interpreter during questioning or preliminary investigations prior to trial: *Kamasinski v Austria* (1989) 13 EHRR 36.

[1095] *K v France* (1983) 35 DR 203; *Bideault v France* (1986) 48 DR 232, EComm HR.

[1096] *X v Germany* (1967) 24 CD 50; *X v United Kingdom* (1978) 2 Digest 916.

[1097] *Luedicke, Belkacem and Koç v Germany* (1978) 2 EHRR 149 para 40.

[1098] See also in *Öztürk v Germany* (1984) 6 EHRR 409.

[1099] *Kamasinski v Austria* (1989) 13 EHRR 36 para 74.

[1100] This may depend on the amount of oral information as to its contents given to the accused; see *Kamasinski v Austria* (n 1099 above), where failure to translate either indictment or judgment was a breach.

[1101] If the accused appoints his own lawyer he must choose one that can communicate with him if such a lawyer is available: *X v Germany* (1983) 6 EHRR 353, EComm HR.

[1102] The Court in *Kamasinski v Austria* (1989) 13 EHRR 36 did not clearly rule on the point, but considered the arguments of the accused as to interpretation at trial, even though his English-speaking lawyer was in attendance.

(5) The provisions of Article 7

(a) Introduction

Article 7 establishes the right to freedom from retroactive penal provisions. More **11.257**
generally, it embodies:

> the principle that only the law can define a crime and prescribe a penalty (*nullum crimen, nulla poena sine lege*) and the principle that the criminal law must not be extensively construed to an accused's detriment, for instance by analogy.[1103]

It follows that:

> an offence must be clearly defined in law. This condition is satisfied where the individual can know from the wording of the relevant provision and, if need be, with the assistance of the court's interpretation of it, what acts and omissions will make him liable.[1104]

In this context, 'law' includes judge made law as well as statute law.[1105] Article 7 does not prohibit a second trial for the same offence.[1106]

The Article applies to convictions for criminal offences and to penalties. Both **11.258**
terms have 'autonomous meanings' under the Convention.[1107] The word 'criminal' in Article 7 must have the same meaning as in Article 6.[1108] In assessing whether or not there has been a 'penalty' it is necessary to consider whether the measure in question is imposed following conviction for a criminal offence, the nature and purpose of the measure, its characterisation under national law, the procedures involved in its making and implementation and its severity.[1109] However, Article 7 does not apply to 'preventive measures',[1110] deportation orders[1111] or to matters of extradition law.[1112] The Convention does not prevent the retrospective application of the criminal law in the accused's favour[1113] and does not guarantee that the accused has the benefit of changes in the law between the offence and trial.[1114]

[1103] *S W and C R v United Kingdom* (1995) 21 EHRR 363 para 35-33; *Kokkinakis v Greece* (1993) 17 EHRR 397 para 52 and see generally, P van Dijk and G van Hoof, *Theory and Practice of the European Convention on Human Rights* (3rd edn, Kluwer, 1998) 480ff.
[1104] *Kokkinakis v Greece* (n 1103, above) para 52.
[1105] *X Ltd and Y v United Kingdom* (1982) 28 DR 77, 80–81, EComm HR.
[1106] This is dealt with by Art 4 of Protocol 7 (not ratified by the United Kingdom).
[1107] As to 'penalty', see *Jamil v France* (1995) 21 EHRR 65 para 30.
[1108] See para 11.174ff above; and see *Brown v United Kingdom* (1998) 28 EHRR 233.
[1109] *Welch v United Kingdom* (1995) 20 EHRR 247 paras 27–28.
[1110] *Lawless v Ireland (No 1)* (1960) 1 EHRR 1.
[1111] *Moustaquim v Belgium* (1991) 13 EHRR 802 para 34.
[1112] *X v Netherlands* (1976) 6 DR 184, 186, EComm HR.
[1113] *Kokkinakis v Greece* (1993) 17 EHRR 397; *G v France* (1995) 21 EHRR 288.
[1114] *X v Germany* (1978) 13 DR 70, EComm HR.

(b) Retrospective offences

11.259   It is clear that any legislation which criminalises conduct which, at the time it was committed was lawful, will be in breach of Article 7. Examples of such legislation are extremely rare.[1115] The same approach applies to legislation which seeks to impose 'retrospective penalties'. Thus, in *Welch v UK*[1116] a confiscation order made under the Drug Trafficking Offences Act 1986 in respect of offences before the Act came into force was held to constitute a 'retrospective penalty' in breach of Article 7.

(c) Interpretation of criminal law

11.260   Article 7 requires that the interpretation of the law must operate so as to conform with the principle of reasonable certainty. This means that:

> constituent elements of an offence such as, e.g. the particular form of culpability required for its completion may not be essentially changed at least not to the detriment of the accused, by the case law of the courts.[1117]

However, this does not prevent the clarification or adaptation of the existing law. Thus, in the case of *S W & C R v UK*[1118] it was held that the removal of the 'marital rape exemption by the House of Lords[1119] did not amount to a retrospective criminalisation of conduct as it was foreseeable continuation of a line of case law. The 'gradual clarification' of common law offences was consistent with Article 7. Similarly, a conviction for 'unnatural indecency' under Austrian law which involved an 'extensive interpretation' of the statutory provision was not a breach of Article 7 because this interpretation was generally accepted at the time that the acts were committed.[1120]

11.261   The criminal law must be sufficiently accessible and precise to enable an individual to know in advance whether his conduct is criminal[1121] but the fact that legal advice is necessary to elucidate the precise scope of the offence does not necessarily mean that it is not 'reasonably certain' for the purposes of Article 7.[1122] The crucial point is that an offence must be clearly defined in law[1123] so that an individual can know from the wording of the relevant provision (and, if need be, with the

---

[1115] For an example under EC law, the European Court of Justice applied the same principle embodied in Art 7, see *R v Kirk* [1984] ECR 2689.

[1116] (1995) 20 EHRR 247; but see *Taylor v United Kingdom* [1998] EHRLR 90, EComm HR (no breach of Art 7 when 1994 order made in respect of drug trafficking going back to 1974 because the applicant was aware of the possibility that such an order could be made at the time of conviction).

[1117] *X Ltd and Y v United Kingdom* (1982) 28 DR 77, para 9, EComm HR.

[1118] (1995) 21 EHRR 363, see para 11.299 below.

[1119] See para 11.148 above.

[1120] *X v Austria* (1970) 13 YB 798 (mutual masturbation), EComm HR.

[1121] *G v France* (1995) 21 EHRR 288, 295 Com Rep para 32.

[1122] See *Cantoni v France*, RJD 1996–V 1614.

[1123] *Kokkinakis v Greece* (1993) 17 EHRR 397 para 52.

assistance of the court's interpretation of it), what acts and omissions will make him liable.

(d) Impact of international law

Article 7(1) makes express reference to acts or omissions which constitute criminal **11.262** offences under international law. The provisions of the Article have no application to such offences. Although the point has not been explored in the case law it is possible that this refers only to breaches of the laws of war and crimes against humanity.[1124] However, it is arguable that a wider range of offences is contemplated, namely those over which states have adopted jurisdiction to try non-nationals.[1125] Such crimes include torture, piracy, hijacking and drug trafficking.[1126]

(e) The exception in Article 7(2)

Article 7(2) provides that the Article shall not prejudice the trial and punishment **11.263** of any person

> for any act or omission which, at the time when it was committed, was criminal according to the general principles of law recognised by civilised nations.

The purpose of this exception appears to be to allow the retrospective application of national and international 'war crimes' legislation.[1127] It is arguably inconsistent with Article 15(2) which provides that there shall be no derogation from Article 7 in times of war.[1128]

The words 'the general principles of law recognised by civilised nations' are taken **11.264** from Article 38 of the Statute of the International Court of Justice.[1129] The nature of conduct which is 'criminal according to the general principles of law recognised by civilised nations' is not clear. It appears to cover the offences described in the Charter of the International Military Tribunal annexed to the Agreement for the Prosecution and Punishment of the Major War Criminals of the European Axis:[1130] that is 'crimes against peace', 'war crimes', and 'crimes against humanity'. It has also been suggested that the words will also cover criminal violations of human rights outside the 'war crimes' context.[1131]

[1124] See I Brownlie, *Principles of Public International Law* (5th edn, Oxford University Press), 308 and 565ff.

[1125] D Harris, M O'Boyle and C Warbrick, *Law of the European Convention on Human Rights* (Butterworths, 1995) 277.

[1126] Ibid. see also, Brownlie, (n 1124 above) 307–308; and cf *R v Bow Street Stipendiary Magistrate, ex p Pinochet Ugarte (No 3)* [1999] 2 WLR 672.

[1127] *X v Belgium* (1961) 4 YB 324, EComm HR.

[1128] See para 6.92ff above; see generally, van Dijk and van Hoof (n 1103 above) 487.

[1129] Art 38.1(c); see generally, Brownlie (n 1124 above) 15ff.

[1130] 8 Aug 1945, 39 AJ (1945), Suppl, 258; see generally, Brownlie, (n 1124 above) 565ff.

[1131] See van Dijk and van Hoof (n 1103 above) 488.

D. The Impact of the Human Rights Act

(1) Introduction

11.265 The Human Rights Act will give further impetus to the increasing focus of the English courts on 'fair trial rights'. Article 6 has already been the subject of detailed discussion in a number of criminal cases.[1132] Its impact on the practice of the criminal courts is likely to be considerable. The complex and frequently changing rules of criminal procedure and sentencing will be subject to re-assessment in the light of Convention 'fair trial' principles. Although it seems unlikely that many criminal statutes will be found to be incompatible with Article 6, the approach of the criminal courts will change in a number of areas.[1133]

11.266 The likely impact of Article 6 on civil cases is less clear. The rules governing civil procedure in the English courts have recently undergone their most substantial overhaul for over a century. Following the Woolf Report on *Access to Justice*, the new Civil Procedure Rules were drafted with Article 6 in mind. Nevertheless, the drive to efficient case management which lies behind many of the new rules does, potentially, generate conflict with Article 6 in a number of areas.[1134]

11.267 The field of regulatory and disciplinary regulation is likely to be a more fertile source of Article 6 challenges. Regulators and disciplinary bodies are of increasing importance, particularly in the area of financial services. At present hearings are often in private without a full range of procedural safeguards. Regulatory and disciplinary bodies will usually be 'functional public authorities' under section 6 of the Human Rights Act.[1135] The many and varied procedural rules of regulatory bodies and disciplinary tribunals are likely to require substantial revision to ensure Article 6 compliance.[1136]

11.268 In addition, there are a number of other areas of substantive law in which English law may be in conflict with the Convention. Articles 6 and 7 are likely to have an impact in the fields of commercial law, education law, employment and discrimination, family, immigration, local government law, planning and environment, police law, prison law and social security law. These are discussed in section (4) below.

[1132] See para 11.93 above.
[1133] See para 11.338ff below.
[1134] See para 11.313ff below.
[1135] See para 5.16ff above.
[1136] See para 11.330ff below.

(2) United Kingdom cases prior to the Human Rights Act

(a) Introduction

More United Kingdom applications to Strasbourg have been based on Article 6 than   **11.269**
on any other provision of the Convention. United Kingdom Article 6 complaints
have been substantively considered by the Court on more than 60 occasions. This is
partly a consequence of the central importance of 'fair trial rights' in the
Convention, and partly the result of the failure of public authorities to give proper
weight to such rights. The Court has found the United Kingdom to be in violation
of Article 6 on 26 occasions[1137] and in violation of Article 7 on one occasion.[1138] The
United Kingdom has entered into one friendly settlement on the basis of undertakings to take steps to rectify a breach of Article 6.[1138a] However, a large number of
areas of criminal and civil procedure have survived scrutiny by the Commission and
the Court. Many of the United Kingdom applications which have been made under
Article 6 fall into four general categories: rights of access to the courts, the conduct
of civil proceedings, the conduct of criminal proceedings and the rights of prisoners.

(b) Access to the courts

One of the most important decisions of the Court concerning access was made in   **11.270**
the early United Kingdom prisoner case of *Golder*.[1139] The applicant was a prisoner who wished to bring defamation proceedings against a prison officer but was
refused permission to consult a solicitor. The Court held that Article 6 contained
an implied right of access to the courts[1140] which had been violated by this refusal.[1141] A violation was found in *Silver v United Kingdom*[1142] on similar facts.

[1137] *Golder v United Kingdom* (1975) 1 EHRR 524; *Silver v United Kingdom* (1983) 5 EHRR 347;
Campbell and Fell v United Kingdom (1984) 7 EHRR 165; *W, B, O, B and H v United Kingdom*
(1987) 10 EHRR 29; *Granger v United Kingdom* (1990) 12 EHRR 469 (Scotland); *Darnell v United
Kingdom* (1993) 18 EHRR 205; *Boner v United Kingdom* (1994) 19 EHRR 246 (Scotland);
Maxwell v United Kingdom (1994) 19 EHRR 97 (Scotland); *McMichael v United Kingdom* (1995)
20 EHRR 205; *Benham v United Kingdom* (1996) 22 EHRR 293; *Murray v United Kingdom* (1996)
22 EHRR 29 (Northern Ireland); *Saunders v United Kingdom* (1996) 23 EHRR 313; *Findlay v
United Kingdom* (1997) 24 EHRR 221; *Robins v United Kingdom* (1997) 26 EHRR 527; *Coyne v
United Kingdom* RJD 1997–V 1842; *Tinnelly and Sons and McElduff v United Kingdom* (1998) 4
BHRC 393 (Northern Ireland); *Osman v United Kingdom* (1998) 5 BHRC 293; *Hood v United
Kingdom* (2000) 29 EHRR 365; *Cable v United Kingdom, The Times*, 11 Mar 1999; *Scarth v United
Kingdom*, 22 Jul 1999; *T and V v United Kingdom* (2000) 7 BHRC 659; *McGonnell v United
Kingdom* (2000) 8 BHRC 56; *Rowe and Davis v United Kingdom, The Times*, 1 Mar 2000; *Condron,
The Times*, 9 May 2000; *Magee v United Kingdom, The Times*, 20 Jun 2000, *Averill v United
Kingdom, The Times*, 20 Jun 2000.
[1138] *Welch v United Kingdom* (1995) 20 EHRR 247.
[1138a] *Faulkner v United Kingdom, The Times*, 11 Jan 2000.
[1139] (1975) 1 EHRR 524.
[1140] Ibid paras 35-36; see para 11.185 above.
[1141] See also the Commission decisions in *Kiss v United Kingdom* (1977) 19 EHRR CD 17 and
Hilton v United Kingdom (1978) 3 EHRR 104.
[1142] (1983) 5 EHRR 347.

11.271   However, Article 6 only provides a right of access in relation to the 'determination' of civil rights and obligations and criminal charges. In a number of cases it has been decided that proceedings of a 'preparatory' or 'investigatory' nature are not subject to Article 6 because no 'determination' is involved. The most important case on this point is *Fayed v United Kingdom*[1143] in which the applicants complained that they had been criticised in a report by DTI inspectors[1144] and that, as a result, their reputations had been damaged. As they could make no effective challenge to the conclusions of the report under English law, they contended that they had been denied effective access to the courts. The Court held that the functions of the inspectors was essentially 'investigative'[1145] and were not 'determinative' of any civil right. The Court went on to hold that the defence of absolute or qualified privilege which was available to DTI Inspectors was in pursuit of a legitimate aim and was proportionate.[1146]

11.272   A number of other types of decision have been held not to involve 'determination' of civil rights and obligations. These include:

- decisions as to the classification of prisoners;[1147]
- deportation decisions;[1148]
- decisions in relation to the right to elementary education;[1149]
- applications for interim relief;[1150]
- orders requiring a person to give evidence;[1151]
- decisions by the Secretary of State as to whether someone was a 'fit and proper person' to conduct insurance business;[1152]
- a decision refusing leave to appeal to the House of Lords.[1153]

11.273   The question as to whether care proceedings are within Article 6 has been considered by the Court in several UK cases. In the linked cases of *W, R, O, B and H v United Kingdom*[1154] the applicants made various complaints about care proceedings which restricted their rights of access to their children. It was held that was a

---

[1143] (1994) 18 EHRR 393.
[1144] Under Companies Act 1985, s 432(2).
[1145] Referring to the analysis of the functions of the US Federal Civil Rights Commission in *Hannah v Larche* (1960) 363 US 420; see *Golder* (n 1139 above) para 61.
[1146] See also, *Tee v United Kingdom* (1996) 21 EHRR CD 108 (investigation by LAUTRO did not involve 'determination' of a civil right).
[1147] *Brady v United Kingdom* (1981) 3 EHRR 297.
[1148] *Uppal v United Kingdom (No 1)* (1979) 3 EHRR 391, EComm HR.
[1149] *Simpson v United Kingdom* Application 14688/89, (1989) 64 DR 188, EComm HR.
[1150] *X v United Kingdom* (1981) 24 DR 57, EComm HR.
[1151] *British Broadcasting Corporation v United Kingdom* (1996) 21 EHRR CD 93 (witness summons re video material).
[1152] Because this did not involve the determination of any 'dispute'. *Kaplan v United Kingdom* (1980) 4 EHRR 64.
[1153] *Porter v United Kingdom* (1987) 54 DR 207, EComm HR.
[1154] (1987) 10 EHRR 29.

dispute between the applicant and local authority which concerned the 'civil' right of access. Article 6(1) did not require that all access decisions had to be taken to the courts but only that they should have power to determine any substantial disputes that arose. Applications for judicial review or the institution of wardship proceedings enabled the courts to examine local authorities' decisions concerning access. However, the Court held that there was

> no possibility of a 'determination' in accordance with the requirements of Article 6(1) of the parent's right in regard to access . . . unless he or she can have the local authority's decision reviewed by a tribunal having jurisdiction to examine the merits of the matter.[1155]

The powers of the English courts did not satisfy this requirement and, as a result, there was a violation of Article 6(1). Furthermore, proceedings for access to a child in care which took two years and eleven months were not concluded within a reasonable time and, as a result, there was a further violation of Article 6(1).[1156] In *McMichael v United Kingdom*[1157] the applicants complained about the procedures at a 'children's hearing' the purpose of which was to consider care orders. The Court accepted that:

> in this sensitive domain of family law there may be good reasons for opting for an adjudicatory body that does not have the composition or procedures of a court of law of the classic kind.[1158]

Nevertheless, the right to fair trial meant the opportunity to have knowledge of and comment on the observations of the other party and the lack of disclosure of such vital documents as social reports meant there had not been a fair hearing.

Proceedings to challenge a planning enforcement notice involve the determination of 'civil rights'.[1159] Because the Secretary of State could revoke the power of the planning Inspector to hear an appeal, the Inspector was not an 'independent and impartial tribunal'. However, since the Inspector was subject to a statutory appeal on a point of law[1160] there was, in the circumstances, no violation of Article 6. It was important that there were no disputes about the primary facts or the factual inferences drawn by the Inspector.   **11.274**

The access of a litigant to the courts can be restricted in many different ways. One possibility is the granting of 'immunity' to particular categories of litigants. This has been considered in a number of cases. In *Ashingdane v United Kingdom*[1161] the   **11.275**

[1155] *W v United Kingdom* (1987) 10 EHRR 29 para 82.
[1156] *H v United Kingdom* (1987) A 120, 10 EHRR 95.
[1157] (1995) 20 EHRR 205.
[1158] Ibid para 80.
[1159] *Bryan v United Kingdom* (1995) 21 EHRR 342.
[1160] Under the Town and Country Planning Act 1990, s 289.
[1161] (1985) 7 EHRR 528.

applicant was a mental patient who complained, inter alia, that he was unable to challenge the lawfulness of a refusal to transfer him from a secure hospital. He had brought an action which had been stayed, the Secretary of State successfully invoking the 'statutory immunity' under the Mental Health Act 1959.[1162]Under this provision, an action could only be brought if there was an allegation of bad faith or want of reasonable care. It was held that there was no violation of Article 6 because the immunity 'did not impair the very essence of Mr Ashingdane's "right to a court" or transgress the principle of proportionality'.[1163]

11.276 The case of *Osman v United Kingdom*[1164] concerned police immunity for actions in negligence arising out of the 'investigation and suppression of crime'.[1165] The Court rejected the government's argument that Article 6 was of no application[1166] and held that the negligence immunity for police acts and omissions during the investigation and suppression of crime amounted to an unjustifiable restriction on an applicant's right to have a determination on the merits of his or her claim. Other applications are pending in relation to public authorities' immunities from actions and the Commission has ruled admissible a complaint concerning negligence of a local authority in taking a child into care .[1167]

11.277 The Commission have held that the imposition of such requirements on 'vexatious litigants'[1168] and bankrupts[1169] is not a breach of Article 6. The requirement of a two-year qualifying period before an employee can bring a claim for unfair dismissal is not a breach of Article 6(1) because it serves a legitimate aim.[1170] The effect of limitation periods on access to the courts was considered in *Stubbings v United Kingdom.*[1171] The applicants' claims for damages for alleged sex abuse in childhood were statute barred under English law and they claimed that they had been denied access to the court under Article 6. The Court pointed out that the right to access to the court was not absolute and that limitation periods in personal

---

[1162] s 141; see now Mental Health Act 1983, s 139(1); see para 11.47 above.
[1163] n 1161 above para 59.
[1164] (1998) 5 BHRC 293; the English decision was *Osman v Ferguson* [1993] 4 All ER 344.
[1165] See para 11.42 above.
[1166] See para 11.195 above.
[1167] *T P and K M v United Kingdom* Application 28945/95, 26 May 1998, EComm HR (admissibility); 10 Sep1999 (merits) the application is the claim against Newham which was struck out in *X (Minors) v Bedfordshire County Council* [1995] 2 AC 633.
[1168] *H v United Kingdom* (1985) 45 DR 281, EComm HR.
[1169] *M v United Kingdom* (1987) 52 DR 269, EComm HR.
[1170] *Stedman v United Kingdom* (1997) 23 EHRR CD 168.
[1171] (1996) 23 EHRR 213; the English decision was *Stubbings v Webb* [1993] AC 498; see generally, E Palmer, 'Limitation Periods in Cases of Sexual Abuse: A Response Under the European Convention' [1996] EHRLR 111; see also *I B v United Kingdom* [1996] EHRLR 524 and *Dobie v United Kingdom* [1997] EHRLR 166.

injury cases were a common feature of the legal systems of Contracting States.[1172] Limitation periods served important purposes and the periods applied were not unduly short. As a result, the very essence of the applicants' right of access were not impaired and the restrictions pursued a legitimate aim and were proportionate. There was, therefore, no violation of Article 6.[1173]

In *Tolstoy Miloslavsky v United Kingdom*[1174] one of the applicant's complaints was that his right of access to the court had been violated by a requirement that he provide substantial security for the costs of an appeal against a jury verdict in a libel action. The Court accepted that, the fundamental guarantees of Article 6 did apply to an appeal system but that the whole of the proceedings had to be considered. It was held that the security for costs order pursued the legitimate aim of protecting the plaintiff in the libel action from an irrecoverable bill for costs and was not disproportionate.[1175]

11.278

(c) The conduct of civil proceedings

The case of *Robins v United Kingdom*[1176] involved a dispute as to costs following a civil action between neighbours over a question of sewerage. The costs proceedings, although separately decided, were to be seen as a continuation of the substantive litigation, to which Article 6 undoubtedly applied. The Court found that four years from the date of judgment to the final appeal was an unreasonable length of time for the resolution of a relatively straightforward dispute over costs. While state authorities could not be held responsible for all of the delays, periods of 10 months and 16 months in which the courts were totally inactive warranted the finding of breach.

11.279

In *Darnell v United Kingdom*[1177] the applicant had been dismissed from his health authority post in 1984 after disciplinary proceedings. After a successful judicial review application, the Secretary of State reconsidered his decision and, in 1988 affirmed it. In 1990 the Industrial Tribunal dismissed the applicant's claim for unfair dismissal. His appeal against that decision was dismissed in 1993. It was accepted by the Government that there had been a violation of Article 6(1) because the applicant's civil rights and obligations had not been determined within a reasonable time.

11.280

Article 6 does not provide for any right to legal aid for civil proceedings and cases may be selected for legal aid on merit with financial contributions being

11.281

[1172] Ibid paras 48–49.
[1173] Ibid paras 53–55.
[1174] (1995) 20 EHRR 442; see generally, para 15.228 above.
[1175] Ibid paras 61–67.
[1176] (1997) 26 EHRR 527.
[1177] (1993) 18 EHRR 205.

required.[1178] The blanket exclusion of legal aid in defamation cases is not a breach.[1179] However, the Commission has found that the lack of a civil legal aid system in Guernsey was a violation of the right of access to the courts.[1180] A friendly settlement was reached on the Government's undertakings to introduce such a system.[1180a]

11.282   The Commission has found that hearings in private are permissible if they are interlocutory[1181] or if they are renewable in open court.[1182] However, in *Scarth v United Kingdom*[1183] the Court held that the denial of a public hearing in a county court arbitration case was a breach of Article 6(1).[1184]

11.283   The case of *McGonnell v United Kingdom*[1185] involved a challenge to the legal system of Guernsey, where the Royal Court is presided over by the Bailiff, who is also the President of the State of Deliberation (the legislature) and of four States Committees (which are part of the executive). The applicant's challenge to a planning decision had been refused by the Royal Court on the basis that it was consistent with the relevant development plan. The Commission[1185a] found that there was a violation of Article 6 as it was incompatible with the requisite appearances of independence and impartiality for a judge to have substantial legislative and executive functions. It was suggested by some commentators that this could have significant repercussions for the position of the Lord Chancellor. However, the Court found a violation on a narrower basis, namely that the Bailiff had presided over the legislature when the relevant development plan had been adopted.[1185b] This narrower ground for decision left open the question as to whether the Lord Chancellor's combination of legislative, executive and judicial roles is incompatible with Article 6.

(d) The conduct of criminal proceedings

11.284   Many UK applications have dealt with the rights of defendants in criminal proceedings. The first issue to be considered is whether the proceedings are 'criminal'

[1178] *X v United Kingdom* (1980) 21 DR 95, 101, EComm HR; see also *Stewart-Brady v United Kingdom* (1997) 24 EHRR CD 38 and *Thaw v United Kingdom* (1996) 22 EHRR CD 100.
[1179] *Winer v United Kingdom* (1986) 48 DR 154, EComm HR; *Munro v United Kingdom* (1987) 52 DR 158, EComm HR; *S and M v United Kingdom* (1993) 18 EHRR CD 172 (the 'McLibel' case).
[1180] *Faulkner v United Kingdom* Application 30308/96, 30 Nov1996, EComm HR.
[1180a] *Faulkner v United Kingdom, The Times* 11 Jan 2000.
[1181] *X v United Kingdom* (1969) 30 CD 70, EComm HR.
[1182] Cf *Monnell and Morris v United Kingdom* (1987) 10 EHRR 205 (application for leave to appeal in criminal cases).
[1183] Application 33745/96, 22 Jul 1999.
[1184] The point had been conceded by the UK Government, see ibid para 24; the hearing would now be held in public under the CPR, see para 11.80 above.
[1185] (2000) 8 BHRC 56.
[1185a] [1999] EHRLR 335, see para 61 of the full decision.
[1185b] Ibid para 57 and see the concurring opinion of Sir John Laws.

in nature, bearing in mind the 'autonomous' Convention meaning of this term.[1186] In *Benham v United Kingdom*[1187] the applicant was imprisoned by magistrates for non-payment of community charge. He complained, *inter alia*, that full legal aid was not available to him for the committal hearing. The Court found that there was a breach of Article 6(1) and 6(3)(c) taken together because:

> where a deprivation of liberty is at stake, the interests of justice in principle call for legal representation.[1188]

In *Perks v United Kingdom*[1189] the applicants were also imprisoned for non-payment of community charge. The Court again decided that the refusal to give the applicants legal aid breached Article 6. The Court said that:

> Having regard to the severity of the penalty risked by the applicants and the complexity of the applicable law, the interests of justice demanded that, in order to receive a fair hearing, the applicants ought to have benefited from free legal representation before the magistrates.[1189a]

The case of *Air Canada v United Kingdom*[1190] was the other side of the line. This **11.285** involved the seizure of an aircraft by the Customs as liable to forfeiture because a consignment of drugs had been found on board. The Court held that, although there was, in effect, a fine, the proceedings were not criminal in nature as the criminal courts were not involved and there was no threat of criminal proceedings.[1191] There was a dispute about civil rights but Article 6 was satisfied because the Customs had to take 'condemnation proceedings' before forfeiting the aircraft. It has been held that the following do not constitute 'criminal charges' for the purposes of Article 6:

- misconduct proceedings before the Solicitors Disciplinary Tribunal;[1191a]
- company directors disqualification proceedings;[1191b]
- proceedings before the General Medical Council involving allegations of indecent behaviour towards a patient.[1191c]

The 'right to silence' of criminal defendants has given rise to several applications. **11.286**

[1186] See para 11.174ff above.
[1187] (1996) 22 EHRR 293.
[1188] At para 61.
[1189] Application 25277/94, 12 Oct 1999.
[1189a] Ibid para 76.
[1190] (1995) 20 EHRR 150; the English decision was *Customs and Excise Commissioners v Air Canada* [1991] 2 QB 446, CA.
[1191] Ibid paras 50–55.
[1191a] *Brown v United Kingdom* (1998) 28 EHRR CD 233.
[1191b] *D C, H S and A D v United Kingdom* Application 39031/97, 14 Sep 1999 (admissibility decision).
[1191c] *Wickramsinghe v United Kingdom* [1998] EHRLR 338.

The applicant in *Murray v United Kingdom*[1192] had been arrested under the Prevention of Terrorism Act and denied legal advice for 48 hours. He had been tried in Northern Ireland under provisions which allowed the judge to draw adverse inferences from his silence. The Court accepted that, despite the fact that they were not specifically mentioned in Article 6:

> there can be no doubt that the right to remain silent under police questioning and the privilege against self-incrimination are generally recognised international standards which lie at the heart of the notion of fair procedure under Article 6.[1193]

However, it was held that the right to silence was not absolute and, as a result it could not be said that:

> an accused's decision to remain silent throughout criminal proceedings should necessarily have no implications when the trial court seeks to evaluate the evidence against him.[1194]

The question as to whether the drawing of adverse inferences from silence infringes Article 6 was a matter to be determined in all the circumstances in each case. On the facts of the case, there had been no breach. However, because such inferences could be drawn, the concept of fairness enshrined in Article 6 required that the accused had the benefit of a lawyer at the initial stages of police interrogation.[1195] As a result, there had been a breach of Article 6(1) in conjunction with 6(3)(c). Breaches of these provisions were also found in the caes of *Averill v United Kingdom*[1195a] and *Magee v United Kingdom*.[1195b]

11.287   The Commission reached a similar view in *Quinn v United Kingdom*[1196] in which the applicant had been convicted of attempted murder and possession of firearms on the basis of forensic evidence, hearsay evidence and inferences drawn from silence in the absence of a solicitor. The Commission concluded that:

> the forensic evidence relating to gunpowder traces and linking him to the car used in the offence could be regarded, on a common sense basis, as a situation attracting considerable suspicion and reasonably allowing inferences to be drawn in light of the nature and extent of any explanations provided by the applicant. The inference drawn from the applicant's silence was thus only one of the elements upon which the judge found the charge proven beyond reasonable doubt. The Commission

---

[1192] (1996) 22 EHRR 29; see R Munday, 'Inferences from Silence and European Human Rights Law' [1996] Crim L Rev 370.
[1193] Ibid para 45.
[1194] Ibid para 47.
[1195] Ibid para 66.
[1195a] *The Times*, 20 Jun 2000 (denial of access to a solicitor fo the first 24 hours of questioning).
[1195b] *The Times*, 20 Jun 2000 (denial of access to a solicitor for 48 hours).
[1196] 17 Dec 1997 (Merits) see also (1996) 23 EHRR CD 41, the original case was *Rv Dermot Quinn* (1993) 10 NIJB 70; see also *Hamill v United Kingdom* (Merits) Application 22656/93, 2 Dec 1997 and *Murray v United Kingdom* Application 22384/93, 2 Dec 1997—no violation in relation to adverse inferences on admissibility hearing.

considers that by taking this element into account the judge did not go beyond the limits of fairness in his appreciation of the evidence in the case.[1197]

In *Condron v United Kingdom*[1197a] the applicants had remained silent on the advice of their solicitor who believed, contrary to the view of the police doctor, that they were not fit to be interviewed. The Court accepted that it was proper to draw adverse inferences from their silence in this situation and to waive privilege on the advice given. There was, however, a breach of Article 6 as a result of an inadequate direction by the trial judge:

> the jury should have been directed that if it was satisfied that the applicants' silence at the police interview could not sensibly be attributed to their having no answer or none that would stand up to cross-examination it should not draw an adverse inference.[1197b]

The Court also expressed concern that the Court of Appeal (Criminal Division) made its decision on the basis of the 'safety' of the applicants' conviction rather than considering whether they received a fair trial:

> the question whether or not the rights of the defence guaranteed to an accused under Article 6 of the Convention were secured in any given case cannot be assimilated to a finding that his conviction was safe in the absence of any enquiry into the issue of fairness.[1197c]

In the well-known case of *Saunders v United Kingdom*[1198] the applicant complained that he was denied a fair hearing because of the use made at his criminal trial of statements obtained by DTI Inspectors under statutory powers of compulsion.[1199] The trial judge and the Court of Appeal had held these statements were admissible[1200] The issue was whether the use of the statements was an unjustifiable infringement of the right to silence which lay at the heart of 'fair procedure' under Article 6.[1201] The Court rejected the Government's argument that the vital public interest in the prosecution of corporate fraud could justify departure from the principles of fair procedure. It concluded that there had been an infringement of the right of a person not to incriminate himself.[1202]   **11.288**

The burden of proof in criminal proceedings must, in general, rest on the prosecution. Nevertheless, this does not prevent the law from relying on 'presumptions'.   **11.289**

[1197] n 1196 above para 63; there was no violation in relation to the admission of hearsay evidence but there was in relation to lack of access to a solicitor.
[1197a] *The Times*, 9 May 2000; see *Averill v United Kingdom*, *The Times*, 20 Jun 2000 (permissible to draw adverse inferences from silence despite the absence of legal advice).
[1197b] *Condron v United Kingdom* (n 1197a above) para 61.
[1197c] Ibid para 65.
[1198] (1996) 23 EHRR 313.
[1199] Under Companies Act 1985, s 432; see generally, para 11.103 above.
[1200] *R v Seelig* [1992] 1 WLR 148.
[1201] *Saunders* (n 1198 above) para 68.
[1202] But see the dissenting judgment of Judges Martens and Kuris.

Thus, the presumptions of fact in the Dangerous Dogs Act 1991 do not breach Article 6.[1203]

11.290 Complaints of 'jury bias' have been unsuccessful in most cases. In *Pullar v United Kingdom*[1204] the applicant complained that the jury trial was unfair because an employee of a key prosecution witness had been a member of the jury. The Court of Appeal had relied on the witness's written statement as to the juror's impartiality. The question was whether or not the jury could be regarded as an 'independent and impartial tribunal' under Article 6(1). The Court held that:

> it does not necessarily follow from the fact that a member of a tribunal has some personal knowledge of one of the witnesses in a case that he will be prejudiced in favour of that person's testimony.[1205]

As a result, it was held that the applicant's misgivings about the impartiality of the jury could not be regarded as being 'objectively justified'. In *Gregory v United Kingdom*[1206] the applicant, who was black, was being tried on an offence of robbery when, after the jury had retired, they handed a note to the judge saying that 'Jury are showing racial overtones'. After consultation with counsel, the judge decided not to discharge the jury but directed them to put thoughts of prejudice out of their minds. It appeared that defence counsel had agreed to this course. The Court found that there was no violation of Article 6.[1207] By contrast, in *Sander v United Kingdom*[1207a] a complaint of bias was upheld in a case involving an Asian defendant. A juror handed up a note anonymously indicating that another juror had made racist jokes; and he was then separated from the other jurors. The judge declined to discharge the jury but recalled them to ask whether they felt able to try the case. The next day the judge received two letters: one from all the jurors rejecting the allegation of bias and another from the juror who had made the jokes, saying that he was sorry that he had given offence and denying that he was racially biased. The judge again declined to discharge the jury but gave them a further direction. The Court took the view that the disclosure of the identity of the juror who had made the complaint had prejudiced his position; and that the admission by a juror that he had made racist jokes should have alerted the judge to the fact that there was something fundamentally wrong with the jury. The Court therefore held the jury should have been discharged on grounds of bias.

11.291 The Commission and Court have also considered complaints concerning the non-disclosure of evidence to defendants in criminal trials. In *Edwards v United*

[1203] *Bates v United Kingdom* [1996] EHRLR 312, EComm HR.

[1204] (1996) 22 EHRR 391 (a Scottish case).

[1205] Ibid para 38.

[1206] (1997) 25 EHRR 577.

[1207] See also, *Hardiman v United Kingdom* [1996] EHRLR 425.

[1207a] Judgment of 9 May 2000.

Kingdom[1208] the applicant complained that evidence which had not been disclosed by the prosecution in the course of his trial rendered the trial unfair. The Court said that its task is to ascertain whether the proceedings in their entirety were fair.[1209] It held that the defects of the original trial were remedied by the subsequent procedure before the Court of Appeal and that, as a result, there had been no breach of Article 6.

Where it is claimed that the material which is not disclosed is subject to 'public interest immunity', the prosecution must make an application to the trial judge, if necessary, without notice.[1210] In *Jasper and Fitt v United Kingdom*[1211] the Court accepted that, in some cases it might be necessary to withhold certain evidence from the defence so as to preserve the fundamental rights of another individual or to safeguard an important public interest. Only such measures restricting the rights of the defence that were strictly necessary were permissible. The Court held that, where the defence had been told of the application for non-disclosure and had been able to outline its position, there was no breach of Article 6(1). However, in *Rowe and Davis v United Kingdom*[1212] the Court held that the failure of the prosecution to make an application to the trial judge to withhold material was a breach of Article 6. The fact that the material had been subsequently reviewed by the Court of Appeal was not sufficient to remedy the unfairness caused at the trial by the absence of any scrutiny of the withheld material by the trial judge.[1213] **11.292**

The reception by a court of the evidence of an accomplice with immunity from prosecution will not be a breach of Article 6.[1214]

In the cases of *T and V v United Kingdom*[1215] the applicants were 10-year-old boys who were convicted of murdering a young boy; they were sentenced to detention at Her Majesty's pleasure. The Court found that there had been violations of Article 6 in respect of the trial because, bearing in mind their age, the application of the full rigours of an adult trial denied them the opportunity to participate effectively in the proceedings. Furthermore, the role of the Home Secretary in fixing the periods for which the applicants should be detained was a breach of Article 6(1). This was because the fixing of the tariff amounted to a sentencing exercise and the Home Secretary was clearly not an 'independent tribunal'. **11.293**

The availability of legal aid in criminal appeals has been considered in several cases **11.294**

[1208] (1992) 15 EHRR 417.
[1209] Ibid, paras 33–34.
[1210] See para 11.98 above.
[1211] *The Times*, 1 Mar 2000.
[1212] *The Times*, 1 Mar 2000.
[1213] Ibid para 79.
[1214] See also *X v United Kingdom* (1976) 7 DR 115, EComm HR.
[1215] See *T v United Kingdom* [2000] 7 BHRC 659 for the English case, see *R v Secretary of State for the Home Department, ex p Venables* [1998] AC 407.

from Scotland. In *Granger v United Kingdom*[1216] the applicant was refused legal aid in an appeal against his conviction for perjury. The Court held that it would have been in the interests of justice for free legal assistance to have been given to the applicant. As a result, there was a violation of Article 6(3)(c). The same point arose in *Boner v United Kingdom*[1217] and *Maxwell v United Kingdom*[1218] in which the Court followed *Granger* and held that there had been a violation of Article 6.

11.295   The protection of Article 6 continues to apply until the charge is finally determined or discontinuance of the proceedings occurs before trial.[1219] In *Monnell and Morris v United Kingdom*[1220] the applicants had unsuccessfully applied for leave to appeal against conviction and sentence. In dismissing these applications in their absence, the Court of Appeal directed that part of the time spent in custody should not count towards their sentences. The Court accepted the applicants' contention that Article 6 applied to such an application but held that there had been no violation. Article 6 also applies to the referral of a case to the Court of Appeal by the Home Secretary many years after conviction.[1221]

11.296   Over recent years, the Court has considered several cases arising out of the operation of the Court Martial procedure in the armed forces.[1222] In *Findlay v United Kingdom*[1223] the Court had to consider whether the court martial was independent and impartial. The convening officer decided which charges should be brought, convened the court martial and appointed its members and the prosecuting and defending officers. The members of the court martial were subordinate in rank to the convening officer and fell within his chain of command.[1224] In these circumstances, the applicant's doubts about the independence and impartiality of the tribunal could be objectively justified and there was a violation of Article 6(1). The Court followed this case and found violations of Article 6 in relation to court-martial proceedings in the cases of *Coyne v United Kingdom*,[1225] *Hood v United Kingdom*[1226] and *Cable v United Kingdom*.[1227]

11.297   The costs orders made at the conclusion of criminal proceedings have been

---

[1216] (1990) 12 EHRR 469.
[1217] (1994) 19 EHRR 246.
[1218] (1994) 19 EHRR 97.
[1219] *Orchin v United Kingdom* (1983) 6 EHRR 391.
[1220] (1987) 10 EHRR 205.
[1221] *Callaghan v United Kingdom* (1989) 60 DR 296, EComm HR, the referral would now be by the Criminal Cases Review Commission.
[1222] See para 11.228 above, the cases concern the former procedure under the Army Act 1955.
[1223] (1997) 24 EHRR 221.
[1224] Ibid paras 74–76.
[1225] RJD 1997–V 1842.
[1226] *The Times*, 11 Mar 1999.
[1227] *The Times*, 11 Mar 1999.

challenged. A violation was found by the Commission in two cases in which the judge refused to allow the defendant's costs for a failed prosecution and made comments implying guilt.[1228] However, there was no violation where the judge refused costs on the basis that the applicant had been greedy and brought the case on himself, as this did not imply guilt.[1229]

(e) Rights of prisoners

In *Campbell and Fell v United Kingdom*[1230] the applicants were prisoners who had **11.298** been subjected to disciplinary proceedings by the Board of Visitors resulting in the loss of remission and of privileges. Both sought permission to consult a lawyer but, when this was finally granted, consultations had to take place in the presence of a prison officer. It was held that, in the light of the character of the offences, the proceedings before the Board of Visitors were subject to Article 6. The Board of Visitors were an independent and impartial tribunal.[1231] The hearings could proceed in private, because

> To require that disciplinary proceedings concerning convicted prisoners should be held in public would impose a disproportionate burden on the authorities of the State.[1232]

However, there was a breach of Article 6 because the decision had not been made public[1233] and legal assistance and representation had been refused.[1234] Furthermore, the delay in allowing the applicants to take legal advice was a denial of access to justice. Finally, the condition that legal consultation had to be in the presence of a prison officer was a breach of Article 6(1).[1235]

(f) Other applications

The applicants in the joined cases of *S W v United Kingdom* and *C R v United* **11.299** *Kingdom*[1236] complained that they had been convicted of rape of their spouses as a result of a change in the law removing the 'marital rape exemption'. The Court held that this was the foreseeable continuation of a line of case law. Furthermore, it was held that:

> The essentially debasing character of rape is so manifest that the result . . . that the applicant could be convicted of attempted rape irrespective of his relationship with

---

[1228] *Moody v United Kingdom* Application 22613/93, 16 Jan 1996; *Lochrie v United Kingdom* Application 22614/93, 18 Jan 1996.
[1229] *D F v United Kingdom* Application 22401/93, 24 Oct 1995.
[1230] (1984) 7 EHRR 165.
[1231] Ibid paras 77–85.
[1232] Ibid para 87.
[1233] Ibid para 89–92.
[1234] Ibid paras 97–99.
[1235] Ibid paras 111–113.
[1236] (1995) 21 EHRR 363; see C Osborne, 'Does the End Justify the Means? Retrospectivity, Article 7 and the Marital Rape Exemption' [1996] EHRLR 406.

the victim—cannot be said to be at variance with the object and purpose of Article 7 of the Convention, namely to ensure that no-one should be subjected to arbitrary prosecution, conviction or punishment.[1237]

No breach of Article 7 was established in relation to the reporting provisions of the Sex Offenders Act 1997 which required the applicant to inform the police of any change of name or address.[1238] The Commission rejected the argument that this involved a 'retrospective penalty' on the ground that the measure was preventative and operated independently of the ordinary sentencing process.

11.300 The Court did, however, find a violation of Article 7 in the case of *Welch v United Kingdom*[1239] This case concerned a confiscation order made under the Drug Trafficking Offences Act 1986. These provisions came into force in 1987 and an order was made against the applicant when he was convicted in 1988 of offences committed in 1986. The Court took the view that the order was a 'penalty' within the meaning of Article 7 and that, looking at the realities of the situation

the applicant faced more far-reaching detriment as a result of the order than that to which he was exposed at the time of the commission of the offences from which he was convicted.[1240]

11.301 In *Tinnelly and Sons and McElduff v United Kingdom*[1241] the applicants were contractors who had been refused contracts in Northern Ireland on the ground that their employees were security risks. Complaints of discrimination made under the Fair Employment (Northern Ireland) Act 1976 were met by a ministerial certificate which, by section 43 were conclusive evidence that the contracts had been refused 'for the purpose of safeguarding national security'. The Court observed that:

The right guaranteed to an applicant under Article 6 §1 of the Convention to submit a dispute to a court or tribunal in order to have a determination of questions of both fact and law cannot be displaced by the *ipse dixit* of the executive.[1242]

There was no proportionality between the protection of national security and the impact which the ministerial certificates had and they constituted a disproportionate restriction on the applicants' right of access to the court. It was pointed out

---

[1237] n 1235 above para 44/42.

[1238] *Ibbotson v United Kingdom* [1999] EHRLR 218, 21 Oct 1998; see also *Adamson v United Kingdom* Application 42293/98, 26 Jan 1999.

[1239] (1995) EHRR 247; for criticism of this decision see D Thomas, 'Incorporating the European Convention on Human Rights its Impact on Sentencing Laws', in J Beatson, C Forsyth and I Hare (eds), *The Human Rights Act and the Criminal Justice and Regulatory Process* (Hart Publishing, 1999) 84–85.

[1240] Ibid para 34.

[1241] (1998) 27 EHRR 249.

[1242] Ibid para 77.

that it was possible to modify judicial procedures in such a way as to safeguard national security concerns while still according the individual 'a substantial degree of procedural justice'.[1243]

A number of cases have established breaches of the Convention in the context of European Community law. In *Johnston v Chief Constable of the Royal Ulster Constabulary*[1244] the European Court of Justice took Articles 6 and 13 of the Convention into account in determining that the applicant did not have an effective remedy in pursuing a claim for sex discrimination. The relevant legislation provided for a certificate of 'conclusive evidence' which, in effect, excluded the exercise of a power of review by the courts. In *R v Kent Kirk*[1245] it was held a Council Regulation validating the UK ban on Danish vessels fishing within a 12-mile limit could not have retrospective effect.   **11.302**

(3) General impact issues

(a) Introduction

Article 6 expressly confers fair hearing rights in broad and unqualified terms. In addition, the Court has recognised an 'implied right' of access to the courts and a series of other 'implied' fair trial rights (such as 'equality of arms' and the right to an adversarial hearing). It has taken the view that implied Article 6 rights can only be restricted in furtherance of a legitimate aim and where the measures taken are necessary for the achievement of this aim and are proportionate. Special additional rights are conferred on those facing 'criminal charges'. There are, therefore, five questions to be asked when considering whether a public body has violated Article 6:   **11.303**

- Is the body engaged in a determination of 'civil rights and obligations' or a 'criminal charge'?
- In the case of a 'criminal charge', has there been any breach of the 'minimum guarantees' in Article 6(2) and 6(3)?
- Has there been an infringement of the express rights to an independent and impartial tribunal, a hearing within a reasonable time, a public hearing and public pronouncement of judgment?
- Has there been an apparent infringement of the applicable implied 'fair trial' rights? if so, was this infringement for a legitimate aim, necessary and proportionate?
- Has the applicant waived the right in question?[1245a]

[1243] Ibid para 78.
[1244] [1987] QB 129.
[1245] [1985] 1 All ER 453.
[1245a] See generally, para 6.148ff above.

In relation to the first question, it is clear that any court dealing with a private law or criminal case will be engaged in such a determination.[1246] In relation to other tribunals or decision-makers, the answer to the first question may not be clear cut although the only decisions likely to be excluded are those relating to purely 'administrative' entitlements.[1247]

11.304 There is one general point which arises concerning the impact of Article 6 on administrative decision-makers. Frequently, a public authority cannot show that its internal procedures are 'independent' because (for example, councillors decide entitlements to council benefits). It is submitted that in such circumstances a public authority under the Human Rights Act[1248] will not be acting *incompatibly* with Article 6 under section 6 of the Act[1249] *even though* a decision-maker himself does not meet the guarantees required by Article 6(1) in some respects: *provided* that decision maker is subject to a body exercising judicial control which has full jurisdiction and does provide the guarantees of Article 6(1).[1250] The position has certain parallels with the question of whether an appeal can cure an unfair procedure as a matter of general administrative law;[1251] and reflects the general approach taken when Article 6 is considered before the Court of Human Rights.[1251a] An alternative view is that the public authority has breached the Article 6 obligation placed on it; but it would not be 'just and appropriate' under section 8 of the Human Rights Act to grant relief.[1251b] It would be surprising if relief was granted against a public authority for breach of Article 6 where the complaint was satisfied by a court hearing itself; and where no breach would be found had the case been heard before the Court of Human Rights.

11.304A However, where a public authority relies on a subsequent court hearing to argue that it has acted compatibly with Article 6, the position under the Human Rights Act will depend on:

[1246] Although, as a result of the 'autonomous meaning' of 'criminal charge', the boundaries will not necessarily be in the same place in English law as they are under the Convention, see para 11.174 above.

[1247] Such as claims in relation to education or housing, see para 11.173 above.

[1248] See generally, para 5.03ff above.

[1249] It will be unlawful for a public authority to act in a way which is not compatible with Convention rights; see, generally, para 5.120ff above.

[1250] *Albert and Le Compte v Belgium* (1983) 5 EHRR 533, para 29; *Bryan v United Kingdom* (1995) 21 EHRR 342 para 40; this only applies to decisions of an administrative or disciplinary nature, not to ordinary civil and criminal cases: see *De Cubber v Belgium* (1984) 7 EHRR 236, para 32.

[1251] See para 11.71 above.

[1251a] See para 11.197ff above.

[1251b] See para 21.01ff below.

- the extent to which the decision-maker has himself satisfied the relevant Article 6 rights;[1252] and
- whether the applicant has been given a sufficient opportunity fairly to put his case where the primary facts are at issue.[1253]

The approach taken in Convention law to Article 6(1) and rights of appeal was considered in *Stefan v General Medical Council*[1254] where Lord Clyde identified the principle as being whether the existence of a right of appeal would enable the requirement of fairness embodied in Article 6(1) to be met.

In particular, difficulties may arise where administrative decisions are subject to judicial review or appeals confined to questions of law. Where the important issues of fact are disputed, it may be argued that the applicant has not been given a proper opportunity to contest them.[1255] It may also be said that because the *Wednesbury* test[1256] is such a high one to overcome,[1257] the applicant has not been given an effective opportunity to challenge a public authority's decision.[1258] **11.305**

(b) Access to the courts and immunities

The right of access to the court which is implied into Article 6[1259] is limited by the various 'immunities' available to public authorities.[1260] Such immunities will only be acceptable under the Human Rights Act if they are necessary and proportionate: the court will, in each case, have to strike a balance between the hardship suffered by the claimant and the damage to be done to the public interest.[1261] This could mean that some blanket public policy immunities can no longer be maintained, for example: **11.306**

[1252] The Art 6 rights are stricter than the standards imposed by general administrative law (see, generally, para 11.69ff above) and comprise the right to be present at an adversarial oral hearing (see para 11.206 above); the right to equality of arms (see para 11.208ff above); the right to fair presentation of the evidence (see para 11.214 above); the right to cross examine (see para 11.217 above); the right to a reasoned judgment (see para 11.218 above); the right to a hearing within a reasonable time (see para 11.219ff above); the right to an independent and impartial tribunal established by law (see para 11.222ff above); and the right to a public hearing and the public pronouncement of judgment (see para 11.230ff above).

[1253] See, generally, para 11.198 above.

[1254] [1999] 1 WLR 1293, 1299, 1300 where he discussed *Bryan v United Kingdom* (1995) 21 EHRR 342; *Wickramsinghe v United Kingdom* [1998] EHRLR 338, EComm HR; and the case brought by the applicant himself, *Stefan v United Kingdom* (1997) 25 EHHR CD 130.

[1255] See para 11.198 above.

[1256] See generally, paras 5.123 above.

[1257] See generally, para 5.126 above.

[1258] See *Smith and Grady v United Kingdom*, 27 Sep 1999 paras 138, 139; and see para 21.178 below.

[1259] See para 11.185ff above.

[1260] See para 11.27ff above.

[1261] Cf *Barrett v Enfield LBC* [1999] 3 WLR 79, 84G–85H.

- 'crown immunity' as applied to the Sovereign in her personal capacity in the event it was challenged;[1262]
- 'negligence immunity' of the police and Crown Prosecution Service in relation to the prevention or investigation of crime;[1263] and related immunities;[1264]
- 'negligence immunity' of local authorities in relation to the performance of their statutory duties to protect children;[1265]
- 'proceedings immunity' in relation to negligence claims against legal advisors;[1266]
- 'judicial immunity' in relation to claims against judges or magistrates for actions outside their jurisdiction.[1267]

However, it seems likely that parliamentary immunity would be held to be compatible with Article 6.[1268]

11.307   The question of whether, and to what extent, negligence immunities can survive the Human Rights Act is highly controversial and uncertain. The European Court of Human Rights held in *Osman v United Kingdom*[1269] that the immunity of the police from actions in negligence[1270] breached the right of access to the courts. The Court's decision has been vigorously criticised. It is claimed that the Court has unjustifiably extended the scope of Article 6 as a procedural guarantee by reformulating the substantive law of a domestic state.[1271] It has also been said that the Court misunderstood the English law of negligence. In *Barrett v Enfield LBC*[1272] Lord Browne-Wilkinson described the decision as 'difficult to understand'[1273] because, on a proper analysis of the position in English law, there was no 'immunity from claims' but, rather, no right to make a claim at all. It is submitted that these concerns are misplaced: although, strictly speaking, an element of the

---

[1262] See para 11.28 above.

[1263] Cf *Osman v United Kingdom* (1998) 5 BHRC 293; and see para 11.40 above.

[1264] See para 11.43 above.

[1265] See para 11.41 above; cf *Barrett v Enfield LBC* (n 1261above).

[1266] See para 11.37 above; and see *Docker v Chief Constable of West Midlands Police, The Times*, 1 Aug 2000.

[1267] See para 11.35 above.

[1268] See para 11.31ff above.

[1269] (1998) 5 BHRC 293.

[1270] The Court of Appeal struck out the claim as disclosing no reasonable cause of action: see *Osman v Ferguson* [1993] 4 All ER 344; and generally, para 11.42ff above.

[1271] See para 11.196 above.

[1272] [1999] 3 WLR 79; the views expressed by Lord Browne-Wilkinson concerning the decision in *Osman v United Kingdom* (1998) 5 BHRC 293 at 84 and their impact on the development of negligence are discussed at para 11.196 above.

[1273] *Barrett v Enfield LBC* (n 1272 above) 84B; see also see Lord Hoffmann, 'Human Rights and the House of Lords' (1999) 62 MLR 159; T Weir, 'Downhill—All the Way' [1999] 1 FLR 193; Sir Richard Buxton, 'The Human Rights Act and Private Law' (2000) 116 LQR 48.

tort is not present[1274] the substance of the position (recognised by the frequent use of the term 'immunity' by the courts)[1275] is that a right to claim in negligence is being removed by a 'policy immunity'. This does constitute a restriction on access to the courts in cases involving public authorities and Article 6 is, therefore, brought into play. Lord Browne-Wilkinson also suggested[1276] that the decision in *Osman* makes it inappropriate[1277] to deal with the issue by applying to strike out the case;[1278] and it will be necessary for the court to carry out a detailed factual inquiry into whether the interference can be justified as being a proportionate and legitimate restriction on the right of access.[1279] The Commission has also ruled in favour of the applicants in a case arising out of one[1280] of the claims which had been struck out in the *X (Minors) v Bedfordshire County Council* litigation;[1281] and there are other cases pending. It therefore seems that all of the public policy based negligence immunities will require close examination as a result of the Human Rights Act.

It is submitted that the courts will take a similar approach to other types of 'negligence immunity' and to 'proceedings immunity' and 'judicial immunity'. A defendant will no longer be able to rely on a broad brush justification for immunity which is not specific to the particular case; and will now need to adduce factual evidence to show that the interference with the implied right of access to the Court under Article 6 is justified. As Lord Slynn emphasised in *Phelps v Hillingdon London Borough Council*[1281a] it must not be presumed that imposing liability will interfere with the performance of a public body's duties. The allegations must be proved and will only be established in exceptional circumstances. Nevertheless, in an appropriate case summary determination may be possible.[1281b] **11.308**

(c) Independence and impartiality

Independence.   Judges who determine ordinary civil and criminal cases must be independent of the executive.[1282] The full time judiciary in England and Wales are **11.309**

[1274] Namely, the requirement that it is 'just and reasonable' to impose a duty of care.

[1275] See para 11.42ff above.

[1276] *Barrett v Enfield LBC* (n 1272 above) 198.

[1277] Although s 2(1) of the Human Rights Act ensures a court is not bound to follow the decision of the Court of Human Rights (see generally, para 3.46ff above), it would almost inevitably result in an application to Strasbourg.

[1278] Under CPR, r 3.4; but see *Kinsella v Chief Constable of Nottinghamshire, The Times*, 24 Aug 1999 and *Kent v Griffiths* [2000] 2 WLR 1 158 123 paras 37–38 (*per* Lord Woolf).

[1279] See generally, para 11.190 above.

[1280] *T P and K M v United Kingdom* Application 28945/95, 26 May 1998 (admissibility), EComm HR.

[1281] [1995] 2 AC 633.

[1281a] *The Times*, 28 Jul 2000.

[1281b] *Kent v Griffiths* (n 1278 above) paras 37–38 (*per* Lord Woolf).

[1282] In such cases, lack of independence cannot be cured by an appeal to an 'independent tribunal', see *De Cubber v Belgium* (1984) 7 EHRR 236 para 32; the position is different in relation to disciplinary and administrative decisions, see para 11.197 above.

clearly independent of the executive for the purposes of Article 6. The position is less clear in relation to part-time judges and lay magistrates.

11.310 The position of temporary judges in Scotland was considered by the High Court of Justiciary in the case of *Starrs v Procurator Fiscal, Linlithgow*.[1283] It was held that temporary sheriffs who were appointed for a period of one year and were subject to a power of recall were not 'independent' for the purposes of Article 6. A number of factors pointed strongly away from independence including:

- the short fixed term of office with the possibility of renewal at the discretion of the executive;
- the fact that temporary sheriffs were very often persons hoping for a permanent appointment and thus had a relationship of dependency with the executive;
- the absence of guarantees against outside pressures, including the power to recall an appointment, to decline to renew it or to fail to provide judicial work.

The court accepted that, in practice, the system was operated with careful regard for judicial independence however the absence of an objective guarantee of security of tenure was fatal. Lord Reed made it clear that protection of independence by convention was not sufficient:

> It is fundamental . . . that human rights are no longer dependent solely on conventions, by which I mean values, customs and practices of the constitution which are not legally enforceable. Although the Convention protects rights which reflect democratic values and underpin democratic institutions, the Convention guarantees the protection of those rights through legal processes, rather than political processes. It is for that reason that Article 6 guarantees access to independent courts. It would be inconsistent with the whole approach of the Convention if the independence of those courts itself rested upon convention rather than law.[1283a]

11.311 If this approach had been followed by the English courts, there would have been strong arguments that assistant recorders, Deputy High Court Judges and various other part time appointees to judicial office would not have constituted 'independent tribunals' for the purposes of Article 6. These potential difficulties were removed by a decision announced on 12 April 2000 that such appointments would, in future, be made for a minimum period of at least five years with various other safeguards.[1284] The position remains unclear in relation to lay magistrates who are subject to removal in circumstances which are not defined by statute.[1285] It is also

---

[1283] [2000] 1 LRC 718; see also *Clancy v Caird, The Times,* 9 May 2000 (Inner House) in which it was held that temporary judges of the Court of Session, appointed for period of three years were 'independent' for the purposes of Art 6.

[1283a] *Starrs v Procurator Fiscal* (n 1283 above) at 771a–c.

[1284] See para 11.61 above.

[1285] Ibid; note that the Canadian courts have rejected an analogous challenge under the Charter, see *Reference re Justices of the Peace Act* (1984) 16 CCC (3d) 193 and see, generally, para 11.409, below.

strongly arguable that 'statutory tribunals' are not 'independent': the lay members having no security of tenure.[1286] If a challenge were made to magistrates or statutory tribunals on the basis they were not independent or impartial, the objection should be taken immediately; otherwise the court may hold the applicant has waived the Article 6 objection which was the approach taken in Scotland by the Court of Session in *Clancy v Caird*.[1286a]

Impartiality.   In English law a tribunal is only disqualified by apparent bias if   **11.312**
there is a 'real danger of bias'.[1287] This is a less stringent test than that under Article 6 which requires only a 'reasonable suspicion' or 'reasonable apprehension' of bias.[1288] It is submitted that the result of the Human Rights Act is that the English courts will be obliged to apply the 'reasonable suspicion' test. In the majority of cases the two tests are likely to lead to the same result[1289] but, in some borderline cases, the stricter Article 6 test may affect the outcome. In Scotland it has been held that a judge who made public criticism of the Convention was disqualified from sitting on an appeal in which Convention issues were to be raised.[1289a]

(d) Impact on civil proceedings

In general, the rules of English civil court procedure have been found to be in   **11.313**
compliance with Article 6.[1290] The common law has generally recognised fair trial rights such as:

- the right of access to the courts;[1291]
- the right to trial within a reasonable time;[1292]
- the right to a public, oral hearing, with the cross-examination of witnesses;[1293]
- the right to a reasoned judgment.[1294]

Although these rights can, under English constitutional law, be expressly limited by statute,[1295] such limitations have been rare.

In 1999, English civil procedure was subject to the most radical revision for over   **11.314**

[1286]   See *Smith v Secretary of State for Trade and Industry* [2000] ICR 69 on this point.
[1286a]   *The Times*, 9 May 2000.
[1287]   *R v Gough* [1993] AC 646, see para 11.68 above.
[1288]   See para 11.225ff above; and see *Locabail (UK) Ltd v Bayfield Properties Ltd* [2000] 2 WLR 870, 884–885 (where this difference is noted); and see P Havers and O Thomas 'Bias Post Pinochet and Under the ECHR' [1999] JR 111.
[1289]   Ibid.
[1289a]   *Hoekstra v Her Majesty's Advocate (No 3)* (2000) GWD 12–417, High Court of Justiciary.
[1290]   Cf Sir Robert Walker, 'Impact of European Standards on the Right to a Fair Trial in Civil Proceedings in English Domestic Law' [1999] EHRLR 4.
[1291]   See para 11.15ff above.
[1292]   See para 11.84ff above.
[1293]   See paras 11.77 and 11.79 above.
[1294]   See para 11.89 above.
[1295]   See para 1.21 above.

a century. The Civil Procedure Rules give the courts a large range of summary powers over the conduct of civil proceedings with a view to achieving more efficient 'case management'.[1296] Many of these powers can be exercised by the court of its own motion, without a hearing taking place.[1297] The effect of such orders can be to place restrictions on the 'access to justice' of litigants:

- the court can order a party to pay a sum of money into court 'if that party has, without good reason, failed to comply with a rule, practice direction or a relevant pre-action protocol'[1298]—this could prevent an impecunious party from proceeding;
- the 'striking out' of statements of case—which means that cases may be disposed of without a full hearing;[1299]
- the 'summary disposal of claims' on the application of either the claimant or the defendant, which also means that cases may be disposed of without a full hearing;[1300]
- the 'summary assessment of costs' on final hearings—which, in practice, means that substantial financial liabilities are determined without substantial investigation.[1301]

In some circumstances, such orders might be regarded as being incompatible with Article 6: particularly if inflexible rules of practice were developed which prevented the court from considering the merits of a particular case.

11.315 Article 6 issues may also arise where the court exercises its power to decide promptly which issues need full investigation and which can be disposed of summarily,[1302] where the court directs that evidence is given by a single joint expert[1303] (particularly, if it results in an inequality of arms[1304] because the forensic issues are complex and one of the parties has insufficient resources and so is unable to formulate his own case effectively) or where the court limits cross examination.[1305] It should, however, be noted that Article 6 does not apply to 'interim' applications or determinations.[1306] Furthermore, the flexibility which is central to the Civil Procedure Rules means that the Courts will have ample opportunity to adjust

---

[1296] See CPR, Pt 3.
[1297] The general power is contained in CPR, r 3.3.
[1298] CPR, r 3.1(5).
[1299] CPR, r 3.4.
[1300] CPR, Pt 24.
[1301] In accordance with CPR, r 44.7; a determination of costs which is the continuation of a substantive dispute is subject to Art 6 guarantees: see *Robins v United Kingdom* (1997) 26 EHRR 527 paras 25–29
[1302] CPR, r 1.4(2)(c).
[1303] CPR, r 37.5; but see *Daniels v Walker, The Times*, 17 May 2000 where Lord Woolf MR strongly discouraged reliance on Art 6 in a dispute arising from the joint instruction of an expert; however, the Court of Appeal decided that the parties were entitled to instruct their own expert.
[1304] See para 11.208ff above.
[1305] CPR, r 32.1(3).
[1306] See *X v United Kingdom* (1981) 24 DR 57, EComm HR, and see para 11.157 above.

their procedures so as to conform with Article 6 as they are required to do by section 6(3) of the Human Rights Act.[1307] In relation to case management issues Lord Woolf MR stressed in *Daniels v Walker*[1307a] that:

> It would be highly undesirable if consideration of these issues was made more complex by the injection into them of Article 6 style arguments. I hope that judges will be robust in resisting any attempt to introduce these arguments.

Where it is claimed that the Rules are being applied in breach of Article 6 rights, it may be appropriate to seek a ruling on that question at an early stage.

11.315A The practice of granting freezing injunctions[1307b] in relation to alleged trust monies which contain no proviso allowing payment for legal advice will be affected by Article 6. Where the court is exercising its discretion about whether it is just to refuse to include such a proviso[1307c] the applicant's right to have effective access to the court[1307d] will be an important factor to weigh in the balance.

11.316 The new general rule that hearings should be in public[1308] brings English civil proceedings into line with Article 6(1). Nevertheless, the fact that no special arrangements have to be made for accommodating members of the public[1309] could, arguably, lead to a breach of Article 6 as many court premises are arranged in such a way that practical public access to 'chambers' is extremely difficult.

11.317 The power to order disclosure of privileged documents may breach Article 6 because the right to confidentiality is a fundamental condition for the adminstration of justice.[1310] Thus, the power of the court to require disclosure of privileged material in child care proceedings under Part IV of the Children Act may require further consideration[1311] because legal representatives are obliged to make full and frank disclosure even where it harms their clients' case.[1312]

11.317A Limitation periods do not breach Article 6 provided they can be justified as a proportionate interference with access to the court.[1312a] It may therefore be difficult

---

[1307] See generally, para 5.38ff above.

[1307a] Above n 1303.

[1307b] Under CPR r 25.1(1)(f): formerly, Mareva injunctions.

[1307c] See *Fitzgerald v Williams* [1996] QB 657 *per* Sir Thomas Bingham at 669; *United Mizrahi Bank v Docherty* [1998] 1 WLR 435.

[1307d] See in particular, *Airey v Ireland* (1979) 2 EHRR 305; and see para 11.189 above.

[1308] CPR, r 39.2(1); see para 11.80 above.

[1309] CPR, r 39.2(2).

[1310] See eg *General Mediteranean v Patel* [1999] 3 All ER 673.

[1311] See *In re L (A Minor) (Police Investigation Privilege)* [1997] AC 16; see, in particular, the dissenting judgment of Lord Nicholls at 34.

[1312] See eg *Oxfordshire County Council v P* [1995] Fam 161; *Essex County Council v R* [1994] Fam 167; *Re D H (A Minor) (Child Abuse)* [1994] 1 FLR 679.

[1312a] See para 11.190ff above.

to justify under Article 6 limitation periods which cannot be extended for good cause or where the power to extend is very limited in scope;[1312b] potential areas of dispute include the power to extend time to refer disputes to arbitration under section 12(3) of the Arbitration Act 1996,[1312c] the strict approach towards extending time for statutory appeals under CPR Sch 1 R 55,[1312d] appeals against the local authority's decisions in homelessness cases to the county court[1312e] and appeals to the Employment Appeal Tribunal.[1312f]

11.317B Article 6 may call into question the enforceability of certain arbitration agreements. Arbitrators will not be a 'court' or 'tribunal' under section 6(3) of the Human Rights Act.[1312g] and will not be prohibited from acting incompatibly with Convention rights under Section 6(1). It is well established under Convention case law that the right of access to the courts under Article 6 may be waived by a voluntary arbitration agreement.[1312h] However, a waiver will only be effective if it is clear and unequivocal, made in the absence of constraint and made in the full knowledge of the nature and extent of the right.[1312i] It is therefore arguable that an arbitration clause will not be effective if, for example, the applicant was effectively compelled to agree an arbitration clause[1312j] or where the arbitration clause was not expressly agreed.[1312k]

11.318 It is possible that 'self-help' remedies such as distress for rent, forfeiture by re-entry or the power of a mortgagee to obtain possession without a court order[1313] will be held to be contrary to Article 6. It is arguable that self help is 'inimical to a society in which the rule of law prevails'[1314] as it prevents access to the courts for the adjudication of disputes. The power of a mortgagee to take possession of a dwelling house without a court order[1315] appears to be a particularly clear breach of Article 6, bearing in mind the importance of the right to occupy the home which is brought to an end by such a step[1316] and the fact that such a procedure allows the

---

[1312b] N Giffen, 'Judicial Supervision of Human Rights: Practice and Procedure', Administrative Law Bar seminar, 5 Feb 2000.

[1312c] See *Harbour and General Works v Environment Agency* [2000] 1 All ER 50.

[1312d] *Regalbourne v East Lyndsey District Council* [1994] RA 1.

[1312e] Housing Act 1996, s 204.

[1312f] See eg *Aziz v Bethnal Green City Challenge* [2000] IRLR 111.

[1312g] See para 5.42ff above.

[1312h] See para 6.149ff above.

[1312i] See para 6.160ff above.

[1312j] Because, for example, all traders in a particular area trade on standard terms including such a clause.

[1312k] Because, for example, it was included in 'small print' or 'incorporated by reference' to standard terms, see eg *Zambia Steel and Building Supplies v James Clark and Eaton Ltd* [1986] 2 Lloyd's Rep 225.

[1313] See *Ropaigealach v Barclays Bank* [1999] 3 WLR 17.

[1314] Cf the South African case of *Lesapo v North West Agricultural Bank*, 1999 (12) BCLR 1420; see para 11.494 below.

[1315] See *Ropaigealach v Barclays Bank*, (n 1313 above).

[1316] The right to respect for home under Art 8, see generally, Chap 12 below.

mortgagee to avoid the statutory procedure for suspension of possession orders in residential mortgagees actions.[1317]

(e) Impact on judicial review proceedings

Introduction. The Human Rights Act will, of course, have a substantial impact on judicial review proceedings: incompatibility with Convention rights will, in effect, be an additional basis for seeking judicial review on the ground of illegality[1318] and, when Convention rights are in issue, the range of 'public authorities' amenable to review may be broadened.[1319] There are three situations in which Article 6 itself could have an impact on judicial review proceedings:[1320]

11.319

- in relation to the court's own procedure for judicial review applications;[1321]
- where the decision under review is alleged to interfere with Article 6 rights;
- where the decision under review itself constitutes a determination of civil rights and obligations or a criminal charge.

Judicial review procedure. The requirement for permission in judicial review applications is consistent with Article 6.[1322] The test to be applied on applications[1323] under the Human Rights Act is unclear: although it might be said that once a *prima facie* violation has been shown, the burden is on the public authority to justify the interference at the substantive stage, the more realistic view is that a claimant will need to show at the permission stage an arguable absence of justification for the interference.[1324]

11.320

A number of statutes contain time limits restricting the period within which statutory appeals can be made.[1325] In some circumstances, such time limits could constitute unjustifiable restrictions on the right of access to the courts under Article 6 although this is unlikely.[1326]

11.321

[1317] Under Administration of Justice Act 1970, s 36.

[1318] Which was defined by Lord Diplock in the *GCHQ* case (*Council of Civil Service Unions v Minister for the Civil Service* [1985] AC 374, 410) as 'I mean that the decision-maker must correctly understand the law that regulates his decision-making powers and gives effect to it'; and see generally, Lord Woolf and J Jowell, *De Smith, Woolf and Jowell, Judicial Review of Administrative Action* (5th edn, Sweet & Maxwell, 1995) III-01–III-04.

[1319] See generally, M Supperstone and J Coppel, 'Judicial Review After the Human Rights Act' [1999] EHRLR 301.

[1320] See generally, Sir Stephen Richards, 'The Impact of Article 6 of the ECHR on Judicial Review' [1999] JR 106.

[1321] See generally, para 22.93ff below.

[1322] See para 11.22ff above.

[1323] See R Clayton and H Tomlinson, *Judicial Review Procedure* (2nd edn, Wiley Chancery Law, 1997) 122ff.

[1324] Cf Richards (n 1320 above) 109–110, para 17.

[1325] See for example Town and Country Planning Act 1990, s 288(3) (six weeks); for a fuller list, see R Gordon, *Judicial Review and Crown Office Practice* (Sweet & Maxwell, 1999), appeals by way of re-hearing (paras 5-094–5-103); tribunals to which the Tribunal and Inquiries Act 1992 (paras 5-104–5-113) and other tribunals (paras 114–119).

[1326] See para 11.191 above.

11.321A   The question as to whether an application for judicial review should be refused because of a failure to use an alternative remedy[1326a] may require reconsideration where the case involves the applicant's 'civil rights and obligations'.[1326b] If the alternative remedy does not involve a determination by an 'independent and impartial tribunal'[1326c] such as a local authority's complaints procedure, then the court may be acting in breach of its own obligations under section 6(1) if it refuses to grant relief in such circumstances.[1326d]

11.322   The limited availability of disclosure of documents[1327] and cross examination of deponents[1328] in judicial review proceedings are unlikely to satisfy the requirements of Article 6 where the applicant disputes the underlying facts of the dispute in a case involving 'civil rights, and obligations'[1328a] or a 'criminal charge'.[1328b] It is possible that the courts may differentiate between judicial review cases in general and cases under the Human Rights Act. Although the court must ensure it is not acting incompatibly with Article 6 when considering an application for discovery or cross examination, the application will have particular force where the judicial review application is based on Article 6 itself.

11.323   **Review of decisions interfering with Article 6 rights.**   Although the English law already recognises a 'constitutional right' of access to the court,[1329] this right is subject to a large number of exceptions. These will be subject to close scrutiny under the Human Rights Act. Any statute which authorises them will be 'read down' under section 3 of the Act to ensure compliance with Article 6.[1330] Other areas of potential challenge include:

- decisions concerning the grant of legal aid in civil and criminal proceedings;[1331]
- decisions concerning the organisation and resourcing of the court system.

11.324   **Review of decisions determining Article 6 rights.**   The Human Rights Act does not impose an obligation on all administrative decision-makers or tribunals to comply with Article 6. Although section 6(3) of the Act states that tribunals (as

---

[1326a] See eg *R v Chief Constable of Merseyside, ex p Calveley* [1986] QB 424; and see generally, *De Smith, Woolf and Jowell, Judicial Review of Administrative Action*, para 18–032ff.

[1326b] See para 11.160ff above.

[1326c] See para 11.222ff above.

[1326d] N Giffen, 'Judicial Supervision of Human Rights: Practice and Procedure', Administrative Law Bar Association seminar, 5 Feb 2000.

[1327] See eg R Clayton and H Tomlinson (n 1323 above) para 7.2.4; R Gordon (n 1325 above) paras 3-658–3-66; and see para 22.102 below.

[1328] See eg Clayton and Tomlinson (n 1323 above) para 7.2.7; R Gordon (n1325 above) paras 3-653–3-657.

[1328a] See para 11.160ff above.

[1328b] See para 11.174ff above.

[1329] *R v Lord Chancellor, ex p Witham* [1998] QB 575; see generally para 11.15ff above.

[1330] For s 3, see, in particular, para 4.27ff above.

[1331] For the position under Art 6, see para 11.189 above.

well as courts) must not act incompatibly with Convention rights, a tribunal is defined in section 21(1) of the Act as any tribunal in which legal proceedings may be
brought.[1332] A decision-maker must not act incompatibly with Article 6 if he is determining 'civil rights and obligations'.[1333] Complying with Article 6 may be
achieved by a combination of the primary decision-maker and the High Court
carrying out judicial review functions.[1334] However, in cases where there are disputes as to the primary facts, it may be necessary for these factual issues to be
investigated by disclosure and cross examination in judicial review proceedings[1335] (contrary to the normal practice).

Furthermore, Article 6 will itself provide a number of additional grounds for ju-   **11.325**
dicial review of decisions by inferior tribunals and administrative decision-makers. The Convention case law imposes more demanding standards than those
which arise under administrative law principles in many situations including
complaints concerning:

- lack of independence from the executive;[1336]
- a failure of the tribunal to be impartial;[1337]
- failure to hold oral public hearings;[1338]
- failure to allow the cross-examination of witnesses;[1339]
- failure to provide for the 'equality of arms';[1340]
- failure to give any sufficient reasons.[1341]

[1332] See generally, para 5.43 above.

[1333] See para 11.154ff above.

[1334] See *Stefan v General Medical Council* [1999] 1 WLR 1293, 1299E; and see para 11.91 above.

[1335] See para 22.102ff below.

[1336] Contrast the Convention principles (see para 11.223ff above) with those of administrative law
(see para 11.53ff above).

[1337] Contrast the Convention principles (see para 11.225ff above) with those of administrative law
(see para 11.66ff above); and see P Havers and O Thomas, 'Bias Post-Pinochet and Under the
ECHR' [1999] JR 111.

[1338] Contrast the Convention principles (see 11.206 above) with those of administrative law (see
para 11.75 above).

[1339] Contrast the Convention principles (see para 11.217 above) with those of administrative law
(see para 11.77 above).

[1340] Contrast the Convention principles (see para 11.208 above) with those of administrative law
(see para 11.72ff above).

[1341] Contrast the Convention principles (see para 11.218 above) with those of administrative law
(see 11.90 above); and see *Stefan v General Medical Council* (n 1334 above) at 1301 where Lord
Clyde reviews developments in the duty to give reasons and goes on to express the view that: 'There
is certainly a strong argument for the view that what was once seen as exceptions to a rule may now
be becoming the norm, and the cases where the reasons are not required may be taking the appearance of being exceptions. But the general rule has not been departed from and their Lordships do
not consider the present case provides an appropriate opportunity to explore the possibility of such
a departure. They are conscious of a possible re-appraisal of the whole position which the passage of
the Human Rights Act 1998 will bring about. The provisions of article 6(1) of the Convention on
Human Rights, which is now about to become directly accessible in the national courts, will require
closer attention to be paid to the duty to give reasons, at least in relation to those cases where a person's civil rights and obligations are being determined. But it is in the context of the application of
that Act that any wide ranging review of the position at common law should take place.'

(f) Impact on ombudsman procedures

11.326   The use of complaints procedures directed to ombudsmen is now well established administrative remedy.[1342] It can be invoked against a diverse range of public bodies including Parliament, local government, the health service, the insurance and banking industry, the legal services and the prison service. It is intended to be an informal mechanism for investigating and resolving complaints. However, there is often no mechanism for bringing a complaint before the court, although judicial review will be available. Where an ombudsman makes binding awards of compensation against public bodies, he is making a determination of 'civil rights and obligations' and the decision-making process must be in accordance with the Article 6 fair trial guarantees.[1343] There are a number of potential difficulties which arise because the 'ombudsman' procedure is often inquisitorial rather than adversarial and there is no disclosure of documents to the complainant or cross-examination of witnesses. It is difficult to see how the guarantees of Article 6 can be provided by judicial review proceedings.[1343a]

(4) Specific areas of impact

(a) Commercial law

11.327   **Introduction.**   In the field of commercial law, the most important area of impact concerns regulatory and disciplinary hearings.[1344] A large range of statutory and non-statutory bodies are now responsible for the regulation of financial and commercial activities.[1345] There are, at present, no general rules governing the operation of such bodies although they are generally subject to judicial review[1346] and must, therefore, conduct themselves in accordance with the flexible standards of fairness which have been laid down by the courts on a case-by-case basis.[1347] Article 6 will provide a much stricter and more uniform framework within which the activities of such bodies must be carried out.[1348]

[1342] See, generally, H W R Wade and C Forsyth, *Administrative Law* (7th edn, Clarendon Press, 1994) 79–105.

[1343] See para 11.183ff above.

[1343a] See Tim Lowe; 'Financial Services: Parliamentary Anatomy of Human Rights' in Wilberforce Chambers, *The Essential Human Rights Act 1998* (Wilberforce Chambers, 2000) 152–156.

[1344] See para 11.267 above.

[1345] Financial services are now subject to regulation by the Financial Services Authority under the provisions of the Financial Services and Markets Act 1999, see generally, B Harris, *The Law and Practice of Disciplinary and Regulatory Proceedings* (2nd edn, Barry Rose, 1999).

[1346] See generally, para 5.23ff above.

[1347] See para 11.69ff above.

[1348] See generally, P Davies, 'Self Incrimination, Fair Trials and the Pursuit of Corporate and Financial Wrongdoing' and N Jordan 'The Implications for Commercial Lawyers in Practice' in B Markesinis (ed), *The Impact of the Human Rights Bill on English Law* (Oxford University Press, 1998); J Beatson 'Which Regulatory Bodies are Subject to the Human Rights Act?', N Jordan,

The first issue in relation to regulatory hearings is whether they involve 'deter-   **11.328**
mination of civil rights and obligations' or criminal charges.[1349] Such bodies will
be subject to Article 6 safeguards if they involve determination of matters such as
fitness to remain in business or awards of compensation.[1350]

Where a regulatory offence is equivalent to a 'criminal charge' the person charged   **11.329**
is entitled to a first instance hearing which fully meets the requirements of Article
6.[1351] However, where no criminal charge is involved, regulatory bodies can meet
the requirements of Article 6 in one of two ways: either the bodies themselves can
comply with the requirements or they are subject to subsequent control by a judicial body which has full jurisdiction and does provide Article 6 guarantees:[1352]

> In cases involving applications for judicial review under English law, the sufficiency
> of the review exercised by the High Court must be assessed having regard to matters
> such as the subject matter of the decision appealed against, the manner in which
> that decision was arrived at, and the content of the dispute including the desired
> and actual grounds of appeal.[1353]

Regulatory proceedings involving 'criminal charges'.   In a limited range of   **11.330**
cases, a 'regulatory' offence may be treated as a 'criminal charge' under Article 6
and the applicant is entitled to procedural safeguards such as the presumption of
innocence,[1354] the right to be informed promptly and in detail of the nature and
cause of the accusations against him,[1355] the right to have adequate time and facilities for the preparation of his defence,[1356] the right to defend himself in person or
through legal assistance of his own choosing (and, if he does not have the means
to pay, to be given free legal assistance when the interests of justice require
it)[1357]and to examine the witnesses against him and to obtain the attendance and
examination of witnesses on his own behalf.[1358]

'Impact of the Human Rights Act upon Compliance: the Taxation Viewpoint', R Nolan 'Human
Rights and Corporate Wrongs: the impact of the Human Rights Act 1998 on Section 236 of the
Insolvency Act 1986', G Staple, 'Financial Services and the Human Rights Act', M Blair, 'Human
Rights and Market Abuse' and Counsels' Opinions on the impact of the ECHR on the Draft
Financial and Markets Bill' in J Beatson, C Forsyth and I Hare (eds), *The Human Rights Act and the
Criminal Justice and Regulatory Process* (Hart Publishing, 1999); Tim Lowe, 'Financial Services:
Parliamentary Anatomy of Human Rights' in Wilberforce Chambers, *The Essential Human Rights
Act 1998* (Wilberforce Chambers, 2000).

[1349] For 'civil obligation' see para 11.163ff above and for 'criminal charge' see para 11.174ff above.
[1350] See eg *Editions Periscope v France* (1992) 14 EHRR 597, 613 para 40.
[1351] See *De Cubber v Belgium* (1984) 7 EHRR 236 paras 31–32; *Findlay v United Kingdom* (1997)
24 EHRR 221 para 79.
[1352] See *Albert and le Compte v Belgium* (1983) 5 EHRR 533 para 29; and para 11.197 above.
[1353] *A P B Ltd, APP and AEB v United Kingdom*, (1998) 25 EHRR CD 141 (admissibility decision); and see *Bryan v United Kingdom* (1995) 21 EHRR 342, 359 para 40, 360–361 paras 44–47.
[1354] Art 6(2); see generally, para 11.236ff above.
[1355] Art 6(3)(a); see generally, para 11.241ff above.
[1356] Art 6(3)(b); see generally, para 11.243ff above.
[1357] Art 6(3)(c); see para 11.245ff above.
[1358] Art 6(3)(d); see para 11.252ff above.

11.331   In a number of recent cases the Commission has held that regulatory proceedings taken to discipline and disqualify certain individuals did not constitute 'criminal proceedings' for the purposes of Article 6. Thus, consideration of whether the applicant was a fit and proper person to carry on investment business,[1359] to be the managing director of an insurance company[1360] or to practice medicine[1361] were treated as determinations of 'civil rights and obligations' rather than as 'criminal charges'. Nevertheless, it is arguable that some types of disciplinary proceedings under the Financial Services and Markets Bill may be characterised as 'criminal' for the purposes of Article 6: in particular, the disciplinary offences which may be committed by a very wide range of persons and may involve substantial financial penalties.[1361a]

11.332   The Government has recognised that 'market abuse' under Part VII of the Financial Services and Markets Bill may be a 'criminal charge' as it is of a generally binding character and has a high degree of overlap with criminal offences of 'insider trading'.[1362] As a result, the Bill has been modified in part to reflect a perceived need to provide the 'criminal charge' guarantees of Article 6(2) and (3) to those charged with market abuse. For example, the Bill now imposes certain limitations on the use of statements made by a person in compliance with a requirement imposed by a regulator;[1363] the Government has indicated that financial support will be provided to defend market abuse proceedings in appropriate cases and a warning notice or decision notice will be taken by a person who is not directly involved in establishing the evidence on which the decision is based.[1364]

11.333   Directors' disqualification proceedings under the terms of the Company Directors Disqualification Act 1986 are also subject to the provisions of Article 6.[1365] It has been suggested that such proceedings should be treated as 'criminal' for the purposes of Article 6[1366] on the basis of the nature of the penalty.[1367] This issue was considered by the Court of Appeal in *R v Secretary of State for Trade and*

[1359] *A P B Ltd, APP and AEB v United Kingdom* (1998) 25 EHRR CD 141.

[1360] *X v United Kingdom* (1998) 25 EHRR CD 88.

[1361] *Wickramsinghe v United Kingdom* [1998] EHRLR 338.

[1361a] See Tim Lowe, 'Financial Services: Parliamentary Anatomy of Human Rights' in Wilberforce Chambers, *The Essential Human Rights Act 1998* (Wilberforce Chambers, 2000) 140–145.

[1362] See generally, G Staple, 'Financial Services and the Human Rights Act' and 'Counsels' opinions on the impact of the ECHR on the Draft Financial and Markets Bill' in J Beatson, C Forsyth and I Hare (eds), *The Human Rights Act and the Criminal Justice and Regulatory Process* (Hart Publishing, 1999).

[1363] Cl 144.

[1364] Cl 340.

[1365] See *E D C v United Kingdom* [1996] EHRLR 189 (the applicant's complaint of over four years' delay in such proceedings was held to be admissible by the Commission).

[1366] See generally, para 11.174ff above.

[1367] See A Mithani, *Directors' Disqualification*, (Butterworths, 1998) VIII, 65 (where the arguments in favour of this contention are conveniently summarised).

Industry, ex p McCormick.[1368] The Court pointed out that not every deprivation of liberty or fine necessarily belonged to the criminal law;[1369] and that the Commission had held that proceedings concerning a prohibition on acting as a business agent were not 'criminal'.[1370] It relied on the fact that:

> The disqualification order does not prevent the person subject to its terms carrying on any commercial activity in his own name (save those of a receiver, liquidator or company promoter, etc.); its effect is to remove the privilege of doing so through a company with limited liability. The consequences of the order are serious for the individual concerned and have been described as penal but they do not involve a deprivation of liberty, livelihood or property'.[1371]

As a result, it was held that the Secretary of State was not bound to treat the proceedings as criminal.[1372] This conclusion was confirmed by the Court of Human Rights in *D C H S and A D v United Kingdom*.[1372a] It has therefore been held that the use of statements obtained under section 235 of the Insolvency Act 1986 in disqualification proceedings did not necessarily involve a breach of Article 6. The issue of fair trial had to be determined by having regard to relevant factors by the trial judge.[1372b]

Regulatory proceedings involving 'civil rights and obligations'.   If the regulatory proceedings are within the scope of Article 6 because they concern 'civil rights and obligations', the 'tribunal' must be independent and impartial. It must, therefore, be independent of the parties[1373] and should have a proportion of lay members. The tribunal should not contain members who have been involved in previous informal or conciliatory stages of the case.[1374] However, the procedure does not have to be formal and the tribunal can, in regulating its own procedure, limit the extent of oral argument and questioning.

11.334

Furthermore, there must be an open and public hearing with judgment being pronounced publicly. This is a fundamental principle which is designed to maintain public confidence in the administration of justice.[1375] However, the 'publicity' requirement is flexible and depends on all the circumstances, including the nature of the proceedings and the other interests protected by a private hearing.[1376] For

11.335

[1368] [1998] BCC 379.
[1369] Relying on *Société Stenuit v France* (1992) 14 EHRR 509.
[1370] *Jaxel v France* (1987) 54 DR 70, EComm HR.
[1371] See n 1368 above.
[1372] Mithani reaches the same conclusion, (n 1367 above) VIII, 81–83.
[1372a] Application 39031/97, 14 Sep 1999 (admissibility decision).
[1372b] *Official Receiver v Stern* [2000] UKHRR 332.
[1373] *Re S (A Barrister)* [1981] QB 683; B Harris, *Law and Practice of Disciplinary and Regulatory Proceedings* (2nd edn, Barry Rose, 1999) 181ff.
[1374] Cf *Procola v Luxembourg* (1995) 22 EHRR 193.
[1375] *Diennet v France* (1995) 21 EHRR 554 para 33.
[1376] *Axen v Germany* (1983) 6 EHRR 195.

example, prison[1377] or medical[1378]disciplinary proceedings can be conducted in private for reasons of 'public order and security' or the 'protection of private life' respectively.

11.336 The right to a public hearing can be waived unless there is some clear public interest to the contrary.[1379] In cases where the issues are technical and no issues of public importance are involved it may be appropriate not to hold oral hearings unless a party requests it.[1380]

11.337 **The use of evidence obtained under compulsory powers.** The use of evidence in criminal proceedings which is obtained under powers to compel witnesses to give evidence to regulators[1381] is unlikely to result in breaches of Article 6[1382] following the amendments to the relevant statutory powers made in 1999.[1383] Evidence acquired under a regulator's compulsory powers could be used in civil proceedings. However, it has been argued that admitting such evidence in civil proceedings would breach Article 6(1) because it would infringe the principle of equality of arms[1384] by giving one party to litigation an unfair advantage over the other.[1385]

(b) Criminal law

11.338 **Introduction.** There are a large number of areas of potential impact in the field of criminal law.[1386] In this section, the potential impact is considered under 12 headings: definition of criminal charge, public hearings, hearings within a reasonable time, right to silence, presumption of innocence, information as to charge, disclosure and public interest immunity, legal advice, conduct of trial, agent provocateurs, interpreters, the giving of reasons and sentencing.

[1377] See *Campbell and Fell v United Kingdom* (1984) 7 EHRR 165, para 11.178 above.
[1378] *Guenuon v France* (1990) 66 DR 181, EComm HR.
[1379] *Håkansson and Sturesson v Sweden* (1990) 13 EHRR 1 para 66; see generally, K Reid, *A Practitioner's Guide to the European Convention on Human Rights* (Sweet & Maxerll, 1998) 124.
[1380] *Schuler-Zgraggen v Switzerland* (1993) 16 EHRR 405, 433 para 58.
[1381] See para 11.101 above.
[1382] See para 11.211ff above.
[1383] See para 11.107 above.
[1384] See para 11.208ff above.
[1385] See R Nolan, 'Human Rights and Corporate Wrongs: the impact of the Human Rights Act on Section 236 of the Insolvency Act 1986' in J Beatson, C Forsyth and I Hare (eds), *The Human Rights Act and the Criminal Justice and Regulatory Process* (Hart Publishing, 1999).
[1386] For general discussions, see D Cheney, L Dickson, J Fitzpatric and S Uglow, *Criminal Justice and the Human Rights Act 1998* (Jordans, 1999); C Baker (ed), *The Human Rights Act 1998: A Practitioners Guide* (Sweet & Maxwell, 1998), Chap 4, Pt I (Richardson) and A Ashworth, 'Article 6 and the Fairness of Trials' [1999] Crim LR 261; S Sharpe, 'Article 6 and the Disclosure of Evidence in Criminal Trials' [1999] Crim LR 273; A Ashworth 'The European Convention and Criminal Law', Rt Hon Lord Justice Buxton, 'The Convention and the English Law of Criminal Evidence', J Spencer, 'The European Convention and the Rules of Criminal Procedure', D Kyle, 'The Human Rights Act: Post Trial and Hearing'in J Beatson, C Forsyth and I Hare (eds), *The Human Rights Act and the Criminal Justice and Regulatory Process* (Hart Publishing, 1999); for a useful summary of the relevant Convention law, see *Archbold Criminal Pleading, Evidence and Practice* (Sweet and Maxwell, 1999) Chap 15 (Emmerson).

Definition of 'Criminal Charge'. Article 6 provides additional protection to   **11.339**
those subject to criminal charges and the term has an 'autonomous Convention
meaning'.[1387] In such circumstances the applicant is entitled to procedural safeguards such as the presumption of innocence,[1388] the right to be informed
promptly and in detail of the nature and cause of the accusations against him,[1389]
the right to have adequate time and facilities for the preparation of his defence,[1390] the right to defend himself in person or through legal assistance of his
own choosing (and, if he does not have the means to pay), to be given free legal
assistance when the interests of justice require it[1391] and to examine the witnesses
against him and to obtain the attendance and examination of witnesses on his
own behalf.[1392]

There are some cases which come before the courts which, although not 'criminal'   **11.340**
in English law will be treated as criminal for Convention purposes and which will,
therefore, attract the full protection of Article 6(2) and (3). There are a number of
possible candidates:

- *'Anti-social behaviour orders':*[1393] Such orders are made by magistrates on complaint to prohibit the conduct described in the order.[1394] The proceedings are
  subject to the civil burden of proof but any breach of such an order attracts a
  potential sentence of imprisonment or a fine[1395] and the court cannot impose a
  conditional discharge.[1396]
- *'Sex offender orders':*[1397] Once again, such orders are made by magistrates to prohibit specified conduct.[1398] The orders are made by magistrates on complaint
  and are subject to the civil burden of proof. Once again, the sanctions for breach
  are a fine or imprisonment and no conditional discharge can be imposed.[1399]
- *Fine enforcement proceedings.* It is uncertain whether, as a matter of English law,
  these proceedings are civil or criminal[1400] but the respondent does face the risk
  of a sentence of imprisonment,[1401] and there is a strong argument that they
  should be treated as 'criminal' for Article 6 purposes.

[1387] See para 11.174ff above; see also the cases under the Canadian Charter of Rights and Freedoms
at para 11.394ff below.
[1388] Art 6(2); see generally, para 11.236ff above.
[1389] Art 6(3)(a); see generally, para 11.241ff above.
[1390] Art 6(3)(b); see generally, para 11.243ff above.
[1391] Art 6(3)(c); see para 11.245ff above.
[1392] Art 6(3)(d); see para 11.252ff above.
[1393] Crime and Disorder Act 1998, s 1, see Baker (n 1386 above) para 4–47.
[1394] s 1(4).
[1395] s 1(10).
[1396] s 1(11).
[1397] Crime and Disorder Act 1998, s 2.
[1398] s 1(3).
[1399] s 1(8) and (9).
[1400] See *Rv Corby Justices, ex p Mort The Times*, 13 Mar 1998.
[1401] See generally, *Benham v United Kingdom* (1996) 22 EHRR 293.

- *Council tax enforcement*: Applications by local authorities to imprison for non-payment of Council tax are likely to be regarded as a criminal charge under Article 6.[1401a]

It seems likely that all these types of proceedings will be regarded as criminal for the purposes of Article 6 and will, therefore, attract the additional protections of Article 6(2) and (3) including the right to legal assistance. In addition, in relation to any charge which is 'criminal' for the purposes of the Convention it may be possible to argue that there has been a breach of Article 7 on the ground that the offence is too vague to allow an individual to foresee to a reasonable degree from the wording of a relevant provision that he is liable to a criminal offence.[1402]

11.341   **Disclosure and public interest immunity.**   It has been suggested that the provisions of the Criminal Procedure and Investigations Act 1994[1403] may be in breach of Article 6 for a number of reasons:[1404]

- *There is no independent assessment of the relevance of material*: The initial assessment for 'primary disclosure' is made by the prosecutor on the basis of schedules prepared by the police. If there is no defence statement there is no right to apply to the court for scrutiny of the adequacy of this disclosure. It is arguable that this could render the trial unfair.[1405]
- *Disclosure is 'conditional' on the service of a 'defence statement'*: It is arguable that this is a breach of the privilege against self-incrimination because the defendant is compelled to provide details of his case.[1406] A failure to serve a defence statement allows the court to draw 'such inferences as appear proper'.[1407]
- *There is no obligation to disclose material obtained in other investigations or held by other people*: It seems that the duty of disclosure under Article 6 extends to material 'to which the prosecution or the police could gain access'.[1408] As a result, the narrower statutory obligation could be a breach of Article 6.
- *There is no obligation to provide disclosure in the case of summary trials*: This would appear to be in breach of the 'equality of arms' obligation under Article 6(1). However, it should be noted that, after a review of the Convention case law, the Divisional Court have held that this practice is compatible with the Convention.[1409]

[1401a] Ibid; and see para 11.282 above.

[1402] *Kokkinakis v Greece* (1993) 17 EHRR 397 para 52; see para 11.257 above.

[1403] See para 11.97ff above.

[1404] See, Baker (n 1386 above) 4–52ff; and see generally, S Sharpe, 'Article 6 and the Disclosure of Evidence in Criminal Trials' [1999] Crim L Rev 273.

[1405] But see Sharpe (n 1404 above) 279–281.

[1406] Cf *Williams v Florida* (1970) 399 US 78 *per* Black J.

[1407] Criminal Procedure and Investigation Act 1994, s 11(3)(b).

[1408] See *Jespers v Belgium* (1981) 27 DR 61, EComm HR.

[1409] *R v Stratford Justices, ex p Imbert* (1999) 2 Cr App R 276.

In addition, there is no obligation to provide disclosure of material relevant to the credibility of defence witnesses.[1410]

The exclusion of evidence on the ground of public interest immunity may, in some circumstances, be incompatible with Article 6. If material is withheld without judicial scrutiny this will, almost certainly, be a breach of Article 6(1).[1411] However, the *ex parte* procedure which is now in place[1412] satisfies Article 6. In *Jasper and Fitt v United Kingdom*[1413] the Court held that where this procedure was followed there was no breach of Article 6(1). **11.342**

Public hearings. Criminal cases are, in general, heard in public. Hearings are held in camera for reasons such as 'national security' or the need to protect informers.[1414] Bearing in mind the approach taken by the English courts in such cases, it seems unlikely that there will be a breach of Article 6 in this regard. During jury trials, reporting restrictions are imposed as a matter of course on the legal argument. It seems unlikely this will be a breach of Article 6.[1415] However, these questions may be considered as raising issues about freedom of expression.[1415a] **11.343**

Hearing within a reasonable time.[1416] At present, under English law a prosecution can only be stayed on the ground of delay if the defendant has been prejudiced.[1417] This is not necessary under Article 6 which requires the court to consider the full period between charge and the final disposal of any appeal in order to ascertain whether there has been a determination within a reasonable time.[1418] It may also be of assistance to refer to the extensive case law that has developed in relation to comparable provisions in other jurisdictions.[1419] Under the Convention, the prosecution cannot rely on arguments about administrative difficulties.[1420] Although the complexity of the investigation can be taken into account, it seems likely that some long running prosecutions will be in breach of Article 6 even where no prejudice can be established. There have been a large number of Human Rights Act cases in Scotland where it is said that delays have breached Article 6(1).[1420a] In *McNab v Her Majesty's Advocate*[1420b] the High Court **11.344**

[1410] See para 11.96 above.
[1411] In *Rowe and Davis v United Kingdom, The Times*, 1 Mar 2000.
[1412] See para 11.292 above.
[1413] *The Times*, 1 Mar 2000.
[1414] See para 11.81 above.
[1415] But see Baker (n 1404 above), para 4–72.
[1415a] See para 15.59ff below.
[1416] See Baker (n 1404 above) para 4–75ff.
[1417] See *A-G's Reference (No 1 of 1990)* [1992] QB 630; see generally para 11.88 above.
[1418] See para 11.219ff above.
[1419] See eg the approach taken by the courts in Canada (para 11.397ff below), New Zealand (para 11.438ff below), South Africa (para 11.502ff below); Trinidad and Tobago (para 11.516ff below) and Zimbabwe (para 11.520 below).
[1420] See para 11.220 above.
[1420a] See generally, para 11.219ff above.
[1420b] 2 Sep 1999.

of Justiciary stressed that there is no universally applicable norm and that a 'reasonable time' must be assessed by reference to the particular circumstances in every case. In *Her Majesty's Advocate v Hynd*[1420c] it was said that in a straightforward case, a delay of 10 months was unacceptable. An application based on unreasonable delay under Article 6(1) does not require the applicant to show that the delay has caused serious prejudice whereas this must be proved to obtain a stay under the court's inherent jurisdiction.[1420d]

11.345   **Right to silence and self incrimination.**   The statutory provisions allowing adverse inferences to be drawn from silence[1421] may be incompatible with Article 6. Although the drawing of adverse inference from silence will not, of itself, be incompatible, proper safeguards must be in place.[1422] It seems unlikely that these provisions will be regarded as constituting 'coercion' to give evidence within the principle in *Funke*.[1423] The Court of Appeal have warned of the need for the judge to give careful directions to the jury to avoid breaches of Article 6.[1424] The amendment of the statute to ensure that adverse inferences will not be drawn when the accused has not had the benefit of legal advice[1425] is, however, likely to ensure that, in ordinary circumstances, there will be no incompatibility with Convention rights.

11.346   The use of evidence obtained from a person under compulsory powers in a subsequent criminal prosecution of that person is a breach of Article 6.[1426] However, following the amendment of certain statutory provisions such evidence is no longer used in practice unless it is introduced by the defence or the prosecution for perjury in relation to the investigation.[1427] There are, however, a number of compulsory powers which are not covered by the new legislation (such as requiring information in relation to planning enforcement proceedings). Where these powers are exercised, there will be strong Article 6 arguments against the admission of evidence obtained as a result although the question of exclusion on grounds of prejudice is a matter of discretion for the trial judge.[1427a] The courts are likely to give

---

[1420c] 9 May 2000.
[1420d] See para 11.88 above.
[1421] See para 11.108ff above.
[1422] See *Murray v United Kingdom* (1996) 22 EHRR 29 (but note, this decision related to a trial by a judge alone, in circumstances in which the other evidence was overwhelming, the position in relation to weaker cases before juries could be different, see A Ashworth, 'Article 6 and the Fairness of Trials' [1999] Crim LR 261, 267).
[1423] See *Funke v France* (1993) 16 EHRR 297; but see D Cheney, L Dickson, J Fitzpatrick and S Uglow, *Criminal Justice and the Human Rights Act 1998* (Jordans, 1999) for a contrary view.
[1424] See *R v Birchall, The Times*, 10 Feb 1998, *per* Lord Bingham CJ; and see *Condron v United Kingdom, The Times*, 9 May 2000 and para 11.287 above.
[1425] See para 11.109 above.
[1426] *Saunders v United Kingdom* (1996) 23 EHRR 313, see para 11.211ff above ; see generally, P Davies, 'Self-Incrimination, Fair Trials and the Pursuit of Corporate and Financial Wrongdoing,' in B Markesinis (ed), *The Impact of the Human Rights Bill on English Law* (Clarendon Press, 1999), 31–62.
[1427] See para 11.107 above.
[1427a] *R v Hertfordshire County Council ex p Green Environment* [2000] 2 WLR 373 (HL).

considerable weight to the approach taken in the Scots case of *Brown v Procurator Fiscal*[1427b] in which it was held that the prosecution could not lead evidence of an admission made to the police exercising the compulsory powers to question motorists under section 172 of the Road Traffic Act 1988. There is a strong argument in favour of this section being 'read down' in a similar way by the English courts.

Presumption of innocence. The common law has a strong presumption of innocence. The issue of reversal of the burden of proof has been considered in a number of jurisdictions.[1428] There are two basic categories of case in which this onus is reversed:[1429] the 'exemption cases' (where the accused bears the burden of proving that he has the benefit of an 'exception, exemption, proviso or excuse') and the 'presumption' cases (in which statute reverses the onus of proof). It seems likely that the reverse onus provisions in 'exemption cases' will not be in breach of Article 6.[1430] In 'presumption cases', the reverse onus provisions must be considered on a case-by-case basis: balancing the rights of the individual against those of society as a whole.[1431]

11.347

The courts have power to make costs orders in favour of acquitted defendants.[1432] Such orders are usually made unless there are positive reasons for not doing so. Under the former Practice Direction, a defendant's costs order could be refused if the defendant had been acquitted on a technicality.[1433] It was strongly arguable that this offended against Article 6(2) and the Practice Direction has now been amended to remove this provision.[1434]

11.348

Information as to charge. In general, the provisions as to the information to be given in charges or indictments[1435] are in accordance with the requirements of Article 6. However, if the prosecution are to rely on particular aggravating features of the offence on a plea of guilty then these features should be undisputed or the accused should be clearly 'charged' with them.[1436] It is, therefore, arguable that the prosecution is under a duty to give the defence formal notice of 'aggravating

11.349

[1427b] 4 Feb 2000; see para 4.28A (under appeal to the Privy Council).

[1428] In addition to the Convention jurisprudence (para 11.236ff above), the issue has been considered, for example, in Canada (para 11.402 below), Hong Kong, in particular the Privy Council case of *A-G of Hong Kong v Lee Kwong-kut* [1993] AC 951 (para 11.471ff below), South Africa (para 11.496ff below) and Zimbabwe (para 11.521 below).

[1429] See para 11.116 above.

[1430] C Baker (ed), *The Human Rights Act 1998: A Practitioners Guide* (Sweet & Maxwell, 1998) paras 4–80– 4–81.

[1431] See *R v DPP, ex p Kebeline* [1999] 3 WLR 972, discussed at para 11.116 above; and see *R v Lambert* [2000] 2 All ER (D) 1135.

[1432] Prosecution of Offenders Act 1985, s 16(2); a costs decision is not subject to judicial review, *Re Sampson* [1987] 1 WLR 194.

[1433] *Practice Direction (Costs in Criminal Proceedings)* (1991) 93 Cr App R 89 para 2.2.

[1434] See *Practice Direction (Crime: Costs in Criminal Proceedings) (No 2)*, The Times, 6 Oct 1999.

[1435] Indictments Act 1915, s 3.

[1436] Cf *De Salvador Torres v Spain* (1996) 23 EHRR 601.

features' which might be relevant to sentencing and which the defence may wish to have resolved at a 'Newton' hearing.[1437]

11.350 **Legal advice.** The common law and statutory right to legal advice appears to comply with Article 6 requirements. However, two areas of potential conflict have been suggested. First, in the light of the importance of the right to communicate with a lawyer without hindrance,[1438] there will be breaches if, as sometimes happens in practice, police officers seek to eavesdrop on telephone calls between persons in detention and their lawyers.

11.351 Secondly, the right to consult with a lawyer is of paramount importance in cases in which the courts can draw adverse inferences from silence.[1439] Until recently, under English law, a person could, in theory, be denied access to legal advice and then be subject to adverse inferences. Adverse inferences could also be drawn from silence prior to the arrival at the police station, when legal advice was not available. It is submitted that these were breaches of Article 6.[1440] The recent amendments to the Criminal Justice and Public Order Act 1994[1440a] are designed to ensure that such inferences cannot now be drawn where there has been no opportunity to obtain legal advice.

11.352 **Conduct of trial.** There are a number of areas in which the English practice at trial may be inconsistent with Article 6:

- The court is, at present, entitled to grant anonymity to witnesses in 'exceptional circumstances'.[1441] A stricter approach is taken under Article 6 where it has been held that granting anonymity to a witness whose evidence is 'decisive' renders the whole proceedings unfair.[1442] It seems, therefore, that the present practice may be inconsistent with Article 6.[1443]
- A conviction can, at present, be based on contested hearsay admitted under the provisions of sections 23 to 26 of the Criminal Justice Act 1988.[1444] The English courts have held that this will not be a breach of Article 6[1445] and this is

---

[1437] For 'Newton' hearings (*R v Newton* (1982) 77 Cr App R 13) see P Murphy (ed), *Blackstone's Criminal Practice 1999* (Blackstone Press, 1999) D17.2ff; and see Baker (n 1430 above) 4–91.
[1438] *S v Switzerland* (1991) 14 EHRR 670 para 48.
[1439] See para 11.108ff above.
[1440] See *Murray v United Kingdom* (1996) 22 EHRR 29 para 67; and cf *Archbold: Criminal Pleading, Practice and Evidence* (Sweet & Maxwell, 1999) 15–401 and *Condron v United Kingdom, The Times,* 9 May 2000, and see para 11.286ff above.
[1440a] See para 11.109 above.
[1441] See para 11.127 above.
[1442] *Kostovski v Netherlands* (1989) 12 EHRR 434; and *Doorsen v Netherlands* (1996) 22 EHRR 330; see para 11.217 above and see also, the discussion of witness anonymity in a 'war crimes' context, A Cassese, 'The International Criminal Tribunal for the Former Yugoslavia and Human Rights' [1997] EHRLR 329, 339-342.
[1443] See D Cheney, L Dickson, J Fitzpatrick and S Uglow, *Criminal Justice and the Human Rights Act 1998* (Jordans, 1999) 97.
[1444] See para 11.128ff above.
[1445] See para 11.129 above.

supported by a number of decisions of the Commission and the Scots courts.[1446] However, if the conviction is based 'solely or to a decisive extent' on the evidence of witnesses who the accused has not had an effective opportunity to challenge (which would be permitted under the Act), there may be a violation of Article 6.[1447]

• The hearsay rule means that the confession of a third party is not admissible in evidence at a criminal trial.[1448] It is arguable that this would render the trial of an accused unfair.[1449]

• The anonymity of the complainant in rape cases[1450] may require reconsideration;[1451]

• The power to clear the court when a child gives evidence[1452] may breach the obligation for proceedings to be heard in public.[1453]

Agents provocateurs.   Under English law, the fact that evidence has been ob-   **11.353**
tained by an agent provocateur will not, of itself, lead to its exclusion in a criminal trial.[1454] It is arguable that this is inconsistent with Article 6. In particular, it is likely that prosecution for any offence which has been 'instigated' by undercover agents of the investigating authority would be a breach of Article 6.[1455] The test to be applied is whether the effect of the evidence of an *agent provocateur* would be to deny the defendant a fair trial. The evidence of undercover police officers who give the defendant an opportunity to commit the offence but who do not 'persuade, pressure, instigate or incite' him to commit it is unlikely to have this effect.[1455a] It has been suggested that, in order to comply with Article 6, it will be necessary to put legal safeguards in place to provide proper regulation of the activities of undercover police agents, perhaps including supervision by an independent third party.[1456] This argument seems to have been accepted by the

---

[1446] *Trivedi v United Kingdom* (1997) 89 DR 136; *Quinn v United Kingdom* Application 23496/94, 11 Dec 1997 (Merits) para 80ff; see also two cases in the High Court of Justiciary *McKenna v Her Majesty's Advocate* 2000 SCCR 159 and *Her Majesty's Advocate v Nulty*, 2000 GWD 11–385.

[1447] See *Quinn*, (n 1446 above) para 80; and generally Cheney, Dickson, Fitzpatrick and Uglow, (n 444, above) 103–104; R Buxton, 'The Convention and the English law of Criminal Evidence' and J Spencer, 'European Convention and the Rules of Criminal Procedure and Evidence in England' in J Beatson, C Forsyth and I Hare, (eds), *The Human Rights Act and the Criminal Justice and Regulatory Process* (Hart Publishing, 1999).

[1448] *R v Blastland* [1986] AC 41; unlike the confession of a co-accused see *R v Myers* [1998] AC 124.

[1449] See Cheney, Dickson, Fitzpatrick and Uglow (n 1443 above) 104; and see the decision of the US Supreme Court in *Chambers v Mississippi* (1973) 410 US 295; but see the contrary view of the Commission in *Blastland v United Kingdom* (1988) 10 EHRR 528, EComm HR.

[1450] Under Sexual Offences (Amendment) Act 1976, s 4.

[1451] See the Canadian decision in *R v Seaboyer* [1991] 2 SCR 577; and see para 11.406 below.

[1452] Under Children and Young Persons Act 1933, s 37.

[1453] See the Canadian case of *Edmonton Journal v Alberta (A-G)* (1983) 146 DLR (3d) 673; QB.

[1454] See para 11.131 above.

[1455] See generally, *Teixiera de Castro v Portugal* (1998) 28 EHRR 101, see para 11.216 above.

[1455a] *Nottingham City Council v Amin* [2000] 1 WLR 1071.

[1456] See generally, O Davies, 'The Fruit of the Poisoned Tree—Entrapment and the Human Rights Act 1998' (1999) 163 JP 84.

Government and a framework for regulation is contained in Part II of the Regulation of Investigatory Powers Bill.

11.354   **Interpreters.**   There is no general right to an interpreter in English law although, in practice, one will be provided where necessary at public expense.[1457] However, the Crown Court has a discretion to order an accused to pay the costs of an interpreter.[1458] It is submitted that this is a breach of Article 6(3)(e) because such costs should always be met by the State.[1459] In addition, there is a strong argument that an accused should have a right to translations of statements and of documents relied on by the prosecution.[1459a]

11.354A   **The giving of reasons.**   The implied Article 6 right to a 'reasoned judgment'[1459b] may give rise to difficulties in criminal cases. There is a strong argument that Crown Court judges and stipendiary magistrates should, in future, give reasons for all decisions which are 'determinative' of rights.[1459c] The position is more difficult in relation to lay magistrates and juries. It is submitted that it is likely to be held that the absence of reasons for their decisions is a justified limitation on the implied right to reasons: lay participation serves the interests of justice and the decisions are reviewable by other courts.

11.355   **Sentencing.**   English law now contains a number of provisions for the confiscation of the proceeds of crime.[1460] These provisions entitle the Court to presume that property which has been in the possession of an offender prior to proceedings is the benefit of a crime. It appears that such a presumption does not breach Article 6(2). In *Welch v United Kingdom*[1461] the Court described the presumption as 'essential to the preventive scheme' and made it clear that it did not 'in any respect' call into question the powers of confiscation conferred on the court as a weapon in the fight against the scourge of drug trafficking.[1461a]

11.356   **Appeals.**   An order 'relating to a trial on indictment' in a Crown Court is not susceptible to judicial review.[1462] This means that certain orders made in the course of criminal trials may not be subject to challenge. It has been suggested that this may lead to a breach of Article 6.[1463] However, the absence of an Article 6

[1457] See para 11.125 above.

[1458] *Practice Direction (Crime Costs)* [1991] 1 WLR 498.

[1459] See *Luedicke, Belkacem and Koç v Germany* (1978) 2 EHRR 149 para 40.

[1459a] Cf the New Zealand case of *Alwen Industries Ltd and Kar Wong v Collector of Customs* [1996] 1 HRNZ 574, see para 11.432 below.

[1459b] See para 11.218 above.

[1459c] For the present practice, see para 11.92 above.

[1460] Criminal Justice Act 1988, Pt IV; Proceeds of Crime Act 1995; Drug Trafficking Act 1994.

[1461] (1995) 20 EHRR 247 para 33.

[1461a] Ibid para 36.

[1462] Supreme Court Act 1981, s 29(3), see generally R Clayton and H Tomlinson, *Judicial Review Procedure* (Wiley Chancery Law, 1997), 19–21.

[1463] See *R v Manchester Crown Court, ex p H & M*, 30 Jul 1999, Div Ct, *per* Forbes J.

'right to appeal' means that, provided that the order was made at a hearing complying with Article 6, there is unlikely to be a breach.

The Court of Appeal (Criminal Division) has the power to allow an appeal where **11.357**
a conviction is unsafe.[1464] This means that the Court could decline to quash a conviction for breach of a Convention right if it took the view that the conviction itself was safe.[1465] It is arguable that this approach is not compatible with Article 6 which requires the court to consider the issue of fairness rather than that of safety,[1465a] but the Court of Appeal held in *R v Davis and Rowe*[1465b] that the two issues of 'fairness' and 'safety' should be kept separate. It is also arguable that the Court of Appeal's approach when receiving new evidence[1466] will breach the requirement of fairness under Article 6 if the court determines the question of whether evidence is capable of being believed as a preliminary to receiving the evidence itself.[1467]

(c) Education

The Commission has held that the right not to be denied an elementary educa- **11.358**
tion falls squarely within the domain of public law, having no private law analogy
or repercussions on private rights or obligations;[1468] and it is difficult to see how
the right to education might fall within the scope of 'civil rights and obligations'.[1469] Some commentators have, nevertheless, argued that the procedure for
school admissions and expulsion are subject to Article 6 and are not compatible
with it.[1470] There may be a stronger argument that Article 6 applies in relation to
independent schools where it is alleged that the school acted in breach of contract.
The inability of a child (as opposed to his parent) to pursue the statutory right of
appeal from the special educational needs tribunal[1471] could be a breach of his
right of access to the court.

[1464] Criminal Appeal Act 1968, s 2(1) as substituted by the Criminal Appeal Act 1995; on this power, see generally *Rv Mullen (Nicholas Robert Neil)* [1999] 3 WLR 777.
[1465] See R Buxton, 'The Convention and the English law of Criminal Evidence' and D Kyle, 'The Human Rights Act: post trial and hearing' in J Beatson, C Forsyth and I Hare (eds), *The Human Rights Act and the Criminal Justice and Regulatory Process* (Hart Publishing, 1999).
[1465a] See *Condron v United Kingdom, The Times*, 9 May 2000 para 65, see para 11.287 above.
[1465b] *The Times*, 25 Jul 2000.
[1466] Under the Criminal Appeals Act 1968, s 23 as amended by the Criminal Appeals Act 1995.
[1467] D Kyle, 'The Human Rights Act: post trial and hearing' in J Beatson, C Forsyth and I Hare (eds), *The Human Rights Act and the Criminal Justice and Regulatory Process* (Hart Publishing, 1999).
[1468] *Simpson v United Kingdom* Application 14688/89, (1989) 64 DR 188, EComm HR.
[1469] See para 11.163ff above.
[1470] J Friel and D Hay, 'Education' in C Baker (ed), *The Human Rights Act 1998: A Practitioner's Guide* (Sweet & Maxwell, 1998), para 11–17; A Bradley, 'Scope for Review: the Convention Right to Education and the Human Rights Act 1988' [1999] EHRLR 395; M Supperstone, J Goudie and J Coppel, *Local Authorities and the Human Rights Act 1998* (Butterworths, 1999) 55.
[1471] *S v The Special Educational Needs Tribunal* [1996] 1 WLR 382.

(d) Employment, discrimination and disciplinary bodies

11.359 It is clear that private law employment rights are subject to Article 6 'fair hearing' protection.[1472] The position in relation to public employees is less clear cut. The Convention case law suggests that disputes concerning the recruitment, careers and termination of service of civil servants are outside the scope of Article 6 because, in many civil law jurisdictions such disputes are regarded as matters of public rather than private law.[1473] The position is different if the public employees work under contracts of employment.[1474] Since it is now generally recognised that civil servants are employed under contracts of employment;[1475] their employment rights will attract the protection of Article 6 insofar as they affect their financial interests.[1476] However, this does not mean that public employer's disciplinary procedures must provide the full range of 'fair hearing' protections for employees. Disciplinary proceedings which do not affect an employee's pay or position will not involve the determination of 'civil rights' at all.[1477] As a result, even though public employees have contractual rights in English law,[1478] it is strongly arguable[1479] that disciplinary proceedings are not ordinarily covered by Article 6.[1480]

11.360 In any event, there will be no violation of Article 6 if an employee who is dissatisfied with the result of disciplinary proceedings has recourse to the courts. The availablity of the court procedure will satisfy Article 6.[1481] The way in which unfair dismissal claims are decided under the Employment Tribunals Act 1996 will be compatible with Article 6, but the arbitration scheme for unfair dismissal disputes under the Employment Rights (Disputes Resolution) Act 1998 could raise issues about its compatibility with Article 6.[1482]

11.361 Employment tribunals are paid for, largely appointed and administered by the employment tribunal service, a Department of Trade and Industry agency. The lay members of the tribunals do not have security of tenure. As a result, it is

---

[1472] See para 11.169 above.

[1473] See *Neigel v France* RJD 1997-II 399; and see para 11.172 above.

[1474] *Darnell v United Kingdom* (1993) 18 EHRR 205.

[1475] *R v Lord Chancellor's Department, ex p Nangle* [1991] ICR 743.

[1476] See also G Morris, 'The European Convention on Human Rights and Employment: to Which Acts Does it Apply?' [1999] EHRLR 498; and the decision of the Commission in *Balfour v United Kingdom* [1997] EHRLR 665 to the contrary and the commentary at [1997] EHRLR 666.

[1477] See, generally, M Supperstone, J Goudie and J Coppel (n 1470 above) 46–48.

[1478] By contrast to public employees in Convention countries such as France.

[1479] However, disciplinary proceedings by professional bodies which affect the ability to practise the profession are within the scope of Art 6: see para 11.167 above.

[1480] See eg *Le Compte v Belgium* [1985] 5 EHRR 533 para 25; *De Compte v European Parliament* [1991] ECR II-781.

[1481] See para 11.197 above.

[1482] See B Hepple, 'The Impact on Labour Law', in B Markesinis (ed), *The Impact of the Human Rights Bill on English Law* (Clarendon Press, 1999), 71.

arguable that the Employment Tribunals are not 'independent' for the purposes of Article 6.[1482a] The lack of independence is particularly clear when Employment Tribunals are considering claims for redundancy payments from the Secretary of State for Trade and Industry.[1483]

11.362 The inability of an applicant to obtain legal aid to pursue a claim before the employment tribunal (such as a lengthy and complex discrimination case) might breach the right of access to the court under Article 6.[1484]

11.363 It is well established that Article 6 applies to disciplinary procedures affecting the professions when the right to practice is in issue.[485] Where the internal procedures fail to comply with Article 6, the critical issue is whether any subsequent judicial control does so. The Commission has recently held that the General Medical Council procedure complies with Article 6;[1486] however, the position may be different where it is necessary to investigate issues of fact and the challenge is by way of judicial review.[1487]

(e) Family law

11.364 Rights dealt with in family law cases are 'civil rights' under Article 6.[1488] The development of English family law has been strongly influenced by decisions under Article 6.[1489] Nevertheless, there are a number of areas of family law where the present English law or practice may be in breach of fair hearing rights.

11.365 The right of access to the courts may be breached by the provisions of section 91(14) of the Children Act 1989 which allows the court to refuse to hear an application if there is no need for renewed judicial investigation.[1490] The test is 'does the application demonstrate that there is any need for renewed judicial investigation?'[1490a] Bearing in mind the fact that the bar is not an absolute one, it seems that section 91(14) will be found to be compatible with the Convention. The child

---

[1482a] See para 11.223ff above.

[1483] *Smith v Secretary of State for Trade and Industry* [2000] ICR 69.

[1484] See para 11.189 above.

[1485] See for example *König v Germany* (1978) 2 EHRR 170 (medicine); *H v Belgium* (1987) 10 EHRR 339 (law); *Guchez v Belgium* (1984) 40 DR 100, EComm HR (architecture); and see, generally, para 11.167 above.

[1486] *Stefan v United Kingdom* (1997) 25 EHRR CD 130; *Wickramsinghe v United Kingdom* [1998] EHRLR 338.

[1487] See para 11.198 above.

[1488] But not the obligation to pay assessments worked out by the Child Support Agency which are public rights outside Art 6: *Logan v United Kingdom* (1996) 22 EHRR CD 178.

[1489] In particular, the Children Act 1989 was, in part, a response to the decision in *R v United Kingdom* (1987) 10 EHRR 74, see para 11.273 above.

[1490] *Re A (Application for Leave)* [1998] 1 FLR 1, CA.

[1490a] See generally, H Swindells *et al*, *Family Law and the Human Rights Act 1998* (Family Law, 1999) para 7.20ff.

himself has no absolute right to make an application under the Children Act; but this appears to be in accordance with the European Convention on the Exercise of Children's Rights.[1491] It is arguable that the length and complexity of public law child proceedings means that they would attract a right to legal assistance under the principle identified in the *Airey* case.[1492] Such legal aid is available at present[1493] but any restriction could be a breach of the right of access to the court.

11.366 Ancillary relief proceedings involve the determination of civil rights and obligations but are held in chambers.[1493a] It is strongly arguable that this is a breach of Article 6(1).[1494] In addition, the present practice in all family proceedings of giving judgment in private appears to be a breach of the express rights in Article 6(1).[1494a] A number of Article 6 issues arise in relation to proceedings under the Child Abduction and Custody Act 1985 which are, by their nature, summary.[1495]

(f) Health care

11.367 Reliance on Article 6 may assist in clarifying the approach to be taken when declarations are sought in relation to medical treatment for mentally handicapped patients.[1496] Although the court must consider the patient's best interests, it often deals with this question by deciding whether the proposed action is in accordance with an accepted body of medical opinion, in accordance with the '*Bolam* test'.[1497] However, it is arguable that the obligation to ensure effective access to the court means that the court will have to address the issue of the patient's best interests directly.

(g) Housing

11.368 Although Article 6 applies to property rights[1498] (and would apply for example, to compulsory purchase orders), the term 'civil rights and obligations'[1499] does not extend to housing management decisions or issues concerning homelessness. At present disputes about admission to and exclusion from the Housing Register are

---

[1491] See generally, M Horowitz, G Kingscote and M Nicholls, *Rayden and Jackson on Divorce and Family Matters: The Human Rights Act 1998, A Special Bulletin for Family Lawyers* (Butterworths, 1999) para 5.10.
[1492] *Airey v Ireland* (1979) 2 EHRR 305; see para 11.189 above.
[1493] Legal Aid Act 1988, s 15(3)(c).
[1493a] For a discussion of the circumstances in which there should be a public hearing in family cases see *Re B (Minors) (Contact)* [1994] 2 FLR 1.
[1494] Cf Horowitz, Kingscote and Nicholls (n 1491 above) para 6.04.
[1494a] See *Re P B (Hearings in Open Court)* [1996] 2 FLR 765 and generally Swindells, *et al* (n 1490a above) para 8.182ff above.
[1495] See *R B (Minors)(Abduction)(No 2)* [1993] 1 FLR 993; see generally, Horowitz, Kingscote and Nicholls (n 1491above), para 6.47ff.
[1496] See generally, I Kennedy and A Grubb, *Principles of Medical Law* (Oxford University Press, 1998) paras 4.133–4.136.
[1497] See *Bolam v Friern Hospital Management Committee* [1957] 1 WLR 582, 586.
[1498] See para 11.166 above.
[1499] See para 11.163ff above.

decided under a local authority's own review procedures without any right of appeal to the court.[1499a] It has been suggested that this may be a breach of Article 6.[1499b] Difficulties also may arise in relation to the procedure for terminating introductory tenancies created under the Housing Act 1996.[1499c] Under section 127(2) of the Act the court is obliged to make a possession order provided the local authority or registered social landlord has served notice of proceedings under section 128. The only way a tenant can protect his position is to request the landlord to review his decision to seek possession under section 129; and that decision may ultimately be challenged in judicial review proceedings.[1499d] However, it is strongly arguable that the procedure breaches the tenant's civil right determined by an 'independent and impartial' tribunal.[1499e] The practice of obtaining a warrant of possession when there has been a breach of a suspended order without a hearing or notice has also been said to breach Article 6.[1499f]

On the other hand, it is well established that Article 6 covers social welfare benefits.[1500] The determination of housing benefit and its review by housing benefit boards does not comply with the obligation to ensure an independent and impartial tribunal.[1501] However, the boards' decision is subject to judicial review; and it can be argued that this is sufficient to ensure compliance with Article 6.[1502] **11.369**

(h) Local government law

Article 6 is likely to have considerable implications over a number of local authority activities. Many of these will involve the determination of what the Convention regards as 'civil rights and obligations'. However, because administrative procedures are involved, it is not necessary to ensure full 'internal Article 6 compliance': the availability of judicial review will usually be sufficient to ensure that, overall, the procedures adopted are 'fair'.[1502a] The following areas are considered: licensing, community care and child protection. **11.370**

Licensing. Local Authorities have extensive licensing powers.[1503] Since a licence to engage in commercial activity is a civil right for the purpose of Article 6,[1504] **11.371**

[1499a] See Housing Act 1996, s 164.
[1499b] J Luba, 'Acting on Rights—The Housing Implications of the Human Rights Act', Lecture, Sep 1999.
[1499c] Housing Act 1996, ss 124–133.
[1499d] *Manchester City Council v Cochrane* (1996) 31 HLR 810.
[1499e] See para 11.222ff above.
[1499f] See Luba (n 1499b above).
[1500] See para 11.170 above.
[1501] See para 11.222ff above.
[1502] See para 11.198 above.
[1502a] See para 11.304ff above.
[1503] For example, taxis, theatres, street trading. For a list of their principal licensing and registration functions, see App D to S Bailey (ed), *Cross on Local Government Law* (9th edn, Sweet & Maxwell, 1996).
[1504] *Tre Traktörer Aktiebolag v Sweden* (1989) 13 EHRR 309 (withdrawal of alcohol licence; *Axelsson v Sweden* (1989) 65 DR 99, EComm HR (refusal to grant taxi licence).

there is a strong argument that 'fair hearing rights' will apply to the grant or withdrawal of licences, including the right to a public oral hearing[1505] before an independent[1506] and impartial[1507] tribunal with a reasoned judgment.[1508] The internal procedures for considering licences are most unlikely to comply with Article 6 guarantees. However, in many instances an applicant will have a right of appeal to the magistrates' or Crown Court. If, on the other hand, the applicant is limited to a judicial review challenge, then compliance with Article 6 will depend on whether he has had a sufficient opportunity to dispute the primary issues of fact.

11.372　A theatre licence may be granted at the discretion of the licensing authority.[1509] The applicant has a right of appeal against a refusal to grant a licence (or to impose conditions and restrictions) to the magistrates' court[1510] which has the power to consider all disputes of fact and law. The licensing authority for cinemas in Greater London is the appropriate borough council;[1511] elsewhere it is the district council.[1512] A person aggrieved by the refusal, revocation or with conditions or restrictions can apply to the Crown Court.[1513] Music and dance licences in Greater London are granted by the appropriate borough council[1514] and a right of appeal to the magistrates' court.[1515] Outside Greater London it is the responsibility, for granting dance and music licences, of the district council.[1516] There are again rights of appeal against the refusal of a licence or against its terms.[1517] In principle, third parties who can show that the 'civil rights and obligations' are affected by granting the licence may have a right to make representations under Article 6.

11.373　The control of licensing sex establishments in Greater London is the responsibility of the relevant borough council (or Common Council of the City of London) and outside Greater London the district councils.[1518] There are some restrictions on the right of appeal to the magistrates[1519] so that the only remedy available is an application for judicial review. In those cases, it may be strongly arguable that

---

[1505]　See para 11.206 above.

[1506]　See para 11.223ff above.

[1507]　See para 11.225ff above.

[1508]　See para 11.218 above.

[1509]　Theatre Act 1968, Sch 1, para 1.

[1510]　Ibid s 14(1).

[1511]　Including the Common Council of the City: see Cinema Act 1985, ss 3(1), 21(1).

[1512]　Ibid ss 3(10), 21(1).

[1513]　Ibid s 16.

[1514]　Or Common Council of the City: see London Local Government Act 1963, s 52(3), Sch 12; Local Government Act 1985, s 16, Sch 7, para 1. Under the Local Government (Miscellaneous Provisions) Act 1982, s 1(1), the Act does not extend to Greater London.

[1515]　Local Government Act 1963, Sch 12, para 19.

[1516]　Local Government (Miscellaneous Provisions) Act 1982, s 1, Sch 1, para 22; for the Scilly Isles, it is the Council of the Isles.

[1517]　Local Government (Miscellaneous Provisions) Act 1982, Sch 1, para 17(1)(2).

[1518]　Local Government (Miscellaneous Provisions) Act 1982, s 2.

[1519]　Ibid Sch 3, para 17.

Article 6 has been breached. The regime for licensing taxis is different in the Metropolitan police area and the City of London[1520] from that which applies for outside those areas.[1521] Inside the Metropolitan area the refusal, suspension and revocation of a licence can be appealed to the magistrates.[1522] Outside the Metropolitan area the refusal of a district council to grant a licence can be appealed to the Crown Court.[1523] A number of local authorities licence the employment of 'bouncers' at night clubs by operating doorman licensing schemes. These procedures are non statutory and might appear to breach the Article 6 requirement that a tribunal must be 'established by law'. However, if such schemes were challenged, the proceedings themselves would be heard before an independent tribunal and it is submitted that these schemes are not incompatible with Article 6.

Community care.   Article 6 may affect a range of decisions in relation to community care. It is well established that social security benefits fall within the scope of Article 6[524] and it is arguable that where an applicant's circumstances are so severe as to require some level of service provision,[1525] decisions about the level and nature of his provision under the Chronically Sick and Disabled Persons Act 1970 must be made in accordance with the fair trial guarantees under Article 6.[1526] Charging decisions[1527] may also be subject to Article 6 in the same way as decisions concerning social security contributions[1528] although the position is not clear cut.[1529]   **11.374**

Article 6 may also require local authorities to take a different approach when considering the cancellation of registration under the Registered Homes Act 1984. It has been suggested that the 'without notice' procedure to cancel registration urgently[1530] may be vulnerable under Article 6.[1531] The practice of many authorities to hear applications to cancel registrations[1532] in private hearings may also be questionable, not least because they are obliged to inform residents and relatives   **11.375**

[1520] Metropolitan Police Carriage Act 1969, s 9, the London Cab Order 1934 (SR & O 1934 No 1346).
[1521] Town Police Clauses Act 1847 ss 37–68, the Town Police Clauses Act 1889, s 76 Public Health Act 1925, the Local Government (Miscellaneous Provisions) Act 1976, Pt II and ss 10–17.
[1522] Transport Act 1985, s 17.
[1523] Public Health Act 1975, s 171(4); Public Health Acts Amendment Act 1980, ss 2(1), 7(1)(b).
[1524] See para 11.170 above.
[1525] *R v Gloucestershire County Council, ex p Barry* [1997] 2 AC 584.
[1526] M Supperstone, J Goudie and J Coppel, *Local Authorities and the Human Rights Act 1998* (Butterworths, 1999) 74.
[1527] Under eg s 22 of the National Assistance Act 1948 or s 17 of the Health and Social Security Adjudications Act 1993.
[1528] *Schouten and Meldrum v Netherlands* (1994) 19 EHRR 432.
[1529] Contrast the views expressed in Supperstone, Goudie and Coppel, (n 1526 above) 74, relying on the decisions holding that tax assessments are not subject to Art 6: see para 11.173 above.
[1530] Registered Homes Act 1984, s 11.
[1531] R McCarthy, 'The Human Rights Act and Social Services Functions', lecture 10 May 1999.
[1532] Registered Homes Act 1984, s 10.

of their intention.[1533] The critical question in any particular case is whether the procedure as a whole breaches Article 6.

11.376 **Child protection register.** It has been argued that entering a child on the child protection register attracts Article 6 protection. A similar argument could be directed to decisions to place a person on the consultancy service index as being unsuitable to work with children.[1533a] However, it is likely that it will be held that such a step does not involve the determination of civil rights but should be characterised as an interim protective measure.[1534]

(i) Planning and environmental law

11.377 **Introduction.** The fair trial rights under Article 6 have been held to apply to a wide variety of situations including any decision granting or refusing planning permission and to any decisions in relation to enforcement proceedings.[1535] The Court has held that Article 6 applies to a decision to grant permission to extract water from a well,[1536] the application of nature conservation laws,[1537] a permit to build a house,[1538] long term planning blight[1539] and enforcement proceedings under the Town and Country Planning Act.[1540] The existing planning appeal procedures were held by the Court in *Bryan v United Kingdom*[1541] to meet the requirements of Article 6(1). However, it should be noted that in that case there was no dispute regarding the primary facts and the position may be different where the underlying factual position is contested.[1542]

11.378 **Third party rights.** The Court has also held that a third party whose property value is adversely affected by the grant of planning permission has Article 6(1) rights.[1543] Under the English planning system a third party has no right of appeal to the Secretary of State and can only challenge planning permission by taking judicial review proceedings. The absence of the ability to challenge a decision on its merits may breach Article 6(1) particularly, where the primary facts are disputed

---

[1533] See eg Ombudsman Complaint No 94/13/1323.

[1533a] See now, Protection of Children Act 1999 (s 4 provides for an appeal to a Tribunal against a decision to include a person on the list).

[1534] Supperstone, Goudie and Coppel, (n 1526 above) 86; and see *R v Secretary of State for Health, ex p C, The Times*, 1 Mar 2000 in which it was held that inclusion on the consultancy index was not 'determinative' of any right.

[1535] See generally, T Corner, 'Planning, Environment and the European Convention on Human Rights' [1998] JPL 301.

[1536] *Zander v Sweden* (1990) 18 EHRR 175.

[1537] *Oerlemans v Netherlands* (1991) 15 EHRR 561.

[1538] *Skärby v Sweden* (1990) 13 EHRR 90.

[1539] *Sporrong and Lönnroth v Sweden* (1982) 5 EHRR 35.

[1540] *Bryan v United Kingdom* (1995) 21 EHRR 342.

[1541] (1995) 21 EHRR 342; see also *ISKCON v United Kingdom* (1994) 76-A DR 90, EComm HR.

[1542] See para 11.198 above.

[1543] *Ortenberg v Austria* (1994) 19 EHRR 524.

although it is again arguable that recourse to judicial review is sufficient for these purposes. Nevertheless, the right to Article 6(1) protection will make it easier to pressurise the Secretary of State to call in controversial planning applications.[1544] Some authorities allow third parties to make representations to planning committees; this practice will go some way to prevent a finding that Article 6(1) has been breached.

Where a person is refused permission to be heard at a public hearing concerning a structure plan,[1545] he is a person aggrieved for the purposes of applying to the High Court to challenge its validity.[1546] However, it may be difficult in these circumstances to demonstrate that the applicant has had access to the court on the factual merits. **11.379**

Plan making powers. The powers of local authorities to make plans will also be affected by Article 6. Decisions on structure plans, local plans or waste plans may in some circumstances affect 'civil rights and obligations'[1547] because of their impact on property or commercial activities. It has been argued that the current procedures for hearing and determining local plan objections may well be in breach of Article 6(1).[1548] A local planning authority makes a final decision on its own proposals so that it is neither independent[1549] nor impartial.[1550] The local planning inspector cannot satisfy Article 6 since his function is not to make a determination but to report with recommendations and the power of the Secretary of State is not sufficient to meet Article 6. It is unclear whether the position is saved by the right of a statutory appeal,[1551] especially if the local authority rejects the inspector's recommendations. **11.380**

It has been suggested that a number of difficulties may also arise for authorities in making development plans.[1552] A planning authority must consult in relation to proposed structure plan policies and to consider representations[1553] and must give adequate reasons when dealing with objections to structure plan policies.[1554] It may be criticised because there is no right of hearing at an examination in public of a structure plan[1555] and it must adequately consult on a proposed local plan or **11.381**

[1544] See generally, T Corner, 'Planning, Environment and the European Convention on Human Rights' [1998] JPL 301.
[1545] Under the Town and Country Planning Act, s 35B(4).
[1546] Under the Town and Country Planning Act, s 287.
[1547] See para 11.163ff above.
[1548] T Kitson, 'The European Convention on Human Rights and Local Plans' [1998] JPL 321.
[1549] See para 11.223ff above.
[1550] See para 11.225ff above.
[1551] On the principles of *Bryan v United Kingdom* (n 1540 above).
[1552] M Supperstone, J Goudie and J Coppel, *Local Authorities and the Human Rights Act 1998* (Butterworths, 1999) 113.
[1553] Town and Country Planning Act 1990, s 33.
[1554] See eg *Modern Homes (Whitworth) v Lancaster County Council* [1998] EGCS 73.
[1555] Town and Country Planning Act 1990, s 35B(4).

urban development plan and consider the objections made.[1556] It must give proper consideration to the inspector's recommendations and give adequate reasons for departing from them[1557] and it may be subject to proceedings for failing to hold a second public inquiry if it accepts changes to the plan which prejudice third parties.[1558]

11.381A **Land development.** There are potential conflicts of interest where a local authority seeks to develop land which it owns and is the relevant planning authority which is empowered to grant planning permission. In such circumstances its decisions will be vulnerable to challenge by persons who are affected on the ground that the decision was not made by an 'independent and impartial tribunal'.[1558a]

11.382 **Evidence under compulsory powers.** The use of evidence in criminal proceedings which is obtained under powers to compel witnesses to give evidence in relation to breaches of planning enforcement[1559] and the regulation of waste on land[1560] could result in breaches of Article 6.[1561] The question of exclusion of potentially incriminating answers on the ground of prejudice is a matter for the discretion of the trial judge.[1562] However, there are likely to be challenges to prosecutions on the basis of evidence obtained by use of these powers. If the evidence is obtained in the course of a criminal investigation it is likely to be excluded but it may be admissible if it was initially obtained by compulsion for non-criminal 'regulatory' purposes.[1562a]

(j) Police law

11.383 Article 6(1) rights apply to those 'charged' with criminal offences in accordance with the special Convention meaning of this term which would cover a person under arrest.[1563] However, the manner in which Article 6 is to be applied during the preliminary investigation depends on the circumstances of the case.[1564] For example, Article 6 does not give an accused the right to examine a witness being questioned by the police.[1565] It seems unlikely that Article 6 will provide arrested suspects with any additional rights.

[1556] See eg *Stirk v Bridgnorth District Council* [1996] 73 P & CR 439; *Miller v Wycombe District Council* [1997] JPL 951; *Tyler v Avon County Council* [1996] 73 P & CR 335.

[1557] See eg *Drexfine Holdings v Cherwell District Council* [1998] JPL 361.

[1558] See eg *R v Teeside District Council* [1998] JPL 23.

[1558a] See para 11.222 above.

[1559] Town and Country Planning Act 1990, s 171C and D.

[1560] Environmental Protection Act 1990, ss 71 and 34(5); and see *R v Hertfordshire County Council, ex p Green Environmental Industries* [2000] 2 WLR 373.

[1561] See para 11.346 above.

[1562] See *R v Hertfordshire County Council, ex p Green Environmental Industries* (n 1560 above).

[1562a] See generally, *Brown v Procurator Fiscal* 4 Feb 2000; see para 11.346 above.

[1563] See para 11.180 above.

[1564] *Imbrioscia v Switzerland* (1993) 17 EHRR 441, 38.

[1565] *X v Germany* (1979) 17 DR 231, EComm HR.

(k) Prison law

The right of access to the courts under Article 6 was, of course, first established in a case involving the rights of prisoners in the United Kingdom.[1566] The question arises as to whether all prison disciplinary hearings fall within the scope of Article 6(3).[1567] It could be argued that the threat of loss of remission means that disciplinary allegations are 'criminal charges'.[1568] If so, prisoners would be entitled to Article 6(3) rights, including the right to legal representation.[1569]

11.384

(l) Social security

It is clear that social security benefits come within the scope of 'civil rights and obligations'.[1570] Nevertheless, it is unlikely that Article 6 will have a substantial impact on English social security law.[1571] Four areas of potential impact have been identified. The first concerns the length of time taken to reach determinations of social security entitlements, particularly where the Social Security Commissioner has set aside a decision and remitted it for a fresh hearing. The delays are often considerable and may breach the requirement to a hearing within a reasonable time.[1572] Secondly, it is arguable[1573] that the approach taken by the Commissioner to refusing an oral hearing where he is satisfied that it can be determined without one may be in breach of Article 6(1).[1574] Thirdly, it might be said that the failure to extend legal aid to appeals before the Commissioner breaches the effective right of access to the court.[1575] Finally, it is arguable that the system for challenging national insurance contributions, which makes no provision for a hearing, contravenes Article 6.[1576]

11.385

[1566] *Campbell and Fell v United Kingdom* (1984) 7 EHRR 165.

[1567] See generally, S Livingstone and T Owen, *Prison Law* (2nd edn, Oxford University Press, 1999) para 9.25.

[1568] See V Treacey, 'Prisoners' Rights Lost in Semantics' (1989) 28 Howard J of Criminal Law 27, but see *Pelle v France* (1986) 50 DR 263, EComm HR (potential loss of 18-days' remission, not sufficient), C Kidd, 'Disciplinary Proceedings and the Right to a Fair Criminal Trial Under the European Convention on Human Rights' (1987) 36 ICLQ 856.

[1569] Livingstone and Owen (n 1567 above) paras 9.35–9.42; this would reverse the decision in *Hone v Maze Prison Board of Visitors* [1988] 1 AC 379.

[1570] *Feldbrugge v Netherlands* (1986) 8 EHRR 425 (sickness benefit); *Deumeland v Germany* (1986) EHRR 448 (industrial injury pensions); in *Salesi v Italy* (1993) 26 EHRR 187 para 19 the Court extended Art 6 from social insurance benefits to welfare assistance where there was no entitlement to insurance based benefits; see also *Schuler-Zgraggen v Switzerland* (1993) 16 EHRR 405; *Schouten and Meldrum v Switzerland* (1994) 19 EHRR 432; and see generally, para 11.170 above.

[1571] See generally R White, 'Social Security' in C Baker (ed), *The Human Rights Act 1998: A Practitioner's Guide* (Sweet & Maxwell, 1998) paras 12-21–12-24.

[1572] See para 11.219ff above.

[1573] For the right to an oral hearing see para 11.206 above.

[1574] Under the Social Security Commissioner Procedure Regulations 1987, SI 1987 214 (as amended).

[1575] See para 11.185ff above.

[1576] J Peacock and F Fitzpatrick, 'Tax Law' in Baker (n 1571 above) para 14–29.

Appendix 1: The Canadian Charter of Rights

(1) Introduction

11.386 A number of sections of the Canadian Charter of Rights and Freedoms deal with 'legal process rights'. The most important of these is the right to 'fundamental justice' to be found in section 7 which provides:

> Everyone has the right to life, liberty and security of the person and the right not to be deprived thereof except in accordance with the principles of fundamental justice

Specific guarantees in relation to 'Proceedings in criminal and penal matters' are set out in section 11 which provides:

> Any person charged with an offence has the right
> (a) to be informed without unreasonable delay of the specific offence.
> (b) to be tried within a reasonable time.
> (c) not to be compelled to be a witness in proceedings against that person in respect of the offence.
> (d) to be presumed innocent until proven guilty according to law in a fair and public hearing by an independent and impartial tribunal.
> (e) not to be denied reasonable bail without just cause.
> (f) except in the case of an offence under military law tried before a military tribunal, to the benefit of trial by jury where the maximum punishment for the offence is imprisonment for five years or a more severe punishment.
> (g) not to be found guilty on account of any act or omission unless, at the time of the act or omission, it constituted an offence under Canadian or international law or was criminal according to the general principles of law recognized by the community of nations.
> (h) if finally acquitted of the offence, not to be tried for it again and if finally found guilty and punished for the offence, not to be tried or punished for it again.
> (i) if found guilty of the offence and if the punishment for the offence has been varied between the time of commission and the time of sentencing, to the benefit of the lesser punishment.

The right in subsection (e) (right to reasonable bail), has been considered in relation to the right to liberty and security of the person[1577] and will not be addressed here.

11.387 Three other sections of the Charter provide 'fair trial rights'. Section 13 is headed 'Self-incrimination' and provides:

> A witness who testifies in any proceedings has the right not to have any incriminating evidence so given used to incriminate that witness in any other proceedings, except in a prosecution of perjury or for the giving of contradictory evidence.

Section 14 deals with interpreters and provides:

> A party or witness in any proceedings who does not understand or speak the language in which the proceedings are conducted or who is deaf has the right to the assistance of an interpreter.

[1577] See para 10.233 above.

(2) The scope of the rights

(a) Fundamental justice

The 'principles of fundamental justice' is not a phrase which had an established meaning **11.388**
in pre-Charter case law; nor is it further defined in the Charter. It did appear in the
Canadian Bill of Rights of 1960,[1578] but because it is used there in connection with a reference to a 'fair hearing', the phrase 'fundamental justice' was regarded as equivalent to the
well-defined notion of 'natural justice'. By comparison, the phrase 'fundamental justice' is
used in section 7 independently of any reference to 'fair hearing' or other concept that
might imply a purely procedural content.

If, as the legislative history of the Charter suggests 'fundamental justice' means simply **11.389**
'natural justice',[1579] the courts are entitled to review only the appropriateness and fairness
of the procedures enacted for a deprivation of life, liberty or security of the person, and
may not review the substantive justice of the deprivation. However, it is now clear that
while the principles of fundamental justice do include a requirement of procedural fairness[1580] which may vary depending on the context,[1581] section 7 also has substantive content.[1582]

In *B C Motor Vehicle Reference*[1583] the Supreme Court of Canada did not follow the leg- **11.390**
islative history of the Charter, but decided that 'fundamental justice' included *both* substantive and procedural justice. On the assumption that sections 8 to 14 are merely
illustrative of the deprivations of fundamental justice caught by section 7, and that they
expressly extend beyond procedural guarantees, Lamer J concluded that section 7 must
provide something more than procedural protection.[1584] The Supreme Court went on to
hold that a strict liability criminal offence which provided for imprisonment in the absence of proving *mens rea* facilitated a deprivation of liberty which was not in accordance
with the principles of fundamental justice; the offence created a substantive injustice in violation of section 7.[1585] However, none of the judgments in *B C Motor Vehicle Reference* defines the principles of fundamental justice beyond the assertion that they are to be found

---

[1578] The Canadian Bill of Rights guarantees the right to a fair hearing in accordance with the principles of fundamental justice for the determination of his rights and obligations.

[1579] The drafters of the Charter sought to avoid the importation into Canada of the American 'due process' doctrine established in *US v Lochner* (1905) 198 US 45, by which the US Supreme Court had struck down substantive federal and state labour laws during 1905 to 1937; see P Hogg, *Constitutional Law of Canada*, (4th edn, Carswell, 1997), para 44.10.

[1580] See *Singh v Minister of Employment and Immigration* [1985] 1 SCR 177; *Pearlman v Manitoba Law Society* [1991] 2 SCR 869, 882; 'The Principles of Fundamental Justice' (1991) 29 Osgoode Hall Law Journal 51; *R v Lyons* [1987] 2 SCR 309.

[1581] *R v Lyons* (n 1580 above) 361.

[1582] In *R v Fisher* (1985) 39 MVR 287, Scollin J said that 'the protection of basic rights by the principles of fundamental justice must mean more than a mere guarantee of a scenic route to the prison-camp', and that 'life, liberty and security of the person are illusory if they can be unjustly taken away with impunity'; see generally, *Singh v Minister of Employment and Immigration* [1985] 1 SCR 177; *Pearlman v Manitoba Law Society* [1991] 2 SCR 869, 882.

[1583] *Reference Re Section 94(2) of Motor Vehicle Act (British Columbia)* [1985] 2 SCR 486.

[1584] Ibid 502-503; this is problematic, as was pointed out by Wilson J in dissent, as ss 8 through 14 are in fact drafted as free-standing provisions rather than as examples of deprivations under s 7.

[1585] See also, *R v Pontes (A-G of Canada intervening)* [1996] 1 LRC 134 (no violation of Art 7 when offence of absolute liability punishable only by a fine).

'in the basic tenets of the legal system'.[1586] Subsequent decisions have not clarified the meaning of 'fundamental justice'.[1587]

11.391 A number of 'principles of fundamental justice' have been suggested in the cases:

- the right to silence;[1588]
- the principle that the law should be fixed, predetermined, accessible and understandable to the public;[1589]
- the right to present full answer and defence;[1590]
- the right to cross-examine witnesses.[1591]

(b) Rights in criminal proceedings: introduction

11.392 Section 11 of the Charter provides constitutional protection for proceedings which relate to the determination of offences that are criminal in nature. In contrast to the Convention, section 11 of the Charter does not provide any such protection for civil proceedings. It does not apply to 'private domestic or disciplinary matters which are regulatory, protective or corrective',[1592] to persons whose conduct is the subject of a public inquiry,[1593] or to proceedings before securities commissions with power to issue cease-trading orders.[1594] Sections 13 and 14, in relation to freedom from incrimination and the right to an interpreter, applies to a witness (and in the case of section 14 a party) who testifies in 'any proceedings', not just criminal proceedings. Section 14 is further limited to situations in which the party or witness is deaf or does not understand or speak the language.

(c) 'Person charged with an offence'

11.393 Section 11 applies to every 'person', whether a natural person or corporation,[1595] who is charged with an offence. A person is 'charged' within the meaning of section 11 either when an information is sworn alleging an offence against him or, in the absence of an information, a direct indictment is laid against him.[1596] It is not sufficient that the person is merely suspected of the offence, or that the impact of the criminal process is felt by him.[1597] An accused is not 'charged' by reason of an application that he be designated a

---

[1586] Lamer J, [1985] 2 SCR 486, at 503 and 512; Wilson J accepts this definition, referring, at 530 to 'a fundamental tenet of our justice system'.

[1587] See *Thomson Newspapers Ltd v Canada (Director of Investigation and Research, Resrictive Trade Practices Commission)* [1990] 1 SCR 425, in which five judges gave five different opinions as to the applicable basic tenet of the legal system; see the criticism in Hogg, (n 1579 above)1079ff.

[1588] see para 11.419ff below.

[1589] *United Nurses of Alberta v Alberta (A-G)* [1992] 1 SCR 901.

[1590] *R v Seaboyer* [1991] 2 SCR 577.

[1591] *R v Osolin* [1993] 4 SCR 595.

[1592] *R v Wigglesworth* [1987] 2 SCR 541; and see *Re James and Law Society of B C* (1982) 143 DLR (3d) 379; see also *Trumbley and Pugh v Metropolitan Toronto Police* [1987] 2 SCR 577.

[1593] *Starr v Houlden* [1990] 1 SCR 1366.

[1594] *Holoboff v Alberta* (1991) 80 DLR (4th) 603.

[1595] See *R v CIP* [1992] 1 SCR 843 (s 11(b) applies to a corporation) and generally, P Hogg, (n 1579 above) para 34.1(b), 835-837.

[1596] See *R v Kalanj* [1989] 1 SCR 1594 *per* MacIntyre J at 1607; also *R v Chabot* [1980] 2 SCR 985 where the term 'charge' in the Criminal Code was interpreted to mean that 'a formal written complaint has been made against the accused and a prosecution initiated'.

[1597] Ibid; the view of dissenting judges Lamer and Wilson JJ was that the accused had been 'charged' upon his initial arrest, as that was the point at which he 'felt the impact of the criminal justice system', even though he was released and an information was not sworn until eight-months later, contrast the position under the Convention, see para 11.182 above.

'dangerous offender',[1598] by the making of an injunction against him for picketing in contempt of court,[1599] or by extradition proceedings to determine whether there is sufficient evidence to warrant his surrender to a foreign jurisdiction.[1600] As a result, section 11 has no application to any of these cases.

(d) 'Offence'

Section 11 rights apply if a person has been charged with an 'offence', meaning any provincial or federal law to which a penal sanction attaches. Two alternative tests as to what constitutes an offence were promulgated in *R v Wigglesworth*:[1601] the matter must either be 'by its very nature' a criminal proceeding,[1602] or lead to a true penal consequence.[1603] In *Wigglesworth*, a police officer, was tried and found guilty by a police tribunal of assaulting a prisoner in the course of interrogation, and was fined $300. Under the first test, the violation was found to constitute an internal and disciplinary matter for regulation within a limited private sphere and was not by nature a criminal proceeding. Nevertheless, because the offence carried the risk of imprisonment of up to one year, it satisfied the second test of attaching a true penal consequence. The Court said that a fine might also constitute a 'true penal consequence' if its magnitude indicated that the purpose of imposing it was to redress a wrong done to society at large.

11.394

In *R v Genereux*[1604] the Supreme Court found that a member of the armed forces faced with court martial proceedings for breach of the Code of Service was charged with an offence under section 11. Because the Code designated as a 'service offence' any act punishable under the federal Criminal Code or other Act of Parliament and substituted service tribunals for ordinary courts where the offence was committed by a member of the armed forces, proceedings were by 'nature' criminal. In addition, the court martial's power to impose imprisonment met the 'true penal consequence' test. In contrast, in *R v Shubley*[1604a] it was held that prison disciplinary proceedings did not constitute a trial for an offence for the purposes of section 11.

11.395

(3) Criminal trial guarantees

(a) Section 11(a): specific information

The section 11(a) right to be informed without unreasonable delay of the specific offence entrenches the right that existed prior to the Charter under the Criminal Code, provincial

11.396

[1598] *R v Lyons* [1987] 2 SCR 309: dangerous-offender designation has been found to be a part of the sentencing process and not a new 'charge' subject to the protections of s 11.

[1599] *BCGEU v British Columbia* [1988] 2 SCR 214: s 11 rights would only apply in the case of a breach of the injunction, upon initiation of proceedings against the individual.

[1600] *R v Schmidt* [1987] 1 SCR 500.

[1601] *R v Wigglesworth* [1987] 2 SCR 541.

[1602] The Court found that a law sanctioned by a penalty would by its very nature be an offence if it was 'intended to promote public order and welfare within a public sphere of activity', but the test would not be satisfied by 'private, domestic or disciplinary matters which are regulatory, protective or corrective and which are primarily intended to maintain discipline, professional integrity and professional standards or to regulate conduct within a limited private sphere of activity'.

[1603] Contrast the position under Art 6(1) of the Convention; see para 11.174 above.

[1604] [1992] 1 SCR 259.

[1604a] [1990] 1 SCR 3; see D Stuart, *Charter Justice in Canadian Criminal Law* (Carswell, 1991) 220, 221.

laws and the common law. This paragraph offers no protection to a person not yet charged.[1605] In considering whether there has been unreasonable delay under this provision, the court should consider: (1) the length of the delay; (2) the waiver of time periods; (3) the reasons for the delay, and (4) prejudice to the accused.[1606] The degree of detail required by the term 'specific' is not entirely clear. It is sufficient if the indictment identifies the relevant time period of the offence, the place of commission, the parties to the offence and its subject matter.[1607] Challenges to the particularity of charges under section 11(a) are very rarely successful.[1607a]

(b) Section 11(b): trial within a reasonable time

11.397 Section 11(b) created a new Charter right:[1608] any person charged with an offence has the right to be tried within a reasonable time. It has been invoked more frequently than any other section of the Charter, because the appropriate remedy for its breach, according to the Supreme Court of Canada, is a stay of proceedings rather than an early trial.[1609]

11.398 The purpose of the right to a reasonable trial is to minimise three detrimental effects of pre-trial detention: time spent by an accused in custody or under restrictive bail conditions; anxiety of the accused awaiting trial; and deterioration of evidence necessary to the accused's defence.[1610] Because the third of these purposes extends equally to corporations as to natural persons, section 11(b) may be invoked by a corporation;[1611] but it can provide no benefit that is not already guaranteed under section 11(d), the right to fair trial. As a corporation can suffer neither imprisonment nor anxiety, the usual presumption of prejudice in the event of unreasonable delay is not applicable and must affirmatively establish prejudice on the sole basis of an impairment of its ability to make full answer and defence.

11.399 The period of time to be considered is that which begins with the charge.[1611a] As mentioned above, the reasonableness of the delay is determined by a process of weighing and balancing four factors:

- the length of the delay;
- waivers of time periods;
- reasons for the delay; and
- prejudice to the accused.[1611b]

The length of the delay is calculated from the point at which the information is laid or the

---

[1605] *R v Heit* [1984] 3 WWR 614.
[1606] *R v Delaronde* [1997] 1 SCR 213.
[1607] *R v Finta* (1989) 61 D R (4th) 85.
[1607a] See Stuart (n 1604a above) 223–224.
[1608] Right to trial within a reasonable time was not previously known to the common law, statute, or the Canadian Bill of Rights.
[1609] *R v Rahey* [1987] 1 SCR 588; *R v Askov* [1990] 2 SCR 1199; 74 DLR (4th) 355.
[1610] *R v CIP* [1992] 1 SCR 843; previously, the third of these purposes was disputed by Lamer J: see *R v Rahey* (n 1609 above).
[1611] *R v CIP* [1992] 1 SCR 843.
[1611a] *R v Kalanj* [1989] 1 SCR 1594, see generally, D Stuart, *Charter Justice in Canadian Criminal Law* (Carswell, 1991) 226–228.
[1611b] See generally, Stuart (n 1611a above) 228–246; P Hogg, *Constitutional Law of Canada* (4th edn, Carswell, 1997) Chap 49.

indictment is preferred[1612] to the final disposition of the case.[1613] Periods of time that are clearly and unequivocally waived[1614] by the accused are not taken into account in computing the length of the delay under section 11(b).[1615] Various reasons for delay have been addressed by the Supreme Court of Canada, most of which fall into one of four categories: delay inherent to the proceedings; delay attributable to the Crown; delay attributable to the accused; delay that is institutional or systemic to the court system. Of these, delay inherent to the case[1616] and delays attributable to the accused[1617] are considered to be reasonably incurred, while delay attributable to the Crown and delay systemic to the legal system[1618] are not. The last of the four factors to be weighed is that of prejudice to the accused. Where there are actual sources of prejudice, such as the impairment of defence evidence or the continuing deprivation of liberty of the accused, the period of time from charge to trial considered reasonable will be short. Even if there are no such apparent sources, the person awaiting trial is nevertheless presumed to be in 'exquisite agony',[1619] resulting in a presumption of prejudice to the accused as a result of the passage of time. On the other hand, a later case has recognised that often the accused is not interested in a speedy trial and delay works to the advantage of the accused,[1620] a conclusion that appears to contradict the presumption of prejudice established in *Askov*.[1621]

(c) Section 11(c): non-compellability

Section 11(c) of the Charter provides that the accused has the right not to be compelled to be a witness in proceedings against him in respect of the offence. Originally Canadian common law provided that the accused was not a compellable witness for the Crown, and was not competent to testify in his own defence. In 1893 the accused became competent as a witness in either case,[1622] though he remains non-compellable as a witness for the

11.400

[1612] There is no remedy for delay in laying the charge: *R v L (W K)* [1991] 1 SCR 1091.

[1613] Final disposition includes all retrials and appeals; such proceedings will be taken into account in the determination of the question as to reasonableness: in *R v Conway* [1989] 1 SCR 1659 a delay of five years from the charge to commencement of the accused's third trial was not unreasonable.

[1614] Such as a delay explicitly incurred in order to secure an adjournment or late trial date. Waiver must be made with full knowledge of the rights that the procedure was enacted to protect and the effect of the waiver on those rights: *R v Morin* [1992] 1 SCR 771. A defence consent to adjournment or a late trial date will not be a waiver unless counsel is alive to the issue of waiver; mere acquiescence in the inevitable may constitute action that falls short of waiver and reasonably extends the proceedings.

[1615] *R v Morin* (n 1614 above).

[1616] Time for preparation of the case, pre-trial procedures, and processing of a case by the court will vary with the complexity and nature of the case.

[1617] Not including the periods explicitly waived by the accused.

[1618] This includes delay caused by court congestion resulting from too few judges or courtrooms and inadequate case management procedures to handle the volume of criminal charges; see *R v Askov* [1990] 2 SCR 1199 in which the SCC stayed proceedings against four accused for unreasonable delays in bringing them to trial. The time elapsed from charge to trial had been two years and ten months, but the court drew the line at six to eight months maximum from committal to trial due to systemic delay.

[1619] *R v Askov* (n 1618 above).

[1620] *R v Morin* (n 1614 above).

[1621] In *R v Morin* (n 1614 above), Sopinka J for the majority implied that delay alone might not support the inference of sufficient prejudice to justify a stay of proceedings. Lamer J dissented on the basis that the decision was a fundamental change from the decision in *Askov*, which the Court ought not to depart from.

[1622] See now Canada Evidence Act, RSC 1985, c c-5.

Crown.[1623] As a result of the Charter provision, any statute which purports to compel a witness to testify against himself would be invalid. The guarantee is a privilege against testimonial compulsion, and not against compulsion generally, so that the accused must, for example, comply with an order to provide a breath test or with a 'reverse onus' provision which could be discharged by calling witnesses other than himself. Oral examinations for discovery in civil proceedings against a party who is charged with an offence arising out of the same facts does not breach this provision.[1624]

11.401 Section 11(c) prohibits only rules that impose a legal obligation on the accused to testify.[1625] If he chooses to testify, he cannot refuse to answer any question on the grounds that it might incriminate him. Instead, Article 13 applies to ensure that the incriminating answer is not used against the witness in other proceedings. If the accused chooses not to testify on his own behalf, the judge is required[1626] to refrain from making any comment to a jury as to an adverse inference that might be drawn from such failure to testify.

(d) Section 11(d): presumption of innocence

11.402 The first part of section 11(d) provides that 'any person charged with an offence has the right to be presumed innocent. . .'.[1626a] The presumption of innocence at common law is found in the rule that the Crown has the burden of proving the guilt of the accused beyond a reasonable doubt. Under the Charter the law is now reinforced and entrenched and capable of overturning legislative provisions that would reverse the common law onus of proof. The Court in *R v Oakes*[1627] held that legislation requiring that the accused disprove, on a balance of probabilities an 'essential element of the offence'[1628] was a breach of section 11(d) because it meant that a conviction was possible, despite the existence of a reasonable doubt as to the accused's guilt. The accused might adduce enough evidence to raise a reasonable doubt as to the purpose of the possession of illegal drugs, but not enough to prove his innocence on a balance of probabilities of the intention of trafficking. The Court found that the lower standard of proof on the reverse onus did not make such a provision constitutional, because it still contravened the requirement that the Crown prove all elements of an offence beyond a reasonable doubt.

11.403 For a reverse onus provision to be reasonable and hence constitutional, the connection between the proved fact and the presumed fact must at least be such that the existence of the proved fact rationally tends to prove that the presumed fact also exists.[1629]

[1623] Pursuant to the Canada Evidence Act and provincial statutes, the accused is now a competent witness for the defence.

[1624] *Saccomanno v Swanson* (1987) 34 DLR (4th) 462; *Municipal Enterprises v Rowlings* (1990) 107 NSR (2d) 88.

[1625] *R v Boss* (1988) 46 CCC (3d) 523.

[1626] Canada Evidence Act, s 4(6).

[1626a] See generally, D Stuart, *Charter Justice in Canadian Criminal Law* (Carswell 1991) 249–267.

[1627] [1986] 1 SCR 103.

[1628] In that case, the Narcotic Control Act required that, once the Crown had proved possession of an illegal drug beyond a reasonable doubt, the onus shifted to the accused to overturn, on a balance of probabilities, the mandatory presumption that the possession was for the purpose of trafficking.

[1629] See *R v Oakes* (n 1627 above); see also, *R v Bray* (1983) 144 DLR (3d) 305, 309; *R v Dubois (No 2)* (1983) 8 CCC (3d) 344, 346–347; *R v Frankforth* (1982) 70 CCC (2d) 488, 491; and see *Leary v United States* (1969) 395 US 6.

The same reasoning was applied in *R v Whyte,*[1630] even though the reverse onus required the accused to prove a 'fact collateral to the substantive offence' rather than an essential element of the offence. The offence was 'care and control of a motor vehicle while intoxicated'; if the accused occupied the driver's seat of a vehicle while drunk, he was deemed to have the care and control of the vehicle unless he could prove on the balance of probabilities that he did not enter it with the intention to set it in motion. The Court said that a reverse onus clause which required an accused to prove anything in order to avoid conviction, whether an element of the offence, a collateral fact, an excuse or a defence,[1631] violated the accused's right to presumption of innocence, but in *Whyte* the provision was saved by section 1 as a measure to prevent drunken driving.

11.404

In *R v Downey*[1632] the Supreme Court dealt with a statutory presumption that a person who lives with or is habitually in the company of prostitutes, is, in the absence of evidence to the contrary, committing the offence of living on the proceeds of prostitution. This presumption was also held to infringe the presumption of innocence (although it was held by a majority to be in all the circumstances a justifiable infringement). Cory J summarised the principles derived from the authorities in seven propositions:[1633]

11.405

   I.   The presumption of innocence is infringed whenever the accused is liable to be convicted despite the existence of a reasonable doubt.

   II.   If, by the provisions of a statutory presumption, an accused is required to establish, that is to say to prove or disprove, on a balance of probabilities either an element of an offence or an excuse, then it contravenes s 11(d). Such a provision would permit a conviction in spite of a reasonable doubt.

  III.   Even if a rational connection exists between the established fact and the fact to be presumed, this would be insufficient to make valid a presumption requiring the accused to disprove an element of the offence.

  IV.   Legislation which substitutes proof of one element for proof of an essential element will not infringe the presumption of innocence if, as a result of the proof of the substituted element, it would be unreasonable for the trier of fact not to be satisfied beyond a reasonable doubt of the existence of the other element. To put it another way, the statutory presumption will be valid if the proof of the substituted fact leads inexorably to the proof of the other. However, the statutory presumption will infringe s 11(d) if it requires the trier of fact to convict in spite of a reasonable doubt.

   V.   A permissive assumption from which a trier of fact may, but must not, draw an inference of guilt will not infringe s 11(d).

  VI.   A provision that might have been intended to play a minor role in providing relief from conviction will nonetheless contravene the Charter if the provision (such as the truth of a statement) must be established by the accused . . .

 VII.   It must of course be remembered that statutory presumptions which infringe s 11(d) may still be justified pursuant to s 1 of the Charter.

The following provisions have been held to violate the presumption of innocence in section 11(d) and were not justifiable under section 1:

11.405A

[1630] [1988] 2 SCR 3.

[1631] But in *R v Holmes* [1988] 1 SCR 914, a majority of the Court held that an excusing provision was not a reverse onus clause.

[1632] [1992] 2 SCR 10; see also *R v Fisher* (1994) 111 DLR (4th) 415 (burden of proving written consent of employee to receipt of commission a violation); *R v Laba* [1994] 3 SCR 965 (burden of proving lawful authority for sale or purchase of ore containing precious metal a violation).

[1633] Ibid at 461.

- a provision requiring an accused to prove insanity;[1633a]
- a provision placing a burden of proving truth on a person charged with wilfully promoting hatred;[1633b]
- a provision requiring the accused to prove ownership, agency or lawful authority for the sale or purchase of ore containing precious metal;[1633c]

In a number of other cases, reverse onus provisions have been held to be justifiable under section 1:

- a 'due diligence' defence to a misleading advertising offence;[1633d]
- the burden on the accused to prove that he had a reasonable excuse for a failure to provide a breath sample;[1633e]
- a requirement that a representation made to the public concerning a product was based on reasonable grounds.[1633f]

(e) Section 11(d): fair and public hearing

11.406   The second part of section 11(d) provides that a person charged with an offence is entitled to a 'fair and public hearing'. The requirement of 'fairness', which is explicitly provided for in section 11(d), has also been found to be implicit in the concept of 'fundamental justice' in section 7 as it applies to the life, liberty and security of the person.[1634] In *R v Seaboyer*,[1635] the Supreme Court of Canada held that both sections 7 and 11(d) guaranteed the 'right to present full answer and defence'. That case overturned the 'rape-shield' provision of the Criminal Code, which restricted the right of a person charged with sexual assault to cross-examine the complainant about her past sexual activity, on grounds that it might exclude relevant evidence that was required to enable the accused to make a full answer and defence. This right has two aspects: the right of the accused to have before him the 'full case to meet' before answering the Crown's case and the right of the accused to defend himself against all the State's efforts to achieve a conviction.[1636] Pre-trial disclosure by the Crown of all information relevant to the offence, once only a voluntary practice, has also been made a constitutional obligation as a result of the accused's right to make full answer and defence,[1637] although the Court referred to section 7 rather than section 11(d).

11.407   The right to a public hearing meant that there was no justification for a requirement that all trials of juveniles should be held in camera.[1638] A complete public trial should be the rule and exceptions should be established on a case-by-case basis.[1639]

[1633a] *R v Chaulk* [1990] 3 SCR 1303.
[1633b] *R v Keegstra* [1990] 3 SCR 697.
[1633c] *R v Laba* [1994] 3 SCR 965.
[1633d] *R v Wholesale Travel Group Inc* [1991] 3 SCR 154.
[1633e] *R v Peck* [1994] 21 CPR (2d) 175.
[1633f] *R v Envirosoft Water Inc* [1995] 61 CPR (3d) 207.
[1634] See para 11.388ff above.
[1635] [1991] 2 SCR 577.
[1636] *R v Rose* (1998) 166 DLR (4th) 385.
[1637] *R v Stinchcombe* (1991) 68 CCC (3d) 1.
[1638] *Edmonton Journal v Alberta (A-G)* (1983) 146 DLR (3d) 673.
[1639] *R v Lefevre* (1984) 17 CC (3d) 277.

(f) Section 11(d): Independent and impartial tribunal

Section 11(d) also provides for a public hearing 'by an independent and impartial tribunal'. In *R v Valente*[1640] it was argued that provincially-appointed judges of Ontario's Provincial Court (Criminal Division) would be biased in favour of the Crown as a result of the degree of control exercised by the Attorney-General over their conditions of employment, salaries, pensions and leave. The Supreme Court of Canada held that the three conditions of judicial independence, were security of tenure, financial security and 'the institutional independence of the tribunal with respect to matters of administration bearing directly on the exercise of its judicial function'. On the facts the three conditions had been met and the Provincial Court was therefore capable of trying criminal cases without violating section 11(d) of the Charter. Neither were part-time municipal court judges who maintained private law practices in Montreal found to be inconsistent with section 11(d) as a result of the judges' oath of office, code of ethics and statutory rules requiring their disqualification to avoid conflicts of interest.[1641] Governments do not infringe the principle of judicial independence by reducing the salaries of Provincial Court judges but they are constitutionally obliged to submit proposed changes to an independent, objective and effective body which depoliticises the process.[1642] Justices of the peace were held to be independent for the purposes of section 11(d).[1642a]

11.408

A jury, however, has been found lacking in impartiality where the ability of the Crown to 'stand by' up to 48 jurors gave the prosecution an undue advantage in the composition of the jury.[1643] The accused's statutory right to challenge potential jurors for cause based on partiality is the only direct means he has to secure an impartial jury.[1644] The trial judge should permit challenges for cause where there is a realistic potential of a racially biased jury.[1645]

11.409

(g) Section 11(f): trial by jury

Although the term 'tribunal' in section 11(d) does not require a jury as an element of 'fairness', section 11(f) creates the independent right to a jury trial, which has never before been recognised in Canada.[1646] A person charged with an offence is entitled, unless the offence is one under military law triable before a military tribunal, to the benefit of a jury trial where the maximum punishment for the offence is imprisonment for five years or a more severe punishment. The threshold level of potential punishment required by the section was not met by the sentence of compulsory confinement of a young offender in an

11.410

[1640] [1985] 2 SCR 673.

[1641] *R v Lippé* [1990] 2 SCR 114, SCC; see also *Reference re: Public Sector Pay Reduction Act (PEI) section 10* (1997) 150 DLR (4th) 577 and *Reference re: Territorial Court Act (NWT) section 6(2)* (1997) 152 DLR (4th) 132.

[1642] *R v Wickman* (1997) 150 DLR (4th) 577; see also *R v Campbell* (1995) 150 DLR (4th) 577.

[1642a] *Reference re Justices of the Peace Act* (1984) 16 CCC (3d) 193.

[1643] See *R v Bain* [1992] 1 SCR 91.

[1644] *R v Parks* (1993) 84 CCC (3d) 353, 362; see also *R v Sherratt* [1991] 1 SCR 509.

[1645] *R v Williams* [1998] 1 SCR 1128.

[1646] The Canadian Bill of Rights does not refer to the right to a jury trial; the drafters of the Canadian Charter appear to have been influenced by the provisions of the Sixth amendment to the US Constitution which provides for trial by an 'impartial jury of the state and district wherein the crime shall have been committed'.

'industrial school' for more than five years;[1647] nor where the offender was a corporation, as it could not be 'imprisoned'.[1648]

11.411   Because section 11(f) grants a right to 'the benefit' of a jury, it is apparent that the right can be waived.[1649] It is also clear that the section does not confer a constitutional right to elect a mode of trial other than by jury. In *R v Turpin*,[1650] the Supreme Court of Canada held that an application by two accused murderers to be tried by judge alone constituted a waiver of their right to a jury trial, and it rejected their attempts to invoke section 11(f) in support of the application. Such a waiver, like waivers of other constitutional rights, must be 'clear and unequivocal' and carried out with full awareness of the consequences.[1651] The failure of an accused to appear at his hearing after having opted for a jury was held not to be an unequivocal indication of waiver. However the Criminal Code legislation provided for trial by judge alone in these circumstances, the provision was therefore upheld under section 1 on grounds that it was appropriate to deny a jury where an accused had abused the system in the first instance.

11.412   Section 11(f) does not apply to military offences to be tried before a military tribunal. Because the National Defence Act[1652] includes in its definition of 'service offences' not only breaches of military law, but violations of the Criminal Code and other statutes applicable to the public at large, it has been suggested that for the purposes of the Charter, 'military offences' should be limited to National Defence Act offences that have a connection with military service.[1653]

(h) Section 11(g): retroactive offences

11.413   Under section 11(g) a person charged with a criminal offence has the right not to be found guilty 'on account of any act or omission unless, at the time of the act or omission, it constituted an offence under Canadian or international law or was criminal according to the general principles of law recognised by the community of nations'. The section limits the power of federal or provincial parliaments to create retroactive criminal offences; other types of laws may still be made retroactive, subject to the interpretative presumption that an ambiguous provision shall not be given retroactive effect. Furthermore, even a criminal law that is clearly intended to be applied retroactively may be in conformity with section 11(g) if it was an offence under international law or was considered criminal under principles of law recognised by the community of nations. This provision does not prohibit uncodified common law crimes.[1654]

[1647] *R v S B* (1983) 146 DLR (3d) 69; as the confinement was intended to treat rather than punish him, the sentence was not 'punishment' for the purposes of entitling him to a jury under s 11(f). The decision has been criticised on the basis that if there are sound policy reasons for denying young offenders a jury trial the limitation of s 11(f) ought to be justified by way of s 1 of the Charter: see P W Hogg, *Constitutional Law of Canada* (4th edn, Carswell, 1999), 1188.

[1648] As the maximum penalty an incorporation can receive is a fine, it is disentitled from a trial by a jury, in spite of the fact that a corporation would have benefited from it. The view of the dissent was that the benefit of the right to a jury in relation to the most serious offences is as relevant to a corporation as to an individual.

[1649] *R v Turpin* [1989] 1 SCR 1296, 1314-1316.

[1650] Ibid.

[1651] *R v Lee* [1989] 2 SCR 1384, 1411.

[1652] RSC 1985, c N-5.

[1653] *R v Macdonald* (1983) 150 DLR (3d) 620: 'military nexus'; see also the pre-Charter case of *R v Mackay* [1980] 2 SCR 370, 380, *per* MacIntyre J.

[1654] *United Nurses of Alberta v Alberta (A-G)* [1992] 1 SCR 901.

(i) Section 11(h): double jeopardy

The common law rules against double jeopardy[1655] are now embodied in the Charter under **11.414**
section 11(h) which provides that a person charged with an offence has the right, 'if finally
acquitted of the offence, not to be tried for it again and if finally found guilty and punished
for the offence, not to be tried or punished for it again'. The section applies only where both
proceedings are in relation to an 'offence', and the latter is substantially identical to or included in the offence of which the accused was convicted. So, for example, where an attack
by one prison inmate on another was dealt with first by way of disciplinary hearing and punishment, the accused was not in a position to resist, on grounds of section 11(f), trial for subsequent Criminal Code charges of assault.[1656] Similarly, in *R v Wigglesworth*,[1657] the
conviction of a police officer for a 'service offence' under the Royal Canadian Mounted
Police Act did not preclude a subsequent trial for assault under the Criminal Code.

In order for attempted 'second' proceedings to trigger section 11(h) protection, the first **11.415**
must result in a final disposition of the charges: where the original proceedings ended in a
stay[1658] or mistrial, the accused could be tried again in relation to the same offence. 'Final'
disposition is not rendered until all appeal proceedings are complete; an appeal from a trial
verdict is not therefore a retrial of the same offence. Where an appeal process took the form
of a 'trial *de novo*',[1659] however, the Supreme Court of Canada held that it was not in fact
an appeal but a disguised retrial in violation of section 11(h).

(j) Section 11(i): variation in penalty

Under section 11(i), any person charged with an offence has the right if found guilty of the **11.416**
offence and if the punishment for the offence has been varied between the time of commission and the time of sentencing, to the benefit of the lesser punishment. The section
applies where the penalty for the offence has been varied after an accused has committed
an offence but before he has been sentenced.[1660] Where the penalty is not strictly a 'punishment', as in the case of the suspension of a driver's licence,[1661] the section will not apply,
but if it is applicable, the accused must have the benefit of the lesser, rather than merely the
latter, of the two penalties in question.

[1655] See *Kienapple v The Queen* [1975] 1 SCR 729 in regard to *res judicata*; special pleas of autrefois
acquit and autrefois convict; issue estoppel; possibly abuse of process: *R v Van Rassel* [1990] 1 SCR
225, 233-239.

[1656] *R v Shubley* [1990] 1 SCR 3; see also *R v Schmidt* [1987] 1 SCR 500 where the accused, who
had been convicted of a federal offence in the US, tried to invoke s 11(f) to avoid Canadian extradition proceedings to return him to the US for a trial on what he claimed was the same offence. The
extradition proceedings, being not determinative of guilt or innocence, did not constitute a trial in
relation to an 'offence' and so the Court left it to the foreign court to deal with the objections of the
accused.

[1657] *R v Wigglesworth* [1987] 2 SCR 541.

[1658] *Re Burrows* (1983) 150 DLR (3d) 317.

[1659] In *Corporation Professionnelle des Médecins v Thibault* [1988] 1 SCR 1033, Quebec legislation
enabled a prosecutor to appeal from an acquittal by trial *de novo* which allowed evidence to be re-
adduced and supplemented as necessary.

[1660] But see *R v Gamble* [1988] 2 SCR 595, where the Court found a breach of s 7 rather than s 11
when an accused mistakenly tried and sentenced under law enacted after the commission of the offence.

[1661] In *Re Bulmer* (1987) 36 DLR (4th) 688 the suspension was a 'civil consequence' rather than a
punishment.

(k) Section 14: right to an interpreter

11.417 This section reflects the common law right to an interpreter which itself derives from the principles of 'natural justice'.[1662] It is the duty of the judge to determine whether the need for an interpreter has been established.[1663] The right applies to all proceedings, civil as well as criminal.[1664] The interpretation must meet the standard of 'continuity, precision, impartiality, competence and contemporaneousness'.[1665] Thus, there was a breach of section 14 when, at the trial of a Vietnamese speaker, a witness testified in English and then gave a brief summary of his testimony in Vietnamese at the end of his evidence in chief and his cross-examination.[1666] Although the accused had suffered no prejudice, the fact that he was unable to follow part of the proceedings meant that his right under section 14 had been infringed. A new trial was ordered.

(4) Freedom from self-incrimination.

11.418 Section 13 of the Charter gives a witness the right not to have incriminating evidence he gives used to incriminate him in any other proceedings.[1667] The rights of an accused under section 13 were infringed when he was cross-examined by prosecuting counsel on testimony he had given on his prior trial for the same offence, a re-trial having been ordered.[1668] However the section does not prohibit cross-examination as to credit.[1669] The section provides no basis for the assertion of a right to remain silent in civil proceedings arising out of the same facts as a criminal charge.[1670]

11.419 The principles of 'fundamental justice' in section 7 of the Charter include the right to silence which is a 'basic tenet of the legal system'.[1671] The essence of the right is the notion that the person whose freedom is placed in question by the judicial process must be given the choice of whether or not to speak to the authorities.[1672] Thus, a confession obtained by disguising a police officer as a fellow prisoner was held to be a breach of this right.[1673] The right can be violated not only by undercover police officers but by any agent of the state.[1674] A statement arising from a prior inadmissible confession cannot be used even for the limited purpose of undermining the credibility of the accused.[1675]

11.420 However, the right to silence is not an absolute one and there must be a careful balance between the interests of the individual and those of the state:[1676] the principle must be considered in the factual circumstances of each particular case.[1677] If a witness is compelled to

---

[1662] *R v Tran* [1994] 2 SCR 361.

[1663] Ibid 979.

[1664] See P W Hogg, *Constitutional Law of Canada* (4th edn, Carswell, 1997), s 53.5(e).

[1665] *R v Tran* (n 1662 above).

[1666] *R v Tran* (n 1662 above) (the witness was the person who had interpreted for the rest of the trial who was called by the defence).

[1667] See generally, Hogg (n 1664 above) Chap 51.

[1668] *R v Mannion* [1986] 2 SCR 272.

[1669] *R v Johnstone and Law Society of British Columbia* (1987) 40 DLR (4th) 550.

[1670] *Caisse Populaire Laurier d'Ottawa Ltée v Guertin* (1983) 150 DLR (3d) 541.

[1671] *R v Hebert* [1990] 2 SCR 151.

[1672] Ibid.

[1673] Ibid; see also *R v Broyles* [1991] 3 SCR 595.

[1674] *R v Broyles* (n 1673 above).

[1675] *R v G* (1999) 6 BHRC 97.

[1676] *R v S (RJ)* [1995] 1 SCR 451.

[1677] *R v Fitzpatrick* [1995] 4 SCR 154, 166-169.

testify he will be entitled to claim effective subsequent derivative-use immunity or other appropriate protection with respect to the compelled testimony.[1678] In *Thomson Newspapers v Director of Investigations and Research*[1679] the Supreme Court considered the relation between the right to silence and compulsory investigative powers.[1680] Although witnesses could be compelled to give evidence, this evidence could not be used in subsequent proceedings. Section 13 was not applicable because the investigation was the first proceeding. The majority held that this 'subsequent use immunity' meant that there had been no infringement of the right to silence. In *R v Fitzpatrick*[1681] the use in evidence of the daily fishing reports made by the accused under the applicable fishery regulations was not a breach of the privilege. The Court relied on the lack of real coercion, the lack of an 'adversarial relationship' at the time the reports were made, the absence of an increased risk of unreliable confessions as a result of statutory compulsion and the absence of an increased risk of abuses of power by the state. In contrast, in *R v White*[1682] the Supreme Court held that the admission in evidence of an accident report made under a statutory requirement was a breach of section 7. In that case there was a potential adversarial relationship between the driver and the police officer taking the statement, a prospect of unreliable confessions and the possibility of abusive conduct by the state.

Appendix 2: The New Zealand Bill of Rights Act

(1) Introduction

The New Zealand Bill of Rights Act 1990 contains a number of provisions granting rights in relation to legal process:

11.421

24. **Rights of persons charged—**

Everyone who is charged with an offence—

- (a) shall be informed promptly and in detail of the nature and cause of the charge; and
- (b) shall be released on reasonable terms and conditions unless there is just cause for continued detention; and
- (c) shall have the right to consult and instruct a lawyer; and
- (d) shall have the right to adequate time and facilities to prepare a defence; and
- (e) shall have the right, except in the case of an offence under military law tried before a military tribunal, to the benefit of a trial by jury when the penalty for the offence is or includes imprisonment for more than three months; and
- (f) shall have the right to receive legal assistance without cost if the interests of justice so require and the person does not have sufficient means to provide for that assistance; and
- (g) shall have the right to have the free assistance of an interpreter if the person cannot understand or speak the language used in court.

[1678] *British Columbia (Securities Commission) v Branch* [1995] 2 SCR 3.
[1679] [1990] 1 SCR 425, see the discussion in Hogg (n 1664 above) 44.10(b).
[1680] Under the Combines Investigation Act 1970—investigations designed to determine whether there had been a breach of competition law.
[1681] [1995] 4 SCR 154.
[1682] (1999) 6 BHRC 120, the case contains a useful survey of the present state of the Canadian law on self-incrimination.

25. Minimum standards of criminal procedure—

Everyone who is charged with an offence, has, in relation to the determination of the charge, the following minimum rights:

(a) the right to a fair and public hearing by an independent and impartial court:

(b) the right to be tried without undue delay:

(c) the right to be presumed innocent until proved guilty according to law:

(d) the right not to be compelled to be a witness or to confess guilt:

(e) the right to be present at the trial and to present a defence:

(f) the right to examine the witnesses for the prosecution and to obtain the attendance and examination of witnesses for the defence under the same conditions as the prosecution:

(g) the right, if convicted of an offence in respect of which the penalty has been varied between the commission of the offence and sentencing, to the benefit of the lesser penalty:

(h) the right, if convicted of the offence, to appeal according to law to a higher court against the conviction or against the sentence or against both:

(i) the right, in the case of a child, to be dealt with in a manner that takes account of the child's age.

26. Retroactive penalties and double jeopardy—

(1) No one shall be liable to conviction of any offence on account of any act or omission which did not constitute an offence by such person under the law of New Zealand at the time it occurred.

(2) No one who has been finally acquitted or convicted of, or pardoned for, an offence shall be tried or punished for it again.

27. Right to justice—

(1) Every person has the right to the observance of the principles of natural justice by any tribunal or other public authority which has the power to make a determination in respect of that person's right, obligations, or interests protected or recognised by law.

(2) Every person whose rights, obligations, or interests protected or recognized by law have been affected by a determination of any tribunal or other public authority has the right to apply in accordance with law, for judicial review of that determination.

(3) Every person has the right to bring civil proceedings against, and to defend civil proceedings brought by the Crown, and to have those proceedings heard, according to law, in the same way as civil proceedings between individuals.

11.422   The scope of these provisions differ from the Convention in a number of respects. First, the Bill of Rights Act provides for an express right to a fair and public hearing only in the context of minimum standards of criminal procedure. The principle of open justice and its exceptions in the civil law in New Zealand therefore remain governed by the common law[1683] and by section 27 which reflects the general right of every person to 'the observance of the principles of natural justice' whenever their interests or obligations are to be determined before a competent tribunal or other public authority. In practice, the Bill of Rights Act is not viewed as the definitive statement on issues of public administration of justice, access to justice or the principles of fairness, but is given consideration in conjunction with other relevant statutory provisions and the common law. It has been suggested that the Bill of Rights Act may be minimised or disregarded altogether as a measure of fairness of criminal and civil proceedings in New Zealand.[1684]

[1683] M McDowell, 'The Principle of Open Justice in a Civil Context' [1995] NZLR 214.

[1684] Cf C Baylis, 'Justice Done and Justice Seen to be Done—The Public Administration of Justice' (1991) 21 Victoria University of Wellington L Rev 177.

There are, however, some signs that the New Zealand courts are taking a 'rights centred' approach which emphasises the primacy of the individual rights and freedoms affirmed in the Bill of Rights.[1685] This would mean that the Bill of Rights Act is given constitutional status. The argument is that the fundamental nature of the affirmed rights is more important than the legal form in which they are declared and that consequently, the reasoning of foreign courts interpreting constitutionally entrenched human rights is applicable to the New Zealand Bill of Rights Act:

> Enjoyment of the basic human rights are the entitlement of every citizen, and their protection the obligation of every civilized state. They are inherent in and essential to the structure of society. They do not depend on the legal or constitutional form in which they are declared. The reasoning that has led the Privy Council and the Courts of Ireland and India to the conclusions reached in the cases to which I have referred . . . is in my opinion equally valid to the New Zealand Bill of Rights Act if it is to have life and meaning.[1686]

11.423

The result in *Baigent's Case*[1687] was that the majority of the Court established an independent civil claim directly against the Crown for infringement of the section 21 freedom from unreasonable search and seizure. As Crown liability is direct liability in public law rather than a vicarious liability in tort for the acts of Crown servants, the usual Crown immunities do not apply. However, this application of the purposive approach to interpretation of the Bill of Rights Act has not escaped criticism.[1688]

11.424

Nevertheless, this approach has far-reaching implications which will potentially affect the right to observance of principles of natural justice and to a fair and public hearing in New Zealand. The New Zealand courts have the power to award damages where 'fair trial rights have been denied'. An award was made in the recent case of *Upton v Green (No 2)*[1689] arising out of a failure by a District Judge to hear a defendant who had pleaded guilty before sentence. Compensation in the sum of NZ$15,000[1690] was awarded for this breach.

11.425

(2) The guarantees

(a) Access to the courts

The New Zealand Bill of Rights Act does not contain any general principle of access to the courts, though a fundamental right to access to justice has been derived from various provisions for access in particular contexts. Whether access to the courts can or needs to be differentiated from the right to access to justice is not clear. Several sections of the Act may be construed to imply a right of access to the courts. They either provide a right of access in a specific criminal context, or appear to assume a right of access to the courts. Section 24(f) recognises the principle of access in its guarantee of a right to legal assistance without cost if the interests of justice so require and the person does not have sufficient means to provide for that assistance. Section 27 is entitled 'access to justice' and establishes that compliance with the rules of natural justice by public decision makers, judicial review and the right to take action in civil proceedings against the Crown must be provided in particular contexts that go beyond criminal law.

11.426

[1685] See in particular, *Simpson v Attorney-General (Baigent's Case)* [1994] 3 NZLR 667.
[1686] Ibid 702.
[1687] Ibid.
[1688] See J Smillie, 'The Allure of "Rights Talk"' (1994) 8:2 Otago L Rev 188.
[1689] (1996) 3 HRNZ 179, affd *sub nom A-G v Upton* (1998) 5 HRNZ 54.
[1690] Approx £4,700.

11.427   It is not clear whether the Bill of Rights Act adds anything to the common law in facilitating access to the judicial process. Sir Robin Cooke has gone so far as to suggest, *obiter*, that even at common law the Court of Appeal

> has reservations as to the extent to which in New Zealand even an Act of Parliament can take away the rights of citizens to resort to the ordinary Courts of law for the determination of their rights.[1691]

This is difficult to reconcile with parliamentary sovereignty, which ensures that, if it does so in sufficiently clear language, Parliament can deny access to the courts.

(b) Fairness: sections 24 and 25

11.428   In contrast to the Convention, the right to a fair (and public) hearing is expressly provided for only in relation to an accused person 'charged with a criminal offence'. In the non-criminal context, persons charged with an offence are guaranteed the specific rights set out in section 24, and the protection of the general principles of 'natural justice' under section 27, including the right to apply for judicial review, or bring a suit against the public authorities. The concept of fairness runs throughout the jurisprudence in relation to both sections 24 and 25. All of the rights specified in subsections of those provisions are treated as elements of a fair trial, with occasional reference to the 'minimum' standards to be afforded in the criminal context when it is section 25 rights that are in issue. There is no reference to another standard of fairness applicable with respect to the determination of civil obligations, as most of the jurisprudence involves determination of criminal charges.

11.429   **The right to be informed promptly of the charge.**   Section 24(a) provides that everyone charged with an offence has the right to be informed promptly and in detail of the nature and cause of the charge. This does not oblige the police authorities to provide the accused with an opportunity to deny charges for the police record and so avoid having to testify in court,[1692] nor to put all the potential charges revealed by his statements to him in an interview, nor to interview the accused at all, if they have sufficient evidence upon which to proceed without doing so.[1693] The 'detail' required by the subsection does not extend to the exact dates of sexual offences that allegedly took place over a period of several years.[1694] The power to amend an information does not conflict with this provision.[1695]

11.430   **Adequate time and facilities to prepare.**   The right in section 24(d) to adequate time and facilities to prepare a defence is an important element of a fair trial designed to put the defence on an equal footing with the prosecution in preparation for trial.[1696] It does not oblige the Crown to call all its witnesses at a preliminary hearing, if the accused will have a chance to cross-examine them at trial,[1697] but it does include the right to adequate access to evidence which the accused requires to present his or her case,[1698] such as the opportunity to obtain evidence that might have an exculpatory effect. In *R v Donaldson*,[1699]

[1691] *New Zealand Drivers' Association v New Zealand Road Carriers* [1982] 1 NZLR 374, 390.
[1692] *R v K* [1995] 2 NZLR 440.
[1693] Ibid.
[1694] *W v A-G* [1993] 1 NZLR 1.
[1695] *Jones v Police* [1998] 1 NZLR 447.
[1696] See Richardson J in *R v Accused* (1994) 12 CRNZ 417.
[1697] See *R v Haig* [1996] 1 NZLR 184.
[1698] Ibid.
[1699] [1995] 3 NZLR 641.

section 24(d) was breached when the appellant, who was arrested on suspicion of driving under the influence of a drug, was denied the right to have a blood sample taken, in spite of the fact that the alcohol breath test conducted at the scene proved negative and a qualified doctor was in attendance at police headquarters. The refusal was considered, in the circumstances, to be an obstruction of the preparation of a defence, implying that the police are required not to obstruct, an obligation narrowly distinguishable in practice from an affirmative duty to assist in the collection of evidence useful for the defence. The Court in *Donaldson* took the view that a breach of section 24(d) could result from a variety of factors, including:

- 'bad faith' on the part of the police which would point towards obstruction;
- the degree and foreseeability or materiality of the lost evidence; and
- the existence and extent of any practical difficulties in obtaining or preserving that evidence.

Where the accused, charged with sexual offences, sought an order that the complainant undergo a medical examination,[1700] the Court was faced with the problem of the competing interests of the complainant who had a right to refuse the examination. The Judge found that the test in determining whether a fair trial has been prevented is whether the evidence denied (in this case, the medical examination) might have provided a reasonable prospect of exculpating the accused. A 'working expression of the test' could be found in the *obiter dictum* of Cooke P: 'there must be a compelling need for the evidence; the Court must be satisfied that justice could not be done without it'.[1701]   **11.431**

In another section 24 case,[1702] the court ordered that a Chinese-speaking defendant charged with illegal importation of goods must be provided with written translations of volumes of documentary evidence briefs delivered by the prosecution prior to the hearing. Using a purposive approach to the interpretation of section 24(g),[1703] and in light of the common law principles,[1704] the phrases 'assistance of an interpreter' and 'language used' were considered broad enough to include both written and spoken language; written interpretation as well as oral translation. Once it is determined that the accused person is incapable of understanding or speaking the language used in Court, section 24(g) is applicable, which in this case meant that the onus was on the court to provide pre-trial translations, at no expense to the accused, in a timely fashion.   **11.432**

The right to a jury. In two cases,[1705] the right to elect trial by jury in section 24(e) has been held to be overridden by section 43 of the Summary Offences Act. Section 43 was clearly intended, with respect to certain specified offences, to abrogate the right to elect a jury trial which was normally afforded in connection with offences punishable by prison   **11.433**

[1700] *R v B (No 2)* [1995] 2 NZLR 752; the first appeal failed in *R v B* [1995] 2 NZLR 172 because the Court of Appeal held that it had no jurisdiction to deal with the matter on an interlocutory appeal.

[1701] *R v B* [1995] 2 NZLR 172, 177.

[1702] *Alwen Industries Ltd and Kar Wong v Collector of Customs* [1996] 1 HRNZ 574.

[1703] The Court found that the aim of the right is to ensure that the defendant receives a fair trial; specifically that he understands the proceedings, and is able to instruct counsel fully and prepare a defence.

[1704] The Court referred to the common law right of the defendant to an interpreter which is an aspect of the fundamental right to a fair trial.

[1705] *Reille v Police* [1993] 1 NZLR 587; *Dreliozis v Wellington District Court* [1994] 2 NZLR 198.

sentences in excess of three months. The offences included assaults involving a police officer[1706] in the execution of his duty which carried a penalty of six-months' imprisonment or a fine of $2,000. There was no meaning consistent with the Bill of Rights Act that could be given the provision; to grant the accused a jury trial would be to impliedly repeal[1707] section 43 or to render it ineffective in relation to such offences, contrary to section 4, an argument decisively rejected by the Court.

11.434 **Section 25: introduction.** The general heading of section 25, which indicates that its provisions are 'minimum standards of criminal procedure' has been referred to in recent cases. In *R v L*,[1708] the court emphasised that the right to a fair trial[1709] and to cross-examine witnesses[1710] are 'minimum rights', affirmed by the parallel provisions of the International Covenant on Civil and Political Rights. Where judicial powers of adjournment or remand in contempt proceedings were challenged because they were not addressed in section 206 of the Summary Proceedings Act,[1711] it was held that they were nevertheless consistent with and 'enhanced' the various 'rights of minimum standards of criminal procedure' in section 25 of the New Zealand Bill of Rights Act 1990. Lastly, 'minimum standards' does not limit the number of retrials that an accused may be subjected to if the jury cannot come to an agreement.[1712]

11.435 **Section 25(a): fair and public hearing before an independent and impartial court.** The right to a fair and public hearing by an independent and impartial court under subsection 25(a) is typically invoked in Bill of Rights cases wherever a challenge under the general category of abuse of process or unfairness is made. All of the subsections of section 25 are, in effect, elements of 'fairness'.[1713] It has been emphasised that, in the absence of compelling reasons to the contrary, criminal justice must be public justice.[1713a] The trial should be disposed of as near as possible to where the crimes occur but, where there is a risk of unfairness, it will be moved to another venue.[1713b] The judge who deals with a 'settlement type' hearing should not preside over the trial.[1713c] A District Court judge sitting with a jury is an independent and impartial Court.[1714] In reaching this conclusion, the Court of Appeal relied heavily on Article 6 of the Convention. The case of *R v L*[1715] emphasised the role of

---

[1706] In *Reille*, a police constable was charged with assaulting a complainant in the course of her arrest under s 9 of the Summary Offences Act; *Dreliozis* involved a charge of assault against a police officer in the execution of his duty under s 10 of the same Act.

[1707] In *Dreliozis v Wellington District Court* [1994] 2 NZLR 198, the Court rejected a further argument that the Bill of Rights Act, while not impliedly repealing s 43, did so expressly, in an indirect fashion.

[1708] *R v L* [1994] 2 NZLR 54.

[1709] s 25(a).

[1710] s 25(f).

[1711] s 206 was alleged to be a codification of the rules of contempt of court.

[1712] *R v Barlow* [1996] 2 NZLR 116.

[1713] See, however, *Martin v Tauranga District Court* [1995] 1 NZLR 491, in which the Court made an express distinction between the right to trial without undue delay under s 25(b) and the right to a fair trial.

[1713a] *R v Bain* [1996] 3 HRNZ 108.

[1713b] *R v Lory* [1996] 3 HRNZ 99.

[1713c] *Pickering v Police* [1999] 5 HRNZ 154.

[1714] See *A-G v McNally* [1993] 1 NZLR 550 (it was also held that there was nothing contrary to the Bill of Rights Act in the fact that only those accused persons to be tried in the High Court can apply for trial by Judge alone).

[1715] [1994] 2 NZLR 54.

cross-examination of witnesses in ensuring a fair trial. In *R v Haig*,[1716] the fairness of the proceedings was unsuccessfully challenged in connection with allegations that a failure of the Crown to call all of its witnesses at a preliminary hearing breached the accused's right to cross-examination of prosecution witnesses under 25(f) and prejudiced the defence preparation for trial under 24(d). A challenge under the same three grounds was successful in *R v B (No 2)*,[1717] in which the complainant refused to undergo a medical examination following her allegations of sexual assault. The test for establishing whether a denial of the opportunity to obtain further evidence prevents the accused from having a fair trial is whether the evidence might have provided a reasonable prospect of exculpating him. There was no unfairness made out when a decision to retry a criminal case for the third time was challenged on the grounds of undue delay and infringement of presumption of innocence.[1718]

A number of grounds were considered together in *R v Coghill*,[1719] where the issue was pre-trial publicity with the complicity of the police. The Court held that the quashing of a trial on the basis of deprivation of fairness requires a 'fatal defect', which on the facts had not been proved. The length of time that had elapsed (which was not 'undue' under section 25(b)) had eradicated any substantial risk that the publicity would be prejudicial to the accused's right to be assumed innocent until proven guilty (section 25(c)).   **11.436**

It has been said in several cases that section 25(a) adds nothing to the arguments made under the common law. The case of *R v Ellis*,[1720] which involved inflammatory media attention given to an accused charged with sexual assault of children in his care, emphasised the need to consider and balance all relevant factors. The Court found that section 25(a) (insofar as it related to fairness) added nothing to the court's inherent jurisdiction to deal with the matter. Similarly in *R v Accused*,[1721] the general submission alleging contravention of the right to a fair trial was said to add nothing to the common law arguments in relation to the admissibility of evidence. However, in *Upton v Green (No 2)*[1721a] it was held that a failure by a District Judge to hear a defendant who had pleaded guilty before sentence was a breach of his rights under section 25(a). Compensation in the sum of NZ$15,000[1721b] was awarded for this breach.   **11.437**

Section 25(b): undue delay. The case of *Martin v Tauranga District Court*[1722] provides a comprehensive overview of principles to be applied in relation to undue delay under section 25(b). On the facts, a period of 17 months from the laying of charges to end of trial, including a period of five months of systemic or institutional delay, was not of such magnitude to be categorised as 'undue'. The Court said that wherever the length of time taken to complete a trial had gone beyond the time in which most cases were able to be disposed of and the accused then raised the issue of undue delay, it is for the Crown to prove on a balance of probabilities that the delay had not become 'undue delay'. It was not appropriate to specify a guideline period as has been done in other jurisdictions.[1723] The Court must   **11.438**

[1716] [1996] 1 NZLR 184.
[1717] [1995] 2 NZLR 752.
[1718] *R v Barlow* [1996] 2 NZLR 116.
[1719] [1995] 3 NZLR 651.
[1720] [1993] 3 NZLR 317.
[1721] [1991] 2 NZLR 187.
[1721a] (1996) 3 HRNZ 179, affd *sub nom A-G v Upton* (1998) 5 HRNZ 54.
[1721b] Approx £4,700.
[1722] [1995] 1 NZLR 491.
[1723] See para 11.399 above.

assess the situation in light of the accused's right to be presumed innocent, taking into account:

- the overall length of delay, calculated from the laying of the charge to the end of the trial;
- the reasons for the delay including the inherent time requirements of the case, actions of the accused, actions of the prosecution, actions of judicial officers, limits on institutional resources, and other reasons;
- any prejudice to the accused arising from the delay; and
- any informed waiver by the accused of the section 25(b) right.

The Court also found that prejudice to the accused was relevant only to the extent that it arose from the delay in bringing charges to trial, not from the delay in laying of the charges, or prejudice in relation to the trial itself. Prejudice might, however, be presumed where there had been an exceptionally long delay. The Court expressed the view that the protection against undue delay under section 25(b) is a guarantee distinct and apart from that which guarantees the right to a fair trial.

11.439   The case of *R v B*[1724] involved two appeals relating to jury trials in a District Court that had been experiencing serious backlogs. Neither case was particularly complex or difficult and in each case the court rejected the complaint that section 25(b) was breached.

11.440   In *Hughes v Police*,[1725] the Court was prepared to dismiss or order a stay of prosecution on the basis that delays in the criminal process, while outside of the scope of application of section 25(b), may nevertheless result in unfairness prejudicial to the accused. Hughes had been the object of a series of investigations for fraud over a period of six years. On the basis of the final investigation, which was completed within 8 months, he was charged with 14 counts of misappropriation of moneys and committed to trial. The Court considered that, even though the specific application of the Act is to the period between initiation of the prosecution and trial, section 25(b) ought to have some significance for the person who is aware that he is under investigation; the pressures imposed are just as real before the formal initiation of the prosecution where the potential accused is aware that it is in contemplation. It found that prejudice could be considered in 'wider terms than merely whether or not ultimately a fair trial in the ordinary sense could take place'; and held that the reopening of the case on the basis of the last investigation involved an 'unfairness' that constituted a 'prejudice' justifying the intervention of the Court.

11.441   In other cases, a decision to go ahead with a second retrial after 19 months of prior proceedings did not constitute 'undue delay', where every effort had been made to expedite the charges against the accused.[1726] A period of 12 months from arrest to the end of a murder trial was not undue delay, in light of the large number of witnesses, the complexity of the case and problems of Court resources.[1727] Neither was a period of three years from police enquiries to sentencing offensive, given that the case had progressed steadily in spite of a history of complexity and difficulties.[1728]

[1724] [1996] 1 NZLR 386.
[1725] [1995] 3 NZLR 443.
[1726] *R v Barlow* [1996] 2 NZLR 116.
[1727] *R v Haig* [1996] 1 NZLR 184.
[1728] *R v Coghill* [1995] 3 NZLR 651.

Subsection 25(c): presumption of innocence until proven guilty.   Section 25(c) ensures   **11.442**
that everyone charged with an offence has, as a minimum right, the right to be presumed
innocent until proved guilty according to law. This reflects the basic principle of the criminal law that the onus of proof beyond a reasonable doubt will lie with the Crown on a
criminal or quasi-criminal allegation unless Parliament gives a reasonably clear indication
that it should be otherwise.[1729] In *R v Rangi*,[1730] the accused successfully appealed against
his conviction of having a sheath knife in a public place where the judge had instructed the
jury that once the Crown had proved possession of the knife, it was for the accused to establish the authority or excuse for the possession on a balance of probabilities. It was held
that the offence of 'having a knife in a public place without lawful authority or reasonable
excuse' indicated no clear legislative intention that the onus was to shift to the accused to
disprove any element of the offence. If the issue of authority or excuse was raised on the evidence, it was incumbent on the Crown to prove beyond a reasonable doubt that no such
defence existed.

In relation to the possession of a cannabis plant for the purpose of sale,[1731] on the other   **11.443**
hand, the legislative intent was clearly to shift the burden of proof. Where the Crown had
proved possession of a certain amount of the substance beyond a reasonable doubt, such
possession was deemed to be for a proscribed purpose (in this case sale) 'until the contrary
is proved'. On appeal against conviction of the accused, the defence argued that by application of section 6 of the Bill of Rights Act, an interpretation consistent with subsection
25(c) of that Act would render 'until the contrary is proved' to mean that the defence had
only to raise sufficient evidence to cast a reasonable doubt on the guilt of the accused and
that it remained for the Crown to prove that sale was the purpose of the possession beyond
a reasonable doubt. The Court rejected the argument, finding it 'strained and unnatural'
and held that the trial judge was correct in his direction to the jury that the onus of proof
shifted to the accused to overturn the presumption as to purpose on a balance of probabilities.

In *R v Coghill*,[1732] the court considered the connection between an offence against the ac-   **11.444**
cused's presumption of innocence and the fairness of the trial itself as a result of alleged
complicity by the police in pretrial publicity. However, the Court failed to address the
question of a separate remedy for a violation of 25(c) and found that the pretrial violation
did not affect the fairness of the trial.

Subsection 25(d): self-incrimination.   The right of an accused not to be compelled to   **11.445**
be a witness in his own case has been asserted in situations in which, had pretrial procedures been conducted in a different manner, the accused may have chosen not to testify at
trial. In *R v K*,[1733] the question was whether the police ought to have interviewed the accused in regard to the specific charge of rape, and thus provide him with the opportunity
to have his denial entered on the police record that would be submitted as evidence at trial.
The Court found that there was no such obligation on the police and that the accused was
not in law compelled to testify. 'Compelled' means 'can be mandatorily required' and
though it should not be unduly refined, it cannot be stretched to mean compelled 'in fact',

---

[1729] *R v Rangi* [1992] 1 NZLR 385.
[1730] Ibid.
[1731] *R v Phillips* [1991] 3 NZLR 175.
[1732] [1995] 3 NZLR 651.
[1733] *R v K* [1995] 2 NZLR 440.

just because a disadvantageous inference might be drawn from a failure of the accused to testify. In light of *R v K*, the reasoning, if not the decision of the earlier case of *Reille v Police*[1734] is difficult to support.

11.446   **Subsection 25(e): the right to be present at the trial and to present a defence.**   The right to be present at the trial was considered in *R v Duval*[1735] where the accused sought a stay of proceedings on the ground that his chronic back pain made it impossible for him to sit through a trial or if he did, to obtain a fair one. The Court found that section 25(e) affirms the requirement of the criminal justice system that an accused must be fit to stand trial. The Court stated that 'the notion that a person must be able to plead and stand trial is not just a matter of procedural fairness . . . , but a substantive requirement firmly rooted in an accused's constitutional rights to a fair trial'; 'a trial would not be fair if the accused suffers a disability which prevents him from effectively defending him or herself, and the section 25(e) right to be present and present a defence would be rendered ineffectual unless the accused is capable of comprehending the case against him and presenting a defence to that case'.

11.447   The second part of subsection 25(e), the right to present a defence, has been asserted in connection with the right to adequate facilities in order to prepare a defence[1736] where the complainant refused to undergo a medical examination which might have provided evidence helpful to the accused's case.[1737]

11.448   **Sub-section 25(f): right to examine prosecution witnesses.**   The purpose of subsection 25(f) is to ensure that the accused has an adequate and proper opportunity to challenge and question witnesses against him at some stage in the proceedings. It does not appear to be necessary that this opportunity is always afforded at trial,[1738] or at a preliminary stage if the accused has the right to examine witnesses at trial.[1739] Where the witness is not available for cross-examination at all, the potential significance of cross-examination ought to be calculated as far as possible,[1740] but will not always be a mandatory element of a fair trial. Where the issue is one of admissibility of evidence, it is a matter of discretion as to the circumstances in which it will be proper to exclude.[1741] The jurisdiction of the Court is 'wide', going beyond the immediate question as to whether the prejudicial effect of the evidence outweighs its probative value, to questions as to overall unfairness to the accused.[1742]

11.449   In *R v Petaera*, the Court excluded a video-taped statement of a witness who had since died, because lack of opportunity to cross-examine would seriously impede a fair trial.[1743] On the other hand, *R v L*[1744] was a 'perhaps rare case' in which the court confidently

---

[1734] [1993] 1 NZLR 587, 593-594.

[1735] [1995] 3 NZLR 202.

[1736] Bill of Rights Act, s 24(d).

[1737] See *R v B* [1995] 2 NZLR 172; *R v B (No 2)* [1995] 2 NZLR 752.

[1738] *R v Haig* [1996] 1 NZLR 184, 192: this can be 'either at the time of the making of the statement or at some later stage of the proceeding'.

[1739] In *R v Haig* [1996] 1 NZLR 184, it was not a breach of s 25(f) that the Crown failed to call all of its potential witnesses at the depositions stage.

[1740] *R v Haig* [1996] 1 NZLR 184.

[1741] In *R v L* [1994] 2 NZLR 54, the Court considered ten principles governing the discretion to exclude otherwise admissible evidence in a series of steps. The last two concerned the applicability of standards of criminal justice under provisions of the New Zealand Bill of Rights Act 1990.

[1742] *R v Petaera* [1994] 3 NZLR 763.

[1743] Ibid.

[1744] [1994] 2 NZLR 54.

concluded that there was no basis for giving any substantial weight to the absence of any practical opportunity to cross-examine the complainant at the preliminary hearing.

In *R v B*[1745] and *R v B (No 2)*[1746] the right to cross-examine prosecution witnesses was one **11.450** of the grounds put forward for justifying the refusal of the complainant to obtain a medical examination anticipated to provide evidence in support of the position of the accused. The connection between such refusal and the right to cross-examination is tenuous, and the decision does not elaborate on the application of section 25(f) specifically.

Sub-section 25(g): benefit of a lesser penalty. This protects the right, if convicted of an **11.451** offence in respect of which the penalty has been varied between the commission of the offence and sentencing, to the benefit of the lesser penalty. In *Norton-Bennett v Attorney General*,[1747] an increase in the period of ineligibility for parole from seven to ten years,[1748] following conviction of the accused, did not constitute a variation in 'penalty' and the prisoner was not entitled to parole upon serving the lesser period.

Sub-section 25(h): right of appeal. This does not guarantee an appeal from a pre-trial **11.452** interlocutory application that does not lead to conviction. The issue was raised when the Court of Appeal denied jurisdiction to hear an appeal from an unsuccessful application for an order that the complainant undergo a medical examination.[1749] It held that the Bill of Rights Act conferred no jurisdiction in relation to appeals from pre-trial applications where there was none granted under the terms of the Judicature Act.[1750]

(c) Freedom from retroactive penalties and double jeopardy: section 26.

Section 26(1) guarantees that no person shall be liable to conviction of any offence on ac- **11.453** count of any act or omission which did not constitute an offence by such person under the law of New Zealand at the time it occurred. The provision recognises the fundamental principle of substantive criminal law that the law should not take effect retrospectively. Where a statutory amendment had broadened the scope of a serious sexual violation following an alleged commission of the offence, the judge, citing subsection 26(1) of the New Zealand Bill of Rights Act, instructed the jury not to apply it to the case before them.[1751]

Subsection 26(2) which prohibits 'double jeopardy', provides that no one who has been **11.454** finally acquitted or convicted of, or pardoned for, an offence shall be tried or punished for it again. This section applies only to criminal proceedings.[1752] In *Bracanov v Moss*,[1753]

[1745] [1995] 2 NZLR 172.

[1746] [1995] 2 NZLR 752.

[1747] [1995] 3 NZLR 712.

[1748] The statute was unambiguous in that it stated clearly that the new minimum non-parole period was to apply to sentences imposed after a specific date, regardless of when the offence had been committed.

[1749] *R v B* [1995] 2 NZLR 172.

[1750] The Court did allow that s 6 of the Bill of Rights Act provides for a liberal interpretation of the Judicature Act and may enable appeals to be brought in habeas corpus proceedings, but those are not proceedings subject to the same appellate limitations as criminal proceedings.

[1751] In *R v King* [1995] 3 NZLR 409 (amendment to the Crimes Act definition of 'sexual violation of a female child' from penetration of the 'vagina' to penetration of the 'genitalia' had the effect of expanding the crime to include acts that had previously been considered indecency).

[1752] *Daniels v Thompson* [1998] 3 NZLR 22.

[1753] *Bracanov v Moss* [1996] 1 NZLR 445.

Mr Bracanov was ordered to enter into a bond of $9000 on his own recognisance to keep the peace, in anticipation of a repeat of his expressions of anti-royalist sentiment that had led to his conviction for breach of the peace on eight previous occasions. The court, rejecting the argument of the accused, held that the peace bond order is not a conviction or an acquittal, so that a breach of the bond together with the conviction for the offence resulting in the breach could not amount to double jeopardy.

(d) Natural justice: section 27

11.455   Section 27 provides that every person has the right to the observance of the principles of natural justice by any tribunal or other public authority which has the power to make a determination in respect of that person's rights, obligations, or interests protected or recognised by law. Wherever those rights have been affected by such a determination a person may apply for judicial review of the decision; in addition, everyone has the right to bring or defend civil proceedings against or by the Crown and to have them heard in the same way as civil proceedings between individuals. A prosecutor is not a 'public authority' within the scope of section 27; the principles of natural justice had no application where a decision was made to transfer proceedings to the High Court to enable the Crown to proceed by way of indictment.[1754]

11.456   The remedy of judicial review in New Zealand, as defined by the Judicature Act, lies only in relation to a refusal to exercise a statutory power; it does not apply in relation to the exercise of a prerogative power where the subject of the decision is not justiciable. In *Burt v Governor-General*,[1755] the prerogative of mercy was said to be a matter of a value or conceptual judgment which had become a (non-reviewable) constitutional safeguard against mistakes in the criminal justice system.

11.457   '**Principles of natural justice**'.   Section 27 requires that any tribunal or other public authority which has the power to make a determination in respect of a person's rights, obligations or interests protected or recognised by law observes the principles of natural justice. It is not clear, however, what 'principles of natural justice' are and how they differ from minimum considerations of fairness protected by section 25 of the Bill of Rights Act. Principles of natural justice provide that the applicant must have an opportunity to place before the decision-maker information relevant to his decision. In order to do so effectively, he must also have a fair opportunity to comprehend the conditions upon which the decision is to be made.[1756] In *Ankers*,[1757] the decision of the authorities in relation to an application for social welfare benefits was in breach of section 27 because the applicant had not been informed as to the principal criteria bearing on his eligibility.

11.458   It is apparent from the case law that the principles of natural justice are to some degree intertwined with the essential elements of a fair trial in criminal cases.[1758] In several cases the

---

[1754] *R v K* [1995] 2 NZLR 440.

[1755] [1992] 3 NZLR 672 (when Mr Burt's application for leave to appeal his murder conviction was refused, he applied to the Governor-General for exercise of the prerogative of mercy and grant of full pardon. When it was declined, he commenced a judicial review proceeding of that decision, alleging that the Justice Department had failed to act fairly and reasonably in dealing with the application. The proceeding was dismissed on the basis that no reasonable cause of action was disclosed, and the applicant appealed).

[1756] *Ankers v A-G* [1995] NZAR 241.

[1757] Ibid.

[1758] Ibid.

overlap between the minimum standards of criminal justice and 'natural justice' is also apparent. It has been found that the section 25(e) right to be present and present a defence would be rendered ineffectual where the accused is not capable of comprehending the case against him as required by the principles of natural justice.[1759] In *W v A-G; P v Wellington District Court*,[1760] a refusal of leave to cross-examine the complainant at a preliminary hearing was found not contrary to the principles of 'natural justice', because there would be an opportunity to cross-examine at trial as required by section 25(f). Compliance with section 27 rested on the existence of one of the minimum elements of fairness required by section 25.

Appendix 3: Human Rights Cases in Other Jurisdictions

(1) Introduction

Over the past 50 years, 'fair trial' issues have been considered by the courts in many jurisdictions. However, the most developed 'due process' jurisprudence remains that decided under the US Constitution. Despite its idiosyncrasies, this jurisprudence continues to influence the development of the law throughout the common law world. There are two specific areas: general 'due process' and 'criminal due process' rights. **11.459**

The general 'due process' rights in the US Constitution are to be found in the Fifth Amendment which provides that: **11.460**

> No person shall . . . be deprived of life, liberty, or property, without due process of law.

The Fourteenth Amendment extends this protection to the States: its 'due process' clause was the means by which provisions of the Bill of Rights were made applicable to the States. A distinction has been drawn between substantive and procedural due process: substantive due process deals with what public authorities can do and procedural due process deals with the way in which the public authorities act.[1761] The due process clauses apply only to deprivations of 'life, liberty or property' and these notions have all been subject to extensive analysis[1762] which is not directly relevant to the subject matter of the present chapter.[1763]

The fair trial rights as dealt with by Article 6 of the Convention, find their equivalent in the US doctrine of procedural due process with its general requirements of prior notice and the right to be heard.[1764] The more significant the interest involved, the stricter the requirement for effective notice.[1765] The right to be heard generally includes the right to **11.461**

[1759] *R v Duval* [1995] 3 NZLR 202.
[1760] [1993] 1 NZLR 1.
[1761] See generally, H Abraham and B Perry, *Freedom and the Court* (7th edn, Oxford Universitgy Press, 1998), Chap 4, 'The Fascinating World of Due Process of Law'; and see also D Galligan, *Due Process and Fair Procedures* (Clarendon Press, 1996), Chap 6 'The American Doctrine of Procedural Due Process'.
[1762] See generally, L Tribe, *American Constitutional Law* (2nd edn, Foundation Press, 1988) 663ff; Galligan (n 1761 above) 192-197.
[1763] But see para 18.116ff below (in relation to the deprivation of 'property').
[1764] See Tribe (n 1762 above) 732ff.
[1765] See for example *Memphis Light, Gas and Water Division v Craft* (1978) 436 US 1 (notice threatening cutting off of utilities must indicate the procedures for challenging the decision); *Greene* v *Lindsey* (1982) 456 US 444 (statute allowing notice of possession proceedings by attachment to door after one attempt at personal service violated due process rights).

present evidence and to cross-examine witnesses.[1765a] However, these rights may be limited or denied in exceptional circumstances.[1766] In determining whether particular procedures satisfy the procedural due process requirements, three factors are considered:[1767]

- the nature of the private interest affected;
- the risk of mistaken deprivation of that interest and the probable value of the additional procedural safeguards;
- the government's interest, including the function involved and fiscal and administrative burden of the additional procedural safeguards.[1767a]

These factors have sometimes led the US courts to deny the right to a hearing: for example, in relation to prison[1768] discipline or dismissal of students for failure to meet academic standards,[1769] the suspension of employees facing criminal charges,[1770] the termination of social security disability benefits[1770a] or issues relating to academic evaluation.[1771] Public employees who have tenure or fixed term contracts have a right to due process in dismissal proceedings.[1771a] The due process clause limits the use of government agents to seize property from one private individual to convey it to another. This covers matters such as pre-judgment garnishee orders[1771b] and prejudgment seizure of property.[1771c]

11.462   Other provisions of the US Bill of Rights provide 'fair trial' rights to those charged with criminal offences. These cover protection against unreasonable search and seizure,[1772] self-incrimination,[1773] cruel and unusual punishment,[1774] double jeopardy,[1775] and excessive bail[1776] as well as the Sixth Amendment rights to counsel, to be confronted with witnesses, to trial by jury and to a speedy trial. In a series of well known cases in the 1960s, the Supreme Court considered the effect of violations of these rights on the admissibility of evidence, holding that evidence was inadmissible in both state and federal courts if obtained

- by searches and seizures in violation of the Fourth Amendment;[1777]
- by secretly taping conversations with a suspect after indictment;[1778]

[1765a] See generally, C Antieau and W Rich, *Modern Constitutional Law* (2nd edn, West Group, 1997) Vol 2, para 35.00ff.
[1766] See generally, Tribe (n 1762 above) 736ff.
[1767] See *Mathews v Eldridge* (1976) 424 US 315.
[1767a] *United States v James Daniel Good Property* (1993) 510 US 43.
[1768] *Wolff v McDonnell* (1974) 418 US 539.
[1769] *Board of Curators v Horowtiz* (1978) 435 US 78; but there will be due process rights in cases of suspension for misconduct: see *Goss v Lopez* (1975) 419 US 565.
[1770] *Gilbert v Homar* (1997) 520 US 924 (state university policeman arrested on drugs charges).
[1770a] *Mathews v Eldridge* (1976) 424 US 319.
[1771] *Board of Curators v Horowitz* (1978) 435 US 78.
[1771a] *Cleveland Board of Education v Loudermill* (1985) 470 US 532.
[1771b] *Sniadach v Family Finance Corporation* (1969) 395 US 377.
[1771c] *Fuentes v Shevin* (1972) 407 US 67.
[1772] Fourth Amendment.
[1773] Fifth Amendment.
[1774] Eighth Amendment.
[1775] Fifth Amendment.
[1776] Eighth Amendment.
[1777] *Mapp v Ohio* (1961) 367 US 643.
[1778] *Massiah v United States* (1964) 377 US 201.

- by the interrogation of a suspect in custody, without his consent, unless a defence lawyer is present;[1779]
- by eavesdropping on or bugging a suspect without a warrant.[1780]

However, the Supreme Court has retreated from strictness of this approach in a number of cases over the past three decades. For example,

- a suspect's confession in the absence of his lawyer can be used to attack his credit;[1781]
- a compulsory blood sample[1782] or videotape of drunk driving suspects[1783] does not violate the self-incrimination rule;
- evidence obtained on a search when the police act in an 'objectively reasonable' reliance on a warrant which turns out to be defective.[1784]

The approach of the US courts to criminal due process issues can be characterised 'pragmatic', on a case-by-case basis.

There is now a substantial body of international human rights 'fair trials' jurisprudence in relation to criminal cases. This is helpfully summarised in the *Fair Trials Manual* published by Amnesty International.[1784a] A wide range of 'international standards' have been suggested including the following:

11.462A

- the right not to be compelled to testify or confess guilt, which includes a prohibition against any form of coercion;[1784b]
- the exclusion of evidence elicited as a result of torture or other coercion (including violence, threats or methods of interrogation which impairs the judgment of detainees);[1784c]
- the right to call and examine witnesses (including a right to know the identity of prosecution witnesses).[1784d]

(2) Australia

Section 80 of the Australian Constitution guarantees that:

11.463

> The trial on indictment of any offence against any law of the Commonwealth shall be by jury.[1785]

This section has been interpreted narrowly. The federal Parliament can itself determine whether a trial is to be on indictment and, as a result, whether there will be a jury trial.[1786]

[1779] *Miranda v Arizona* (1966) 384 US 436.
[1780] *Katz v United States* (1967) 389 US 347.
[1781] *Harris v New York* (1971) 401 US 222; see also *Michigan v Harvey* (1990) 494 US 344.
[1782] *Schmerber v California* (1966) 384 US 757.
[1783] *Pennsylvania v Muniz* (1990) 496 US 582.
[1784] *Massachusetts v Sheppard* (1984) 468 US 981.
[1784a] Amnesty International, 1998.
[1784b] Ibid para 16.1.
[1784c] Ibid Chap 17.
[1784d] Ibid Chap 22.
[1785] See generally, G Williams, *Human Rights Under the Australian Constitution* (Oxford Univeristy Press, 1999) 103-110.
[1786] See *R v Archdall and Roskruge, ex p Carrigan and Brown* (1928) 41 CLR 128 and *R v Federal Court of Bankruptcy, ex p Lowenstein* (1939) 59 CLR 556.

This point has, however, been the subject of a number of powerful dissenting judgments[1787] in which it has been argued that section 80 should be given substantive meaning. However, it has been held that once an accused has a right to trial by jury this right cannot be waived[1788] and the verdict must be unanimous.[1789]

11.464   In addition, the High Court has recognised an 'implied constitutional right'[1790] to a 'fair trial'.[1791] This is recognised as the 'central thesis of the administration of criminal justice' in Australia.[1792] In *Dietrich v The Queen*[1793] it was held that lack of legal representation could mean that an accused is unable to receive a fair trial. In that case where a person charged with a serious offence was, through no fault of his own, without legal representation, the court ordered that the trial should be stayed until representation was available.

11.465   The privilege against self-incrimination is not a constitutionally protected right[1794] and is not available to corporations.[1795] The courts have considered the role that the privilege plays in ensuring a fair trial. The fact that evidence is obtained by deception or trickery does not mean that it should be excluded at trial.[1796] However in *R v Swaffield, Pavic v R*[1797] the High Court held that covertly recorded confession evidence could be excluded if the police tactics caused unfairness to the accused.[1798]

11.466   The High Court has also recognised a limited form of procedural due process guarantee. Thus,

> to cause a court to act in a manner contrary to natural justice would impose a non-judicial requirement inconsistent with the exercise of judicial power[1799]

Some support has also been expressed for an implied constitutional right to equality before the law.[1800] but such an approach was rejected by the majority of the High Court in *Kruger v The Commonwealth*[1801] The Court rejected the argument that a statute which allowed the removal of Aboriginal children from their families was invalid because it was discriminatory.

[1787] See eg *per* Dixon and Evatt JJ in *R v Federal Court of Bankruptcy, ex p Lowenstein* (n 1786 above); Deane J in *Kingswell v The Queen* (1985) 159 CLR 264.
[1788] *Brown v The Queen* (1986) 160 CLR 171.
[1789] *Cheatle v The Queen* (1993) 177 CLR 541.
[1790] See generally, para 1.39 above.
[1791] See *Jago v District Court of New South Wales* (1989) 168 CLR 23; this right has been recognised for many years, see *R v Macfarlane, ex p O'Flanagan and O'Kelly* (1923) 32 CLR 518, 541-2; see generally, J Hope, 'A Constitutional Right to a Fair Trial? Implications for the Reform of the Australian Criminal Justice System' (1996) 24 FLR 173; and G Williams (n 1786 above) 214-225.
[1792] *McInnis v R* (1979) 143 CLR 575.
[1793] (1992) 177 CLR 292.
[1794] *Sorby v Commonwealth of Australia* (1983) 152 CLR 281.
[1795] *Environment Protection Authority v Caltex Refining Pty Ltd* (1993) 178 CLR 477.
[1796] *Ridgeway v The Queen* (1995) 129 ALR 41, 53; see the discussion in Williams (n 1785 above) 218-219.
[1797] (1998) 151 ALR 98.
[1798] Referring to *R v Hebert* [1990] 2 SCR 151 (SCC) and *R v Broyles* [1991] 3 SCR 595.
[1799] *Leeth v Commonwealth* (1992) 174 CLR 455, 470 (Mason CJ, Dawson and McHugh JJ).
[1800] Ibid, *per* Deane and Toohey JJ (dissenting).
[1801] (1997) 190 CLR 1.

(3) Bermuda

The Supreme Court of Bermuda held in *Fubler v A-G*,[1802] that the constitutional right to **11.467**
a fair trial included legal professional privilege. That case concerned a police search of a
lawyer's office under a lawful warrant. The police also made a back-up tape of the office's
word-processing system. The lawyer objected that the tape contained confidential information. The court noted that privilege in documents on a word-processing system was not
breached until those documents were reviewed. The police were accordingly permitted to
sort documents on the back-up tape in the same way that hard-copies were sorted.

(4) Hong Kong

(a) Introduction

Articles 10, 11 and 12 of the Hong Kong Bill of Rights contain the 'fair trial rights' in the **11.468**
terms of Articles 14 and 15 of the International Covenant on Civil and Political
Rights.[1803] It has been held that an arrested person cannot rely on Articles 10 and 11 to
challenge the evidence gathering process of the prosecuting authorities.[1804] This was because these articles relate to the determination of a criminal trial whereas the process of evidence gathering did not form part of the trial. At that stage, the rights and liberty of a
suspected person were not at stake or in jeopardy.

(b) Scope of the rights

The rights in Article 10 come into play with respect to 'suits at law'. Accordingly, the rights **11.469**
do not apply to an administrative hearing which is part of a planning process;[1805] an initial classification of an article by the Obscene Articles Tribunal, without the institution of
criminal proceedings;[1806] a tax assessment by the Commissioner of Inland Revenue;[1807] or
extradition proceedings.[1808] However, Article 10 has been successfully utilised in some administrative law contexts. In *Re Otis Elevator Co (HK) Ltd*,[1809] for example, the court
found that Article 10 was breached when a Director of Electrical and Mechanical Services
brought charges against a lift contractor for negligence or misconduct, and then sat as a
member of the disciplinary board. This was a clear case of a person sitting as a judge in his
own cause. However, the court issued a warning in *R v The Town Planning Board, ex p The
Real Estate Developers Association of Hong Kong*[1810] that an argument based on the rules of
natural justice which would not succeed on the basis of the common law was unlikely to
be improved by the invocation of the Bill of Rights.

In *Chan Po Ming v Chow Tat Ming; Re Lau San Ching; Fung Chan Ki v Chow Tat Ming*[1811] **11.470**

[1802] [1996] 2 CHRLD 268.
[1803] See App J in Vol 2.
[1804] *A-G v Osman* [1992] 1 HKCLR 35.
[1805] *Kwan Kong Co Ltd v Town Planning Board* 11 Jul 1996, CA, *Hong Kong Law Digest*, Jul 1996,
G 168; see also *Auburntown Ltd v Town Planning Board* [1994] 2 HKLR 272.
[1806] *Re Loui Wai Po* [1994] HKLY 200.
[1807] *Commissioner of Inland Revenue, Hong Kong v Lee Lai Ping* [1993] HKLY 178.
[1808] *Re Suthipong Smittachartch* [1993] 1 HKLR 93.
[1809] [1995] 2 HKLR 1.
[1810] 8 Jun 1996, *Hong Kong Law Digest*, Jul 1996 G8.
[1811] [1995] 2 HKLR 14.

legislation which restricted the remedies available to electoral candidates to election petitions, as opposed to judicial review, was upheld as being in conformity with Article 10, even though a candidate would be unable to assert his rights until the outcome of the election. One of the most important considerations under the legislation was to preserve the integrity of the electoral process. The procedure laid down for election petitions was designed to protect this in an orderly manner. Having regard to the tight timetable for each of the successive steps in an election, it would be most unsatisfactory if interested parties were able to resort to the courts during the currency of the election and perhaps cause confusion and uncertainty.

(c) The presumption of innocence

11.471 A large number of cases concerning whether reverse onus clauses contravene the presumption of innocence have been considered under the Hong Kong Bill of Rights. The leading decision in this area is *A-G of Hong Kong v Lee Kwong-kut*.[1812] The Privy Council stated in that case that it would be difficult to justify a criminal law presumption unless it can be said with substantial assurance that the presumed fact is more likely than not to flow from the proved fact on which it is made to depend. There is also a requirement of proportionality, in that the presumption must go no further than necessary having regard to the evil that it was aimed at and the difficulty the Crown would have in combatting it without the aid of the presumption.[1813]

11.472 The following presumptions have been struck down by Hong Kong courts:

- That a person who possessed a certain quantity of drugs was trafficking in them (the quantity which triggered that presumption was very low, and failed the test of rationality and proportionality);[1814] and
- That any person who obtained property by means of a cheque which is dishonoured would, until the contrary is proved, be deemed to have obtained the property with knowledge that the cheque would be dishonoured.[1815] Further, the court refused to interpret the provision as imposing an evidential burden only on the accused.

The courts have, however, upheld the presumption that a person present in a gambling establishment was taking part in the gambling;[1816] the presumption that a person proved to be in physical possession of dangerous drugs knew what the drugs were, a presumption which could be rebutted on the balance of probabilities;[1817] the presumption that a Crown servant maintaining a standard of living above that which was commensurate with his official emoluments was involved in bribery.[1818]

[1812] [1993] AC 951.

[1813] *R v Sin Yau Ming* [1992] 1 HKCLR 127.

[1814] *R v Sin Yau Ming* [1992] 1 HKCLR 127.

[1815] *R v Lau Shiu Wah* [1992] HKDCLR 11.

[1816] *R v Choi Kai On* [1995] 1 HKCLR 79.

[1817] *R v Sin Yau Ming* [1992] 1 HKCLR 127.

[1818] *A-G v Hui Kin Hong* [1995] 1 HKCLR 227. See also: *R v Chong Ah Choi* 1994 3 HKC 68 (presumption concerning possession of offensive weapons); In *R v Chan Chak Fan* 1994 3 HKC 145; *R v Lai Yiu Pui* [1994] 2 HKCLR 17 (presumption relating to ships smuggling unauthorised entrants); *R v Wong Hiu Chor* [1993] 1 HKCLR 107 (if it was proved that a person possessed a restricted article in circumstances that gave rise to a reasonable suspicion that there is an intent to evade a restriction it would be presumed that a person had the requisite intent in the absence of evidence to the contrary; presumption upheld, particularly as the burden on the accused was evidential only).

The presumption of innocence was held not to apply to presumptions in drug trafficking **11.473** legislation that sums received by a person convicted of drug trafficking were the proceeds of such drug trafficking. That was because those presumptions were not being used to penalise drug traffickers, but instead to disgorge drug traffickers of their ill gotten gains. When a prison term in default was fixed, it was not to punish the drug trafficker for trafficking, but rather to enforce the court's order for payment. In any event, the presumptions were rational and realistic, and proportionate to the grave danger to society of leaving drug traffickers rich and to that extent powerful even when behind bars.[1819] This approach can be contrasted to that taken in *R v Chan Suen Hay*,[1820] in which a discretionary disqualification order under companies legislation was found to be a 'penalty' within the meaning of Article 12 (ban on retrospective penalties).

(d) The right to legal assistance

Article 11(2)(d) provides that a person facing a criminal charge has the right 'to have legal **11.474** assistance assigned to him, in any case where the interests of justice so require, and without payment by him in any such case if he does not have sufficient means to pay for it'. This provision was considered in *R v Wong Cheung Bun*,[1821] in which a defendant charged with robbery was refused legal aid because his assets exceeded the maximum specified in the relevant legal aid rules. The reason for this decision was the defendant's ownership of a village house. The defendant succeeded in obtaining a stay of the prosecution based on a breach of Article 11(2)(d). The defendant required legal representation, and could not realistically pay for it. Reasonable but unsuccessful efforts had been made to mortgage the property. Further, it was clear that sale was not a practical possibility because of the nature of the property and the family circumstances.

(e) Double jeopardy

The court considered the prohibition on double jeopardy in Article 11(6) in *R v Wan Kit* **11.475** *Man*.[1822] That case concerned a driver's disqualification based on the accumulation of fixed penalty offences. The driver argued that he should not have been disqualified after he had duly paid all the fixed penalties. The court held that disqualification was not a punishment but the civil consequence of an offence. Even if disqualification was a punishment, it did not constitute double punishment. A single act (namely, the final fixed penalty offence which resulted in disqualification) could have more than one consequence.

(5) India

Article 20 of the Indian Constitution provides that: **11.476**

(1) No person shall be convicted of any offence except for the violation of a law in force at the time of the commission of the act charged as an offence, nor be subjected to a penalty greater than that which might have been inflicted under the law in force at the time of the commission of the offence.
(2) No person shall be prosecuted and punished for the same offence more than once.
(3) No person accused of any offence shall be compelled to be a witness against himself.

[1819] *R v Ko Chi Yuen* [1994] 2 HKCLR 65.
[1820] [1995] HKLY 205.
[1821] [1992] 1 HKCLR 240.
[1822] [1992] 1 HKCLR 224.

11.477   The prohibition in Article 20(1) of conviction under *ex post facto* law does not apply to a trial under procedural rules enacted after the commission of an offence;[1823] sanctions by a civil or revenue authority, to enforce a civil liability;[1824] preventive detention;[1825] or the retrospective creation of a new rule of evidence or presumption relating to an existing offence.[1826] The privilege against self-incrimination in Clause 3 extends to production of documentary evidence, but does not extend to giving thumb impressions, specimen writing or showing parts of the body by way of identification.[1827]

(6) Ireland

11.478   Article 38.1 of the Irish Constitution provides that:

> No person shall be tried on any criminal charge save in due course of law.[1828]

In *Goodman International v Hamilson (No 1)*,[1829] the Supreme Court held that the establishment of a tribunal to investigate alleged criminal (or potentially criminal) conduct could not 'in any circumstances' amount to a trial of a criminal charge. That was because the tribunal's findings could not form the basis of a conviction or an acquittal, nor could the tribunal impose penalties on any person.

11.479   The question of what constitutes a 'criminal charge' under Article 38 has been considered in a number of customs and excise cases. The indicia of a criminal offence are:

- its character as an offence against the community at large rather than an individual;
- the punitive nature of the sanction; and
- the requirement of *mens rea*.[1830]

Thus, in *McLoughlin v Tuite*,[1831] the imposition of a penalty under a tax statute was held to be a civil matter. Although the penalty was payable to the community at large, there was no imprisonment if the penalty was not paid; and the fact that liability to pay the penalty did not cease on death but continued against the estate of the deceased indicated that *mens rea* was not an essential ingredient.[1832]

11.480   The phrase 'in due course of law' has been described as:

> a phrase of very wide import which includes within its scope not merely matters of statutory and constitutional jurisdiction, the range of legislation with respect of criminal offences, and matters of practice and procedure, but also the application of basic principles of justice which are inherent in the proper course of the exercise of the judicial function.[1833]

[1823] *Shiv Bahadur v State of U P* A 1953 SC 394.

[1824] *Brij Bhukan v S D O* A 1955 Pat 1, SB; *State of W B v S K Ghose* 1963 SC 255; *Shiv Dutt v Union of India* A 1984 SC 1194.

[1825] *Prahlad v State of Bombay* A 1952 Bom 1.

[1826] *Sajjan Singh v State of Punjab* A1964 SC 464, 468.

[1827] *State of Bombay v Kathi Kalu* A 1961 SC 1808, 1816.

[1828] See generally, J M Kelly, *The Irish Constitution* (3rd edn, Butterworths Ireland, 1994) 572–623.

[1829] [1992] 2 IR 542.

[1830] *Melling v Mathghamhna* [1962] IR 1.

[1831] [1986] IR 235.

[1832] See also: *DPP v Downes* [1987] IR 139 (fixed mandatory revenue penalty where there had been failure to comply with statutory requirements created a non-criminal liability: statutory language was not criminal); cf *DPP v Boyle* [1993] ILRM 128 (statutory provisions which referred to 'excise penalties', 'offence' and 'summary conviction' created a criminal offence).

[1833] *The State (Healy) v Donoghue* [1976] IR 325.

The requirement of 'in due course of law' encompasses both procedural and substantive rights. Thus, a defendant who was convicted by a judge after a summary trial on a charge of robbery, not having been informed of his right to be tried by jury for that offence, had not been tried 'in due course of law';[1834] a statutory provision which made certain conduct an offence if committed by a 'suspected person or reputed thief' was held not to be 'in due course of law', because of vagueness.[1835] The concept incorporates traditional common law principles of criminal law, such as the prohibition against double jeopardy and retroactivity;[1836] and the principle that sentences must not be arbitrary or disproportionate.[1837] Finally, the phrase 'in due course of law' has been relied upon to overturn convictions where there has been a delay in the trial. An important factor in such cases is the prejudice to the defence.[1838]

11.481 Legal process rights have also been considered in the context of Article 40.3.1 of the Irish Constitution, which provides that:

> The State guarantees in its laws to respect, and, as far as is practicable, by its laws to defend and vindicate the personal rights of the citizen.

The right to have access to the courts is an unenumerated right under Article 40.3.1.[1839] In *Macauley v Minister for Posts and Telegraphs*[1840] it was decided that the requirement for the Attorney-General's consent in order to bring actions against government ministers was an infringement of that right. Common law immunities may be vulnerable to the right to litigate. The Supreme Court stated in *Ryan v Ireland*[1841] that the state's immunity from suit in respect of negligence occurring during armed conflicts would be inconsistent with Article 40.3.1. However, the state is not obliged to assist litigants financially in order to bring claims.[1842]

11.482 The right of access to the courts has had an impact on civil procedure. Thus, litigants should not be denied access to a court by fixing security of costs at too high a level.[1843] In *Bula v Tara Mines Ltd*[1844] the court stated that the right of access to courts gave rise to a right to inspect property which was part of the subject matter of a claim, and also to inspect documents, without having to prove a *prima facie* case.

11.483 In the context of criminal cases, where a constitutional breach is committed 'for the purpose of securing a confession', the confession must be excluded, 'on that ground alone'.[1845] The Supreme Court held in *Cahalane v Murphy*[1846] that delay in charging the defendant

---

[1834] *The State (Vozza) v O'Floinn* [1957] IR 227.

[1835] *King v A-G* [1981] IR 233.

[1836] Kelly (n 1828 above) 577–585.

[1837] *Cox v Ireland* [1992] 2 IR 503.

[1838] See *State (O'Connell) v Fawsitt* [1986] IR 362 (applicant tried in 1985 for alleged assault in 1981; delay had led to unavailability of important defence witnesses).

[1839] *Macauley v Minister for Posts and Telegraphs* [1996] IR 345.

[1840] Ibid.

[1841] [1989] IR 177.

[1842] See eg *M C v Legal Aid Board* [1991] 2 IR 43. But see *The State (O'Healy) v Landy* High Court, 10 Feb 1993 (legal aid required for mother to contest wardship proceedings which, like criminal proceedings, pitted a litigant against the power of the state, and had very serious consequences).

[1843] *Fallon v An Bord Pleanála* [1992] 2 IR 380.

[1844] [1987] IR 85.

[1845] See *People (The) (DPP) v Lynch* [1982] IR 64, 79, following *People (The) (A-G) v O'Brien* [1965] IR 142; *People (The) (DPP) v Kenny* [1990] 2 IR 110.

[1846] [1994] 2 ILRM 383.

can be taken into account when assessing whether a defendant has been tried within a reasonable time.[1847]

(7) Jamaica

11.484 By section 20 of the Constitution of Jamaica it is provided that:

> Whenever any person is charged with a criminal offence he shall, unless the charge is withdrawn, be afforded a fair hearing within a reasonable time by an independent and impartial court established by law

It has been held that the accused did not have to show any specific prejudice before being entitled to have charges against him dismissed because of unreasonable delay.[1848] In determining whether the accused had been deprived of a fair trial by reason of delay, factors which are relevant are the length of the delay, the reasons given by the prosecution to justify it, the efforts made by the accused to assert his rights and the prejudice to the accused.[1849]

11.485 The issue of bias in criminal appellate proceedings was considered in *Berry v DPP (No 2)*.[1850] In that case, the appellant appealed against his conviction for murder to the Court of Appeal of Jamaica. The Court dismissed his appeal, finding his version of facts to be 'incredible'. As a result of prosecution and trial irregularities, the Privy Council allowed the appellant's further appeal and remitted the case to the Jamaican Court of Appeal with a direction to quash the conviction and either enter a verdict of acquittal or order a new trial. The Court of Appeal, which included two of the same judges who had earlier dismissed the appellants' appeal, ordered a new trial. The appellant brought proceedings claiming there was a reasonable suspicion that he had not received a fair hearing by reason of the judges' participation in the earlier decision. The Privy Council rejected that argument. The Court's task on remission was to balance competing considerations in order to determine whether the interests of justice required a new trial. The Court of Appeal was best equipped to perform this balancing. The fact that two judges participated in an earlier judgment which expressed strong views about the guilt of the appellant in light of the evidence before them did not mean there was any danger of bias in the Court of Appeal's decision to order a new trial. Further, the scrupulous care the judges took in weighing the relevant considerations in their judgment on the issue of a new trial confirms that there is no reason to believe that they were not wholly impartial.

11.486 In *Robinson v the Queen*[1851] the Privy Council held that the right to legal representation of choice was not an absolute right, in that it was not necessary for an adjournment to be granted to ensure than any defendant in a criminal matter who desired legal representation was duly represented.[1852] In exercising its discretion whether to grant an adjournment the court had to consider matters such as present and future availability of witnesses. As the absence of legal representation in this case was caused by the conduct of the

---

[1847] See also *EO'R v DPP* [1996] 2 IR 128 (prosecution prohibited for sexual offences committed several years prior to charge).

[1848] *Bell v DPP of Jamaica* [1985] AC 937.

[1849] Following *Barker v Wingo* (1972) 407 US 514.

[1850] [1996] 3 LRC 697.

[1851] [1985] 1 AC 956.

[1852] It should be noted that Lord Scarman and Lord Edmund-Davies dissented.

defendant's counsel and also by the defendant's failure to ensure that his counsel were paid or otherwise to apply in advance for legal aid, the judge's failure to adjourn the trial in order to instruct an alternative legal representative did not deprive the defendant of his right to be represented by an advocate of his own choice. It should be noted that the judge's failure in this case to adjourn led to the defendant being unrepresented in a capital case.[1853]

The case of *Huntley v A-G for Jamaica*[1854] concerned a statutory provision whereby every **11.487** person under a sentence of death for murder was to be reviewed by a judge of the Jamaica Court of Appeal with a view to determining whether the murder was to be treated as capital or non-capital. There was no provision for prior notice of the judge's classification to be given to the convicted person but a person whose case had been classified as capital murder had the right to have that classification reviewed, and the right to be represented at that review. The appellant argued that the classification process was unconstitutional because it denied a person charged with a criminal offence the opportunity to be heard. That challenge was rejected by the Privy Council. The classification was a limited exercise whereby a judge would review the trial record and ask whether a properly directed jury could have reached any conclusion other than that the murder had been capital murder. That process did not involve the determination of guilt or innocence.

(8) Mauritius

Section 10(1) of the Constitution of Mauritius provides that: **11.488**

> Where any person is charged with a criminal offence, then, unless the charge is withdrawn, the case shall be afforded a fair hearing within a reasonable time by an independent and impartial court established by law.

The effect of this provision is that a trial must take place within a reasonable time after arrest and, in some cases, it may be proper to take into account the period before the arrest.[1855] This provision:

> injects the need for urgency and efficiency into the prosecution of offenders and demands the provision of adequate resources for the administration of justice but, in determining whether the constitutional rights of an individual have been infringed, the courts must have regard to the constraints imposed by harsh economic reality and local conditions.[1856]

It is a fundamental requirement of justices that those required to deliver the verdict must have heard all the evidence and a conviction was quashed when one of the convicting magistrates had not heard all the evidence.[1857]

(9) Namibia

In *Mwellie v Ministry of Works*[1858] the High Court of Namibia upheld a limitation period **11.489** of 12 months for bringing wrongful dismissal proceedings against the State. The Court

---

[1853] For an example of a case where a court's refusal to adjourn following withdrawal of counsel led the Privy Council to quash a conviction, see *Dunkley v R* [1995] 1 AC 419.
[1854] [1995] 2 AC 1.
[1855] *Mungroo v R* [1992] LRC (Const) 591, 594.
[1856] Ibid, 594-595 (four-years' delay from arrest to hearing, no breach).
[1857] *Curpen v R* [1992] LRC (Crim) 120; see also *Ng (alias Wong) v R* [1987] 1 WLR 1356.
[1858] 1995 (9) BCLR 1118.

stated that different limitation periods were not unconstitutional provided parties had a reasonable time to bring actions, and they were based on a reasonable classification. The distinction between state and non-state employees was reasonable and rationally connected to a legitimate objective, considering factors such as the size and geographical spread of the public service, the number of individual ministries and departments, staff turnover, budgetary constraints and the need for detailed and urgent investigations of challenges to dismissals.

11.490 In *State v Scholtz*[1859] the Supreme Court considered the information to which a criminal defendant is entitled. The court held that, upon service of an indictment, an accused person should ordinarily be entitled to the information contained in the police docket relating to the case prepared by the prosecution against the accused (including copies of witness statements) whether or not the prosecution intended to call those witnesses at trial. The state would be entitled to withhold any information, however, if it satisfied the court on the balance of probabilities that it had reasonable grounds for believing that disclosure might reasonably impede the ends of justice or otherwise be against the public interest. The time at which such disclosure should occur would depend on the circumstances of the case, but the overriding principle should be to give the accused reasonable time to prepare his case thoroughly. The duty of disclosure did not apply to the defence. In magistrates' courts, disclosure is not always necessary: it will be required in cases involving any complexity of fact or law.[1860] The right to 'adequate facilities' for the defence includes the opportunity to view and listen to material video and audio recordings.[1861]

11.491 Article 12(1)(d) provides that:

> All persons charged with an offence shall be presumed innocent until proven guilty according to law, after having had the opportunity of calling witnesses and cross-examining those called against them.

The Namibian courts have considered reverse onus provisions in a number of cases. A provision to the effect that a person who had rights in a forfeited article had to prove that he had taken all reasonable steps to prevent the use of the article in connection with the offence has been held to be unconstitutional.[1862]

(10) Pakistan

11.492 In *Al-Jehad Trust v Federation of Pakistan*[1863] certain judicial appointments, and non-appointments and transfers were challenged. It was alleged that those actions had been politically motivated. The Supreme Court of Pakistan upheld the challenges. The court noted that the right to an independent judiciary was a fundamental right. The constitutional consultation requirements concerning judicial appointments required effective, meaningful, purposive and consensus-oriented consultation. The opinion of the Chief Justice of Pakistan and the Chief Justice of a High Court as to the suitability of a candidate for judicial office should be accepted in the absence of very sound reasons, which should

---

[1859] [1997] 1 LRC 67.
[1860] *State v Angula* [1998] 1 LRC 14.
[1861] *State v Nassar* [1994] 3 LRC 295, 328.
[1862] *Freiremar SA v Prosecutor-General of Namibia* [1994] 2 LRC 251; see also *State v Van den Berg* [1995] 2 LRC 619.
[1863] PLD 1996 SC 324; [1996] PLR 394.

be recorded, and are justiciable. Political affiliation was not a sufficient ground in itself for disqualifying a candidate, if the candidate had unimpeachable integrity, sound legal knowledge, and had been recommended by the Chief Justice of the High Court concerned and the Chief Justice of Pakistan. Although judges will normally sever their political connections, it was not desirable to appoint strong political activists, as it might not be possible for them to avoid unconscious favouritism. Finally, the court added that it is contrary to the principle of independence of the judiciary to appoint acting judges when permanent vacancies existed, as acting judges had no security of tenure.

(11) Singapore

In *Balasundaram v Public Prosecutor*[1864] the High Court of Singapore held that the right of the accused to be defended by a legal practitioner of his choice applied only if counsel was willing and able to represent the accused. If counsel failed to attend or was not willing or able to act for the accused, he could not, by reason of that fact alone, claim that his constitutional right had been violated. There was no miscarriage of justice when the trial judge refused the appellant's application for an adjournment in order to let the accused's preferred counsel represent him, when the preferred counsel had made it clear that he would not be available for the trial date, and another counsel was willing to represent the accused.

11.493

(12) South Africa

(a) Introduction

Section 34 of the South African Constitution provides that:

11.494

> Everyone has the right to have any dispute that can be resolved by the application of law decided in a fair public hearing in a court or, where appropriate, another independent and impartial forum.

The rights of arrested, detained and accused persons are dealt with in detail in section 35.[1865] It has been said that the right of access to the courts is 'foundational to the stability of society'.[1866] The Constitutional Court has held that 'self-help' remedies are inimical to the rule of law and contrary to Section 34.[1867] The rule against self-help is necessary to protect individuals against 'arbitrary and subjective decisions and conduct of an adversary'. In view of the importance of access to the court, statutory self-help remedies were not a justifiable limitation on Section 34 rights.

Fair trial rights were held not to apply in the case of *Nel v Le Roux NO*,[1868] as the applicant was not an 'accused'. The applicant was summoned under statutory powers to appear before a magistrate to provide relevant information in connection with alleged offences committed by his associate. Failure to answer questions without 'just excuse' made an examinee liable to summary imprisonment. The applicant challenged the provision on

11.495

[1864] [1996] 4 LRC 597.
[1865] See generally, M Chaskalson, J Kentridge, J Klaaren, G Marcus, D Spitz and S Woolman (eds), *Constitutional Law of South Africa* (Juta, 1996) Chaps 26–28.
[1866] *Concorde Plastics (Pty) v NUMSA* 1997 (11) BCLR 1624; *Lesapo v North West Agricultural Bank* 1999 (12) BCLR 1420.
[1867] *Lesapo v North West Agricultural Bank* (n 1866 above).
[1868] [1996] 4 LRC 126.

the grounds that it infringed his right not to be detained without trial, the right to personal privacy, the right to freedom of expression, the right to procedural fairness in administrative matters, and the right to a fair trial. Those challenges failed. A 'just excuse' not to answer questions at an examination included situations where to do so would infringe any of a person's fundamental constitutional rights. Further, the fair trial rights were not applicable because the applicant was not, at that stage, 'an accused person'. The examinee was, however, entitled under the Constitution to have proceedings conducted with procedural fairness. It held further that the summary proceedings before a judicial officer which could lead to imprisonment were not inconsistent with the right not to be detained without trial, as they complied with the requirement that an impartial entity, independent of the executive and the legislature, act as arbiter between the individual and the state.

(b) The presumption of innocence

11.496 There have been a number of decisions by the Constitutional Court concerning reverse onus clauses. The basic approach of the Court is the same as that of the Canadian Supreme Court. In other words, the presumption of innocence is breached where a person can be convicted despite the existence of reasonable doubt as to his guilt. If the reverse onus provision is reasonable, however, it may be upheld under the general limitations clause. The decision in *Osman v A-G, Transvaal*[1869] contains a useful discussion of when onus in a criminal case is regarded as having shifted to the accused. That case concerned a provision that any person found in possession of any goods in regard to which there is a reasonable suspicion that they have been stolen and is unable to give a satisfactory account of such possession shall be guilty of an offence. The Court stated that it was the inability and not the failure or unwillingness to give a satisfactory account of possession that constituted the offence in section 36. The inability to give a satisfactory account of possession was an element of the offence, and the burden of proving it remained with the state. At no point did the onus of proof shift, nor did the accused ever lose the protection of the presumption of innocence. Accordingly, there was no violation of the presumption of innocence.[1870]

11.497 The Court has struck down reverse onus clauses on a number of occasions. The case of *S v Zuma*[1871] concerned a statutory rebuttable presumption that confessions recorded in writing by a magistrate were free and voluntary. The applicant successfully argued that the presumption violated his right to a free trial because it required him to prove, on the balance of probabilities, that such a confession was not free and voluntary. The fact that an accused could be required to prove on a balance of probabilities that a confession was not voluntary would permit a conviction in spite of a reasonable doubt as to its voluntariness. This was contrary to the constitutional rights to be presumed innocent, in addition to the rights to remain silent, not to be compelled to make confession and not to be a compellable witness against himself. The claim that the presumption acted to discourage

---

[1869] 1998 (11) BCLR 1362.

[1870] The Court also held that there was no breach of the right to silence, or not to be compelled into making a confession. The provision neither compelled an arrested or detained person to do anything, nor constituted pressure being applied on such person to make a statement. Such persons had a choice as to whether or not to provide an explanation for the possession of the goods. Arrested or detained persons suffered no prejudice at trial stage in the absence of a prior explanation, because they retained the express right to furnish an explanation at trial if no explanation had previously been given.

[1871] 1995 (4) BCLR 401.

dishonest retractions of confessions and thus shortened trials did not justify such a substantial infringement of fundamental rights. Therefore the breach of fair trial rights was not justified under section 33.

In *S v Bhulwana; S v Gwadiso*[1872] the Constitutional Court declared contrary to the presumption of innocence the inference of drug dealing from possession of a specified quantity of drugs, unless the accused could prove the contrary, on a balance of probabilities. The court noted that the possible penalties for drug dealing were very high. Langa J stated, at para 23:

> It does not appear to be logical to presume that a person found in possession of 115g of dagga [cannabis]is more likely than not to have been dealing in dagga . . . [the state] conceded that it would not be unreasonable for a regular user of dagga to possess that quantity of dagga . . . No explanation was proffered by the State as to why this particular quantity was selected. It appears to be an arbitrary figure, nowadays, whatever sense, if any, it may have made in the socio-economic environment that prevailed when it was originally introduced.[1873]

11.498

The case of *Scagell v A-G*[1874] concerned two presumptions in a gambling statute. The first was that where gambling devices, or other items capable of being used in gambling, were found at any place, it shall be prima facie evidence that the person in control of that place permitted gambling at that place, and that any person found on the place was visiting with the intention of gambling. The second presumption was that where a police officer was authorised to enter any particular place, but was refused entry, it was to be presumed that the person in charge of the place permitted gambling at that place. Those presumptions were declared to be unconstitutional.

11.499

In *S v Mbatha; S v Prinsloo*[1875] the presumption relating to the offence of unlawful possession of arms and ammunition was declared unconstitutional. That presumption was that where it was proved that arms and ammunition had been on any premises at any time, any person who was at that time in charge of or present at those premises, or any part thereof, would be presumed to have been in possession of the arms or ammunition, until the contrary was proved. The Court also found that the breach was not justified under the limitations clause. Although South Africa had high levels of crime, the presumption was widely phrased, and included within its reach many categories of potentially innocent people.

11.500

The reverse onus clauses challenged in *S v Coetzee*[1876] were struck down. The first clause provided that, where in criminal proceedings an accused is charged with an offence of which false representation is an element and it is proved that a false representation was made by the accused, the accused shall be presumed to have made the representation

11.501

[1872] 1995 (12) BCLR 1579.
[1873] See also following cases concerning drug related presumptions: *S v Julies* 1996 (4) SA 313 (Court declared unconstitutional presumption that a person found in possession of any quantity of an undesirable dependence producing substance was presumed to be dealing in that substance); *S v Ntsele* 1998 (11) BCLR 1543 (Court declared unconstitutional presumption that anyone in charge of cultivated land which has dagga [cannabis] plants growing on it is dealing in dagga); *S v Mello; S v Van Nell* 1988 (3) SA 712 (Court declared unconstitutional presumption that person found in immediate vicinity of drug would be presumed unless the contrary was proved to be in possession of drug).
[1874] 1996 (11) BCLR 1446, CC.
[1875] 1996 (3) BCLR 263.
[1876] 1997 (4) BCLR 437.

knowing it to be false, unless the contrary is proved. The second presumption was that where a corporate body has committed an offence, a servant or director of the corporate body is deemed to be guilty of that offence and personally liable to punishment unless the accused can show on a balance of probabilities that he did not participate in the offence and could not have prevented it. As regards the latter clause, although the Court recognised that directors bear a special responsibility to society, the presumption was too wide ranging in that it applied to any possible offence, and any type of liability. In *S v Baloyi*[1876a] the Constitutional Court adopted a construction of a statute relating to domestic violence which did not impose a reverse onus on the accused: although this involved some erosion of the right to silence it was a constitutionally appropriate balancing of the rights of all concerned.

(c) Trial within a reasonable time

11.502 A person charged with a criminal offence is entitled to a trial 'within a reasonable time'. The Constitutional Court considered the meaning of that phrase in *Sanderson v A-G*.[1877] In that case, the appellant teacher had been charged with committing sexual offences against two female pupils at a school at which he had previously taught. The appellant's first court appearance was in December 1994, but he had still not been brought to trial almost two years later. He applied for a permanent stay of prosecution, alleging that the delay had infringed his constitutional right to a trial within a reasonable time. The Court stated that in deciding what a reasonable time is, a court must make a value judgment, considering such factors as the kind of prejudice suffered by the accused, the nature and complexity of the case and lack of state resources which might hamper the investigation or prosecution of the case. The only prejudice suffered by the appellant had been social embarrassment. Because this social prejudice had not been seriously aggravated by the delay, the right in question had not been infringed. The right to be tried within a reasonable time was designed to protect both trial related prejudice, such as impairment to the accused's defence, and other forms of prejudice such a pre-trial incarceration, restrictive bail conditions, anxiety and stress, loss of income and social ostracism.[1878]

11.503 Delays in appellate proceedings were considered in *S v Pennington*.[1879] In that case, it held that appellate delays were materially different from trial delays. In the former, there could be no question of prejudice because the appeal is settled on the record, and when the appeal fails, the trial court's finding of guilt is merely confirmed. The Court left open the question of whether an appeal delay might, in some circumstances, constitute a violation of this or some other right.

(d) Access to the court

11.504 The right of access to courts for the settlement of justiciable disputes was considered in *AZAPO v President of RSA*.[1880] That case concerned the amnesty granted to people who had committed offences for political offences, and made a full disclosure to the Truth and

---

[1876a] 2000 (1) BCLR 86.
[1877] 1997 (12) BCLR 1675
[1878] See also *Wild v Hoffert NO* 1998 (6) BCLR 656 (stay of prosecution was not an ordinarily appropriate form of relief for failure to be tried within a reasonable time, unless there was trial related prejudice).
[1879] 1997 (12) BCLR 1413.
[1880] 1996 (4) SA 672.

Reconciliation Commission, from criminal and civil prosecution. The applicants argued that the amnesty was unconstitutional because it limited their rights under section 22 of the interim Constitution to have justiciable disputes settled by a court of law or other independent or impartial forum. The Court accepted that the amnesty limited rights to have justiciable disputes settled by a court of law but held that the limitation was sanctioned by the epilogue to the interim Constitution. Further, the Court noted that the amnesty was a crucial component of the negotiated transition to democracy, without which the Constitution would not have come into being. The amnesty provisions were not inconsistent with international norms and did not breach any of the country's obligations in terms of public international law instruments.

11.505 The right of access to civil courts was also considered in *Mohlomi v Minister of Defence*.[1881] The applicant in that case challenged a provision whereby any civil action against the state or any person arising from the conduct of armed forces be instituted within six months of the cause of action arising. Further, notice in writing of such civil action had to be given to the defendant at least one month before its commencement. The basis of the challenge was that the provision challenged the applicant's right to have justiciable disputes settled by a court of law or, where appropriate, another independent and impartial forum. The Court struck down that provision, stating that its overall effect was to require that notice be given no later than five months after the cause of action arose. Each particular limitation period must be scrutinised to see whether its terms were compatible with the rights embodied in section 22. The key question was whether there was, in all the circumstances characterising the class of case in question, a real and fair initial opportunity available to exercise the right. This limitation period was too short. The Court's finding was made against the background of conditions prevailing in South Africa, namely poverty, illiteracy, cultural and language differences and the inaccessibility of legal assistance.

(c) Other issues

11.506 The right of an accused not to be compelled to give testimony was considered in *Ferreira v Levin NO*.[1882] That case concerned a provision in companies legislation which stated that the Master of the Court may require any person to answer questions in winding up proceedings notwithstanding that the response might tend to incriminate that person and that the answer may thereafter be used as evidence against him. Failure to answer was an offence. It was held that use of such evidence in criminal proceedings was a breach of the privilege against self-incrimination, and therefore was not admissible at criminal proceedings. As regards the use in a subsequent criminal trial of evidence derived from compelled testimony, as distinct from the compelled testimony itself, the fairness of admitting or excluding such 'derivative evidence' was a matter to be decided by the judge or other officer presiding over the criminal trial.

11.507 The accessibility of police dockets to the defence was considered in *Shabalala v A-G of the Transvaal*.[1883] The accused in that case, charged with murder, applied before the trial for copies of the relevant police dockets, containing witness statements, and lists of exhibits in the possession of the state. Their application was refused at first instance because the trial court was not satisfied that the accused required the documents in order to exercise

---

[1881] 1996 (12) BCLR 1559.
[1882] 1996 (1) BCLR 1.
[1883] 1995 (12) BCLR 1593.

his rights to a fair trial. A related application for an order directing the state to make state witnesses available to the defence legal representatives for the purposes of consultation was also refused by the trial court, on the ground that the court was unable to conclude that the applicants would not be given a fair trial unless the court departed from the practice that the accused or his legal representatives could only consult with a state witness with the consent of the prosecutor. The Court stated that whether the right to a fair trial includes the right to have access to a police docket depends on the particular circumstances of each case, and is in the discretion of the court. The accused normally should have access to documents in the police docket, including statements of witnesses, unless the state can justify the denial of such access on the ground it is not required for the exercise of a fair trial. The claim to consult state witnesses can only be justified in circumstances where the accused's right to a fair trial would, in the special circumstances of the case, be impaired if the opportunity to consult is denied. The discretion to direct access to state witnesses rests with the court, which may refuse it where the prosecution is able to establish a reasonable risk of intimidation or of other prejudice to the proper ends of justice. Further, no state witness could be compelled to such consultation.

11.508 The right to appeal in criminal cases was considered in *S v Ntuli*.[1884] That case concerned a challenge to a criminal statute whereby convicted prisoners who lacked legal representation and who were convicted in a magistrates' court did not have an automatic right of appeal to the Supreme Court. Such prisoners could only appeal against their convictions or sentences if a Supreme Court judge certified that there were reasonable grounds for appeal. All other types of convicted prisoners did not require such permission to appeal from a decision of the magistrates' court to the Supreme Court. Didcott J stated, in a judgment with which all the other justices concurred, that the constitutional right to have recourse by way of appeal or review to a higher court at the minimum implied the opportunity to have an adequate reappraisal of every case and an informed decision on it. The relevant statute made no provision for such reappraisal. The decision on whether a certificate should be granted was generally made by a judge in chambers, without the benefit of oral argument. Moreover, there was no requirement or practice that the judge obtain a full copy of the criminal record from below. The requirement to obtain a judge's certificate also breached the equality rights in section 8(1) of the interim Constitution. The scheme impermissibly differentiated between appellants who were legally unrepresented, and those who were represented.

11.509 However, in *S v Rens*[1885] the requirement for leave to appeal in criminal cases was upheld. That leave could be obtained from the judge before whom conviction occurred, or the Chief Justice by way of a petition procedure. As stated by Langa J, with whom the other members of Constitutional Court concurred:

> It cannot be in the interests of justice and fairness to allow unmeritorious and vexatious issues of procedure, law or fact to be placed before three judges of the appellate tribunal sitting in open court to re-hear oral argument. The rolls would be clogged by hopeless cases, thus prejudicing the speedy resolution of those cases where there is sufficient substance to justify an appeal.
>
> In my view the petition procedure which is available to every accused whose application for leave to appeal has been refused [by the trial judge] allows such accused recourse to a higher court to review, in a broad and not a technical sense, the judgment of a trial court. The

---

[1884] 1996 (1) BCLR 141.
[1885] 1996 (2) BCLR 155.

procedure involves a re-assessment of the disputed issues by two judges of the higher court, and provides a framework for that assessment, which ensures that an informed decision is made by them as to the prospects of success. In this respect the procedure is materially different to the procedure for judges' certificates which we found to be inconsistent with the Constitution in . . . *S v Ntuli*.[1886]

The right of appeal in civil cases was challenged in *Besserglik v Minister of Trade, Industry and Tourism*[1887] as in breach of the right of access to courts. The Court expressed some doubt as to whether the right of access to courts included a right to appeal. Even if such a right were included, a screening process excluding unmeritorious appeals was not a denial of a right of access to a court. In *Beinash v Ernst and Young*[1888] the Constitutional Court held that the procedure whereby a person is declared a vexatious litigant and may not institute legal proceedings without first obtaining court permission limited that person's right of access to the courts, but was reasonable and justifiable.

11.510

(13) Sri Lanka

Article 13(4) of the Constitution provides that:

11.511

> No person shall be punished with death or imprisonment except by order of a competent court, made in accordance with procedure established by law. The arrest, holding in custody, detention or other deprivation of personal liberty of a person, pending investigation or trial, shall not constitute punishment.[1889]

Preventive detention under emergency regulations is not punishment within the terms of this article, as such detention is a precautionary rather than punitive measure.[1890]

Article 13(6) prohibits retrospective criminal legislation, but with a proviso for the trial and punishment of any person for any act or omission which at the time when it was committed was criminal, according to the general principles of law recognised by the community of nations, even though it was not an offence under local law. That proviso was applied by the Supreme Court in a decision concerning the constitutionality of the Offences Against Aircraft Bill of 1982. That Bill sought to give effect to certain conventions relating to the safety of aircraft. The Supreme Court held that the offences referred to in the Bill were all criminal according to the general principles of law recognised by the community of nations.

11.512

(14) Trinidad and Tobago

Section 5 of the Constitution of Trinidad and Tobago protects a number of fair trial rights. By section 5(2), Parliament may not, subject to limited exceptions,

11.513

> (c) deprive a person who has been arrested or detained—
>
>> (i) of the right to be informed promptly and with sufficient particularity of the reason for his arrest or detention;

[1886] Paras 25–26.

[1887] 1996 (6) BCLR 745.

[1888] 1999 (2) BCLR 125.

[1889] See generally, J Wickramaratne, *Fundamental Rights in Sri Lanka* (Navrang, 1996) Chap 6; S Sharvananda, *Fundamental Rights in Sri Lanka* (Arnold's International Printing House Private Ltd, 1993) Chap XI.

[1890] *Kumaratunga v Samarasinghe* FRD (2) 347.

   (ii)   of the right to retain and instruct without delay a legal adviser of his own choice and hold communication with him;

   (iii) of the right to be brought promptly before an appropriate judicial authority;

   (iv) of the remedy by way of habeas corpus for the determination of the validity of his detention and for his release if the detention is not lawful;

(d) authorise a court, tribunal, commission, board or other authority to compel a person to give evidence unless he is afforded protection against self-incrimination and, where necessary to ensure such protection, the right to legal representation;

(e) deprive a person of the right to a fair hearing in accordance with the principles of fundamental justice for the determination of his rights and obligations;

(f) deprive a person charged with a criminal offence of the right

   (i)   to be presumed innocent until proved guilty according to law, but this shall not invalidate any law by reason only that the law imposes on any such person the burden of proving particular facts;

   (ii) to a fair and public hearing by an independent and impartial tribunal; or

   (iii) to reasonable bail without just cause;

(g) to deprive a person of the right to the assistance of an interpreter in any proceedings in which he is involved or in which he is a party or a witness before a court, commission, board or other tribunal if he does not understand or speak English; or

(h) deprive a person of the right to such procedural provisions as are necessary for the purpose of giving effect and protection to the aforesaid rights and freedoms.

11.514   The Privy Council has held that section 5(2)(c)(ii) conferred a right to communicate with a legal adviser. Furthermore, since that right would be ineffective without a procedure whereby the person should be informed of it, a person arrested or detained had a constitutional right to be informed of his right to communicate with a legal adviser as soon as possible.[1891] A confession obtained in breach of this right is *prima facie* (but not automatically) inadmissible.[1892]

(a) Pre-trial publicity

11.515   In *Boodram v A-G of Trinidad and Tobago*[1893] the appellant was charged with murder. In the time up to his trial, there were several newspaper articles about the appellant, which he claimed were calculated and intended to create prejudice in the mind of potential jurors, and would deny him the right to receive a fair trial by an independent and impartial tribunal. The appellant sought a stay of the trial in order for the prejudice to dissipate. He sought further a declaration that the DPP had done nothing to stem the tide of adverse and hostile publicity, in particular by instituting contempt of court proceedings. The Court of Appeal of Trinidad and Tobago rejected the appellant's claim. The state did not guarantee in advance that a person charged would receive a fair trial. If the trial judge failed to ensure that the appellant obtained a fair trial, resulting in clear prejudice and amounting to a miscarriage of justice, his action would be corrected on appeal. As regards the alleged prejudice of the newspaper articles, it is insufficient to establish that the articles were likely to have a prejudicial effect on the minds of potential jurors. It had to be further established that the prejudice was so widespread and so indelibly impressed in the minds of potential jurors that it was unlikely that an impartial jury would be empanelled.

[1891] *A-G of Trinidad and Tobago v Whiteman* [1991] 2 AC 240; see also *Thornhill v A-G of Trinidad and Tobago* [1981] AC 61 (on the identical provision under the 1962 Constitution).

[1892] *Mohammed (Allie) v The State* [1999] 2 WLR 552.

[1893] [1996] AC 842.

(b) Trial within a reasonable time

The Privy Council dealt with pre-trial delay in *DPP v Jaikaran Tokai*.[1894] The Privy   **11.516**
Council noted that the Constitution of Trinidad and Tobago did not include a right to a
speedy trial or trial within a reasonable time. It did however, include a right to a fair trial.
That right to a fair trial was primarily secured by the traditional procedures available to the
criminal trial judge, including, in an exceptional case of delay, the power to grant a stay.
Where a stay is not granted, the trial judge must direct the jury as to all matters arising
from the delay which tell in favour of the accused. It is only possible to claim constitutional relief in advance of the trial where the procedures available to the trial judge are ob-
viously and inevitably going to be insufficient to secure a fair trial.

The case of *Sookermany v DPP*[1895] also concerned the issue of pre-trial delay. The Court   **11.517**
of Appeal of Trinidad and Tobago noted that the framers of the Constitution had omitted
to include a right to trial within a reasonable time and no such right could be inferred from
pre-constitutional common law or statutory sources. Further, any infringement of the
right to liberty and security of the person caused by long pre-trial detention could be remedied by granting bail. Fairness was the touchstone in determining whether an accused's
constitutional rights had been infringed by undue delay. An accused is constitutionally
entitled to a stay of prosecution if the delay was not attributable to the accused and the case
of the accused had suffered significant impairment which could not be remedied by the
powers of the trial judge, for example in jury directions or the exclusion of evidence. Privy
Council decisions from jurisdictions whose constitutions expressly protect the right to be
tried within a reasonable time provide important guidelines which apply to cases based on
common law rights. The right of the accused to be tried within a reasonable time should
be balanced against the public interest in having the accused tried and, in performing this
balancing exercise, the court is entitled to take into account the prevailing system of legal
administration and the economic, social and cultural conditions of the country.[1896] The
right at common law was more extensive than that formulated constitutionally, as it could
take into account time elapsed from the commission of the offence, as opposed to time
elapsed from charge. There is a difference in approach to the common law right and the
constitutional right. For example, the question of whether the accused has suffered actual
prejudice is more important in a common law case, whereas damage to an accused's security interest is given a greater weighting in cases based on express constitutional provisions.
Also, the trial judge's powers to remedy prejudice, while highly relevant for the common
law right, may be disregarded in enforcing an explicit written right. Similarly, systemic delays can only be used in a very limited extent to deny an explicitly given right but may be
more relevant in a common law situation. The appellant had not suffered any actual prejudice in his case other than his and his witnesses' fading memories. However, that disadvantage was shared with the prosecution. Nor was it a case where the appellant had spent
a long time in prison pending trial. The appellant had, however, suffered the stigma, anxiety and uncertainty of being charged with a serious criminal offence for much longer than
was reasonable. He had, therefore, suffered damage to his security interest. A stay, if
granted in this case, would have far reaching effects in pending cases as it would affect the

---

[1894] [1996] AC 856.
[1895] [1996] 2 LRC 292.
[1896] See *Bell v DPP* [1985] 1 AC 937.

safety of citizens, leave victims with no recourse, and provoke resentment against and loss of confidence in the law and administration. Moreover, persons already convicted after similar delays might bring claims to be released and for compensation. The interest of society in requiring the appellant to stand trial outweighed any injury to the appellant. The court noted that the same result would be reached even if the court had adopted the more stringent approach to delays required by an express constitutional provision.

(15) Zimbabwe

(a) Introduction

11.518   The Constitution of Zimbabwe contains extensive 'fair trial' rights for those charged with criminal offences and in relation to the determination of 'civil rights and obligations'.[1897] A statutory provision which allows a minister to determine civil rights and obligations without according a hearing in accordance with the principles of natural justice is unconstitutional and will be struck down.[1898]

11.519   Section 18(2) provides that:

> If any person is charged with a criminal offence, then, unless the charge is withdrawn, the case shall be afforded a fair hearing within a reasonable time by an independent and impartial court established by law.

This section embodies a 'constitutional value of supreme importance' and must be interpreted in a 'broad and creative manner'.[1899] As a result, it covers not only the impartiality of the decision-making body but also:

> the absolute impartiality of the prosecutor himself whose function as an officer of the court, forms an indispensable part of the judicial process. His conduct must, of necessity reflect on the impartiality or otherwise of the court.[1900]

(b) The right to a hearing within a reasonable time

11.520   In *Re Mlambo*[1901] the Supreme Court considered the right to a hearing 'within a reasonable time' contained in section 18(2). The Court followed the US Supreme Court[1902] in holding that the purpose of this right was to minimise the adverse effects of a charge:

> Trials held within a reasonable time have an intrinsic value. If innocent, the accused should be acquitted with a minimum disruption to his social and family relationships. If guilty, he should be convicted and an appropriate sentence imposed without unreasonable delay.[1903]

In addition, the Court emphasised the important practical advantages arising from the expeditious resolution of the charges.[1904] It was held that, for the purposes of 'fair trial

---

[1897] See Zimbabwe Declaration of Rights, s 18 (1979) 3 EHRR 418.
[1898] See *Holland v Minister of the Public Service, Labour and Social Welfare* [1998] 1 LRC 78 (provision allowing minister a discretion to suspend members of the executive committee of a registered private voluntary organisation struck down).
[1899] See *Smyth v Uhsewokunze* [1998] 4 LRC 120, 129b.
[1900] Ibid 129b-c.
[1901] [1993] 2 LRC 28; see also *Smyth v Uhsewokunze* (n 1899 above).
[1902] See eg *US v Loud Hawk* (1986) 474 US 302, 311.
[1903] *Re Mlambo* (n 1901 above) 34e–f.
[1904] Cf *R v Askov* [1990] 2 SCR 119.

rights', the 'charge' was not the formal charge but 'the start of the impairment of the individual's interests in the liberty and security of his person'.[1905] In considering the factors to be taken into account in determining whether the hearing was within a 'reasonable time' the Court adopted the analysis of Powell J in *Barker v Wingo*.[1906] The applicant had been arrested in October 1986 and his trial was not listed to take place until April 1991. In the circumstances, there was a breach of the right to a fair trial and the prosecution was stayed.

(c) The presumption of innocence

By section 18(3)(a) a person charged with a criminal offence is presumed to be innocent until proved guilty. However, by section 18(3)(b) there will be no breach of this presumption if a law imposes the burden of proving particular facts on the person charged. It has been held that this cannot place the entire onus on the accused and that reverse onus provision must be in accordance with guidelines developed by the common law.[1907] In *State v Chogugudza*[1908] it was held that statutory presumption in the Prevention of Corruption Act that an action by a public officer showing favour or disfavour was done for that purpose was not a breach of the constitutional presumption of innocence.

11.521

(d) Other cases

The case of *Mutasa v Makombe*[1909] concerned disciplinary proceedings within Parliament. A Member of Parliament, while addressing a seminar of senior public servants, voiced the opinion as to the low calibre and intelligence of MPs. The Speaker of Parliament ruled that the MP's statements were a breach of parliamentary privilege, and a Select Committee was appointed to look at the matter. The committee took evidence in the MP's absence, and also questioned the MP himself, though he was not permitted to engage legal counsel or to recall for further examination witnesses who had testified. The committee reported its findings to the House, which resulted in the MP being severely reprimanded. The MP challenged proceedings based on a lack of fair trial, and breach of freedom of expression. The Speaker issued a certificate which the presiding judge deemed to be conclusive of the matter and thereafter proceedings were stayed. The Supreme Court upheld that stay, stating that proceedings in Parliament for contempt were not a trial for a criminal offence. Further, the right to freedom of expression did not assist the MP, as that was limited for the purpose of maintaining the authority and independence of Parliament.

11.522

In *Banana v A-G*[1910] the Supreme Court considered an application for a stay of proceedings on the ground that widespread hostile pre-trial publicity had made a fair trial impossible. The Court accepted that, in exceptional circumstances, media reporting could be so irresponsible and prejudicial as to make unfairness irreparable and the administration of justice impossible. The test was whether the accused person had established 'that there was a real or substantial risk that . . . he could not obtain a fair trial'.[1911] The Court noted that although the English courts had recently granted a stay of proceedings on the ground of a

11.523

[1905] *Re Mlambo* (n 1901 above) 36c; relying on *Foti v Italy* (1982) 5 EHRR 313 and *United States v Marion* (1971) 404 US 307.
[1906] (1972) 407 US 514, 530–532; see para 11.88 above.
[1907] See *State v Chogugudza* [1996] 3 LRC 683, 690b.
[1908] [1996] 3 LRC 683, afer considering the Canadian and European law.
[1909] (1997) 2 BHRC 325.
[1910] 1999 (1) BCLR 27.
[1911] Ibid 34.

real or substantial risk of jurors being influenced by what they had read in the newspapers, a stronger line appeared to have been taken in Canada and Australia.[1912] The application was refused.

11.524   In *Lees Import and Export (Pvt) Ltd v Zimbabwe Banking Corp Ltd*[1913] the applicant company argued that the rule that a company had to be represented by a lawyer infringed its right to access to justice. The Supreme Court held that this rule breached the right to a fair hearing: the right given to 'every person' included a corporate body appearing through its alter ego. This was an exception to the general rule and did not permit a corporation to appear through a mere director, officer or servant.

[1912] Ibid 39, relying on *R v Vermette* (1989) 34 CRR 218 and *The Queen v Glennon* (1991–1992) 173 CLR 592.
[1913] (2000) 7 BHRC 647.

INDEX

For reference, we reproduce here the Summary Table of Contents of *The Law of Human Rights* (OUP, 2000, 0–19–826223–X) from which this chapter is extracted.

THE LAW OF HUMAN RIGHTS

CONTENTS

Foreword by Lord Bingham of Cornhill

VOLUME 1

IV REMEDIES AND PROCEDURES

VOLUME 2

APPENDICES

FAIR TRIAL RIGHTS